The Pharmaceutical Studies Reader

Blackwell Readers in Anthropology

This series fulfils the increasing need for texts that do the work of synthesizing the literature while challenging more traditional or subdisciplinary approaches to anthropology.

Each volume offers seminal readings on a chosen theme and provides the finest, most thought-provoking recent works in the given thematic area. Many of these volumes bring together for the first time a body of literature on a certain topic. The series thus both presents definitive collections and investigates the very ways in which anthropological inquiry has evolved and is evolving.

1. *The Anthropology of Globalization: A Reader*, Second Edition
   Edited by Jonathan Xavier Inda and Renato Rosaldo
2. *The Anthropology of Media: A Reader*
   Edited by Kelly Askew and Richard R. Wilk
3. *Genocide: An Anthropological Reader*
   Edited by Alexander Laban Hinton
4. *The Anthropology of Space and Place: Locating Culture*
   Edited by Setha Low and Denise Lawrence-Zúñiga
5. *Violence in War and Peace: An Anthology*
   Edited by Nancy Scheper-Hughes and Philippe Bourgois
6. *Same-Sex Cultures and Sexualities: An Anthropological Reader*
   Edited by Jennifer Robertson
7. *Social Movements: An Anthropological Reader*
   Edited by June Nash
8. *The Cultural Politics of Food and Eating: A Reader*
   Edited by James L. Watson and Melissa L. Caldwell
9. *The Anthropology of the State: A Reader*
   Edited by Aradhana Sharma and Akhil Gupta
10. *Human Rights: An Anthropological Reader*
    Edited by Mark Goodale
11. *The Pharmaceutical Studies Reader*
    Edited by Sergio Sismondo and Jeremy A. Greene

The Pharmaceutical Studies Reader

Edited by

Sergio Sismondo
and
Jeremy A. Greene

WILEY Blackwell

This edition first published 2015

Registered Office
John Wiley & Sons, Ltd, The Atrium, Southern Gate, Chichester, West Sussex, PO19 8SQ, UK

Editorial Offices
350 Main Street, Malden, MA 02148-5020, USA
9600 Garsington Road, Oxford, OX4 2DQ, UK
The Atrium, Southern Gate, Chichester, West Sussex, PO19 8SQ, UK

For details of our global editorial offices, for customer services, and for information about how to apply for permission to reuse the copyright material in this book please see our website at www.wiley.com/wiley-blackwell.

Library of Congress Cataloging-in-Publication data

The pharmaceutical studies reader / edited by Sergio Sismondo and Jeremy A. Greene.
p. ; cm.
Includes bibliographical references and index.
ISBN 978-1-118-48883-6 (cloth) – ISBN 978-1-118-49015-0 (pbk.)
I. Sismondo, Sergio, editor. II. Greene, Jeremy A., 1974– , editor.
[DNLM: 1. Drug Industry. 2. Intellectual Property. 3. Pharmaceutical Preparations.
4. Translational Medical Research. QV 736.1]
RA401.A3
338.4′76151–dc23

2014048334

A catalogue record for this book is available from the British Library.

Cover image: © David Lougheed

Set in 9.5/12pt Sabon by SPi Publisher Services, Pondicherry, India
Printed in Singapore by C.O.S. Printers Pte Ltd

1 2015

Contents

Acknowledgements

We would like to thank Jason Millar and Khadija Coxon for their excellent work helping us to edit the chapters here. Jason contributed to giving many chapters shapes appropriate for many of the varied potential uses of this volume. Khadija's sharp eye and rigorous reading ensured the continuity and integrity of each chapter. Khadija was also responsible for producing an index that helps to unify the volume.

We would like to thank all of the authors of articles in this volume for doing such fine work and making a contribution to pharmaceutical studies. But we also would like to particularly thank Maurice Cassier, Marilena Correa, Joe Dumit, Nate Greenslit, Cori Hayden, and Anne Pollock for their efforts to help us secure permissions to reprint their articles.

Wiley-Blackwell's Editor Rosalie Robertson first saw the value of this volume and gave us tremendous encouragement to put it together. We really appreciate Elizabeth Swayze support of Rosalie's initiative. Ben Thatcher's work on the logistics of gaining and paying for permissions was crucial to our being able to reprint a number of the best articles in the field.

Sergio Sismondo's contributions to this volume were supported by a generous grant from the Social Sciences and Humanities Research Council of Canada (410-2010-1033). Jeremy Greene's efforts on this volume were supported in part by a Science, Technology & Society Scholars Award from the National Science Foundation (NSF 1126132).

1

Introduction

Jeremy A. Greene and Sergio Sismondo

Why Study Pharmaceuticals?

The evolution of the modern pharmaceutical industry over the 20th century—from its early intersection with the image and later the structure of scientific research, to its dramatic post-WWII expansion and late-century saturation of medical and marketing media—has implications stretching far beyond medicine and business. That evolution has involved and affected much broader social, cultural, economic, and political developments. Pharmaceuticals are not merely used by doctors to control objective diseases, by patients to control subjective symptoms, or by manufacturers and marketers to control lucrative markets. Their uses and meanings are fluid and take shape at the intersection of many interests and disciplines.

Prescription drugs embody our ardent hopes in biomedical futures (for relief of suffering and prevention of morbidity and mortality) and also great fears (of medicalization, medical control, and side effects). Lurking in every capsule or tablet is a version of the *pharmakon* analyzed by Jacques Derrida—a thing that is both cure and poison.[1] But the pharmaceutical does not simply collapse into this binary alone. Drugs take on value because they simultaneously alter the chemistry and biology of our bodies, the expectations and categorization of our experiences, and the potentialities and networks of our social relations.

In the past decade, a number of ethnographic and historical studies, speaking to very different audiences, have framed pharmaceuticals as an ideal "sampling device" to study the interactions of medical science, clinical practice, consumerism, culture, industry, and the marketplace in the 20th and early 21st centuries. This volume draws together seventeen important works from this field over the past decade to give an introduction to this robust and vital new field of study.

We use the term "pharmaceutical studies" to encompass these humanistic and social scientific studies of prescription drugs.[2] From the point of view of the anthropologist, historian, sociologist or philosopher, a pharmaceutical can serve as a narrative device for exploring the politics, economics, cultures, and beliefs that potentiate and sustain its use.

The Pharmaceutical Studies Reader, First Edition. Edited by Sergio Sismondo and Jeremy A. Greene.

It can serve as a tracer tool that can be used to elaborate complex global flows of knowledge, capital, and people. Any pharmaceutical on the market today has been the focus of intense research and marketing efforts, expert regulation, and vernacular interest. It is an object that mediates borders between medical science and popular belief, health and disease, and spheres of licit and illicit. It is also—unlike other interesting biomedical matters such as research protocols, standards, or ethical codes—always a *thing*, a part of the material world invested with specific forms of value and stamped with highly regulated forms of knowledge. In their varied approaches to studying such "informed materials," scholars working in the area of pharmaceutical studies both demonstrate the interdisciplinarity of science and technology studies (STS) and illustrate some of the field's broader problematics.[3]

This volume cannot claim to present a synthesis of all of the important new research in the expanding field of pharmaceutical studies. On the one hand, economic analyses of pharmaceutical markets, ethics, adverse effects, or speculative innovations continue to fill pages in a number of dedicated and general journals on a monthly basis. On the other hand, a steady stream of exposé journalism—some highly nuanced, some crude—documents the role of the pharmaceutical industry in gouging consumers, selling sickness, exploiting research subjects, and selling life-saving drugs at prices that are inaccessible to many who would benefit from them. In selecting the contributions to this volume, however, we have chosen research that highlights social relations often obscured by conventional narratives of triumph and tragedy, of assumed biomedical realism, or conversely of the fabrication of disease by pharmaceutical marketing. We wish to show the value of an STS approach to describing important transformations of biological and social worlds brought about by developments in the field of pharmaceuticals.[4] The STS approach opens the door for analyses of drugs in both social and biological environments, by situating the scientific, organizational, and rhetorical work to produce a successful (or failed) pharmaceutical in these contexts. There can be no pharmaceuticals without that work: bare molecules do not become pharmaceuticals without ties to health concerns, scientific knowledge, appropriate regulation, effective marketing, and receptive prescribers and publics. Therefore, while there are many potential fields and areas of pharmaceutical studies, this volume focuses on those that draw from close empirical attention to key social contexts. We have chosen some exemplary articles that illuminate the multiple and complex social connections that pharmaceutical studies can make visible.

A Prehistory of Pharmaceutical Studies

It is not a new thing to argue that one can learn much about a society by studying how it tries to cure what ails it. Critical writings about Western therapeutics have been connected to broader forms of social critique for centuries. When, in June of 1527, the young Phillippus Aureolus Theophrastus Bombastus von Hohenheim, later known as Paracelsus, publicized his critique of the Galenic pharmacopoeia in favor of the more rational therapeutics of chemical pharmacy, he burned books of Galen and Avicenna on the front steps of the University of Basel, just as Martin Luther had burned a papal bull a few years earlier on the front steps of the Elster Gate of Wittenberg. Likewise, the acerbic pen of the mid-19th century Boston physician and social commentator Oliver Wendell Holmes was appealing to broader popular critiques of orthodoxy when he stated that "I firmly believe that if the whole *materia medica*, as now used, could be sunk to the bottom of the sea, it would be all the better for mankind, and all the worse for the fishes."

The popular genre of therapeutic skepticism grew in size and scope over the 20th century, coincident with the growth of the principal firms that now constitute the global pharmaceutical industry. The work of investigative journalists Samuel Hopkins Adams and Ida Tarbell helped build popular support for the passage of what became the 1906 Pure Food and Drugs Act, which founded the US Food and Drug Administration and the modern age of pharmaceutical regulation in the United States. This lineage of pharmaceutical muckraking can be traced through the middle of the 20th century to a burgeoning genre of literature in the early 21st century and is closely related to the growth of the consumer movements in Europe, North America, Latin America, and Southeast Asia.[5] Such critical accounts have been matched by an equally popular series of paeans to medical progress, including a host of popular works that continue to celebrate the forward march of the pharmaceutical industry.[6] Already by the middle of the 20th century, much popular and scholarly literature on the role of pharmaceuticals in society was heavily polarized between triumphalist and muckraker accounts. One might switch from one ideological position to another—as did journalist Milton Silverman somewhere between his rose tinted *Magic in a Bottle* (1943) and his much darker *Prescriptions for Death* (1982) —but relatively few authors found suitable space between the two camps.[7]

Into this highly polarized field, a few islands of nuanced empirical scholarship on the role of pharmaceuticals in society have developed in the past 50 years. In 1959, the young sociologist Renée Fox—a student of Talcott Parsons who would go on to become perhaps the leading medical sociologist of her generation—published her first book, *Experiment Perilous: Physicians and Patients Facing the Unknown*, a multilayered account of uncertainty in the ethics and practice of innovative pharmaceutical research at the Brigham and Women's Hospital in Boston, Massachusetts. Although cortisone, one of the experimental pharmaceuticals described in her account, would become an iconic "wonder drug" of the late 1940s and 1950s, in Fox's account, the pharmaceutical research enterprise was a sphere of ambivalence: no black hats or white hats walked the halls of the Brigham, just an array of people working from their own limited positions of knowledge and possibility. Working from another center of the sociology of science, the Bureau of Applied Social Research at Columbia University, James S. Coleman, Elihu Katz, and Herbert Menzel conducted a careful study of the utilization of new pharmaceuticals among the medical communities of several small Midwestern cities as a test site for studying the diffusion of medical knowledge. The resulting text, *Medical Innovation*, became an immediate staple in the field of the sociology of knowledge upon its original publication in 1966.[8]

Historians of medicine initially approached the modern pharmaceutical industry with caution: when James Harvey Young published his history of patent medicines, *Toadstool Millionaires* (1961), the 20th century research-based pharmaceutical industry, appeared as a rational therapeutic solution to the 19th century huckster of patent medicines. In turn, insider histories of the pharmaceutical industry, such as Miles Wetherell's *In Search of a Cure* (1975), tended to take the production of new drugs and successful organization of companies as natural correlates.[9] But Young's careful cultural history of the persuasiveness of patent medicine promotion would be extended by later historians—including authors in Charles Rosenberg and Morris Vogel's edited volume *The Therapeutic Revolution* (1979)—to account for the sociocultural significance of late 20th century pharmaceuticals as well. Judith Swazey's *Chlorpromazine in Psychiatry* (1974) was perhaps the first careful book-length pharmaceutical biography to narrate the social life of a single medication, from conception to development to wide-scale deployment, exploring the transformative potential that pharmaceuticals could effect upon the social institutions governing the management of the mental illness. It would be followed by Michael Bliss's *Discovery of Insulin* (1982), Mickey Smith's study of the social life of Valium, *Small Comfort* (1985), and by a series of more sweeping social histories of the modern pharmaceutical industry and its tangled relations with academic science and clinical practice over the 20th century.[10] In a very different historical theater, Daniel Headrick's *Tools of Empire* (1981) chronicled the transformative role of the fever-reducing drug quinine in allowing the spread of European empires in tropical Africa, Australasia, and Latin America over the 19th and early 20th centuries.[11]

In its colonial and early postcolonial manifestations, an incipient field of medical anthropology concerned itself with questions of ethnobotany (often connected to bioprospecting for medically useful materials) on the one hand, and the comparison of local indigenous medical *beliefs* to apparently universal biomedical forms of medical knowledge on the other. Following the inversion of the ethnographic lens in the 1970s and 1980s, however, the modern pharmaceutical itself became an increasingly important subject for ethnographic inquiry.[12] An early focus on the significance of Western pharmaceuticals as a component of cargo cultures gave rise to more in-depth accounts of how therapeutics as commodities became invested with different layers of performative and ritual meanings in the global North as well as South.[13] By the late 1970s, anthropologists such as Jean Comaroff could use ethnographic materials from sub-Saharan Africa to complicate understandings of the placebo effect in American medical practice, while Susan Reynolds Whyte traced the different meanings and efficacies of an apparently universal cure like penicillin across different locales of therapeutic action in Uganda.[14] Many anthropologists in the 1970s and 1980s, working in field sites marked by scarcity of essential medications and/or overabundance of inessential or harmful medications, incorporated activism and advocacy along with their analysis of the political economy of pharmaceuticals. Michael Tan, Hildebrak Haak, and Anita Hardon were just a few of the many anthropologists whose work in Southeast Asia, Latin America, and sub-Saharan Africa led them to join the pharmaceutical advocacy network Health Action International, whose founding manifesto at the steps of the World Health Organization in 1981 called for a more rational use of medications. By the 1990s, new developments in the anthropology of consumption (especially Arjun Appadurai and Igor Kopytoff's "biographical approach" to consumer goods as charted in the 1986 *Social Life of Things*) became the backbone to a series of calls for the organization of a new field of pharmaceutical anthropology, such as by Mark Nichter and Nancy Vukovic in 1994, and by Sjaak van der Geest, Susan Reynolds Whyte and Anita Hardon in 1996.[15] The second of these calls was made via a thorough survey of earlier anthropological studies of the production, marketing, prescription, distribution, and use of medicines. These categories demonstrated the utility of a biographical approach to commodities, but also showed how the social lives of medicines mapped onto political economies. This juxtaposition would influence much thinking about pharmaceuticals, including the current volume as a whole.

By the turn of the 21st century, a series of sociological, historical, and anthropological tool kits were available for those interested in charting the social lives of pharmaceuticals.[16] As more and more Americans were consuming prescription drugs for an increasing number of chronic conditions, and more and more radio advertisements, billboards, and websites advertised prescription drugs directly to consumers, and more and more scandals involving new (and often suppressed) risks of blockbuster developed in the early 2000s, the social study of the pharmaceutical became an interdisciplinary field of wide interest in investigative journalism and scholarly research.

Key Themes in Pharmaceutical Studies

These early links among the sociology, history, and anthropology of pharmaceuticals have since stretched further afield toward social epidemiology, legal studies, bioethics, political science, and philosophy. This increasingly interdisciplinary field nonetheless coheres around a series of key thematic foci: (1) using pharmaceutical as "sampling device" to open up and study broader social phenomena, (2) situating the pharmaceutical as an object at the boundaries of the licit and illicit, enhancement and treatment, and normal and pathological, (3) interpreting pharmaceutical consumption as a cultural text and a site of identity politics, (4) charting the movements of pharmaceuticals as global commodities with heterogeneous maps of access, cost, risk, and benefit, (5) understanding the pharmaceutical as a site of knowledge production, through organized clinical trials and through the more inchoate experience with drug risks in the general population, (6) analyzing the creation and maintenance of markets for drugs and knowledge about them, and (7) examining the politics and economies involved in regulating pharmaceutical markets on local and global scales.

1. *The pharmaceutical as sampling device*

In his 1962 work, *The Cholera Years,* Charles Rosenberg argued that a disease—like cholera—could be used as a methodological "sampling device" for historians interested in tracing more intangible qualities of cultural history like the role of expertise in governance and the secularization of civic discourse.[17] Pharmaceuticals, too, serve as tools to study networks of social relations. The production of drugs requires certain networks of social relations in the first place, facilitates other, new formations, and can even obviate longstanding traditions. Drugs are not just of interest in their own right but, as Susan Reynolds Whyte, Sjaak van der Geest, and Anita Hardon consider, tools for studying the social lives of medicines. The trajectories of otherwise quite distant groups of people become closely linked in the production, circulation, and consumption of a single pharmaceutical agent.[18]

In one way or another, the chapters in this volume use pharmaceuticals as both methodological and narrative devices to study broader social and cultural phenomena; thus we might take this first very general theme as intersecting with all of the others below. For example, Gabriele Soto Laveaga's "biography of a drug" (Chapter 12) explores among other things the work and organization of Mexican peasants to harvest the root of the barbasco plant, previously considered a noxious weed, as the key ingredient in the synthesis of cortisone.[19] Or, to take only one other example, we might look to Jongyoung Kim's study (Chapter 11) of how Korean medicine is reinventing itself to fit with different and changing therapeutic cultures, becoming a different kind of treatment in hybrid contexts in Korea, and then different again as it is exported to the United States.

2. *The pharmaceutical as a mediating agent*

Why is a prescription required for a prescription drug? The answer lies somewhere in the *pharmakon*: all prescription drugs are both poisons and cures, prescriptions are required for those agents that are seen to sit on the knife-edge of risk and benefit without expert guidance. The prescription and the prescription drug constitute a boundary between lay and expert knowledge.[20] They also lie at boundaries of legal remedy and illegal succor and pleasure. Most drugs of abuse are or were at one point products of the pharmaceutical industry: amphetamines, opioids, barbiturates, tranquilizers, all were licit drugs before they became illicit ones.[21] How they are dealt with legally has depended crucially on medical prescriptions, in conjunction with especially issues of race, gender, and class.[22]

Of late, pharmaceuticals have taken on increased roles in mediating the distinction between health and disease, between treatment and enhancement and between the extent to which health is understood as a right or as a good.[23] As Simon Williams et al. (Chapter 2) and many others in this volume illustrate in different ways, some of these processes of transformation might now better be termed "pharmaceuticalization" than "medicalization."[24] Medicalization became a key word in critical scholarship in the 1960s and 1970s, especially to those who railed against medical profession's authority to take control over intimate events and processes, often simply through classification. Yet with the relative weakening of the medical profession in the political economy of health care in the 21st century, the implicit professional focus of medicalization has lost some of its traction: physicians today appear to be only one set of actors in struggles for control over bodies, health, and illness. Williams et al. suggest that a comparable array of intimate events are now interpreted and addressed through the medium of the pharmaceutical. Joseph Dumit's chapter here (Chapter 3) is part of his larger argument that the past fifty years have seen the instauration of a new model of health and disease, on which we are all less than healthy, and could be treating—typically with pharmaceuticals—our shortcomings.[25]

Historians, anthropologists, sociologists, and others have increasingly looked to pharmaceuticals to understand changes in disease and illness categories: as part of the construction of disease, or "selling sickness" and "disease mongering," in the terms of the pharmaceutical industry's critics.[26] In this volume, Jeremy Greene (Chapter 5) describes the emergence of asymptomatic hypertension as a disease in its own right, rather than as a sign of some other condition; this emergence has much to do with a new drug, Diuril, which could be used to treat hypertension. Jennifer Fishman (Chapter 7) looks at the actors attempting to construct a new illness, female sexual dysfunction, in a way that can make it amenable to treatment with drugs, even in the absence of specific available drugs. The connections between drugs and diseases are especially apparent, and have been widely studied, in the arena of psychopharmaceuticals, where the boundaries between health and illness seem particularly malleable.[27] However, drugs have been crucial to establishing the boundaries of other diseases: menopause, osteoporosis, hypercholesterolemia, and irritable bowel syndrome, to name a few.[28]

3. *Pharmaceutical consumption as a cultural text*

Prescription drugs have also served as a key focus of consumer activism. From the journalistic work that led to the passage of the 1906 Pure Food and Drugs Act, to the foundational texts of Consumers Union in the 1930s that led to the passage of the 1938 Food Drugs and Cosmetics Act, to the anti-monopolistic hearings of Estes Kefauver in the 1960s, pharmaceuticals have played a key role in animating key moments in American consumer history. A significant part of consumer activisms around pharmaceuticals have related to the identity politics of specific consumers, as understood across axes of gender, race, or sexuality. Organized inquiry and protest about the safety of oral contraceptives, diethylstilbestrol (DES), and hormone replacement therapy (HRT) were crucial to the development of health feminism in the 1960s and 1970s. Likewise, the gendered marketing of diet pills, minor tranquilizers, and sleep aids has been the nidus of a complex series of critiques about the medicalization of gendered inequity in American society.[29] A robust strand of feminist scholarship has expanded beyond studies of reproductive technologies in America and Europe to their deployment in the global marketplace[30] and beyond women's health in the spheres of obstetrics, gynecology, and psychiatry toward the gendering of other forms of pharmaceuticals, such as cardiovascular medications.

The pharmaceutical consumer, as subject or object, also has been characterized along racial lines. Anne Pollock's study of BiDil (Chapter 6), the heart drug approved by the US Food and Drug Administration for treating heart failure in African Americans, shows how contours of race become revealed in the context of discussions of prices and patronage. BiDil brings the issue of race into sharp relief, but other work on the conjunction of race and pharmaceuticals has looked at metaphors, genetic research, and technologies used to label some bodies as racialized in particular ways.[31]

Several cultural texts and subtexts can be enacted when a pharmaceutical is prescribed, purchased, and consumed. Particular drugs come with meanings attached, and thus are often understood to be taken (and often even prescribed) by particular kinds of people. Pills become social and cultural signifiers whose meanings are not fully controlled by prescribers or by the legal and regulatory frameworks that govern pharmaceutical consumption. They are often closely connected with ideas of the self, of the social world, of community and nation.[32]

Nathan Greenslit (Chapter 5) looks at the drug Sarafem, which is chemically identical to Eli Lilly's antidepressant Prozac, but is packaged, culturally coded, and marketed for premenstrual dysphoric disorder. The result, arguably, is that Sarafem is a different drug than Prozac; the people who consume the two drugs understand their problems and identities differently. Likewise, Cori Hayden's account (Chapter 18) of the jockeying of competing kinds of copied drugs in the early 21st century Mexican pharmacy shows the challenges posed to would-be consumers of generic drugs when "the same thing" can be purchased along several different lines of guarantee of therapeutic equivalence. What does it mean to purchase a brand-name drug when a cheaper product exists that claims to do the same thing? What risks are entailed in purchasing a cheaper *similar* pharmaceutical in place of an authenticated *generic*? How and why do different consumers choose to consume the same thing differently?[33]

4. *The pharmaceutical as a global commodity*

Although the themes discussed so far have not focused exclusively on American and European examples, the field of pharmaceutical studies presented in this book is tipped toward American studies. Yet the pharmaceutical is, as it turns out, an excellent device for studying transnational flows of commodities and connected economies of knowledge.

Pharmaceuticals have played a role in the mediation of global economies of knowledge and goods, since the first European voyages of discovery in the 15th century and before. The spices sought by Vasco da Gama in his nautical exploration of the East Indies, and Columbus and others in developing the West Indies trade were understood to be powerful therapeutic objects. Many of the new objects brought back from the New World—including anti-syphilitic guaiac bark, antipyretic Peruvian bark, and stimulant coca leaves—would pose significant challenges to previously stable Galenic *materia medica* and would help to enable new systems of thinking about therapeutics, like the 16th century iatrochemistry of Paracelsus mentioned earlier.

Though pharmaceuticals have long moved in global markets, the structure of the research-based pharmaceutical industry shifted dramatically in the second half of the 20th century toward a more explicitly globalizing model, in which research, production, and distribution of drugs within a single company could take place in a series of 10–20 countries scattered across several continents. It has been a bitter irony that this increased globalization in the business of pharmaceutical production and research has not resulted in global equity in pharmaceutical access, or in the adequacy of regulatory regimes to safeguard consumers. Consumer activism around pharmaceuticals in the late 20th century became a key site for critique of multinational corporations—a form of "anti-globalization" critique *avant la lettre*.[34] As the International Organization of Consumers Unions shifted its policy center to the global South in the 1970s (literally moving its offices from the Hague to Penang, Malaysia), its new president, Anwar Fazal, created a transnational network of advocacy groups around pharmaceutical overuse and underuse in the developing world.

One key area of contemporary pharmaceutical studies then, is to demonstrate the relevance of reading the pharmaceutical as a global commodity that nonetheless takes on different forms of meaning and value within local markets. Some notable works to focus in this balance in recent years range from ethnographies of counterfeit drugs in Nigeria to studies of the availability or unavailability of neoplastic drugs in East Africa or antiretroviral drugs in West Africa to the general non-visibility of endemic killers of the global South (malaria, trypanosomiasis, tuberculosis) as markets for firms based in the global North.[35] Stefan Ecks, in this volume (Chapter 17), likewise demonstrates the pluralistic understanding of markets for what would seem to be the same anticancer drug, Glivec, in North American and South Asian markets. Cori Hayden's essay (Chapter 18) traces the differential marketing of the "same things" in generic pharmaceutical markets in Mexico as opposed to the United States. Adriana Petryna's contribution (Chapter 14) notes with some alarm the distance between the geographies of pharmaceutical consumption (understood as a geography weighted toward North, and West) and the geographies of pharmaceutical knowledge production (increasingly weighted further East, and South).

5. *The pharmaceutical as a site of knowledge and value production*

As "informed materials," pharmaceuticals take on value through association with new forms of knowledge.[36] Conversely, the existence of pharmaceutical interventions help bring other forms of knowledge into being and have helped to stabilize certain forms of biomedical knowledge-making, most notably the randomized controlled trial (RCT). The study of pharmaceuticals opens up key windows into how biomedical objects take on value—and lose value—in relation to the production and adherence of new biomedical facts.[37]

Pharmaceutical knowledge was validated through a variety of means in the nineteenth and early 20th centuries. But by the middle of the 20th century, pharmaceutical value was increasingly associated with the rise of RCTs as an ascendant form of biomedical knowledge-making, from the 1948 MRC streptomycin trials in the UK onward. The rise of the RCT is a result, among other things, of reform movements that distrusted practitioners. At the same time as clinical trials came to validate pharmaceuticals, however, pharmaceuticals also helped establish clinical trials as the new "gold standard" in biomedical epistemology.[38] Clinical trials became key means to consolidate popular controversies over the safety and efficacy of experimental therapeutics, but as critics have since established, comparison with placebo alone is rarely sufficient to ensure that new pharmaceuticals are effective—or safe—in all relevant senses of the term.[39] Concerns over the safety of pharmaceuticals emerge frequently, despite negative findings in initial, short-term RCTs. Many discoveries of the harmful qualities of drugs—from DES to HRT, sulfanilamide to Avandia—depend on the accumulation of "drug experience" through lay and professional forms of pharmacoepidemiology, but as a result are often easily discredited or devalued in relation to institutionally conducted RCTs.[40]

Pharmaceutical knowledge is increasingly produced across many locations, often by contract research organizations.[41] Thus, understanding how knowledge of pharmaceutical safety, efficacy, or quality is produced and attached to specific products requires attention to broader social networks of knowledge production and ratification. Several essays in this volume—from Jill Fisher (Chapter 13) to Adriana Petryna (Chapter 14) to Kaushik Sunder Rajan (Chapter 15)—describe infrastructure needed for commercial trials and processes by which subjects are recruited for those trials.[42] The pharmaceutical industry has attempted to reduce its costs by standardizing requirements internationally; this allows companies to use the same research for their applications for a drug's approval in many jurisdictions. In creating the International Conference on Harmonization (ICH), it helped to make the testing of drugs a global phenomenon, even though it has been tempered by local therapeutic cultures, and has been challenged by countries insisting on the racial or ethnic differences of their populations.[43] It has been argued that the ICH agreement has tended to harmonize standards "downward," resulting in overall weaker carcinogenicity testing, weaker reporting of adverse events, and less long-term monitoring of adverse events.[44]

Production of drugs themselves, as material objects, is understudied, relative to the production of knowledge about those drugs. Because of their association with advanced science, pharmaceutical production may often be imagined as an activity taking place in isolated and sterile laboratories. Gabriela Soto Laveaga's contribution (Chapter 12) takes us into the Mexican jungles, where through the middle of the 20th century, a raw ingredient for the synthesis of steroids was collected by *campesinos* on a vast scale; endocrinological drugs posed particular organizational challenges because of the minute quantities of the precursor substances available from animal organs (from slaughterhouses) or urine (collected from pregnant women or horses).[45] Other works have looked at pharmaceutical production facilities as chemical plants, with attendant environmental consequences.[46]

6. *The pharmaceutical and its markets*

Of all of the relationships mediated by pharmaceuticals, one enables all others: the relationship of good to market. Pharmaceuticals have circulated through mass markets as long as mass markets have existed; much of the earnings of the early advertising industry were supported by patent pharmaceutical firms; by the end of the 19th century, the Lydia E. Pinkham Medicine Company could boast that it was the largest advertiser by volume in the world.[47] Since the expansion of direct-to-consumer advertising of drugs in the United States, and the permission of some forms of it in Europe and elsewhere, marketing has become visible to far broader audiences and has helped to create broader markets. The visibility of direct-to-consumer advertising has led to an extensive conversation about whether the promotion of medicines should or should not be subject to a different code of ethics than other consumer goods.[48]

Drugs may be taken up in new markets because of local forces, such as physicians' efforts to treat more patients.[49] What may be most striking about pharmaceutical marketing, though, is companies' integrated efforts, encompassing not just advertising, but efforts that work through medical science journals, regulation, medical education, one-on-one contact with doctors, and many other media.[50] Kalman Applbaum shows (Chapter 9) that drugs are created along with markets, as companies try to make salient certain cultural texts for the different actors necessary for mass consumption of a new product. There need not be a clearly defined preexisting demand for a pharmaceutical to be successful, if its marketers can have enough power to shape the different terrains they wish to occupy.[51] In particular, pharmaceutical companies can attempt to structure and restructure medical knowledge in different ways, whether through innovative drug discovery or through hegemony over medical knowledge production and communication. The latter, it has been argued, can often be shown to be a better investment of resources.[52] This may be why, as Sergio Sismondo's study (Chapter 10) of "publication planning" indicates, pharmaceutical companies invest significantly in the planning, creation, and circulation of scientific articles tied to their products.[53] To physicians, some of the most visible conduits of both pharmaceutical marketing and communication are sales representatives, who can be important shapers of medical opinion. These "detailers" beat paths from office to office, trying to earn a minute or so of a physician's time to make a sales pitch.[54] They bring food for doctors and staff and drug samples to be given away to patients and information companies have shaped to give scientific backing to their pitches. As Adriane Fugh-Berman and Shahram Ahari describe (Chapter 8), sales representatives have carefully honed approaches to classifying doctors and then tailoring their approaches to methods most likely to succeed.

7. *The pharmaceutical as subject of regulation*

Concerns about pharmaceutical piracy can be found in earlier regimes of intellectual property regulation, including 17th century disputes.[55] It is notable that pharmaceuticals became patentable in Europe early in the 20th century; the histories of these patent laws are varied and revealing.[56] More recently—in the early 1980s—a group of companies within which the pharmaceutical industry was very prominent put intellectual property at the top of the US trade agenda. They helped to design international agreements and a successful strategy for convincing other countries to sign onto those agreements.[57] The result was the Agreement on Trade-Related Aspects of Intellectual Property Rights or TRIPs, which has formed the basis for new intellectual property laws in countries around the world.

Even though it has reacted strongly against many government attempts at regulation[58] (TRIPs being an exception), the multinational pharmaceutical industry has influenced, adapted to, and profited from those regulations. It is today very much a creature of its regulation. The distinction between legitimate pharmaceuticals and their legitimate counterparts—such as patent medicines, herbal remedies, supplements, illegal drugs, and traditional medicines—has depended and continues to depend on demarcations that require certain medicines to be scientifically tested for their safety and efficacy, approved for particular uses, and then prescribed by licensed physicians or sold through licensed pharmacies.[59]

In general, state-based regulators are receptive to pressures to balance interests in safety and effectiveness with the financial interests of a thriving industry that, it is argued, provides long-term health and economic benefits. Thus, the experts who evaluate drug applications are expected to be "friendly" to the industry even as they apply strict standards, and the regulator as a whole is expected to support the industry even as it upholds laws.[60] Several studies have drawn attention to the alliances of organized medicine and the organized pharmaceutical industry, especially the US-based Pharmaceutical Research and Manufacturers of America (PhRMA).[61] These alliances have been important in lobbying for particular policies and in defending the legitimacy of pharmaceutical knowledge in contrast with alternative forms of therapeutics.[62] Physician/industry relationships— which grew very close and relatively uncontested, for much of the late 20th century—are now increasingly reexamined as social ties with significant potential for individual and institutional conflicts of interest.

Regulation happens at many different levels and not just by states. Adopting E.P. Thompson's well-known concept of "moral economy," we can understand how particular forms of collaboration between researchers, doctors, and pharmaceutical companies are and are not acceptable.[63] The idea of moral economies as forms of regulation, at least of justifications of behaviors, has been picked up by a number of researchers in pharmaceutical studies.[64]

In its public relations efforts, the pharmaceutical industry justifies its monopolies, its prices, and its marketing practices in terms that invoke moral economies. The industry's astronomically high estimates of the cost of bringing a new drug to market are used to justify—to consumers, political actors, and states—high prices and restrictive patent regimes. Despite numerous challenges, these estimates have been widely circulated and are deeply ingrained in debates in the public sphere.[65] Alternate moral economies are at play in the case described by Stefan Ecks (Chapter 17), in which corporate philanthropy is used as a justification for high prices in wealthy markets, even as it undercuts local competition in places like India. The claim that copying or reverse engineering drugs, as Brazil has threatened to do for AIDS drugs, is mere piracy and a rhetorical plank used to defend international patent regimes in the face of humanitarian demands. Maurice Cassier and Marilena Correa (Chapter 16), though, challenge this claim, arguing that copying and innovation are continuous activities, that copying is a form of innovation with its own productive capacities.

Guide to this Volume

This volume is the result of two decades observation of a developing field of study and of teaching courses for undergraduates and graduate students on the social study of pharmaceuticals. We intend the book to be used as an entry point into the field for students and teachers and others interested in thinking critically about living with pharmaceuticals. The articles and chapters here are ones that we have found particularly useful and that we believe can fit together to form a coherent sample of excellent work in pharmaceutical studies.

But this representation can only be partial. As the extensive footnotes to this brief introduction suggest, a great many excellent works are not represented in the volume. We had to make some difficult decisions to keep the length down and make the volume affordable. Even so, almost every chapter here has been shortened from its originally published form, many of them significantly shortened. We have tried to keep the central examples, narratives, and theoretical points intact but sometimes at the expense of subthemes and particularly interesting asides.

We have clustered the chapters into five sections: (1) pharmaceutical lives, (2) new drugs, diseases, and identities, (3) drugs and the circulation of medical knowledge, (4) political and moral economies of pharmaceutical research, and (5) intellectual property in local and global markets. However, each of these chapters could have been placed in one or more different sections. As the earlier discussion has suggested, the thematic connections that link these chapters cut across all sections of the book. There is no need to read the chapters in order. Indeed, many chapters refer to others in the volume or other works by authors represented here, and so it would be possible to read the volume simply by tracing connections across chapters.

We hope that readers will find new productive routes through the book and out into the expanding and dynamic field that is pharmaceutical studies.

NOTES

1 Jacques Derrida, *Dissemination* (Barbara Johnson, trans., University of Chicago Press, 1981).
2 The term "pharmaceutical studies" sometimes is also used to refer to coursework offered toward a career in pharmacy or pharmacology, clearly far from our purposes here.
3 Andrew Barry, "Pharmaceutical Matters: The Invention of Informed Materials," *Theory, Culture & Society* 22.1 (2005): 51–69.
4 See Sergio Sismondo, *An Introduction to Science and Technology Studies*, 2nd ed. (Wiley-Blackwell, 2010).
5 For example: Samuel Hopkins Adams, *Great American Fraud* (P.F. Collier & Son, 1907); Morton Mintz, *The Therapeutic Nightmare* (Houghton Mifflin Co., 1965); Arthur Kallet and Frederick John Schlink, *100,000,000 Guinea Pigs: Dangers in Everyday Foods, Drugs and Cosmetics* (Vanguard Press, 1932); Allan Klass, *There's Gold in Them Thar Pills: An Inquiry into the Medical-Industrial Complex* (Penguin, 1975); Milton Silverman, Philip Lee, and Mia Lydecker, *Prescriptions for Death: The Drugging of the Third World* (University of California Press, 1982); Marcia Angell, *The Truth About the Drug Companies: How They Deceive Us and What to Do About It* (Random House, 2004); Greg Critser, *Generation Rx: How Prescription Drugs Are Altering American Lives, Minds, and Bodies* (Houghton Mifflin, 2005); Peter C. Gøtzsche, *Deadly Medicines and Organized Crime: How Big Pharma Has Corrupted Healthcare* (Radcliffe Publishing, 2013).
6 For example: John Christian Krantz, *Fighting Disease with Drugs* (Baltimore: Williams & Willkins, 1931); Milton Silverman, *Magic in a Bottle* (Macmillan Co., 1948); Tom Mahoney, *The Merchants of Life: An Account of the American Pharmaceutical Industry* (Harper, 1959), Edward Kremer and George Urdang, *Kremer's and Urdang's History of Pharmacy*, 3rd ed., revised by Glenn Sonnedecker (J.B. Lippincott, 1964), and, in a more focused way, John E. Lesch, *The First Miracle Drugs: How the Sulfa Drugs Transformed Medicine* (Oxford, 2007).
7 Milton Silverman, *Magic in a Bottle: Being the True Narratives of Ten Wonder-Working Drugs and the of the Doughty Men Who, Wittingly or Unwittingly, Discovered Them* (Macmillan, 1943), Milton Silverman, Philip Lee, and Mia Lydecker, *Prescriptions for Death: The Drugging of the Third World* (University of California Press, 1982).

8 Renee Fox, *Experiment Perilous: Physicians and Patients Facing the Unknown* (Transaction Books, 1959); 1966 James Samuel Coleman Elihu Katz and Herbert Menzel. *Medical Innovation: A Diffusion Study* (Bobbs-Merrill, 1966).

9 Henry George Lazell, *From Pills to Penicillin: The Beechams Story* (Henemann, 1975); Miles Weatherall, *In Search of a Cure: A History of the Pharmaceutical Industry* (Oxford, 1990).

10 Jonathan Liebenau, *Medical Science and Medical Industry: The Formation of the American Pharmaceutical Industry* (Johns Hopkins University Press, 1987); Jonathan Swann, *Academic Scientists and the Pharmaceutical Industry: Cooperative Research in Twentieth-Century America* (Johns Hopkins University Press, 1988); Judith Swazey, *Chlorpromazine in Psychiatry: A Study in Therapeutic Innovation* (MIT Press, 1974); Morris J. Vogel and Charles E. Rosenberg, eds., *The Therapeutic Revolution: Essays in the Social History of American Medicine* (University of Pennsylvania Press, 1979); Michael Bliss, *The Discovery of Insulin* (University of Chicago Press, 1982); Mickey Smith, *Small Comfort: A History of the Minor Tranquilizers* (Praeger, 1985).

11 Daniel R. Headrick, *Tools of Empire: Technology and European Imperialism in the Nineteenth Century* (Oxford University Press 1981).

12 Byron J. Good, *Medicine, Rationality, and Experience: An Anthropological Perspective* (Cambridge University Press, 1994). George Stocking and Byron Good, "Medical Anthropology and the Problem of Belief".

13 A.F. Bagshawe, G. Maina and E.N. Mngola, *The Use and Abuse of Drugs and Chemicals in Tropical Africa* (East African Literature Bureau, 1974); Jagdish C. Bhatia et al., "Traditional healers and modern medicine," *Social Science & Medicine* 9.1 (1975): 15–21.

14 Jean Comaroff, "A Bitter Pill to Swallow: Placebo Therapy in General Practice," *Sociological Review* 24.1 (1976): 79–96; see also Clark. E. Cunningham, "Thai 'Injection Doctors': Antibioticlark Mediators," *Social Science & Medicine* 4.1 (1970): 1–24; Susan Reynolds Whyte, "Penicillin, Battery Acid, and Sacrifice: Cures and Causes in Nyole Medicine," *Social Science & Medicine* 16.23 (1982): 2055–2064.

15 Mark Nichter and Nancy Vuckovic, "Agenda for an Anthropology of Pharmaceutical Practice," *Social Science & Medicine* 39.110 (1994): 1509–1525. Sjaak van der Geest, Susan Reynolds Whyte and Anita Hardon. "The Anthropology of Pharmaceuticals: A Biographical Approach," *Annual Review of Anthropology* 25 (1996): 153–178.

16 Keith Wailoo, *Drawing Blood: Technology and Disease Identity in Twentieth-Century America* (Johns Hopkins University Press, 1997); Harry M. Marks, *The Progress of Experiment: Science and Therapeutic Reform in the United States, 1900-1990* (Cambridge University Press, 1997); David Healey, *The Antidepressant Era* (Harvard University Press, 1997).

17 Charles E. Rosenberg, *The Cholera Years: The United States in 1832, 1849, and 1866* (University of Chicago Press, 1962); see also Charles E. Rosenberg, "Introduction," in Charles E. Rosenberg and Janet Golden (eds), *Framing Disease: Studies in Cultural History* (Rutgers University Press, 1992).

18 Susan Reynolds Whyte, Sjaak van der Geest, and Anita Hardon, *The Social Lives of Medicines* (Cambridge University Press, 2004).

19 For a more full version of this account, see Gabriela Soto Laveaga, *Jungle Laboratories: Mexican Peasants, National Projects, and the Making of the Pill* (Duke University Press, 2009).

20 Jeremy A. Greene and Elizabeth S. Watkins (eds), *Prescribed: Writing, Filling, Using and Abusing the Prescription in Modern America* (Johns Hopkins University Press, 2012); see also Harry M. Marks, "Revisiting the Origins of Compulsory Prescription," *American Journal of Public Health* 85.1 (1995): 109–115; Peter Temin, *Taking Your Medicine: Drug Regulation in the United States* (Harvard University Press, 1980).

21 David F. Musto, *The American Disease: Origins of Narcotic Control (expanded edition)*, (Oxford University Press, 1987); David T. Courtwright, "The Controlled Substances Act: How a 'Big Tent' Reform Became a Punitive Drug Law," *Drug and Alcohol Dependence* 76.1 (2004): 9–15.

22 David Herzberg, *Happy Pills in America: From Miltown to Prozac.* (Johns Hopkins University Press, 2009); Nicolas Rasmussen, *On Speed: The Many Lives of Amphetamine* (New York University Press, 2008).

23 Rein Vos, *Drugs Looking For Diseases: Innovative Drug Research and the Development of the Beta Blockers and the Calcium Antagonists* (Springer Science+Business Media, 1991); Chris Feudtner, *Bittersweet: Diabetes, Insulin, and the Transformation of Illness* (University of North Carolina Press, 2003); Carl Elliott, *Better than Well: American Medicine Meets the American Dream* (W. W. Norton, 2003); Sheila Rothman and David Rothman, *The Pursuit of Perfection: The Promise and Perils of Medical Enhancement* (Pantheon, 2003); João G. Biehl, *Vita: Life in a Zone of Social Abandonment* (University of California Press, 2013); also Thomas Pogge, *Incentives for Global Public Health Patent Law and Access to Essential Medicines* (Cambridge University Press, 2014).

24 Peter Conrad, *Identifying Hyperactive Children: The Medicalization of Deviant Behavior* (D. C. Heath & Co., 1976); Peter Conrad, "Medicalization and its Discontents," in *The Medicalization of Society: On the Transformation of Human Conditions into Treatable Disorders* (Johns Hopkins University Press, 2007).

25 Joseph Dumit, *Drugs for Life: How Pharmaceutical Companies Define Our Health* (Duke University Press, 2012).

26 For example: Ray Moynihan and Alan Cassels, *Selling Sickness: How the World's Biggest Pharmaceutical Companies Are Turning Us All into Patients* (Greystone Books, 2005); Ray Moynihan and David Henry, "The Fight Against Disease Mongering: Generating Knowledge for Action," *PLoS Medicine* 3.4 (2006): e191; Leonore Tiefer, "Female Sexual Dysfunction: A Case Study of Disease Mongering and Activist Resistance," *PLoS Medicine* 3.4 (2006): e178; Steven Woloshin and Lisa M. Schwartz, "Giving Legs to Restless Legs: A Case Study of How the Media Helps Make People Sick," *PLoS Medicine* 3.4 (2006): e170; Nancy Tomes, "Merchants of Health: Medicine and Consumer Culture in the United States, 1900-1940," *Journal of American History* 88.2 (2001): 519–547; Nancy Tomes, "The Great American Medicine Show Revisited," *Bulletin of the History of Medicine* 79.4 (2005): 627–663; Shannon Brownlee, *Overtreated: Why Too Much Medicine Is Making Us Sicker and Poorer* (Bloomsbury Publishing, 2007).

27 David Healy, *Let Them Eat Prozac: The Unhealthy Relationship Between the Pharmaceutical Industry and Depression* (New York University Press, 2004); David Healy, *Mania: A Short History of Bipolar Disorder* (Johns Hopkins University Press, 2010); Andrea Tone, *The Age of Anxiety: A History of America's Turbulent Affair with Tranquilizers* (Basic Books, 2009); Christopher Lane, *Shyness: How Normal Behavior Became a Sickness* (Yale University Press, 2008).

28 Ray Moynihan and Alan Cassels, *Selling Sickness: How the World's Biggest Pharmaceutical Companies Are Turning Us All into Patients* (Greystone Books, 2005); Jeremy Greene, *Prescribing by Numbers: Drugs and the Definition of Disease* (Johns Hopkins University Press, 2007).

29 David L. Herzberg, "'The Pill You Love Can Turn on You': Feminism, Tranquilizers, and the Valium Panic of the 1970s," *American Quarterly* 58.1 (2006): 79–103; Jonathan Metzl, *Prozac on the Couch: Prescribing Gender in the Era of Wonder Drugs* (Duke University Press, 2003); Elizabeth Siegel Watkins, *The Estrogen Elixir: A History of Hormone Replacement Therapy in America* (Johns Hopkins University Press, 2007); Susan E. Bell, "Gendered Medical Science: Producing a Drug for Women," *Feminist Studies* 21.3 (1995): 469–500.

30 Adele Clarke, *Disciplining Reproduction: Modernity, American Life Sciences, and the Problems of Sex* (University of California Press, 1998); Amy Kaler, *Running After Pills: Politics, Gender and Contraception in Colonial Zimbabwe* (Heinemann, 2003).

31 Anne Pollock's chapter is part of her book *Medicating Race: Heart Disease and Durable Preoccupations with Difference* (Duke University Press, 2012). Other recent works on the connections of race and pharmaceuticals include: Jonathan, Kahn "How a Drug Becomes Ethnic: Law, Commerce, and the Production of Racial Categories in Medicine," *Yale Journal of Health Policy, Law & Ethics* 4.1 (2004): 1–46; Keith Wailoo, *Drawing Blood: Technology and Disease Identity in Twentieth-Century America* (Johns Hopkins University Press, 1997); Duana Fullwiley, "The Biologistical Construction of Race: 'Admixture' Technology and the New Genetic Medicine," *Social Studies of Science* 38.5 (2008): 695–735; Adam Hedgeco, "Bioethics and the Reinforcement of Socio-technical Expectations," *Social Studies of Science* 40.2 (2010): 163–186.

32 Janis H. Jenkins, "Psychopharmaceutical Self and Imaginary in the Social Field of Psychiatric Treatment," in *Pharmaceutical Self: The Global Shaping of Experience in an Age of*

Psychopharmacology (School for Advanced Research Press, 2011): 17–40; Emily Martin, *Bipolar Expeditions: Mania and Depression in American Culture* (Princeton University Press, 2009); João G. Biehl, "The Activist State: Global Pharmaceuticals, AIDS, and Citizenship in Brazil," *Social Text* 22.3 (2004): 105–132; Andrea Tone, *The Age of Anxiety: A History of America's Turbulent Affair with Tranquilizers* (Basic Books, 2009).

33 We were able to include only a short version of Hayden's study here. For a longer version that includes more analysis, see Cori Hayden, "A Generic Solution?" *Current Anthropology* 48.4 (2007): 475–495. See also Andrew Lakoff, "The Anxieties of Globalization: Antidepressant Sales and Economic Crisis in Argentina," *Social Studies of Science* 34.2 (2004): 247–269.

34 Milton Silverman, *The Drugging of the Americas: How Multinational Drug Companies Say One Thing About Their Products to Physicians in the United States, and Another Thing to Physicians in Latin America* (University of California Press, 1976); Milton Silverman, Philip R. Lee and Mia Lydecker, *op. cit.* note 5; Diane Melrose, *Bitter Pills: Medicine and the Third World Poor* (OXFAM, 1982); Matthew Hilton, *Prosperity for All: Consumer Activism in an Era of Globalization.* (Cornell University Press, 2009).

35 Kristin Peterson, "AIDS Policies for Markets and Warriors: Dispossession, Capital, and Pharmaceuticals in Nigeria," in Kaushik Sunder Rajan (ed.) *Lively Capital: Biotechnologies, Ethics, and Governance in Global Markets* (Duke University Press, 2012); Paul Farmer, *Infections and Inequalities: The Modern Plagues* (University of California Press, 1999). João G. Biehl, *op. cit.* note 21; Vinh-Kim Nguyen, *The Republic of Therapy: Triage and Sovereignty in West Africa's Time of AIDS* (Duke University Press, 2010); Melinda Cooper, *Life as Surplus: Biotechnology and Capitalism in the Neoliberal Era* (University of Washington Press, 2008).

36 Andrew Barry, *op. cit.* note 3.

37 E.g. Toine Pieters, *Interferon: The Science and Selling of a Miracle Drug* (Taylor & Francis, 2005); Nelly Oudshoorn, *The Male Pill: A Biography of a Technology in the Making* (Duke University Press, 2003).

38 Harry M. Marks, *op. cit.* note 16; Stefan Timmemans and Marc Berg, *The Gold Standard: The Challenge of Evidence-Based Medicine and Standardization in Health Care* (Temple University Press, 2003).

39 For example, David Healy, *Pharmageddon* (University of California Press, 2012). There have been a great many focused criticisms of trial design; for a few that develop in connection with the STS literature, see Trudy Dehue, "Comparing Artificial Groups: On the History and Assumptions of the Randomised Controlled Trial," in Catherine Will and Tiago Moreira (eds.) *Medical Proofs, Social Experiments: Clinical Trials in Shifting Contexts* (Ashgate Publishing, 2010); Andrew Lakoff, "The Right Patients for the Drug: Managing the Placebo Effect in Antidepressant Trials," *BioSocieties* 2.1 (2007): 57–71; Linsey McGoey, "Profitable Failure: Antidepressant Drugs and the Triumph of Flawed Experiments," *History of the Human Sciences* 23.1 (2010): 58–78.

40 John Abraham and Courtney Davis, "Discovery and Management of Adverse Drug Reactions: The Nomifensine Hypersensitivity Syndrome, 1977–1986," *Social History of Medicine* 23.1 (2010): 153–173.

41 Philip Mirowski and Robert Van Horn, "The contract research organization and the commercialization of scientific research," *Social Studies of Science* 35.4 (2005): 503–548.

42 In each of these cases, the authors have written wider treatments of these issues. For an exploration of U.S. human and material infrastructure for commercial trials, see Jill A. Fisher *Medical Research for Hire: The Political Economy of Pharmaceutical Clinical Trials* (Rutgers University Press, 2009). For international commercial trials, especially focusing on the recruitment of subjects, see Adriana Petryna, *When Experiments Travel: Clinical Trials and the Global Search for Human Subjects* (Princeton University Press, 2009); and Kaushik Sunder Rajan, *Biocapital: The Constitution of Postgenomic Life* (Duke University Press, 2006). Peter Keating and Alberto Cambrosio, *Cancer on Trial: Oncology as a New Style of Practice* (University of Chicago Press, 2012), provides a close look at large cancer trials, showing ways in which the substantial infrastructures created do subtle research. The essays in Catherine Will and Tiago Moreira (eds.) *Medical Proofs, Social Experiments: Clinical Trials in Shifting Contexts* (Ashgate Publishing, 2010), explore different facets of the modern clinical trial, including its transformation and the

ways in which different locations affect its value and implementation. Roberto Abadie, *The Professional Guinea Pig: Big Pharma and the Risky World of Human Subjects* (Duke University Press, 2010) presents a detailed study of subjects for North American trials, mostly on the basis of an ethnographic study of a community of trial participants.

43 Arthur A. Daemmrich, *Pharmacopolitics: Drug Regulation in the United States and Germany* (University of North Carolina Press, 2004); Wen-Hua Kuo, "Understanding Race at the Frontier of Pharmaceutical Regulation: An Analysis of the Racial Difference Debate at the ICH," *The Journal of Law, Medicine & Ethics* 36.3 (2008): 498–505. The trend toward homogenization for purposes of testing drugs goes against U.S. pushes to differentiate and represent groups in biomedical research, as described by Steven Epstein, *Inclusion: The Politics of Difference in Medical Research* (University of Chicago Press, 2007).

44 John Abraham and Tim Reed, "Trading Risks for Markets: The International Harmonisation of Pharmaceuticals Regulation," *Health, Risk & Society* 3.1 (2001): 113–128.

45 E.g. Christer Nordlund, *Hormones of Life: Endocrinology, The Pharmaceutical Industry, and the Dream of a Remedy for Sterility, 1930-1970* (Science History Publications, 2011).

46 Alexa S. Dietrich, *The Drug Company Next Door: Pollution, Jobs, and Community Health in Puerto Rico* (New York University Press, 2013).

47 See Peter Conrad and Valerie Leiter, "From Lydia Pinkham to Queen Levitra: Direct-to-Consumer Advertising and Medicalisation," *Sociology of Health & Illness* 30.6 (2008): 825–838.

48 For example, Joel Lexchin and Barbara Mintzes, "Direct-to-Consumer Advertising of Prescription Drugs: The Evidence Says No," *Journal of Public Policy & Marketing* 21.2 (2002): 194–201; Barbara Mintzes, "For and against: Direct to Consumer Advertising Is Medicalising Normal Human Experience," *British Medical Journal* 324.7342 (2002): 908–911.

49 For example, Stefan Ecks, "Polyspherical Pharmaceuticals: Global Psychiatry, Capitalism, and Space," in Janis H. Jenkins (ed.) *Pharmaceutical Self: The Global Shaping of Experience in an Age of Psychopharmacology* (School for Advanced Research Press, 2011): 97–115.

50 For a summary focused on doctors' interactions with pharmaceutical companies, see Carl Elliott, *White Coat, Black Hat: Adventures on the Dark Side of Medicine* (Beacon Press, 2010).

51 For a related study of education of Japanese physicians to recognize and treat depression, see Kalman Applbaum, "Educating for Global Mental Health: The Adoption of SSRIs in Japan," in Adriana Petryna, Andrew Lakoff and Arthur Kleinman (eds.) *Global Pharmaceuticals: Ethics, Markets, Practices* (Duke University Press, 2006): 85–110; in Argentina, depression and anxiety are given both psychoanalytic and economic readings, yet remain treatable with drugs, as seen in Andrew Lakoff, *Pharmaceutical Reason: Knowledge and Value in Global Psychiatry* (Cambridge University Press, 2005).

52 Marc-André Gagnon, *The Nature of Capital in the Knowledge-Based Economy: The Case of the Global Pharmaceutical Industry* (Dissertation, York University, Toronto, 2009).

53 See also Alastair Matheson, "Corporate Science and the Husbandry of Scientific and Medical Knowledge by the Pharmaceutical Industry," *BioSocieties* 3.4 (2008): 355–382; Adriane Fugh-Berman, "The Haunting of Medical Journals: How Ghostwriting Sold 'HRT'," *PLoS Medicine* 7.9 (2010): e1000335.

54 Michael J. Oldani, "Thick Prescriptions: Toward an Interpretation of Pharmaceutical Sales Practices," *Medical Anthropology Quarterly* 18.3 (2004): 325–356. See also Jeremy A. Greene, "Attention to 'Details': Etiquette and the Pharmaceutical Salesman in Postwar America," *Social Studies of Science* 34.2 (2004): 271–292. It is interesting to juxtapose these academic treatments of the sales and marketing with former sales representatives' tell-all accounts, such as Jamie Reidy, *Hard Sell: The Evolution of a Viagra Salesman* (Andrews McMeel Publishing, 2005); Kimberly Cheryl, *Escape from the Pharma Drug Cartel: My Life as a Member of the Pharmaceutical Drug Cartel* (Outskirts Press, 2007), and John Virapen, *Side Effects: Death. Confessions of a Pharma-Insider* (Virtualbookworm.com, 2010).

55 Adrian Johns, *Piracy: The Intellectual Property Wars from Gutenberg to Gates* (University of Chicago Press, 2010).

56 See Jean-Paul Gaudillière, "How Pharmaceuticals Became Patentable: The Production and Appropriation of Drugs in the Twentieth Century," *History and Technology* 24.2 (2008): 99–106.

57 Peter Drahos, "Global Property Rights in Information: The Story of TRIPS at the GATT," *Prometheus* 13.1 (1995): 6–19.

58 Dominique A. Tobbell, *Pills, Power, and Policy: The Struggle for Drug Reform in Cold War America* (University of California Press, 2011).

59 Jeremy Greene and Elizabeth Watkins, *op. cit.* note 18; Marc A. Rodwin, *Conflicts of Interest and the Future of Medicine: The United States, France, and Japan* (Oxford University Press, 2011).

60 John Abraham, "Sociology of Pharmaceuticals Development and Regulation: A Realist Empirical Research Programme," *Sociology of Health & Illness* 30.6 (2008): 869–885.

61 This was earlier known as the Pharmaceutical Manufacturers Association (PMA).

62 Milton Silverman and Philip R. Lee, *Pills, Profits, and Politics* (University of California Press, 1974); Dominique A. Tobbell, *op. cit.* note 56.

63 Edward P. Thompson, "The Moral Economy of the English Crowd in the Eighteenth Century," in Edward P. Thompson, *Customs in Common: Studies in Traditional Popular Culture* (New Press, 1993): 185–258.

64 See Nicolas Rasmussen, "The moral economy of the drug company–medical scientist collaboration in interwar America," *Social Studies of Science* 34.2 (2004): 161–185. Following Rasmussen's in the use of the "moral economy" concept to study acceptable marketing practices and justifications by doctors to speak on behalf of pharmaceutical companies are Emily Martin, "Pharmaceutical Virtue," *Culture, Medicine and Psychiatry* 30 (2006): 157–174; Sergio Sismondo, "Key Opinion Leaders: Valuing Independence and Conflict of Interest in the Medical Sciences," and Christer Nordlund, "The Moral Economy of a Miracle Drug: On Exchange Relationships between Medical Science and the Pharmaceutical Industry in the 1940s," both in Isabelle Dussauge, Claes-Fredrik Helgesson, and Francis Lee (eds.) *Value Practices in the Life Sciences* (Oxford, 2014).

65 The most prominent industry estimates, now at over US $1 billion, are the product of one think tank created by the pharmaceutical industry in conjunction with radical neoliberal activists, as argued in Edward Nik-Khah, "Neoliberal pharmaceutical science and the Chicago School of Economics," *Social Studies of Science* 44 (2014, forthcoming). The figures have been challenged by, among others, Donald W. Light and Rebecca Warburton, "Demythologizing the High Costs of Pharmaceutical Research," *BioSocieties* 6.1 (2011): 34–50.

Part I
Pharmaceutical Lives

The Pharmaceutical Studies Reader, First Edition. Edited by Sergio Sismondo and Jeremy A. Greene.
© 2015 John Wiley & Sons, Inc. Published 2015 by John Wiley & Sons, Inc.

Pharmaceuticals play diverse and increasingly important roles in people's lives. In the Global South, many highly visible public health measures such as the global health campaigns against HIV/AIDS and malaria are tied to pharmaceutical delivery. In most of the Global North, the number of prescriptions per capita ranges from the low to high teens. It is not unusual for elderly people in these countries to consume ten or more different drugs on a daily basis. Health problems are strongly expected to be paired with pharmaceutical solutions. Thus, patients generally expect a successful trip to the doctor to end with at least one prescription, and chronic health conditions are usually accompanied by indefinitely long daily use of multiple drugs.

Sociologists Simon Williams, Paul Martin, and Jonathan Gabe offer us an umbrella term, pharmaceuticalization, to describe the increasing roles of pharmaceutical interventions. In Chapter 2, they describe how pharmaceuticalization can be driven by increased awareness or perceptions of disease; drug companies are often accused of "selling sickness" or "disease mongering." But they also draw attention to a number of other dimensions of pharmaceuticalization that can serve as entrees into other sections and essays in this volume: social identities that revolve around particular drugs or classes of drugs, changing regulatory landscapes that affect access to drugs, and non-medical uses of medical drugs. Williams, Martin, and Gabe ask us to consider the value of moving from a sociology of medicalization (which studies how human conditions come to be defined in terms of specific pathological categories) toward one of pharmaceuticalization (which studies instead how human conditions come to be defined in terms of our responses to them with specific therapeutic agents).

Is pharmaceuticalization an inevitable process, or is it driven by specific actors with specific agendas? In Chapter 3, anthropologist Joseph Dumit looks at two central pressures toward pharmaceuticalization. The first is the use of pharmaceutical marketing to recast individual experience in terms of disease and treatment; this is frequently seen in direct-to-consumer advertisements that simultaneously promote particular disease awareness and sell products. The second is the proliferation of risk factors, which turn all bodies into unhealthy ones: we are all at risk, differing only in our degrees of risk. This transformation of the normal and the pathological from a binary into a gradient helps to generate concern about and demand for health, a fact that can be exploited by pharmaceutical companies. As most of these conditions of risk are chronic, the prospect of treatments can extend indefinitely. And since we are all unhealthy in many ways, treatment—even successful—of risk factors or conditions allows us to focus on new ones, always increasing demand for health.

2

The Pharmaceuticalisation of Society? A Framework for Analysis

Simon J. Williams, Paul Martin and Jonathan Gabe

Drawing on insights from both medical sociology and science and technology studies, this article provides a critical analysis of the nature and status of pharmaceuticalisation in terms of the following key dimensions and dynamics: (i) the redefinition or reconfiguration of health 'problems' as having a pharmaceutical solution; (ii) changing forms of governance; (iii) mediation; (iv) the creation of new techno-social identities and the mobilisation of patient or consumer groups around drugs; (v) the use of drugs for non-medical purposes and the creation of new consumer markets; and, finally, (vi) drug innovation and the colonisation of health futures. Pharmaceuticalisation, we argue, is therefore best viewed in terms of a number of heterogeneous socio-technical processes that operate at multiple macro-levels and micro-levels that are often only partial or incomplete. The article concludes by drawing out some broader conceptual and reflexive issues this raises as to how we might best understand pharmaceuticalisation, based on our analysis, as a framework for future sociological work in this field.

Introduction

Medicalisation is a key concept in medical sociology and also has been employed in both professional and popular discourse on medicine and society. It is not a static concept, however, and there has recently been discussion about the changing engines or drivers of medicalisation (Conrad 2005, 2007), the costs of medicalisation (Conrad et al. 2010), the shift to a new techno-scientific era of biomedicalisation (Clarke et al. 2003) and other calls to rethink or go beyond medicalisation (Rose 2007, Moynihan 2002).

Simon J. Williams, Paul Martin and Jonathan Gabe. "The pharmaceuticalisation of society? A framework for analysis," in Sociology of Health & Illness 33 (5) (2011). pp. 710–725. Reproduced with permission from Wiley.

The Pharmaceutical Studies Reader, First Edition. Edited by Sergio Sismondo and Jeremy A. Greene.

One key development has been recognition of the growing importance of the pharmaceutical industry in medicalisation. While physicians are still the gatekeepers for many drugs, the role of pharmaceutical promoters is increasing by aggressively targeting the public as well as physicians (Conrad 2007). This article provides a further contribution to these debates through a detailed consideration of the related yet distinct notion of pharmaceuticalisation.

Definition, Delineation and Dynamics: What is Pharmaceuticalisation?

Pharmaceuticalisation is a not an entirely new sociological concept. While there has been an increase in the use of the term in recent years (see, for example, Abraham 2009a, Fox and Ward 2009, Williams et al. 2009), there has been little sustained effort, to date, to define and delineate its sociological credentials in a fashion comparable to that of medicalisation. So what then is pharmaceuticalisation?

At its simplest, 'pharmaceuticalisation' denotes the translation or transformation of human conditions, capabilities and capacities into opportunities for pharmaceutical intervention. These processes potentially extend far beyond the realms of the strictly medical or the medicalised (Conrad 2007) to encompass other non-medical uses for lifestyle, augmentation or enhancement purposes (amongst 'healthy' people). Relations between pharmaceuticalisation and medicalisation, as this suggests, are complex and contingent. Those taking up this term have often raised questions similar to those addressed about medicalisation and about the legitimacy of pharmaceuticalisation, thereby engaging in an element of social critique. Despite this, both medicalisation and pharmaceuticalisation should ideally be treated as value-neutral descriptive terms and may include both gains and losses to society. Furthermore, the degree or extent to which they are occurring remains open to empirical investigation on a case-by-case basis. Pharmaceuticalisation, in this respect, may be partial or incomplete.

It is useful, therefore, to frame pharmaceuticalisation as a dynamic and complex heterogeneous socio-technical process that is part of what we might call a 'pharmaceutical regime'. This can be understood as the networks of institutions, organisations, actors and artefacts, as well as the cognitive structures associated with the creation, production and use of new therapeutics (Goodman and Walsh 1993). Such a regime has been built around the development of pharmaceutical products since their introduction in the 19th century and is centred on the chemistry-based technology embodied in the pill. As we discuss below, one of the key dynamics of this regime is its continuing commercial, clinical and geographical expansion. This, in turn, alerts us to both upstream (macro) level processes concerning the development, testing and regulation of pharmaceuticals and downstream (micro) processes pertaining to the meaning and use of pharmaceuticals in medical practice and everyday life. As with medicalisation, pharmaceuticalisation is potentially at least a bidirectional process in which de-pharmaceuticalisation remains possible, though in practice, even in cases of drug withdrawal, it is more likely to be a matter of one type of drug or generation of drugs replacing another or a decline in usage rather than the complete phasing out of such interventions altogether, particularly if de-medicalisation does not occur as well. The history of pharmaceutical drug development, indeed, is one in which new drugs are often designed to offset the adverse effects of previous ones. Furthermore, we can identify social resistance to the process of pharmaceuticalisation as medicine use encroaches ever further, as well as its advocacy by patients and clinicians in completely new areas.

Pharmaceuticalisation therefore is a multidimensional, multi-level concept that lends itself to a variety of different perspectives. We focus on recent changes in the pharmaceutical regime that are making the use of drugs more expansive or pervasive, despite limited scientific evidence and a decline in pharmaceutical innovation regarding any genuine or significant therapeutic advances. What Busfield (2010) dubs the 'progressive' or scientific account of this expansion—in other words, the account based on professional or pharmaceutical industry appeals to advances in pharmacology, scientific progress and benefits to patient or public health—is of limited explanatory value here, as she convincingly shows. At the same time we hope to demonstrate not simply the value of pharmaceuticalisation as a social scientific concept and the light that different theoretical perspectives shed on these processes but the reasons why pharmaceuticalisation is becoming increasingly important.

Trends and Transformations

There are at least six key sociological dimensions to explore concerning trends and transformations in the pharmaceuticalisation of society.

Selling sickness? The redefinition and reconstruction of health problems as having a pharmaceutical solution

The first way in which an expansion of the pharmaceutical regime is visible is in the massive growth of drug markets internationally and in particular in the USA and Europe. As a consequence, pharmaceutical solutions to health problems have become much more widespread. Undoubtedly the pharmaceutical industry is one of the most profitable industries in the world, with leading companies reportedly enjoying profits of 25 per cent for most of the 1990s (Law 2006). Worldwide pharmaceutical sales now amount to over US$700 billion a year, with North American sales alone constituting around half of this market and North American and European sales amounting to three-quarters of all sales (IMS 2010). Although starting from a lower base, sales in middle-income countries such as China, India and Brazil are now increasing at a faster rate than in countries like the USA or the UK (Busfield 2010). Moreover there has been a phenomenal growth in pharmaceutical sales since the 1980s. While prescribed drug sales in the US, for example, remained fairly stable as a percentage of GDP from 1960 to 1980, they tripled between 1980 and 2000, thereby transforming what looked like a 'good' business into a 'stupendous' one (Angell 2005: 3–5). Similarly the global drugs bill increased thirty-fold between 1972 and 2005 (Law 2006). Overall, though, the distribution of pharmaceutical sales across the world remains uneven—a picture which reflects the more chronic health problems of those in affluent (ageing) societies who require long-term medication.

It is not, however, simply a case of the manufacture of drugs but the marketing, if not manufacture, of disorders for these drugs to treat. Pharmaceutical companies, as Conrad notes, 'are now marketing diseases, not just drugs' (2007: 19). Moynihan has been a particularly vocal critic on this count (Moynihan 2002, Moynihan and Henry 2006; see also Blech 2006). He contends that some forms of medicalising ordinary life may now better be described as disease mongering or selling sickness—that is, 'widening the boundaries of treatable illness in order to expand markets for products' (Moynihan 2002: 886). Pharmaceutical companies, it is claimed, are 'actively involved in sponsoring the definition of diseases and promoting them to both prescribers and consumers': a process in which the social construction of illness is being replaced by the 'corporate construction of disease' (2002: 886). This involves: (i) turning ordinary ailments into medical problems; (ii) seeing mild symptoms as serious; (iii) treating personal problems as medical; (iv) seeing risks as diseases; and (v) framing prevalence estimates to maximise potential markets (Moynihan 2002).

In support of these contentions, in recent years a range of studies has appeared on conditions ranging from erectile dysfunction (Lexchin 2006) to restless leg syndrome (Woloshin and Schwartz 2006). As with medicalisation, however, these processes may result in various forms of resistance, as Tiefer's (2006) study of female sexual dysfunction suggests.

These critiques are undoubtedly important and valuable. Compared to both medicalisation and pharmaceuticalisation, however, disease mongering is clearly a value-laden rather than a value-neutral term, with an in-built element of normative judgement and social critique. While disease mongering thus captures an important range of issues pertinent to the broader concept of pharmaceuticalisation, its analytic value is clearly restricted. Pharmaceuticalisation may or may not involve elements of disease mongering on the part of the pharmaceutical industry.

Another important vehicle for pharmaceutical market expansion is direct-to-consumer (DTC) advertising. To date this is limited to countries such as the USA and New Zealand, although attempts to overturn the ban, or at least to change the rules to enable pharmaceutical companies to provide more 'information' to patients, continue in Europe. One of the great ironies of DTC advertising, as Conrad and Leiter (2004) note, is that it extends the relationship between drug companies, physicians and consumers in ways that return us to the advertising of patent medicines in the past, when drug manufacturers had a direct and independent relationship with consumers. This shift is explored further below, along with a range of other ways of marketing disorders as well as drugs, including what Angell (2005) appositely dubs 'marketing masquerading as education' and 'marketing masquerading as research'.

Changing forms of governance: Globalisation and the new role of regulatory agencies in promoting innovation

The second important dimension of pharmaceuticalisation is manifest in the changing relationship between regulatory agencies and the pharmaceutical industry. This has three components; firstly, reforms that have reduced the regulatory hurdle and increased the dependency of regulatory agencies on industry; secondly, new policies that have increased the role of regulatory agencies in promoting drug innovation; and thirdly, the globalisation of established models of governance based on the interests of the pharmaceutical industry in the developed world.

Important sociological work on the science and politics of medicines regulation has occurred over the past two decades. Abraham (1995, 2009a, 2009b, 2010, Abraham and Davis 2005), for example, has been at the forefront of these developments through detailed empirical case studies of the regulation of medicines such as anti-inflammatories, antidepressants and sleeping tablets and comparative analyses of regulatory institutions and processes. This work has provided evidence of a corporate bias and privileged access by pharmaceutical companies to regulatory bodies such as the Food and Drug Administration (FDA) in the USA and the Medicine and Health Care Products Regulatory Agency (MHRA) in the UK. Other work in this area has focused on regulatory responsiveness to patients' demands for the accelerated approval of new drugs (Daemmrich 2004) and the fragmentation of expert authority and its consequences for regulatory decision-making (Gabe and Bury 1996a). This research raises questions about the extent to which pharmaceutical regulation is failing to act in the interests of public health: a failure that is camouflaged by claims that regulators can promote the interests of the pharmaceutical industry and the interests of public health simultaneously, when they are, in fact, in conflict (Abraham 2009b: 66).

At the same time there are clear signs that the relationship between the pharmaceutical industry and state regulatory agencies is getting even closer. For example, the industry has been required to pay most of the cost of funding of regulatory agencies—a 100% funding for the MHRA since 1989, with similar trends in the EU (70% funding) and the USA (50% funding) since the mid-1990s. In return it has seen a significant reduction in the regulatory review times for new patentable drugs, which have tumbled by half in the USA since 1993, with similar dramatic falls evident in Europe (Abraham 2009b: 60). Furthermore, new measures, such as fast-tracking approval of drugs for 'serious' or 'life-threatening' conditions with less data than would normally be expected to demonstrate safety or efficacy has resulted in around 14 per cent of new drugs receiving such approval over the last 15 years in the EU (Garattini and Bertele 2001). While reductions in review times may be in the interests of patients who need these drugs as soon as possible, the upshot of these changes, as Abraham (2009b) rightly stresses, is that they leave regulatory agencies vulnerable to the pressures of the market. In effect, these agencies are encouraged to compete with each other by making themselves attractive to drug companies who have come to be defined, in keeping with neoliberal ideology, as the regulator's 'customers'. Having said this, it is important to recognise that the pharmaceutical industry broadly supports the existing regulatory regime despite the high cost associated with compliance. This is for a number of reasons, including the consumer confidence that is associated with a rigorous regulatory regime and the high barrier to market entry this poses for new entrants.

In recent years a number of the major international drug regulatory agencies, including the FDA and the European Medicines Evaluation Agency, have started to play an increasing role in supporting pharmaceutical innovation. New activities such as the FDA's critical path initiative explore how new forms of regulatory science and technology used in the drug approval process can be developed to streamline the route to market. This change in the role of regulators from guardians of the public health to also having a key role in promoting innovation has to be set against the background of the continuing productivity crisis in the pharmaceutical industry (Hopkins et al. 2007, Nightingale and Martin 2004).

At the same time, there has been a globalisation of the dominant western regulatory system through such initiatives as the International Conference on Harmonisation, which brings together regulators from Europe, Japan and the USA with the aim of creating greater harmonisation in the interpretation and application of regulatory guidelines for drug development and approval. There are two main drivers of this expansion of the western regulatory model: (i) the opening-up of new markets for global pharmaceutical companies to sell their products in emerging economies, such as India; and (ii) the outsourcing of important aspects of the drug development process to developing countries where the costs of clinical trials are much lower. However, this is not a simple repeat of the drug dumping in the 1970s and 1980s, as minimum standards of clinical care and safety are now required to enable the data collected in non-western clinical trials to be useful for drug approvals in North America and Europe. This shift to testing new drugs in developing countries has also been accompanied by the globalisation of manufacturing and, to a lesser extent, the process of drug discovery itself through investment in new research facilities in countries like China (Kuemmerle 1999).

Mediation: The (re)framing of health problems in the media and popular culture as having a pharmaceutical solution

Everything these days, it seems, is mediated one way or another. In particular, as the earlier discussion of disease mongering suggests, media involvement, witting or unwitting, facilitates processes of pharmaceuticalisation. Woloshin and Schwartz (2006), for example, in their study of news coverage of restless leg syndrome, suggest that the media have been co-opted into disease mongering about this condition given stories that: (i) exaggerated the prevalence of the disease and the need for treatment (with drugs such as ropinirole); and (ii) failed to consider the problem of over-diagnosis (2006: e170).

Kroll-Smith (2003), too, in a provocative article on the social construction of sleepiness in popular culture, points to the critical role the media now play in processes of medicalisation and, by extension, pharmaceuticalisation: extra-institutional, textually mediated forms of authority are cast in the rhetoric of medicine yet are far removed from the traditional doctor–patient relationship.

To the extent, then, that the media, directly or indirectly, are complicit in these processes of disease mongering and in so far as framing problems in this way promotes pharmaceutical interests, mediation of this kind is clearly important in relation to pharmaceuticalisation. The media, however, are not so much creators or catalysts as conveyors and amplifiers of these processes over time; the drivers lie elsewhere. Perhaps the clearest example of this is DTC advertising where the media effectively become a marketing tool in the service of pharmaceutical interests, alongside other forms of marketing masquerading as education, information or research (Angell 2005). These techniques include the voices of both experts and patients, as well as celebrity endorsements and offers of symptom based self-testing. This, in turn, provides diagnostic validity to the condition in question and the proposed pharmaceutical solution on offer—albeit with the proviso, 'Ask your doctor if [drug x] is right for you'. It also creates the impression that the condition is one that could happen to anyone (Conrad 2007: 18), thereby ensuring fertile ground for potential market expansion of the kind discussed earlier.

The media, nonetheless, are no mere puppets of pharmaceutical interests. Media coverage of pharmaceuticals may be contradictory or condemnatory, oscillating between oppositional extremes of both idealisations on the one hand, and demonisation on the other (Seale 2002). A temporal pattern may be discerned here, with early media coverage of new drugs such as Prozac and Viagra being largely uncritical if not celebratory in tone and content. If or when unwelcome side effects become apparent, however, or misuse of some kind (by doctors, patients or consumers) is detected, then negative or critical portrayals soon follow. This is clearly demonstrated by the changing media coverage of benzodiazepines over time (Gabe and Bury 1996b). Rarely, it seems, do the media present a balanced portrayal of the risks and benefits contained in a single substance (Seale 2002: 148): doubtless as a product, in part, of the imperative for newsworthy stories.

Other so-called new media are also important to consider here, not simply in terms of access to pharmaceutical information or support via the Web, but in terms of the purchase of pharmaceutical products online, thereby effectively bypassing the traditional doctor–patient relationship. Fox and Ward (2009), for example, in their study of the pharmaceuticalisation of daily life, identify two broad processes at work. These are: first, a domestication of pharmaceutical consumption through computer-mediated access and consumption in the home, particularly in the bedroom (e.g. Viagra and Cialis for sexual potency) and the kitchen (for example, Xenical, Alli and Apidex for weight loss); and second, the pharmaceuticalisation of everyday life, as pharmaceuticals are treated as magic bullets for a range of day-to-day life problems. As with other media, however, these processes are far from straightforward. Indeed, the internet may provide both new channels for the pharmaceuticalisation of daily life (Fox et al. 2005a) and new spaces or forums for challenging or reworking prevailing understandings and practices. This is clearly demonstrated in the case of pro-anorexia websites (Fox et al. 2005b).

Patients, consumers and the life world: The creation of new social identities and the mobilisation of patient or consumer groups around drugs

It is one thing to map these macro-level processes to do with the regulation of medicines and related questions of market expansion and mediation but this of course gives rise to further important questions about the role of patients or consumers in these processes of (de-)

pharmaceuticalisation. Much has been written in recent years about the increasingly active, if not critical, role patients and consumers play in their own healthcare. Previous sociological work on the meaning and use of medicines (for example, Gabe and Lipshitz-Phillips 1984, Williams and Calnan 1996) has been joined by a variety of other recent work in which attention has increasingly focused on users of pharmaceuticals as knowledgeable reflexive actors, assessing risks and benefits and making informed choices about their treatment (Stevenson et al. 2002, 2009). These developments, in turn, are reflected and reinforced through current health policies in both the USA and the UK that construct patients as experts, particularly the chronically ill, working in partnership with healthcare professionals (Taylor and Bury 2007). Furthermore, there have been attempts to reclassify some prescription-only medicines as over-the-counter (OTC), and policies to make the arrangements for the prescribing and supplying of medicines more flexible, including delimited prescribing by nurses and pharmacists (Weiss and Sutton 2009). And these in turn chime with broader trends towards a knowledge-based society in which health-related information and products are readily available on-line at the click of a mouse (Nettleton et al. 2005).

On the one hand the rise of the articulate or information rich consumer, and associated forms of patient expertise, suggest the potential for various challenges or forms of resistance to pharmaceuticalisation. On the other hand, however, these developments may themselves fuel or facilitate further processes of pharmaceuticalisation, including patient-driven demand for pharmaceuticals (of which more in the next section of this article), with or without the aid of DTC advertising and other forms of 'marketing' on the part of the pharmaceutical industry. Certainly there is evidence, as we have already seen, of new forms of pharmaceutical consumption through computer-mediated access which effectively bypass traditional patient-professional relations and existing forms of governance (Fox and Ward 2009, Fox et al. 2007, Seale 2005). This in turn suggests that consumerism is an important driver of pharmaceuticalisation, with or without the aid of professional input or industry influence.

Questions arise regarding not simply the implications of these processes for individual subjectivity or selfhood (cf. Rose 2007) but the multiple ways in which patients and consumers of medicines act collectively to represent their interests as members of self-help groups, patient advocacy organisations or health social movements in the public sphere (Brown et al. 2004, Gibbon and Novas 2008, Kelleher 2004). These issues are further complicated when some of these groups, with pharmaceutical company support, press for early access to as yet unlicensed medicines while others demand that pharmaceutical companies remove what they claim to be unsafe drugs from the market. Overall, the apparent power of patient activism or collective consumer mobilisation may therefore 'significantly depend on whether it is supporting or contravening the fundamental interests of the pharmaceutical industry' (Abraham 2009a: 113). This may go some way to explaining the apparent meagre success of citizen activism in battles against pharmaceutical companies over drug injury to patients, compared with the success of patient groups seeking access to drugs in alliance with pharmaceutical manufacturers (Abraham 2009a). The latter includes recent high-profile cases, attracting considerable media attention, of demands to obtain new drugs on the National Health Service for breast cancer (Herceptin), multiple sclerosis (Beta Interferon) and (early onset) Alzheimer's disease (Aricept).

Whether or not such success amounts to the industry 'capture' of consumer groups' agendas is a subject of ongoing debate. Jones (2009), for example, in her recent research on health consumer groups and the pharmaceutical industry in the UK, finds little to confirm the notion of industry capture. Further questions also arise here, however, regarding pharmaceutical companies' attempts to educate or inform patients and consumers and their convergence with expert patient agendas. 'Expert patient' discourses have proved particularly useful in various pharmaceutical campaigns on this front, both in countries where DTC advertising is permitted and in others, as in Europe, where it is not. Appeals to expert patients serve a dual purpose: legitimising pharmaceutical education campaigns on the one hand, while challenging the ban on DTC advertising by characterising patients as informed consumers about drugs on the other hand. Viewed in this more critical light the industry, it appears, wishes to 'use patients as a means of de-regulation and market expansion, without regard to wider health interests' (Abraham 2009a: 114).

It therefore appears that trends toward consumerism in healthcare and associated developments such as the expert patient programme, in the main are congruent with, rather than a challenge to, the interests of the pharmaceutical industry. Indeed, patients and consumers may actively and willing collaborate in processes of pharmaceuticalisation, particularly when much needed treatments are sought.

From treatment to enhancement? The use of drugs for non-medical purposes and the creation of new consumer markets

These discussions of consumerism in turn mesh with another important set of developments regarding the pharmaceuticalisation of everyday life: drugs for enhancement purposes among healthy people. The desire to improve ourselves in one way or another, of course, is as old as human history. Enhancement itself, however, remains a contested term, not least because it is frequently employed to denote going beyond treatment or health to become 'better than well' (Elliot 2003)—distinctions which themselves are socially constructed and changeable over time.

Conrad (2007), for example, usefully refers to three main types of biomedical enhancement: firstly, normalisation, where biomedical enhancements are used to bring the body in line with what doctors or patients deem to be normal or with socially expected standards; secondly, repair, in which biomedical interventions are used to restore or rejuvenate the body to its previous condition; and thirdly, augmentation, in order to improve or boost life performance in ways that confer the user with a competitive edge (2007: 87–9). Context, of course is also important to consider in the sense that the very notion of enhancement inheres 'not in the biomedical composition of the intervention, but in when and how it is used' (Conrad 2007: 89). Enhancement, moreover, represents a social temptation in a culture that values 'bigger, faster and more' and where competitive difference amongst otherwise similar individuals offers personal advantage and social rewards for those who have 'an edge' (Conrad 2007: 89).

One issue attracting considerable attention on this count at the moment is the promise of a new era of cognitive enhancement drugs designed to boost alertness, concentration, memory and other aspects of cognitive functioning. A flurry of recent reports and articles has emerged in response to these developments, in which the ethical, legal and social implications of cognitive enhancement drugs and the degree to which they should be regulated loom large (Academy of Medical Sciences 2008, British Medical Association 2007, Office of Science and Technology 2005). Consider, for example, a recent controversial commentary, provocatively entitled 'Toward responsible use of cognitive enhancing drugs by the healthy', which appeared in *Nature* (Greely et al. 2008). Many drugs used to treat psychiatric and neurological conditions such as methylphenidate (attention deficit hyperactivity disorder), Ritalin and Aricept (Alzheimer's) and modafinil (narcolepsy), it is noted, also improve cognitive performance amongst the healthy and are being re-marketed for this purpose, particular on 'university campuses around the world' (Greely 2008: 702). Cognitive enhancement, these authors state, has 'much to offer individuals and society', including extending work productivity and delaying normal and pathological age-related cognitive decline. A 'proper societal response', therefore, they conclude 'will involve making enhancements available while managing their risks' (2008: 702).

Given that neither the medical nor the social risks of such cognitively enhanced futures are understood at present, caution is indeed needed here when evaluating the use of such drugs amongst healthy people (Williams and Martin 2008). Critically, attempts to reconstruct the use of medicines as enhancement can be understood as another example of the move to create new drug markets through direct relationships with consumers that lie outside the control of the medical profession. The prospect of cognitive enhancement, therefore, clearly demonstrates both the potential of consumerism to drive these processes of pharmaceuticalisation and the ways in which any such pharmaceuticalisation may take us beyond medicalisation.

Pharmaceutical futures in the making: Drug innovation and the colonisation of health futures

Our sixth and final set of issues concerns questions of innovation, imagination and the making of pharmaceutical futures. Recent work in the sociology of expectations has drawn attention to the key role of the future in shaping the present. In particular, it highlights the dynamic role that expectations play in attracting support and investors and building mutually binding obligations or communities of hope or promise (Brown 2003, van Lente 1993). It also shows how these expectations differ between various groups or stakeholders (such as scientists, the industry, consumers, policy communities, patients and publics), and how the futures envisaged are contingent, contested and fought over (Brown and Michael 2003, Hedgecoe and Martin 2003). In the process, this work emphasises the considerable hope that patients, both individually and collectively, invest in future pharmaceutical breakthroughs in the treatment of their conditions (Novas 2006).

Take, for instance, the field of pharmacogenetics and pharmacogenomics (that is, the use of genetic or genomic knowledge to predict drug reactions). This field has engendered much speculation about a new era of personalised or tailor-made medicine with prevention and treatment geared to an individual's genetic profile. This, in turn, holds the promise of greatly reducing adverse drug reactions that are commonly associated with current one-size fits all interventions. In addition, by targeting drugs at particular genotypes it is argued that the effectiveness of treatment will be enhanced.

Such pharmaceutical innovation also forms the basis for much policy planning and the imagining of future healthcare scenarios (Department of Health 2003). In this way pharmacogenetics can be thought of as colonising the future and crowding out other alternative paths for development. This pharmaceuticalisation of the future may help to maintain the hegemony of a dominant biomedical discourse that constructs investment and innovation in the search for new medicines as the best way of improving human health. However, the reality of how new pharmaceutical technologies are translated into practice is rather more complex.

Certainly, pharmacogenetic data of the kind described above is now feeding into all stages of the research and development process (Webster et al. 2004). At present, however, progress remains slow and uneven and there appears to be little evidence of widespread benefits of the kind envisaged by these expectations (Hopkins et al. 2007: 8). At the same time these developments have generated a range of concerns from diverse constituencies, including potential worries about over-segmented (that is, unprofitable) markets, the proliferation of genetic testing and the racial politics they stimulate (Hedgecoe 2004, Hedgecoe and Martin 2003). Even the very notion of personalised medicine is something of a misnomer (that is, it is neither especially personalised nor tailor-made). It is also important to bear in mind that the clinical acceptability and utility of genomic-based therapies has to be placed in the context of particular regimes of treatment and practice. For example, Barr and Rose (2009) found in their study of the pharmacogenomics of antidepressant medications that there was considerable ambivalence regarding the use of antidepressant medication amongst patients with depression and a commonplace tendency to conflate a pharmacogenomic test for antidepressant medication with a genetic test for depression.

Furthermore, despite much talk of a medicinal biotechnology revolution, in which pharmaceutical innovation looms large, evidence drawn from a variety of empirical indicators highlights a major productivity crisis in the industry (Hopkins et al. 2007, Nightingale and Martin 2004). Despite the rise in potential drug targets flowing from genomics, a very significant increase in research and development expenditure since the 1970s, and the aforementioned neoliberal acceleration of regulatory approval times over the past 20 years, pharmaceutical innovation has actually been static or declining world wide over the past two decades (as measured by the number of new chemical entities approved in a given year, or the number of new patented drug compounds launched on the world market) (Hopkins et al. 2007, Law 2006). This is not to say that biotechnology will not deliver on these counts in the future. However, rather than producing revolutionary changes, medicinal biotechnology appears to be following a well-established path of slow, incremental technological diffusion (Nightingale and Martin 2004). Caution, at the very least, is therefore needed with respect to the pharmaceutical present if not to pharmaceutical futures in the making.

Viewed in this light, then, one may perhaps be forgiven for asking why the belief in the biotechnology revolution remains so influential. Expectations, in part at least, provide the answer. They are critical to the very processes of technological change, successful or otherwise. Or, to put it more strongly, the claims underpinning the biotechnology revolution may best be viewed as 'rhetorical devices employed to generate the necessary political, social and financial capital to allow perceived promise to emerge' (Hopkins et al. 2007: 21). Sociologists and other social scientists studying these processes, moreover, are far from innocent bystanders. Indeed, one of the reflexive messages the sociology of expectations teaches us is the need to examine our own expectations and their role in the very co- production of the field in question, including the various pharmaceutical futures we profess to analyse.

Discussion

Where then, returning to the questions posed at the beginning of this article, does this leave us? What is pharmaceuticalisation? Is it a useful sociological term? Why is it important to consider it now? And what remains to be done in terms of future sociological research agendas?

Pharmaceuticalisation, we have argued, can be understood as a dynamic and complex heterogeneous socio-technical process that is part of the long-term and ongoing construction of the pharmaceutical regime, including distinct socioeconomic activities and diverse actors such as clinicians, patients or consumers and regulators. These activities are part of the ongoing process of the pharmaceutical industry, extending its power and reach.

Six key sociological dimensions of pharmaceuticalisation have been identified as a framework for analysis, namely: (i) the redefinition or reconfiguration of health problems as having a pharmaceutical solution; (ii) the changing relationship between state regulatory agencies and the pharmaceutical industry; (iii) the mediation of pharmaceuticals in popular culture and daily life; (iv) the creation of new techno-social identities and the mobilisation of patient or consumer groups around drugs; (v) the use of drugs for non-medical (enhancement) purposes and the creation of new consumer markets, and finally; (vi) drug innovation and the colonisation of health futures, albeit in an industry plagued by a major crisis over productivity and innovation.

Looking over these sociological dimensions of pharmaceuticalisation a number of common features are apparent, notably: a) the expansion of drug markets outside traditional areas, including new medical indications and conditions, new territories in developing countries and new applications in healthy individuals; b) the increasing dominance of state regulatory and public health agendas; c) increasing moves to bypass the dominance of the medical profession through reconstructing the role of patients and consumers and creating more direct relationships with these groups; and d) the colonisation of the life world, everyday life and health futures by pharmaceutical solutions. We suggest that, taken together, these are important recent changes that provide a comprehensive picture of pharmaceuticalisation that is distinct from medicalisation in important respects and of particular relevance to contemporary developments. These changes can be thought of as an important shift in the types both of markets and applications targeted by the pharmaceutical industry and a transformation in the socio-technical relationships between key actor groups, with industry increasingly dominating regulatory agencies, bypassing medical control and reconstructing the role of patients and consumers. This highlights the analytic value of pharmaceuticalisation as a specific sociological concept that is of increasing relevance. In particular, it is valuable in drawing attention to the work of the pharmaceutical industry as one of the key actors in contemporary biomedicine, providing an analytical framework for empirical and theoretical research and helping to prompt a shift in the gaze of medical sociology.

It would be wrong, however, to overstate the speed or scope of pharmaceuticalisation. As mentioned in the introduction, the expansion of the pharmaceutical industry and its products and markets has been happening for over a century, although this has arguably intensified in the last few decades. Furthermore, as we have stressed, the complex relationship between the industry, the state and the medical profession places real structural limits on the extent to which drug companies can operate outside the control of either government or medicine, as both provide vital sources of legitimation. State sanction through the regulatory process plays a key role in both regulating market entry and ensuring consumer confidence, while the medical profession's role as gatekeeper is rooted in mediating the sick role and regulating people's access to healthcare. Finally, there are important sources of resistance to the expansion of pharmaceutical markets from the media, government, medicine, patients and diverse publics thereby making de-pharmaceuticalisation a possibility in principle, if infrequent in practice.

It is not our intention in this article to provide some sort of grand theoretical synthesis. To do so may well be premature, if not unnecessary, at this particular juncture. To the extent, moreover, that pharmaceuticalisation is a multi-level and multidimensional concept, there is strength or merit in theoretical eclecticism. Keeping our theoretical options open, in other words, may well be wise at this point. There are also significant opportunities here, through concepts linked to multi-level and multiple dimensions, such as pharmaceuticalisation, to foster further fruitful links between ongoing work in medical sociology and Science and Technology Studies (STS) on these matters.

Future research agendas might, therefore, consider a number of key issues, including studies of the role of industry in expanding pharmaceutical markets to cover new diseases, disorders and other non-medical conditions, the changing role of regulatory authorities, the reconstruction of the role of patients and consumers in the development and use of drugs and the way in which the life world, everyday life and health futures are being colonised by pharmaceutical solutions. In doing so, sociologists must also be reflexive about their own role in the creation or, to borrow a much favoured term from STS, the co-production of these very matters concerning both the pharmaceuticalisation of society to date and the contested or colonised futures to which they speak.

REFERENCES

Abraham, J. (2009a) The pharmaceutical industry, the state and the NHS. In Gabe, J. and Calnan, M. (eds) *The New Sociology of the Health Service*. London: Routledge.

Abraham, J. (2009b) Sociology of pharmaceuticals development and regulation: a realist empirical research programme. In Williams, S.J., Gabe, J. and Davis, P. (eds) *Pharmaceuticals and Society: Critical Discourses and Debates*. Oxford: Blackwell.

Abraham, J. (2010) On the prohibition of conflicts of interest in pharmaceutical regulation: precautionary limits and permissive challenges. A commentary on Sismondo and O'Donovan and Lexchin, *Social Science and Medicine*, 70, 648–51.

Abraham, J. and Davis, C. (2005) Risking public safety: experts, the medical profession and 'acceptable' drug injury, *Health, Risk and Society*, 7, 379–95.

Abraham, J.W. (1995) *Science, Politics and the Pharmaceutical Industry*. London: University College London Press.

Academy of Medical Sciences (2008) *Brain Science, Addictions and Drugs*. London: AMS.

Angell, M. (2005) *The Truth about Drug Companies*. New York: Random House.

Barr, M. and Rose, D. (2009) The great ambivalence; factors likely to affect service user and public acceptability of the pharmacogenomics of antidepressant medication. In Williams, S.J., Gabe, J. and Davis, P. (eds) *Pharmaceuticals and Society: Critical Discourses and Debates*. Oxford: Blackwell.

Blech, J. (2006) *Inventing Diseases and Pushing Pills*. London: Routledge.

British Medical Association (2007) *Boosting Your Brain Power: Ethical Aspects of Cognitive Enhancements*. London: BMA.

Brown, N. (2003) Hope against hype: accountability in biopasts, presents and futures, *Science Studies, The Medicalisation of Society* 16, 3–2.

Brown, N. and Michael, M. (2003) A sociology of expectations: retrospecting prospects and prospecting retrospects, *Technology Assessment and Strategic Management*, 15, 3–18.

Brown, P., Zavestoski, S., McCormick, S., Mayer, B., et al. (2004) Embodied health movements: new approaches to social movements in health, *Sociology of Health and Illness*, 26, 1, 50–80.

Busfield, J. (2003) Globalization and the pharmaceutical industry revisited, *International Journal of Health Services*, 33, 581–603.

Busfield, J. (2010) 'A pill for every ill': explaining the expansion in medicine use, *Social Science and Medicine*, 70, 931–41.

Clarke, A, Fishman, J., Fosket, J.R., Mamo, L. and Shim, J. (2003) Biomedicalization: technoscientific transformations of health, illness and US biomedicine, *American Sociological Review*, 68, 161–94.

Conrad, P. (2005) The shifting engines of medicalization, *Journal of Health and Social Behavior*, 46, 3–14.

Conrad, P. (2007). Baltimore: Johns Hopkins University Press Conrad, P. and Leiter, V. (2004) Medicalization, markets and consumers, *Journal of Health and Social Behavior*, 45, 158–76.

Conrad, P. and Leiter, V. (2009) From Lydia Pinkham to Queen Levitra: direct-to-consumer advertising and medicalization. In Williams, S.J., Gabe, J. and Davis, P. (eds) *Pharmaceuticals and Society: Critical Discourses and Debates*. Oxford: Blackwell.

Conrad, P., Mackie, T. and Mehrota, A. (2010) The costs of medicalization, *Social Science and Medicine*, 70, 1943–47.

Daemmrich, A. (2004) *Pharmacopolitics*. Chapel Hill: University of North Carolina.

Department of Health (2003) *Our Inheritance, Our Future: Realising the Potential of Genetics in the NHS*. UK Government White Paper. London: Department of Health.

Elliot, C. (2003) *Better Than Well: American Medicine Meets the American Dream*. New York: W.W. Norton.

Fox, N.J. and Ward, K.J. (2009) Pharma in the bedroom ... and the kitchen. *The pharmaceuticalisation of daily life*. In Williams, S.J., Gabe, J. and Davis, P. (eds) *Pharmaceuticals and Society: Critical Discourses and Debates*. Oxford: Blackwell.

Fox, N.J., Ward, K.J. and O'Rourke, A.J. (2005a) The 'expert patient': empowerment or medical dominance? *The case of weight loss, pharmaceutical drugs and the internet, Social Science and Medicine*, 60, 1299–309.

Fox, N.J., Ward, K.J. and O'Rourke, A.J. (2005b) Pro-anorexia, weight-loss drugs and the internet: an 'anti-recovery' explanatory model of anorexia, *Sociology of Health and Illness*, 27, 7, 944–71.

Fox, N.J., Ward, K.J. and O'Rourke, A.J. (2007) A sociology of technology governance for the information age: the case of pharmaceuticals, consumer advertising and the internet, *Sociology*, 40, 315–34.

Gabe, J. and Bury, M. (1996a) Halcyon nights: a sociological account of a medical controversy, *Sociology*, 30, 447–69.

Gabe, J. and Bury, M. (1996b) Risking tranquilliser use: cultural and lay dimensions. In Williams, S. and Calnan, M. (eds) *Modern Medicine*. London: University College London Press.

Gabe, J. and Lipshitz-Phillips, S. (1984) Tranquillisers as social control? *Sociological Review*, 32, 524–46.

Garattini, S. and Bertele, V. (2001) Adjusting Europe's drug regulation to public health needs, *The Lancet*, 358, 66.

Gibbon, S. and Novas, C. (eds) *Biosocialities, Genetics and the Social Sciences*. London: Routledge.

Goodman, J. and Walsh, V. (1993) Little and Big Heuristics: medicine, chemistry and pharmaceutical production in nineteenth-century Europe. Paper given at Society for the History of Technology (SHOT), Conference on Technological Change, Oxford, 8-11 September 1993.

Greely, H., Sahakian, B., Harris, J., Kessler, R.C., et al. (2008) Towards responsible use of cognitive-enhancing drugs by the healthy, *Nature*, 456, 702–5.

Hedgecoe, A. (2004) *The Politics of Personalised Medicine*. Cambridge: Cambridge University Press.

Hedgecoe, A. and Martin, P. (2003) The drugs don't work: expectations and the shaping of pharmacogenetics, *Social Studies of Science*, 33, 327–64.

Hopkins, M.H., Martin, P.A., Nightingale, P., Kraft, A., et al. (2007) The myth of the biotech revolution: an assessment of technological, clinical and organisational change, *Research Policy*, 36, 566–89.

IMS Heath (2010) Press releases: IMS health forecasts. Available at http://www.imshealth.com/ portal/site/imshealth (last accessed 6 December 2010).

Jones, K. (2009) In whose interest? Relationships between health consumer groups and the pharmaceutical industry in the UK. In Williams, S.J., Gabe, J. and Davis, P. (eds) *Pharmaceuticals and Society: Critical Discourses and Debates*. Oxford: Blackwell.

Kelleher, D. (2004) Self help groups and their relationship to medicine. In Kelleher, D., Gabe, J. and Williams, G. (eds) (2004) *Challenging Medicine*. 2nd edition, London: Routledge.

Kuemmerle, W. (1999) Foreign direct investment in industrial research in the pharmaceutical and electronics industries – results from a survey of multinational firms, *Research Policy*, 28, 179–93.

Kroll-Smith, S. (2003) Popular media and 'excessive sleepiness', *Sociology of Health and Illness*, 25,6, 625–43.

Law, J. (2006) *The Big Pharma*. London: Constable and Robinson.

Lexchin, J. (2006) Bigger and better: how Pfizer redefined erectile dysfunction, *Public Library of Science Medicine*, 3, e132.

Moynihan, R. (2002) Disease-mongering: how doctors, drug companies, and insurers are making you feel sick, *British Medical Journal*, 324, 923.

Moynihan, R. and Henry, D. (2006) The fight against disease mongering: generating knowledge for action, Public Library of Science Medicine, 3e, 191.

Nettleton, S., Burrows, R. and O'Malley, L. (2005) The mundane realities of the everyday lay use of the internet for health, and their consequences for media convergence, *Sociology of Health and Illness*, 27, 7, 972–92.

Nightingale, P. and Martin, P.A. (2004) The myth of the biotech revolution, *Trends in Biotechnology*, 22, 564–69.

Novas, C. (2006) The political economy of hope: patients' organizations, science and biovalue, *Biosocieties*, 1, 289–305.

Office of Science and Technology Department of Trade and Industry (2005) *Drugs Futures 2025*. London: DTI.

Rose, N. (2007) *The Politics of Life Itself*. Princeton: Princeton University Press.

Seale, C. (2002) *Media and Health*. London: Sage.

Seale, C. (2005) New directions for critical internet health studies, *Sociology of Health and Illness*., 27, 4, 515–40.

Stevenson, F., Britten, N., Barry, C., Bradley, C. and Barber, N. (2002) Perceptions of legitimacy: the influence on medicine taking and prescribing, *Health*, 6, 85–104.

Stevenson, F., Leontowitsch, M. and Duggan, C. (2009) Over-the-counter medicines: professional expertise and consumer discourses. In Williams, S.J., Gabe, J. and Davis, P. (eds) *Pharmaceuticals and Society: Critical Discourses and Debates*. Oxford: Blackwell.

Taylor, D. and Bury, M. (2007) Chronic illness, expert patients and care transition, *Sociology of Health and Illness*, 29, 1, 27–45.

Teifer, L. (2006) Female sexual dysfunction: a case study of disease mongering and activist resistance, *Public Library of Science –Medicine*, 3, e.178.

Van Lente, H. (1993) *Promising Technology: the Dynamics of Expectations in Technological Development*. Enschede: University of Twente.

Webster, A., Martin, P.A., Lewis, G. and Smart, A. (2004) Integrating pharmacogenetics into society: in search of a model? *Nature Reviews Genetics*., 5, 663–69.

Weiss, M.C. and Sutton, J. (2009) The changing nature of prescribing, *Sociology of Health and Illness*, 31, 3, 406–21.

Williams, S.J. and Calnan, M. (eds) (1966) *Modern Medicine: Lay Perspectives and Experiences*. London: University College London Press.

Williams, S.J. and Martin, P.A. (2008) Risks and benefits may turn out to be finely balanced, *Nature*, 457, 532.

Williams, S.J., Seale, C., Boden, S., Lowe, P., et al. (2009) Waking up to sleepiness: modafinil, the media and the pharmaceuticalisation of everyday / night life. In Williams, S.J., Gabe, J. and Davis, P. (eds) *Pharmaceuticals and Society: Critical Discourses and Debates*. Oxford: Blackwell.

Woloshin, S. and Schwartz, L.M. (2006) Giving legs to restless legs: a case study of how the media help make people sick, *Public Library of Science Medicine*, 3, e170–8.

3

Pharmaceutical Witnessing: Drugs for Life in an Era of Direct-to-Consumer Advertising

Joseph Dumit

This article interrogates a relatively new grammar of illness, risk, experience and treatment—one in which the body is inherently disordered and in which health is no longer the silence of the organs, but it is illness which is silent, often with no symptoms. The article examines how the new grammar involves an image of health as risk reduction, and an image of information as full of partial facts. Together, these images underpin a logic of accumulation of pharmaceuticals in the U.S. such that it becomes natural and imperative to treat one's body with more and more drugs for life. In fact, it is so commonsensical that even critics of the pharmaceutical industry and advocates of alternative medicine share in this logical growth.

> *People come into my office, throw down an ad and say, 'That's me.'*
> Psychiatrist
>
> *It's a disease that often has no symptoms.*
> Advert for Peripheral Artery Disease
>
> *If you answered 7 or less for question 10, you probably aren't feeling like yourself.*
> Website for Depression Awareness.

As an anthropologist studying pharmaceuticals in the U.S., I am constantly tripped up by statements that seem to challenge my common sense, ones made by pharmaceutical marketers, advertisers, doctors and patients. A life on drugs is not alien to me, nor to most readers of this article. But the easy emission of these statements points to a cultural inflection

Joseph Dumit, "Pharmaceutical Witnessing: Drugs for Life in an Era of Direct-to-Consumer Advertising," in Jeanette Edwards, Penny Harvey, and Peter Wade (eds.), Technologized Images, Technologized Bodies. Berghahn Books, 2010. pp. 37–64. Reproduced with permission from Berghahn Books Inc.

that I want to investigate here using what Victor Turner called "the method of processuralism" in anthropology, attending to processes that we are involved in and to how actors perceive, mutate and communicate their embodied worlds (Turner and Turner 1992: 172–73). All of the opening statements, I want to argue, share a relatively new grammar of illness, risk, experience and treatment – one in which the body is inherently disordered and in which health is no longer the silence of the organs, but it is illness which is silent, often with no symptoms. In this article, I want to interrogate this grammar, examining how it involves an image of health as risk reduction, and an image of information as full of partial facts. Together, these images underpin a logic of accumulation of pharmaceuticals in the U.S. such that it becomes natural and imperative to treat one's body with more and more drugs for life. In fact, it is so commonsensical that even critics of the pharmaceutical industry and advocates of alternative medicine share in this logical growth.

Here I examine advertisements for their grammar of facts and health. I also analyse the 'grey literature' written by pharmaceutical marketers to each other to improve their practices. I aim to show how our ways of talking articulate with theirs such that we may get what we want, but it may not be what we need. *Pharmaceutical Executive* (*PE*) is one journal that concentrates on marketing strategies towards doctors and the public. I trace a key shift in marketing towards what I call factual persuasion and what *PE,* in its first branding seminar in April 2002, termed 'Pharma's challenge to convert science into marketing' (Shalo and Breitstein 2002: 84).

Using tools from many disciplines, pharmaceutical marketers are building on a much longer tradition of public relations aimed at calibrating emotions for maximum effect in concert with the authoritative discourses of science and medicine that dissociate viewers from their own bodies and experiences (Tye 1998; Chomsky and Barsamian 2001; Herman and Chomsky 2002). I begin with an early pharmaceutical commercial.

Remaking the Body at Risk

The following table shows a direct-to-consumer (DTC) television commercial for a Depression Kit (manufactured by Lilly), which begins as a checklist in the form of an interrogation.

The commercial features simple questions that are very general: are you sleeping too much or too little? But their seriousness is transmitted in the follow-up: 'These can be signs of clinical depression.'

This conclusion converts the questions into a medical algorithm, a logical process of following a series of steps. But the grammar arrests: 'these can be signs' is a peculiar phrase. It is retroactively transformative: aspects of one's life are inscribed as symptoms. What you had previously thought of – if at all – as personal variations are brought into heightened awareness. The first implication is that you are, maybe, suffering from a serious disease and do not know it. Your body, in other words, is potentially deceptive, concealing its own decline. This is not a presymptomatic form of awareness. Unlike the situation in Nelkin and Tancredi's *Dangerous Diagnostics* (1989), where a brainscan or genetic test reveals a disease before it manifests symptoms, here you find out that you have been suffering from symptoms without feeling them.

The grammar of the phrase 'these can be signs of X' or 'you could be suffering from X' are also not simple performatives. They do not assert that you have depression, they do not diagnose (Austin 1962; Kahn 1978). For legal, marketing, and health reasons, the grammar is explicitly modalized as possibility: 'these *can* be,' 'you *could* be,' 'you *might* be.' But they are giving new possibility.

Table 3.1 Text of TV advert for Lilly's Depression Kit

Voiceover	Audio-visuals
Have you stopped doing things you used to enjoy? Are you sleeping too much, are you sleeping too little? Have you noticed a change in your appetite? Is it hard to concentrate? Do	Sombre music playing over black-and-white stills of unhappy people.
you feel sad almost every day? Do you sometimes feel that life may not be worth living? These can be signs of clinical	Text on screen: 'Depression strikes one in eight.'
depression, a real illness, with real causes. But there is hope, you can get your life back.	Text on screen: 'Get your life back'
Treatment that has worked for millions is available from your doctor. This is the number to call for a free confidential information kit, including a personal symptoms checklist, that can make it easier to talk with your doctor about how you're feeling. Make the call now for yourself, or for someone you care about.	Woman looking at pamphlets, phone number on screen, pictures of checklists and other information pieces. Fade to logo for Lilly.

Information about the *possibility* of pathology transforms modalization into mobilization. You cannot ignore the possibility morally because your status has changed (Sacks and Jefferson 1992). This can produce a very strong duty to be healthy (now that you know you are not) and a rational 'having to try' (since you know there is something you can do), that is as deeply moral as the imperative to be tested identified by Nelkin and Tancredi (1989; see also Franklin 1997). You are *now* at risk, you now *know* that you have been at risk, you *have* to try to do something about it. Since treatments are available, '[t]here is hope.'

From a marketer's point of view, once you are aware of the disease in general, the question is how to get you to add depression, breast cancer, cholesterol to *your* lived anxieties, to your personal agenda, enough so that you attend to it, find out more information, and talk to your doctor about it. This is what they term 'personalization.' Their problem is how to get their particular facts into your head as facts that you come to depend on. This practice recalls and builds on an older generation of advertisements teaching you that you might be suffering from bad breath or be overweight and not realize it (Marchand 1986; Bordo 1993), but amplifying this personalizing effect by passing it through tests and diagnostic algorithms.

The challenge of thinking through how these commercials work dialogically lies in the fact that they aim for a retroactive status change. Rather than illness punctuating ordinary life, the everyday conceals illness. Once this is identified, once you identify with it, then your true, real life can be returned to you. The process here is a counterpart to interpellation. Althusser's process of interpellation involved the always, already self-recognition of the subject, where the teacher or policeman hails you or asks you a question, and your response confirms the self-evidence of your being a subject: 'I am I' (Pecheux 1982; Althusser 1984). Here your self-evidence is directly assaulted. Your self-identity is called into question via the algorithm. You are not who you think you are. Your body is not what you think it is. Your feelings are not what you think they are. The algorithm offers in tum to identify your objective self for you. So, instead of the interpellated response, 'Yes, it's me', we instead say, 'Oh! so that's who I am.'

The challenge in studying pharmaceutical marketing is that the commercials do not usually work this easily. In fact they do not work well at all, but they do work well enough. Both the number of prescriptions and the amount of drugs per prescription are projected to continue to grow at 5-15 per cent per year for almost all classes of drugs for chronic conditions (Express Scripts 2006). For marketers, *some* people responding *some* of the time is all that they need: their processes of persuasion are designed to work in percentages, or market share. If they can get even a small percent more Americans to consider the possibility that they might be depressed or have high cholesterol, and a small percent of those people actually go to a doctor and request a prescription, the profits on these tens to hundreds of thousands of additional patients are more than enough to cover advertising costs (Kaericher 2007). It does not matter whether those people 'believe' that they are sick, only that they *act* in accordance with that belief as delineated by the marketing campaigns. The studies that have been done on direct-to-consumer advertising suggest that these commercials are successful at generating concern and anxiety, and that they drive pharmaceutical sales just enough to justify continuing to invest in them (Aikin 2002). My ethnographic challenge is therefore to account for this aggregate growth. I am thinking of this as an ethnography of the aggregate. Thus I begin with a study of how marketers *imagine* people to be manipulable *enough*.

As businessmen, pharmaceutical marketers know exactly what their endpoint is: profit in the form of ongoing mass pharmaceutical consumption. This profit ultimately boils down to prescription maximization which can be achieved through growing the absolute number of new prescriptions, extending the time a patient stays on a prescription, or shortening the time between having a condition and getting a prescription for it (Bolling 2003).

Most pharmaceutical marketing overviews start with the product cycle. A pharmaceutical in the U.S. must go through an extensive regulatory process in order to be approved for use. This process includes testing the drug for safety, first in animals, then in humans. Its potential efficacy is then assessed, and finally its actual efficacy is tested in a clinical population for a specific illness through clinical trials. When all of these have been successfully accomplished, the pharmaceutical company applies to the FDA for approval. If granted, the company gains a number of years of exclusive right to market that drug to doctors and public for that illness.

Marketers therefore divide their strategies into stages: pre-launch, launch, market exclusivity, and transition to generic competition. Embedded in their articles about direct-to-consumer marketing, however, is also a complex theory of the mass market as potential patients who do not know that they are ill, and must be led, step by step, toward a prescription. Marketers have a highly developed language for articulating the steps of conversion through which non-patients come to see themselves as undiagnosed patients, then actively visit and persuade their doctor to give them a prescription. Using their terms, but focusing on how marketers approach a person as someone who does not even know that they require a drug, I have mapped their implicit strategy onto five distinct steps. They are:

1. Awareness through education
2. Personalizing the risk
3. Motivation to self-diagnose
4. Seeing and convincing a doctor
5. Branded compliance

Most DTC commercials are aimed broadly at addressing people in any step, at reinforcing this step-wise progression as logical and natural, and at helping people move onto the next step. This process involves much more than just advertisements, it includes the design of clinical trials, arranging screening programmes, constructing databases, and monitoring compliance. As we, patients and potential patients, try to learn facts about our risks and illnesses and come to incorporate these into our identities and bodies, almost every aspect of the medical world we encounter is being modulated (not constructed, but adjusted) in accordance with profit motives. That is capitalism, you might say, but it is also an opportunity to understand *how,* in our capitalist culture, facts, risks and illnesses work in and on us, transforming how we experience, understand and measure health.

Awareness Through Education

> So companies realize that an effective way to reach commercial goals is to cultivate long-term patients through education, rather than acquiring new consumers through brand-awareness advertising. (Hone and Benson 2004: 98)

Medical sociologists have recognized how the neutrality of health information can be manipulated through selection and amplification, privileging one form of explanation over others. The idea that information empowers can be turned into structured or controlled empowerment, what Dixon Woods has called 'information for compliance' in contrast to 'information for choice' (Dixon-Woods 2001, cited in Henwood et al. 2003:591). One key strategy for producing a market is direct education of both doctors and the public. Even before the launch of a new drug, time is spent crafting messages about the disease that shape it towards market ends. The logical premise of education as patient cultivation is that the public, doctors and medical institutions are ignorant. The status quo is harming people in a most dangerous way because they are not even aware of the harm they are doing to themselves.

Being ignorant of medical issues justifies an emergency public health response: explicit manipulation or 'facilitated awareness'. There are two main approaches to awareness through education: preparing the market and health literacy. At different levels of generality, each aims at hanging the status quo of common knowledge through critical presentation: redefining what health is, what treatment is, what a smart person does to be healthy, and so on. They aim, in other words, to reframe how we see the world working and what we take for granted. In this manner, fact-based marketing creates a receptive climate.

The aims of health-literacy campaigns as envisioned by marketers are to cement this relationship between knowing and doing. Targeting a sixthgrade reading level allows imagining a market of 110 million people who could be addressed with health information. The health - aware individual is thus presented as one who can and will act on medical facts. While facts are typically seen as descriptive, health education is only seen as meaningful and successful if its knowledge induces action. Non-compliance with facts is thus framed as a problem of literacy. Health literacy grammatically frames the public as well-intentioned but ignorant, illiterate, uneducated and disempowered.

The moral grammar of 'health information' is that facts will of course be acted upon. This grammar precludes resistance: if you do not act on what you know, you must be doing so for psychological reasons. You are confused, embarrassed, intimidated or ignorant. Each of these reasons offers an opportunity for strategic intervention to fix the problem of people who have encountered the information but are not acting on it.

In Europe, this challenge is acute because brand-name pharmaceutical advertising to consumers is not allowed. Sandoz (Novartis), with an antifungal agent Lamisil to promote, needed to find another way 'to encourage patients to talk with their doctors about onychomycosis and its treatment options. So the company renamed the condition the more consumer-friendly 'fungal infection' and took out newspaper ads asking readers to call or write to "Step Wise" for a free brochure on foot care' (Hone and Benson 2004: 96). Besides capturing future patients through the informational relationship, the phrase 'fungal infection' became an indirect brand, an illness fused with Lamisil as its treatment. The challenge for pharmaceutical companies is managing education that is not directly branded without giving too much away to competitors. Mechanisms include quasi-branded cues that will later be branded explicitly when the drug that works on just that mechanism is launched. Even the colour schemes and typography are tied into this process of managing awareness in anticipation of a future market (Prounis 2004).

Personalizing the Risk

When its efforts to market to physicians had reached the saturation point, the manufacturer of a prescription health product for women decided to launch a DTC campaign to expand product sales. The company's goal was to pull through new prescriptions by increasing the target audience's awareness of the need for treatment to prevent the onset of osteoporosis. The first communication objective was to get patients to 'personalize' the risk so they regarded the disease state as important enough to warrant taking further action (2003).

Once a prospect is aware of a risk and accepts that it is possible, he or she must then be made to personalize the risk. Having been introduced to a fact, one needs to enter into a relationship with it. Personalizing involves having the risk become part of an existing internal and external dialogue. It has to become part of my story, how I talk about and represent myself to myself and others. Personalizing requires that the possibility of risk in general now becomes my possible risk. What is needed is that I worry about this possibility that it go from being an object of my attention (awareness) to becoming an object of my concern.

Medicalization is a term used by sociologists to describe the historical process through which conditions, complaints, normal variation and socially undesirable traits are turned into medical conditions and interventions (Conrad 1992; Klawiter 2002; Lock 2002; Clarke et al. 2003). Analysed as power conflicts, medicalization can be a coercive force making people into patients in order to control and manage them. Alternately, medicalization can be a tactic by sufferers to become objects of attention and care through becoming patients (Dumit 2006). Within DTC, these problems of 'my status' and 'my bodily state' are 'offered' to me as explanations for what I am and should now be concerned about. It appears non-coercive, even empowering. I am offered a gift to evaluate freely. However, as Ronald Frankenberg has noted, characterizing this process of medicalization is fraught with narrative and conceptual difficulties for everyone involved (Frankenberg 1993).

How does medical identification happen? In pharmaceutical marketing, a switch often turns on some sort of bodily hook. This is a facilitated recognition in which I come to understand that what I had previously taken for granted or overlooked in my body is in fact an object of concern. In this manner, my attention to a risk possibility and my selfconcern become linked, and the temporal fact that I had overlooked this before adds an emotional surprise and worry to the mix. The archetypal form of this identification is the 'ouch test' as described by virtual contributing editor Vern Realto in *Pharmaceutical Executive*.[1]

> Of course, in the world of DTC, it helps to have a product indication in which patients can point to a spot on their bodies and say, 'Ouch!' Prilosec [for acid indigestion] has such luck. And its DTC creative makes full use of the fact. Patient self-selection is the point. For a heartburn sufferer, looking at the campaign's ever-present cartoon figures is like looking in the mirror. Does it hurt? Yes. Would you like 24-hour relief with a single pill? Yes! (Realto 1998: 14).

The grammar of this concise description conceals the interpellation at work. 'Patient self-selection' is the retroactive effect of the campaign when it is successful. A person who does not consider herself a patient or even necessarily a sufferer comes to recognize a complaint as suffering and as treatable and therefore recognizes herself as a patient. Althusser called this process of coming to see oneself as having already been a patient a 'subject effect'. I call this process, when it happens through a scientific fact, 'objective self-fashioning' because one's new identity appears to have been verified as one's real and objectively true identity (Dumit 2004).

This retroactive effect can also happen at a bodily level, within a subject's body, when an ache or complaint is reframed as a symptom. In the following description, by patient compliance expert Dorothy L. Smith, the headache is always already a symptom that the unaware consumer has mistakenly ignored.

> A person who suffers from frequent headaches may learn from a DTC ad that those may be the symptoms of a migraine and that there is treatment available. Those ads can give us hope. They can help us identify positive steps to take. They can motivate us to talk with the doctor about subjects we find embarrassing. (Smith 1998)

Furthermore, one recognizes that a third-party expert enabled this objective redescription of one's 'symptom' as the truth of one's experience. In addition to a subject-effect here, there is also a truth-effect. At this point in the DTC process, the target is common sense. First, in the awareness step, I recognize that heartburn is a *treatable* medical condition and also that I should have known this. As a fact, it should have been part of my taken-forgranted background against which I examine the world. 'If we think there is no treatment available for our symptoms, we may decide it's not worth spending the money on an office visit' (Smith 1998). Now, with personalization, I see that *I* may be suffering from this treatable medical condition. I may be a patient. What I now *know* is that I am a *possible* patient.

Realto's account of Prilosec (above) notes that it is 'lucky' to have this built-in auto-identification 'ouch' test. Then, the problem is only one of medicalizing a portion of experience. The bigger challenge for marketers is producing identification with an asymptomatic condition, '*making* patient recognize themselves' despite feeling healthy. Medical sociologists and anthropologists have long used a distinction between *illness* as lived experience framed by lay notions of suffering and *disease* as biomedical knowledge (cf. Kroll-Smith et al. 2000). The aim of risk and symptom personalization is precisely to fuse these understandings of illness and disease together so that one talks in terms of medical facts, risk factors and biomarkers, so that one literally experiences risk factors as symptoms.

The lived body must be reframed as no longer giving forth symptoms, but instead as naturally concealing them. One's body itself, as marked or measured, then takes the place of a bodily symptom. Even a basic demographic attribute like sex, race or age can become the basis for risk personalization and marketing.

A series of commercials for Zocor feature grandmothers and grandfathers, including the famous football coach Dan Reeves, discussing how much they enjoy their time but how much they want to see the future, their grandchildren's graduations, etc. They narrate having had a heart attack and how diet and exercise were not enough to lower their cholesterol:

> I could dance all night back there. So I was thrilled when my grandson wanted to follow in my footsteps. But before our first lesson, I had a heart attack. I needed to lower my cholesterol. How will you take care of your high cholesterol and heart disease?

Their doctor's information about Zocor gives them a salvationary solution: 'Be good to yourself. It's your future. BE THERE.' This mode of storytelling provides an image of a responsible rational actor who upon healing a new fact incorporates it through concern and then action. The very act of reciting this tale repeats this process, passing on the informational possibility of risk to the listener, and the personalized possibility of taking it up responsibly.

Rhetorically repeating a tale about a fact is a mode of passing on the grammar through witnessing. The tale is told in the exact words that the viewer can in tum state for themselves, to others, and to their doctor. 'Because I want to be there.' At the same time, the risk information is translated from an 'odds' sense of possibility to a powerfully imperative one of probability. If you too are a woman or middle aged, how can you not 'be ready', 'get checked'?

Motivation to Informing Self-diagnosis

> The goal during this pre-launch stage is not to motivate patients to see their doctors but to motivate them to respond for more information. (Bolling 2003)

Once identification has taken place and the person accepts a possible risk as their own, marketers see the next step as converting the possible into actual risk, or in the case of symptoms, getting the patient to self-diagnose. The next step of motivation then confirms this personal possibility as a probability through some kind of objective self-assessment: a self-diagnosis through a checklist or another external tool. Self-help is promoted as a 'free' activity, it does not cost anything to 'see' if you fit the criteria. You do not risk anything, you just take this simple quiz. Ambiguities of language in ads and teaser articles aim to induce curiosity and concern about one's apparently neutral and healthy status.

Checklists and risk-factor charts are provided in DTC commercials, ads, news articles, on websites and in direct-mail pieces. The personalized patient is still a patient-in-potential, and these self-help techniques aim to create empowered self-identified patients whose next task will be visiting and convincing their doctors of their condition and need for treatment. Checklists empower and disempower at the same time. The paradox of checklists is that while they appear to be a form of self-help they take the question of diagnosis, 'Am I sick?', out of the subject's hands. Even if feelings and experience are used to fill out the checklist, the algorithm then decides whether or not these *count* as objective symptoms. The score one receives thus takes the place of a lived experience of illness, the score can even become its own experience. In this manner, one comes to verify that indeed the possible risk or symptom is a true risk or symptom. One has gained not just a fact about oneself but also a vocabulary, rationale and moral judgement about the unfinished process.

Checklists thus function as a kind of rite of passage. Anthropologist Victor Turner described rites of passage as liminal processes in which a person is socially unmade and then remade into a different person – a boy into a man. Within DTC campaigns, nominally healthy persons (prospects) become secretly sick persons – patients in waiting (Sunder Rajan 2007) – who are oriented towards becoming healthy again. In the DTC rite of passage, one gives up one's sense of self and health – the body becomes a silent traitor that has concealed its condition. One then submits to the ritual of questions in order to discover that the body

Table 3.2 Zoloft TV commercial

Voiceover	Audio-visuals
You know when you're not feeling like yourself. You're tired all the time.	Drawing of fuzzy egg (or neuron?) with sad face.
You may feel sad, hopeless, and lose interest in the things you once loved.	Egg cries. A ladybug approaches egg and egg loses interest, sighing.
You may feel anxious, can't even sleep. Your daily activities and relationships suffer. You KNOW when you don't feel right.	Nighttime, a crescent moon comes out and egg starts walking
Now here's something you may not know: These are some symptoms of depression. A serious medical condition affecting over twenty million Americans.	Text at bottom of screen: 'Symptoms persist every day for at least two weeks'. Egg looks surprised, then sad again.
While the cause is unknown, depression may be related to an imbalance of naturally occurring chemicals between nerve cells in the brain.	Shifts to a picture labelled 'Chemical Imbalance', with 'nerve A' and 'nerve B' with little balls going from A to B. Text at bottom: 'Dramatization'.
Zoloft, a prescription medicine, works to correct this imbalance.	Zoloft symbol appears as 'chemical imbalance' words fade and black boxes appear on 'nerve A'.
When you know more about what's wrong, you can help make it right.	Birds chirping, shift back to egg, who is happy and has grass growing near it.
Only your doctor can diagnose depression.	Butterfly comes and egg smiles at it, then chases it. Text at bottom: 'Depression is a serious medical condition'.
Zoloft is not for everyone. People taking medicines called MAOIs shouldn't take Zoloft. Side-effects may include dry mouth, insomnia, sexual side-effects, diarrhoea, nausea and sleepiness. Zoloft is not habit-forming. Talk to your doctor about Zoloft – the number one prescribed brand of its kind.	Egg bounces past large Zoloft logo, chasing butterfly. Text at bottom: 'Zoloft is approved for adults 18 and older' then 'See our ad in People magazine' then 'www.ZOLOFT.com'
Zoloft. When you know more about what's wrong, you can help make it right.	Text says same thing with egg bouncing along. Then text at bottom: '1-800-6-ZOLOFT'

really is disordered. If one is sick, the promise is that one will then be treated and reunited with one's true self and true community. This process is enacted explicitly in many DTC commercials.

The story in the Zoloft commercial of Table 3.2 mimics a Van Gennepian rite of passage as delineated by Turner. The subject, 'you', begins separated, alienated by a series of descriptions that are aligned into accusations. The biomedical facts are then introduced in a reflexive, subjunctive voice, the voice of liminality. These may not be your fault, they may be symptoms of a biology. 'You' at this point in the story is in the liminal state of being both this and that, both mental and physical, accused and sick. You "know" you don't feel right, but you need the commercial to tell you that the feeling is a real symptom. And the grammatical voice, as Turner observed, can then shift from the subjunctive to the optative, from hypothesis and possibility into emotion, wish and desire (Turner 1982). 'There is hope' a narrator explains, 'treatments are available'. The conclusion of the story is of course re-aggregation, a return to society with a new status, a new, true 'you'.

These commercials and hundreds like them engage in a form of biomedical informing we might call pharmaceutical witnessing. Through passing on facts embedded in stories where the subject of the story is potentially you, the viewer is put in a position of having to make sense of the story or ignore the risk it portrays altogether.

Steve Kroll-Smith uses the self-test as an example in which the voice of experience and the voice of medicine are 'beginning to converse outside of the once solid container of institutionalized medicine' (Kroll-Smith 2003: 639). Kroll-Smith has studied the development, deployment and use of 'excessive daytime sleepiness' (EDS) as definite illness defined publicly through a Likert measure of excessive sleepiness, a self-test. He suggests that 'a person who self-diagnoses with EDS after taking [self-test] ... is exercising, if only momentarily, an alternative authority [to that of modem medicine]' (Kroll-Smith 2003: 640). Calling for a both-and approach to illness and disease, he suggests that popular media plays a crucial role in fashioning medicine and bodily knowledge.

Sufferers often form their own communities online in discussion groups, and offline in mutual-help groups. In these sites, they actively invent ways of living with their conditions (Dumit 2006; Martin 2007). Of course there are often many different groups with different approaches to the same condition. Marketers with treatments to sell actively court these groups whose interests align with their needs. They accelerate the circulation of these social innovations in ways that also help sell products. The result is often a public service 'educational advertising' campaign that draws attention to an illness by reifying it as treatable, and by destigmatizing it.

The marketers I have talked with regularly monitor online discussions of pharmaceuticals, they hold focus groups with patients, and some of them have hired anthropologists to conduct ethnographies of diseases. They consider one of their greatest strengths to be finding a patient who eloquently expresses a private insight about an illness that accords with their mission to increase prescriptions. Their job is then to amplify that insight so that others may come to identify with it. Cutting and pasting is thus a fitting description of the general circulation and mediation of pharmaceutical experiences and practices. Communicational media, mass media, everyday discussions and research techniques feed back on one another (Strathern 1992; Melucci 1996).

Michel Pecheux, in his study of language, ideology and discourse, found that motivation and identification were mediated by specific word choices (Pecheux 1982). Questionnaires are 'meticulously' designed through 'extensive market research'. Each question on surveys and checklists is a psychological tool. At the conclusion of this step, concerned consumers have become worried, self-diagnosed potential patients who know what they have and want treatment for it. From a marketing point of view, they are empowered patients ready and motivated to see their doctor.

Convincing the Doctor, the Critical Moment

With self-diagnosis accomplished, the goal of pharmaceutical promotion is still only half-way done. The potential patient must now get to the doctor, convince the doctor to diagnose and prescribe treatment, and the patient must then take the drug and continue taking it. Marketing must now aim at 'pass-through persuasion', giving the patient the tools to convince their doctors. Doctors in turn, are seen as obligatory obstacles to be overcome without authority actually to make a diagnosis. Any resistance on the doctor's part is seen as a lack of knowledge, of interest or of time. This reading may seem harsh, but it is constantly reinforced in DTC campaigns in spite of their required acknowledgement that 'only your doctor can make the diagnosis'. Some campaigns make doctor incompetence a direct theme, where the patient has to diagnose herself through seeing a commercial and filling out an online checklist in order to convince the doctor of her true condition.

The problem is that doctors also depend on these checklists which are essentially the only measure of an illness and treatment effectiveness that otherwise is not perceptible to anyone, doctor or patient. In many cases, checklists developed in order to conduct clinical research have become both marketing and self-diagnostic tools (Healy 2002). This blindness and disempowerment is all too visible in both the descriptions of emplotment of doctors by patients online – in which they discuss how to get what they want from their doctor by saying the right things – and in commercials which directly encourage such behaviour. The virtual world for the clinician is precisely the self-identified world of the advertisement grammar.

Medical anthropologists Cheryl Mattingly, Maryjo Delvecchio Good and others have shown convincingly that even as they appear to be offering patients a choice, many doctors ask questions and phrase responses that elicit the response that the doctor thinks is right. They have identified this process as 'therapeutic emplotment' (Del Vecchio Good et al. 1994; Mattingly 1994). Similarly, when Martinez-Hemaez describes doctors' conversion of patient stories into 'a language of facts', he was launching a critique of 'the conversion of symptoms into physical signs; the suppression of authorship; avoidance of the message; and the meaningful intention of the complaint. In short, the intention of the reader comes to dominate, limiting the symptom to his own interpretation' (Martinez-Hemaez 2000:248).

These critiques are quite perspicacious. The reification of symptoms often results in the evacuation of the meaning of suffering and delegitimates the speaker's authority. But as patient social movements and DTC marketing show, there is a counter-politics to this semiotics: patients often discuss in support groups and online the possibilities to take this increasingly mechanical form of diagnosis and use it to emplot their doctors, telling them exactly what needs to be said to get what they want (Dumit 2000, 2006). Martinez-Hemaez's notion of the 'reader's domination' here becomes the domination of both reader and speaker, patient and doctor, by the code or algorithm, or symbolic domination (Melucci 1996).

Much DTC marketing, therefore, offers a consumer the precise language with which to accomplish this counter-emplotment. Through the focus groups, interviews and fieldwork, marketers attempt to fuse personal stories with the rules of diagnosis. Calibrated for maximum effectiveness, the scripts thus simultaneously dumb down and reify the patient's experience into generic branded stories of suffering, and in so doing, empower them to translate these stories into effective action in their doctors' offices – in order to get what they 'now' know they want. The doctors are in the end even more dumbed down and reified. For if a patient should arrive in the doctor's office saying these words, the doctor will have little choice but to observe that the patient has stated all the right things in the right way (Kravitz et al. 2005).

The isomorphism of marketing is here aligned with that of patient groups against a healthcare system, that for good or ill is attempting to resist the *costs* of increasing pharmaceutical interventions and maintenance. The net result is the aggregate increase in patients asking for and receiving prescriptions for daily medicines. The final stage of marketing is then to have patients complete the purchase and to continue to refill these prescriptions as long as possible.

Branded Compliance

> Companies are increasingly using physician-supplied patient starter packs containing user leaflets, tips, FAQ advice, and patient diaries at the initial prescribing consultation to help ensure the right patient/brand compliance from the start. Those packs create the basis of initial patient expectations with resulting patient treatment outcomes fostering repeat brand loyalty in terms of prescribing decision making and user preference. (Hone and Benson 2004: 104)

The final stage is the payoff – one prescription purchased and hopefully many more in the future. Compliance refers to patients staying on the prescriptions they are given and refilling them. For marketers, compliance also refers to the general gap between those who should be on life-long meds and those not.

The aim at this point is to cement a relationship between self-assessment, diagnosis and branded treatment – to integrate the pharmaceutical into the everyday and reinforce a notion of dependent normality. The notion of a 'healthstyle', requires support from many different directions. The initial one is through community with other patients. Second, brands are proposed as anchoring a patient's healing to future purchases. With brand loyalty comes 'product advocacy'.

> And there's nothing more powerful than patient-to patient endorsements. Although a physician's recommendation may be highly credible, it doesn't carry the power of empathy and understanding that a fellow sufferer typically conveys. (Bolling 2003)

Achieving this integration starts with knowing as much about patients as possible, and making sure that they understand 'the need to take medication daily', 'how to convert education to action', and to 'associate their medication with being sick or well'. Above all, researchers need to determine: 'Do patients accept that they have a chronic disease or condition and need to continue to take medication for it, or are they in denial that they need to do that?' (Bolling 2003). Contrary to writing on chronic illnesses that stem from pain or fatigue or suffering, none of these issues are taken for granted with these lifelong pharmaceuticals aimed at asymptomatic conditions.

This explicit manipulation of unfounded fears offers insight into the single-mindedness of marketing. The war here is between companies, branded versus generic multinationals, in which patients are the means, their minds the instruments used in waging the battle. Bolling goes to recommend: 'Overall, the key is to increase consumers' comfort level so they're resistant to change if faced with the option to switch' (2003: 117).

Conclusion

In liminal situations, Turner argues, we develop our grammar, 'ways of talking about indicative ways of communicating…We take ourselves for our subject matter' (Turner and Turner 1992: 137). Perhaps even in subliminal marketing experiences, we develop and refine our modes of expressivity, changing our minds in order to change our bodies. In addition to his careful attention to the grammar and creativity of process, Turner constantly attended to the role of the anthropological writer who must always make choices in where to locate agency in process: in the individual, the social structure, or to strive for some sort of balance. Here I have portrayed the pharmaceutical marketing encounters with an emphasis on how they can convict some people some of the time. In other work,

I have stepped back, behind the focus groups to see how activists and everyday acts of creativity and resistance have shaped the terrain of the doctor-patient encounter and invented most of the forms of informing that marketing has in tum taken up and amplified (Dumit 2006).

Many drugs work, much of the time, for most of the people they are intended for. The issue at stake in DTC for marketers is how to continue to grow the market big enough and fast enough to keep up with investors' expectations, often stretching the evidence from clinical trials. Many of the currently used pills do work to modulate our bodies in ways that we may not be able to describe completely, but which we nonetheless desire for curative, preventative, experiential or experimental reasons. However, we have far too little data and are not in fact collecting data as to the long-term effects and side-effects of most drugs, as to the interactions between chronic drugs, nor of the positive dimensional effects like enhanced school performance, mood brightening, and so on. Especially consider the increasing tendency to add drugs in treatment algorithms for the side-effects of a previous drug.

The expressivity of the commercials, websites and marketing efforts remains my key concern. To the extent that they do posit objective self-identification of feelings and possible risk symptoms, I wonder where, when and how self-talk adopts and deploys this new grammar within and alongside other modes. As much as marketing provides potential patients with the exact words with which to emplot their doctors into providing them with their pills of 'choice', people also share and disseminate counter-strategies to avoid certain drugs, to calibrate their own doses through splitting pills, and to explore alternative treatments, alternative diagnoses and alternative explanations.

For the moment, though, the average patient, by which I mean the marketer's average, comes to experience his or her body under pharmaceutical conviction. This body is silently disordered, counterexperiential, waiting to be evaluated and measured in order to speak. This body is always under construction. For more and more Americans, health is a sign of concern, health is something they must see a doctor for in order to ward off the invisible risk they have been taught to worry about. Treatment is neither an imposition nor a choice, it is increasingly ordinary.

NOTE

1 According to his byline, 'Vern Realto is a virtual contributing editor to DTC Times, a composite of regular staffers and other advisors.' As a composite, Realto thus speaks the collective wisdom of the pharmaceutical marketing industry, precisely the level of enunciation I am interested in analysing.

REFERENCES

Aikin, KJ. 2002. 'Direct-to-Consumer Advertising of Prescription Drugs: Physician Survey Preliminary Results'. Division of Drug Marketing, Advertising, and Communications, Center for Drug Evaluation and Research, U.S. Food and Drug Administration. http://www.fda.govIcderlddmac/globalsummit2003/index.htm.

Althusser, L. 1984. 'Ideology and Ideological State Appearances (Notes toward an Investigation)', in L. Althusser, *Essays on Ideology*. London: Verso, pp.61–139.

Bolling, J. 2003. 'DTC: A Strategy for Every Stage', *Pharmaceutical Executive* 23(11): 110–117.

Chomsky, N. and D. Barsamian. 2001. *Propoganda and Public Mind: Conversations with Noam Chomsky*. Cambridge, MA: South End Press.

Clarke, A., J. Shim, L. Mamo, J. Fosket and J. Fishman. 2003. 'Biomedicalization: Theorizing Technoscientific Transformations of Health, Illness, and U.S. Biomedicine', *American Sociological Review* 68: 161–94.

Conrad, P. 1992. 'Medicalization and Social Control', *Annual Review of Sociology* 18: 209–32.

Del Vecchio Good, M., T. Munakata, Y. Kobayashi, C. Mattingly and B. Good. 1994. 'Oncology and Narrative Time', *Social Science and Medicine* 38: 855–62.

Dixon-Woods, M. 2001. 'Writing Wrongs? An Analysis of Published Discourses about the Use of Patient Information Leaflets', *Social Science and Medicine* 324: 573–77.

Dumit, J. 2000. 'When Explanations Rest: "Good-enough" Brain Science and the New Sociomedical Disorders', in M. Lock, A. Young and A. Cambrosio (eds), *Living and Working with the New Biomedical Technologies: Intersections of Inquiry*. Cambridge: Cambridge University Press.

—.2004. *Picturing Personhood: Brain Scans and Biomedical Identity*. Princeton: Princeton University Press.

—.2006. 'Illnesses You Have to Fight to Get: Facts as Forces in Uncertain, Emergent Illnesses', *Social Science and Medicine* 62: 577–90.

Express Scripts. 2006. 'Drug Trend Report'. http://www.exptressscripts.com/ourcompany/newsindustryreports/.

Frankenberg, R. 1993. 'Risk: Anthropological and Epidemiological Narratives of Prevention', in S. Lindenbaum and M. Lock (eds), *Knowledge, Power, and Practice: The Anthropology of Medicine and Everyday Life*. Berkeley: University of California Press.

Franklin, S. 1997. *Embodied Progress: A Cultural Account of Assisted Conception*. London: Routledge.

Harding, S. 1987. 'Convicted by the Holy Spirit: The Rhetoric of Fundamental Baptist Conversion', *American Ethnologist* 14: 167–81.

—.2000. *The Book of Jerry Falwell: Fundamentalist Language and Politics*. Princeton, NJ: Princeton University Press.

Healy, D. 2002. *The Creation of Psychopharmacology*. Cambridge, MA: Harvard University Press.

Henwood, F., S. Wyatt, A. Hart and J. Smith. 2003. '"Ignorance is Bliss Sometimes": Constraints on the Emergence of the "Informed Patient" in the Changing Landscapes of Health Information', *Sociology of Health and Illness (Print)* 25: 589–607.

Herman, E.S. and N. Chomsky. 2002. *Manufacturing Consent: The Political Economy of the Mass Media*. New York: Pantheon Books.

Hone, F. and R. Benson. 2004. 'DTC: European Style', *Pharmaceutical Executive* 24(3): 96–106.

Kaericher, C. 2007. 'Pharmaceuticals and Direct to Consumer Advertising'. Manuscript. Kelly School of Business, Indiana University. http://kelley.iu.edu/cbls/research/articles.html (accessed 11 January 2008).

Kahn. J.Y. 1978. 'A Diagnostic Semiotic', *Semiotica* 22: 75–106.

Klawiter, M. 2002. 'Risk, Prevention and the Breast Cancer Continuum: The NCI, the FDA, Health Activism and the Pharmaceutical Industry', *History and Technology* 18: 309–53.

Kravitz, R.L., R.M. Epstein, M.D. Feldman, C.E. Franz, R. Azari, M.S. Wilkes, L. Hinton and P. Franks. 2005. 'Influence of Patients' Requests for Direct-to Consumer Advertised Antidepressants: A Randomized Controlled Trial', *JAMA* 293: 1995–2002.

Kroll-Smith, S. 2003. 'Popular Media and "Excessive Daytime Sleepiness": A Study of Rhetorical Authority in Medical Sociology', *Sociology of Health and Illness*. 25: 625–43.

Kroll-Smith, J.S., P. Brown and V.J. Gunter. 2000. *Illness and the Environment: A Reader in Contested Medicine*. New York: New York University Press.

Lock, M.M. 2002. *Twice Dead: Organ Transplants and the Reinvention of Death*. Berkeley: University of California Press.

Marchand, R. 1986. *Advertising the American Dream: Making Way for Modernity, 1920-1940*. Berkeley: University of California Press.

Martin, E. 2007. *Bipolar Expeditions: Mania and Depression in American Culture*. Princeton: Princeton University Press.

Martinez-Hermiez, A. 2000. *What's Behind the Symptom? On Psychiatric Observation and Anthropological Understanding, trans.* S.M. DiGiacomo and J. Bates. Amsterdam: Harwood Academic Publishers.

Mattingly, C. 1994. 'The Concept of Therapeutic "Emplotment"', *Social Science and Medicine* 38: 811–22.

Melucci, A. 1996. *Challenging Codes: Collective Action in the Information Age*. Cambridge: Cambridge University Press.

Nelkin, D. and L. Tancredi. 1989. *Dangerous Diagnostics: The Social Power of Biological Information*. New York: Basic Books.

Pecheux, M. 1982. *Language, Semantics, and Ideology*. New York: St Martin's Press.

Prounis, C. 2004. 'The Art of Advertorial', *Pharmaceutical Executive* 24(5): 152–64.

Realto, V. 1998. 'Prilosec Spot Hits All the Hot Buttons', *Pharmaceutical Executive* 1 May, p. 14.

Sacks, H. and G. Jefferson. 1992. *Lectures on Conversation*. Oxford: Blackwell.

Shalo, S. and J. Breitstein. 2002. 'Science + Marketing = Branding', *Pharmaceutical Executive* 22(7): 84.

Smith, D. 1998. 'It's Our Health ... And We Want More Than Adveritising', *Pharmaceutical Executive* 1 July, p. 23.

Strathern, M. 1992. *Reproducing the Future: Essays on Anthropology, Kinship, and the New Reproductive Technologies*. New York: Routledge.

Sunder Rajan, K. 2007. 'Experimental Values: Indian Clinical Trials and Surplus Health', *New Left Review* 45: 67–88.

Turner, V. 1982. *From Ritual to Theatre: The Human Seriousness of Play*. New York: Performing Arts Journal Publications.

Turner, V.W. and E.L.B. Turner. 1992. *Blazing the Trail: Way Marks in the Exploration of Symbols*. Tucson: University of Arizona Press.

Tye, L. 1998. *The Father of Spin: Edward L. Bernays and the Birth of Public Relations*. New York: Crown Publishers.

Part II

New Drugs, Diseases, and Identities

The Pharmaceutical Studies Reader, First Edition. Edited by Sergio Sismondo and Jeremy A. Greene.

Pharmaceuticals, to paraphrase Claude Lévi-Strauss, are good to think with, especially for those interested in the definition of new categories of patients and diseases. New drugs can come to influence the definition of disease in a host of ways. They can transform an acute and fatal disease into a manageable and chronic condition, as antiretrovirals did for HIV/AIDS or insulin did for type I diabetes. New drugs can also produce new diseases, either as an intentional marketing strategy (consider the role of paroxetine in the popularization of social anxiety disorder) or as unintended consequence (consider the role of the antibiotic methicillin in the emergence of the "superbug" methicillin-resistant *Staphylococcus aureus*). Pharmaceutical agents can serve as a catalyst for the production of medical knowledge (in the form of randomized controlled trials and epidemiological studies) and as a site for civil society activism. Relations of drug and disease can be simultaneously understood as the relation of weapon to target, on the one hand, and the relation of product to market, on the other. At this complex intersection, the identities of diseases as pharmaceutical targets and patients as pharmaceutical consumers are constantly in flux.

Jeremy Greene, in Chapter 4, explores the complexity of this interaction by narrating the genesis and development of Merck's blockbuster drug, Diuril, one of the first pills widely used in the treatment of hypertension. Using materials from Merck's corporate archives, Greene demonstrates that the interplay of research and marketing influenced the development of new drugs and new diseases far earlier than we might think—but that this process was never fully in control of either researchers or marketers. In Chapter 5, anthropologist Nathan Greenslit describes the complex role of psychopharmaceuticals in the creation of new diseases and new identity practices. Greenslit narrates the launch of a new drug that was not really new: Sarafem, a product chemically identical to Prozac but rebranded (quite literally) from a green-and-yellow antidepressant to a pink-and-purple remedy for a new gender-specific pathological category, premenstrual dysphoric disorder. In Chapter 6, Anne Pollock narrates a different tale of an old drug made new again through association with identity politics, in this case through the association of BiDil—a repackaging of two generically available drugs—with racially-specific claims of efficacy in the treatment of heart failure in African American patients. In Chapter 7, sociologist Jennifer Fishman examines some pharmaceutical companies' attempted creation of a pathology of "female sexual dysfunction," using scientific and cultural mediators to establish and promote the condition within medicine and on the larger cultural landscape.

4

Releasing the Flood Waters: Diuril and the Reshaping of Hypertension

Jeremy A. Greene

This article narrates the development and promotion in the 1950s and 1960s of Merck, Sharp & Dohme's Diuril (chlorothiazide), an antihypertensive drug, which played a significant role in the redefinition of high blood pressure as a widespread target for chronic pharmaceutical consumption. The joined careers of Diuril and hypertension in the late twentieth century demonstrate the connections between the clinical research, clinical practice, and marketing practices through which pharmaceuticals and disease categories come to define one another. By examining a series of internal documents preserved in the Merck Archives alongside a careful reading of the clinical literature and industry journals of the time, this article explores how the ambitions of marketers, physicians, and public health advocates found convergence in the expanding pharmaceutical prevention of chronic diseases.

Introduction

Thousands of small white tablets of Diuril emerged from Merck, Sharp & Dohme production plants to appear in pharmacies and clinics across America in January 1958, surrounded by a dazzle of research symposia, journal advertisements, and record prescription rates for a novel agent. Diuril—generically known as chlorothiazide—represented the first palatable pill for hypertension, and although its story is less well known than the saga of antibiotics discovery, the drama of antipsychotic drug development, or the cultural hand-wringing surrounding the minor tranquilizers, the impact of this agent on clinical practice was equally

Greene, Jeremy A., "Releasing the Flood Waters: Diuril and the Reshaping of Hypertension," in Bulletin of the History of Medicine 79:4 (2005). pp. 749–794. ©2005 The Johns Hopkins University Press. Reprinted with permission of Johns Hopkins University Press.

The Pharmaceutical Studies Reader, First Edition. Edited by Sergio Sismondo and Jeremy A. Greene.

profound. As late as the Second World War a patient with high blood pressure and no symptoms would not be likely to receive any treatment. A few decades later, hypertension had become a radically different entity: mild, largely asymptomatic, detected routinely in primary-care screening, and increasingly treated with specific pharmaceutical agents long before any symptoms had developed. This transformation, and the broader shift it marked in the definition of chronic disease in the postwar era, was highly contingent upon the emergence of novel therapeutic agents like Diuril and upon the promotional apparatus set in place to market their broader and earlier use by physicians and patients across the country.

Most existing chronicles of Diuril belong to a familiar genre that casts pharmaceuticals as milestones in the progressive unfolding of scientific medicine, in which the discovery of the pharmaceutical agent is heralded as the dividing line between "premodern" and "modern" approaches to disease. As Albert Brest, editor of the journal *Clinical Therapeutics*, has written:

> The introduction of thiazide diuretics in 1958 ushered in the modern era of antihypertensive drug therapy. The advent of these diuretics and the subsequent availability of other groups of antihypertensive drugs made it possible to control all grades of hypertension, and the concomitant morbidity and mortality of hypertensive disease were significantly reduced.[1]

Two crucial themes are often found in this type of narrative—namely, (1) that a disease both predates its remedy and serves as a fixed "target," and (2) that there is a sharp division between a scientific sphere in which diseases and cures are researched and a commercial sphere in which they are marketed. But in Diuril's life history the ease and clarity of this structure break down: marketing is not merely an endpoint, but a phenomenon that suffuses the entire process; drug defines disease at least as much as disease defines and elicits drug.

And yet drug marketers cannot simply fashion any disease of their liking in order to sell their drug; even the largest research-and-marketing budget is ultimately limited in some way by the material nature of therapeutic and pathologic processes. To understand the interplay between drug and disease in late twentieth-century therapeutics—and the contesting positions of doctors, patients, researchers, pharmaceutical executives, and others with a stake in their mutual definition—it is vital to pay attention to simultaneous interactions between the research, the clinical, and the market arenas in which pharmaceuticals operate.[2]

The history of Diuril's development and launch provides insight into the process by which pharmaceutical marketing expanded in the postwar era and came to overlap with arenas of clinical research and clinical practice, at a time when the pharmaceutical industry was a rapidly ascending force in American medicine. Hypertension became a different disease after Diuril. It is equally true, however, that Diuril became a different drug after it encountered hypertension.

Diuril in the Life of the Pharmaceutical Firm

The American pharmaceutical industry in the two decades following the Second World War witnessed an increase in the scope and pace of therapeutic innovation unanticipated by physicians, consumers, or even the industry itself. Infrastructural links between academic medicine, industry, and governmental institutions were swiftly adapted in the postwar environment to yield a robust "pipeline" of novel and efficacious medicines that proved highly profitable for growing American drug companies.[3] Entirely new classes of therapeutic compounds were emerging almost every year, supported by an increasingly systematic literature. By 1947, it was estimated that fifty cents of every dollar of pharmaceutical sales was made from products not available ten years earlier.[4]

Nonetheless, the expanded pharmacopoeia of the postwar era was accompanied by heightened rates of pharmaceutical consumption. Between 1939 and 1959, sales of pharmaceuticals increased from $300 million to $2.3 billion.[5] Ironically, this rapid expansion of the drug market—popularly known as the "drug explosion"—was considered potentially threatening by the two organizations most poised to benefit from it: the medical profession and the pharmaceutical industry. Indeed, the rapidity of therapeutic expansion and the consequent inundation of practicing physicians with novel therapeutic compounds produced substantial challenges for both groups. In 1953, the American Medical Association (AMA) publicly cited bureaucratic overload in the face of excessive numbers of new compounds, and formally disbanded the "Seal of Acceptance" program that had served since 1908 to evaluate new drugs and educate physicians regarding their usage.[6]

Meanwhile, in the midst of such extraordinary growth, pharmaceutical executives perceived a set of threats to their former promotional practices. Growth of the industry meant increased product competition and an increasing concern with the competitiveness of any particular product. Amid the rising swell of competing products, the old principles of "ethical" promotion—with emphasis on chemical name and dry, factual advertising in medical journals—were increasingly perceived to be insufficient means of persuading physicians to use novel products. By the late 1950s, pharmaceutical companies had developed sophisticated and integrated systems for the promotion of their products that involved a tight intertwining of research and marketing.[7] This shift is particularly well illustrated in the institutional history of Merck, Sharp & Dohme (MSD) at the time of Diuril's release.

By the early 1950s, the Merck Company's research laboratories were the pride of the American pharmaceutical industry, and could boast a set of internationally recognized researchers with a substantial role in the production of "miracle drugs" like penicillin, streptomycin, vitamin B_{12}, and cortisone.[8] Financially, however, Merck had made almost all of its revenues as a supplier of pure chemicals—rather than pharmaceutical formulations such as pills or injectables—to pharmacists and the pharmaceutical industry. For the first half of the century, most of the pills, tablets, elixirs, or capsules that reached the ultimate consumer were physically assembled, or "compounded," in the pharmacy, even if their contents were provided by major pharmaceutical firms; but by the late 1940s, the role of chemical supply was declining. As fewer and fewer pharmacies compounded their own medications, the role of pharmaceutical "specialties"—prepackaged prescription medicines made by only one firm—increased dramatically.[9] The core products of the pharmaceutical industry were shifting from equivalent and chemically standardized medicinal substances to a set of proprietary, branded, and mass-marketed commodities.

Rather than building up a marketing force de novo, Merck's directors set out to acquire one, ending their search on the other side of the Delaware River at the Philadelphia pharmaceutical house of Sharp & Dohme. Sharp & Dohme was not known for its research laboratories, and most of the products it sold by 1951 were available from other houses as well in other formulations. The firm was, however, known for its dynamic and well-trained sales force and marketing teams that were highly effective at getting Sharp & Dohme brands onto physicians' prescription pads. Perceiving that they had much to gain from Merck's deep research pipeline, executives at Sharp & Dohme listened carefully to the proposal. The merger was announced in 1953, and analysts predicted that the combined firm would be an ideal marriage of research and marketing.[10] The launch of Diuril was to consummate this union.

Diuril, however, did not develop out of any targeted search for an antihypertensive therapy. Indeed, the drug did not have any therapeutic contact with hypertension until after it had left the company's research laboratories. Rather, Diuril's material genealogy can be traced back to wartime shortages of penicillin. Under the leadership of Karl Beyer, the Renal Program of Sharp & Dohme's newly minted research laboratories in West Point, Pennsylvania, was established in 1943 with the explicit task of devising an agent that could block the body's excretion of penicillin, in order to stretch the value of a single dose of the precious substance. Although this project ultimately did produce an agent that effectively blocked penicillin excretion with minimal side effects—Benemid (probenicid)—the product did not appear on pharmacy shelves until the mid-1950s. By that point, a wartime collaborative effort had already rendered penicillin widely available and relatively inexpensive.[11]

After this partial and costly victory, Beyer and his team quickly sought another field in which to demonstrate the utility of renal physiology for pharmaceutical development. A 1949 paper suggesting that sulfonamides had diuretic side effects had sparked their interest: if that diuresis could be translated from side effect to therapeutic indication, the Renal Program's existence would be more than justified.[12] As agents of fluid reduction in congestive heart failure and edema, diuretics were already known to be a substantial market, although their role in hypertension had not been explored. Because all available diuretics in 1957 were either heavily toxic or largely ineffective, a diuretic that was both palatable and effective would fetch a large market.[13] By the time of the merger, Beyer had assembled a team of pharmacologists and chemists and was working toward just that goal.

After the failure of several precursors such as Dirnate and Daranide, the Renal Program announced in 1956 that Diuril had been demonstrated through in-house animal experimentation to be a safe and surprisingly efficacious diuretic, a compound with significant potential as a prescription product.[14] On 25 October 1956 the drug was first demonstrated to a set of potential clinical researchers, and by the spring of 1957 Diuril had been distributed to a network of 250 clinicians in the United States and 54 physicians in eighteen other countries.[15] Two million patient-days' worth of chlorothiazide was moved through this network in 1957, and by July of that year, as case-series data mounted into the hundreds, the team filed a new drug application (NDA) with the Food and Drug Administration; in early September, Merck, Sharp & Dohme received clearance to market Diuril as a novel diuretic agent.

Attachment: Diuril Meets Hypertension

That same spring, however, two groups of clinical investigators happened to give the drug to patients with congestive heart failure who, in addition to edema, also suffered from severe hypertension, and a dramatic reduction in blood pressure was noted. These researchers—two in Boston and two in Washington, D.C.—followed up with a small case-series of severely hypertensive patients, and by the fall of 1957 a case-series of clinical encounters had documented Diuril's antihypertensive effects.[16] At that point the Boston group went public, holding a press conference in early October that was reported in newspapers and newsmagazines across the country.[17]

Paradoxically, this new therapeutic indication introduced several complications into the Merck, Sharp & Dohme marketing effort. As late as May of that year a detailed marketing plan had been drawn up based solely on Diuril's value as a safe and effective fluid-remover; this document did not include any information regarding blood-pressure effects.[18] Diuretics were not known as antihypertensives, and an unexpected physiological activity—particularly something like a drop in blood pressure—could seriously undermine a drug's safety profile. The launch, originally slated for late October, was delayed indefinitely. George

Schott, Merck's head of publicity, distributed a memorandum to the marketing teams in the immediate aftermath of the Boston press release:

> With interest in "Diuril" picking up momentum, I feel it is high time to bring our side of the story into focus, so that we will be identified with these reports, as a company and as a trade mark specialty. *I fear that our failure to adjust our program to outside pressures which are beyond our control may lead to our loss of identity with the product.*[19]

Schott feared that the November conference originally planned for the drug's release might "be an anticlimax ... although we plan to follow through with as much publicity as possible"; "however," he continued, "interest is high now, and we should be flexible enough to take advantage of it. It may never return."[20]

Karl Beyer, who would later receive a Lasker Award for his role in Diuril's development, recalls how this collision with hypertension altered the drug's therapeutic trajectory:

> It wasn't certain at all, prior to chlorothiazide. ... How in hell can a diuretic agent be antihypertensive from a marketing standpoint? How can we promote this thing, even if it works? And our top Nobel consultant in medicine thought that was a lot of nonsense too. ... But all you have to do was have those first two little papers by Freis and Wilson and by Hollander and Wilkins on hypertension come out, and we were in hypertension for whatever it cost. Everybody knew the size of the hypertension field.[21]

This is no story of serendipity. Though it was not planned as an antihypertensive, Diuril did not just "happen" into hypertension either—it arrived there through a concerted confluence of clinical, research, and marketing practices. That a marketing attitude penetrates even to the basic researcher is particularly visible in Beyer's narration, which reflects a pragmatic understanding that the research enterprise and the marketing enterprise were intimately interconnected in the process of new product development.

As Beyer suggested, the size of the hypertension field was indeed promising. A national health survey begun in 1957 concluded that 5.3 million Americans were suffering from some form of hypertension.[22] Initial sales projections for Diuril as a diuretic had been set at $8 million; hypertension now added at least another $10 million to the projection.[23] A few days after the press conference, Schott sent out a second memorandum in which he formulated a plan to refashion the Diuril campaign, emphasizing the antihypertensive qualities of the drug as a central indication and opportunity for market expansion. Hypertension was to become the central claim of the drug.

Along with cancer, heart disease was increasingly central to the health concerns of the Eisenhower era, and the heart was where MSD now positioned itself. A new launch date was set for January 1958, resources were made available to clinical researchers investigating Diuril for hypertension, and expanded focus was given to other "heart-related" indications for diuresis, particularly congestive heart failure.[24]

Schott's revised plan was circulated to Merck's marketing, research, and medical divisions. This program was meticulously orchestrated, set to simultaneously launch Diuril as a treatment for hypertension and MSD as a company visibly situated in the vanguard of heart disease and preventive medicine. To successfully plant the idea of an unfamiliar drug's relevance to a conservative physician population and consuming public, Diuril's marketers worked to develop strategies in multiple overlapping arenas of influence, staggered at different phases to form an integrated chronology of promotion with continuity between the pre-launch, launch, and postlaunch periods. Juxtaposed with the externally visible events of Diuril's launch, the content of these internal documents serves to sketch out the tactical framework of pharmaceutical promotion taking shape in the 1950s.

Clinical Research as a Marketing Arena

As late as 1948, pharmaceutical marketing textbooks made no mention of the relationship between marketing and clinical research.[25] By the 1950s, however, the industry explicitly recognized that clinical research did not precede or determine pharmaceutical marketing but was instead an essential and interwoven part of the marketing process. Paul de Haen, a marketing consultant to the industry and a frequent contributor to the journal *Drug and Cosmetic Industry,* illustrated the necessary parallels between research and marketing in the development of a new drug. As de Haen insisted, "the successful development of a new pharmaceutical product depends not only on the coordination of research and marketing, but on the synchronization of these activities."[26] Over the course of the 1950s, as marketing departments grew and the "marketing concept" spread through the industry, pharmaceutical executives began to speak more confidently about the relationship between research and marketing. Surveying the spread of marketing in the field, one executive wrote in the late 1950s:

> If Marketing should not dictate to or control the scientists in our laboratories, it is equally true that Research and Development must not assume control over marketing. … [Product planning] should function in such a way as to permit the scientist and the commercial man to meet on common ground. … The important consideration here is that under the marketing concept the laboratories will not put a finished product in a bottle, unveil it before a sales manager, and say, "Here it is, take it out and sell it."[27]

Sharp & Dohme's marketing staff were only gradually allowed into meetings at Merck research facilities, and at first those who were admitted were expressly forbidden to speak.[28] Nonetheless, by the time of Diuril's launch, clinical research was clearly understood in explicit relation to marketing. Fred Heath, the head of the medical division at MSD, articulated a vision of clinical research that was intended both to generate data for the more convincing promotion of Diuril—especially in regard to hypertension—*and* to serve as a promotional structure in itself. External researchers were all treated equally well by Merck (each was given a color TV as a bonus—no small prize in 1957), but internally the marketers divided these clinicians into a marketing structure of two concentric spheres. The outer ring comprised incidental researchers of negligible importance, but at the core was a group of eighty-four clinician-researchers selected as influential figures within their local areas, carefully chosen to be "scattered in each of the Merck, Sharp & Dohme marketing areas excepting Memphis and Minneapolis."[29] These were clinicians who might, in addition to performing research, act as models for their peers in their endorsement of Diuril, and might even circulate samples of the experimental drug within their academic and private practices.[30] This geography of clinical research was then used to generate a precise map of Diuril's premarket acceptance.

In addition to their roles in regional promotion, researchers were also mobilized by the MSD marketing team to form a series of symposia that traveled across the country. This Diuril road show had its kick-off event at the New York Academy of Sciences (NYAS) on 8 November 1957, and featured a lineup of prominent cardiologists and nephrologists from influential academic medical institutions. Known as the "third-oldest scientific organization in America," the NYAS was seen as a prestigious neutral space, a conference setting with a more protected public-relations image than Merck's Rahway, New Jersey, headquarters.[31] Following the symposium, a speaking tour of clinical researchers was mobilized with talks evenly spaced from January to November 1958, covering twenty states that represented all regions of the country. Fred Heath attended every talk and sent detailed notes back to the Rahway offices after each meeting.[32]

Symposia were good for generating publicity, but were bound in time and place; consequently, Diuril's marketers recognized the importance of journal publications that introduced larger numbers of physicians to novel medications and encouraged their prescription. Sometimes the symposium itself could become a publication, as when the proceedings of the NYAS conference were published two weeks later as a special volume of the *Annals of the New York Academy of Sciences*. Most peer-reviewed journals, however, required a longer and more complicated process to reach publication. This, too, marketers sought to manage as well as they could, and Diuril's development timeline plotted out when and how news of the product would ideally reach the general and specialty peer-reviewed journals. Setting quotas and timetables for research publications was crucial to the prelaunch marketing project, and marketers kept careful track of the publications that Diuril had managed to accrue. As an internal prelaunch Diuril memorandum described: "The importance of publications in promotion of the drug was stressed, [and] it is estimated that some 6–12 more papers will be submitted this year. It is also estimated that we can reach a goal of some two dozen papers by the end of 1958."[33] This estimate proved to be low: by the end of 1958 at least 50 articles on Diuril had appeared in the medical literature, and by June 1960 there was a literature of more than 150 articles specifically detailing the attributes of Diuril in the treatment of hypertension.[34]

Publications were particularly important in establishing Diuril as an antihypertensive agent, for this was a novel clinical application and therefore the most vulnerable aspect of the promotional program. Edward Freis's and Robert Wilkins's early case studies connecting Diuril with hypertension demanded further substantiation.[35] MSD's investment in the explicit clinical testing of Diuril in hypertension yielded further publications in early December 1957, when Freis published an eight-month study of one hundred severely hypertensive patients that suggested that Diuril in combination therapy reduced blood pressure "more effectively than any other drugs generally used."[36] At the time of launch, publications became even more important in influencing potential prescribers. The crowning jewel of Diuril's journal campaign was the 11 January 1958 issue of the *Journal of the American Medical Association*, which devoted itself almost exclusively to articles detailing the efficacy and safety of chlorothiazide. The publication of this issue, timed to match the launch month of Diuril, may have been facilitated by the journal's editor-in-chief, Austin Smith, a member of the AMA's Council on Drugs who was also elected president of the Pharmaceutical Manufacturers' Association in the same year.[37]

Public Relations and Popular Media

Publicity was only partially controllable, but marketers worked to manage what variables they could. Press kits were prepared with publication-ready illustrations that would explain the principles of hypertension and diuretics to a lay audience; symposia and press luncheons were planned in detail to maximize media attention.[38] In 1953, the American Pharmaceutical Manufacturers' Association (APMA) had commissioned a public-relations primer that advised firms to develop institutional relationships with science writers and other specialized journalists.[39] This advice was clearly heeded in the fall of 1957 as Merck publicity director George Schott ordered the creation of a "Diuril Research Report" for distribution to science writers for newspapers and newsmagazines. "This is frankly a fishing expedition," Schott added, "designed to see if any writer may be gathering material for a piece on any of the areas for which 'Diuril' may be indicated. If we strike a responsive chord, we may find ourselves in a piece from which we would otherwise be excluded. Make whatever personal contacts may be desirable."[40] Public relations required a degree of creativity in order to maximize possible venues for public contact while not violating the sanctions against advertising prescription drugs directly to consumers. In addition to the general-interest magazines, Schott argued, it was essential to "promote special stories for publications with limited interests," such as a story for *Lifetime Living* "stressing benefits to Senior Citizens,"[41] and a story for *Medical Economics* highlighting the role of the physician as clinical investigator "with 'Diuril' work the specific case."[42]

These efforts met with considerable success. Paul de Kruif, one of the best-known science writers in the health field—who, in addition to his popular *Microbe Hunters* and collaboration with Sinclair Lewis on *Arrowsmith*, had written numerous popular articles—was engaged to promote chlorothiazide to a popular audience.[43] By April 1959, *Reader's Digest* and the *Saturday Evening Post* had published full-length articles entitled "New Hope for Overloaded Hearts" and "The Pill with the Built-In Surprise," respectively. De Kruif's *Reader's Digest* article rated Diuril as the biggest medical breakthrough in recent years,[44] and the *Saturday Evening Post* article concluded with similar praise:

> On the basis of the number of [prescriptions] being written, the drug, known commercially as Diuril, would be a contender for the title of Pill of the Year, if there were such a thing. ... if no long-range flaw turns up in its surprising and still unexplained action in reducing high blood pressure, many of the 20,000,000 Americans who suffer from that have hit a medical jack pot.[45]

The publisher of the *Saturday Evening Post*, Curtis Publications, sent an analysis of the article's reception to Merck executives, reporting that "The Pill with the Built-In Surprise" was rated as the article most interesting to the largest number of readers in that issue of the *Post*. Curtis analysts estimated from their sample that more than seven million Americans learned of Diuril through that article alone.[46] *Reader's Digest* sent a similar memorandum to Merck in early 1959, suggesting that more than 1.5 million patients who used Diuril each month had likely seen the de Kruif article.[47]

Technically, Merck's publicity department was not advertising Diuril, since advertising to the lay public was forbidden by convention of the American prescription drug industry. And yet these magazine articles, along with paid institutional advertisements that highlighted "Diuril" as a "development to showcase Merck research," constituted an acceptable and malleable public-relations operation that could be coordinated with the drug's development schedule.[48] Lest the company be perceived as overstepping its bounds, however, publicity personnel carefully monitored physicians' responses to media coverage on Diuril. The 1953 APMA primer had counseled that too much pharmaceutical publicity could arouse defensive responses from physicians, pointing out that "the physician resents pressure from the public for new drugs or methods of treatment."[49] As a prophylactic measure, George Schott created a file service listing all Diuril-related publicity by radio, television, newspaper, and magazine, which it circulated on a monthly basis to all salesmen and marketers. This *Diuril News Report* notified salesmen about particular articles that physicians might have recently read. As one issue warned, "the prescribing physician sometimes objects to lay articles about drugs he uses in his practice. ... Review the article in the attached copy of CORONET so that you can intelligently discuss it, SHOULD a doctor bring up the subject."[50]

As Diuril's marketers worked with MSD public-relations specialists, they sought to popularize and manage public expectations of the basic clinical and scientific breakthrough that chlorothiazide represented. These tasks, however, were always performed within a tightly constrained space, so as not to overstep the boundaries of "ethical" drug marketing and thus jeopardize Merck's relationship with the physician community. As we will see, the marketers had far more sophisticated means of getting their message out to physicians.

"Ethical Marketing": The Detail Man and the Diuril Man

From the founding of the American pharmaceutical industry in the mid-nineteenth century, the marketing of "ethical" (i.e., prescription) pharmaceuticals had defined the physician, and not the ultimate consumer, as its principal target.[51] At a time when physicians and pharmaceutical firms alike were concerned with establishing the legitimacy of their services in contradistinction to quacks, sectarians, and patent-medicine salesmen, both institutions had agreed to codes of ethics forbidding the direct advertising of their services to the general public.[52] In the twentieth century, as prescription-drug marketers worked to follow the regulatory demands of the Federal Trade Commission (FTC) and, in the wake of the 1938 sulfanilamide scandal, the Food and Drug Administration (FDA), they also sought to meet the ethical demands of the American Medical Association. "Unless acceptance is obtained from the medical and dental organizations and unless great care is taken to keep the sales approach definitely on the professional basis," a 1940s text on drug marketing observed, "ill will can be created that can well prove disastrous."[53] Initially, this "professional basis" referred mainly to dry, factual journal advertising and direct mailings to physicians, but by the late 1950s, visually complex advertising and the expanded use of the pharmaceutical salesman became a more important way to provide physicians with new information about new drugs.[54]

The restriction of marketing to physicians was not entirely a limitation. Rather, focusing on a small and well-bounded elite created clear advantages for the marketers, as Richard Hull, director of marketing for Smith, Kline and French in the late 1950s, pointed out in a lecture given to the National Pharmaceutical Council: Placing a single advertisement in four medical journals in 1958, he argued, would cost under $3,000 and would provide a "very complete, duplicated coverage of their marketplace."[55] On the other hand, presenting the same copy to the lay public in the four most prominent popular magazines—*Life, Time, Saturday Evening Post*, and *Reader's Digest*—would cost in excess of $80,000 while reaching only a fraction of the consumer market. Moreover, in addition to being a smaller target for promotion, physicians represented a highly visible and easily studied population. "Thanks to the fact that physicians must be licensed," Hull continued, "and because the American Medical Association maintains what has been called the best professional directory service in the world, we have accurate lists of physicians, together with good information on the nature of the individual doctor's practice and his specialty, if any."[56] Marketers used this demographic data set to weed out older and retired physicians in order to focus marketing efforts on the 125,000 actively "prescribing physicians," as well as to subdivide the profession for purposes relevant to the promotion of specific products.[57]

Promotional materials for Diuril were targeted toward an audience of general practitioners as well as specialists in cardiology, internal medicine, and other relevant fields.[58] Physicians licensed in these fields were sent a series of "Dear Doctor" letters and a pamphlet entitled *Information for the Physician on Diuril (Chlorothiazide), a New Diuretic and Antihypertensive Agent*—a technical publication that emphasized Diuril's safety and efficacy and provided an annotated bibliography of publications in peer-reviewed journals related to chlorothiazide.[59] And yet marketers recognized the limitations of direct mail as a modality for convincing conservative physicians to feel comfortable using a novel therapeutic agent. In the late 1950s, a growing literature of pharmaceutical market research began to document the effectiveness of both journal advertising and sales representatives in influencing physicians' prescribing habits. Using various sampling methods, these studies quantified the role of journal advertisements as the crucial factor in 9–25% of prescriber decision-making, and suggested that contact with salesmen constituted 31–52% of the information that physicians used to make prescribing decisions.[60] As medical journals became increasingly important to drug marketers, the journals themselves changed dramatically: the number of advertising pages per medical journal increased by 34% between 1953 and 1958, to make up nearly 40% of all printed pages in medical journals; by that time the pharmaceutical industry accounted for more than $30 million of medical journal advertising revenue.[61]

Where Merck had formerly spent a negligible amount on advertising, the Diuril campaign quickly commanded a $5 million yearly budget for journal advertising and direct mailings.[62] Diuril was not advertised in the 11 January 1958 issue of the *Journal of the American Medical Association*, but the following week the advertising campaign began in full. The resulting campaign was polished and penetrating, uniting all mailings, advertisements, and associated trinkets with the iconic figure of the "Diuril Man". The Diuril Man was described to the Merck sales force in a feature article in their in-house monthly magazine, *MSD Sales Dispatch*:

> Standing just a shade under six inches on a tiny platform, the Diuril man is a transparent figurine, not quite filled with liquid, showing the heart, lungs, kidneys, ureters, and bladder. He has set the theme for the entire campaign, for he emphasizes wordlessly how an edematous man can actually drown in his own excess body fluid. As a result, hardly a promotional piece or an advertisement appears without this picture.[63]

As a visual aid in journal advertisements, the Diuril Man presented an idealized image of physiology, health, and disease; as a six-inch-high desk trophy, however, it took on added significance as an early example of the pharmaceutical gift that detail men were increasingly providing to physicians as part of their routine promotional activities. Like the "Diuril Heart" and the "Diuril Kidney" that would be given to physicians in future years, the Diuril Man could be presented as a prop to be used in educating patients about their conditions: the doctor could point out the organs involved in high blood pressure (the heart and the great vessels) and the site of action of chlorothiazide (the kidneys).[64] Perhaps the most ingenious aspect of the Diuril statuette was its fluid-filled base: when the figurine was inverted, the body filled with transparent mineral oil; once righted, the fluid level slowly drained out of the body back into the base—cleverly simulating both the pathological mechanism of excess body fluid and its therapeutic removal via Diuril.

However much they might serve to educate patients, however, Diuril promotional materials were primarily designed to educate physicians to see hypertensive disease in terms of Diuril. From Merck's perspective, much of the Diuril Man's value was that he sat on the doctor's desk, continually radiating the name "Diuril" and the mechanism of fluid removal to all physicians, nurses, and patients who might pass by or pick him up and turn him over. Later advertisements that emphasized the accumulated "weight of evidence" clearly made a visual pun about the role of the Diuril Man as a ubiquitous paperweight in physicians' offices. Another illustration that appeared around the same time was an unusual cartoon posted in the *MSD Sales Dispatch*, in which a confused physician sees a Diuril Man (wearing pants) appear in his office instead of a human patient. The beleaguered physician's question—"Haven't I seen you somewhere before?"—is humorous, but underlying the joke is a wry sense that physicians were learning to see their patients in terms of the promotional imagery of the drug.

Reception: Diuril and Hypertension in Practice

For the most part, physicians responded favorably to the advertising and publicity surrounding Diuril. In its first year of release, thirteen million prescriptions for Diuril were written, and in 1958 MSD recorded $20 million in Diuril sales, making it the most financially successful drug launch the firm had yet seen. Whereas the entire market for diuretics had amounted to $7 million in 1957, a stunning $25 million in diuretic prescriptions were sold in 1958, with Diuril accounting for 75% of the market.[65] By 1959 MSD's prescription volume had more than doubled, and in that year, every other prescription written for a Merck drug was written for Diuril. Merck's showcase drug had not just done well: it had, to paraphrase one analyst, created its own market.[66]

Hypertension was crucial to that lucrative and newly fabricated market, for Diuril's launch took place in the midst of a fundamental debate over the diagnosis and treatment of hypertension.[67] The recent emergence of specific therapeutics with demonstrated efficacy at lowering pressure—as well as a significant set of adverse effects—demanded a pragmatic consensus as to which patients truly had a *disease* that merited treatment, and which merely had an above-average measurement. As the question of "whom to treat" began to trump the question of "what was normal," Diuril became materially involved in altering the definition of hypertension in America, helping to transform a degenerative and symptomatic condition into a symptomless and treatable category of risk.

By the late 1950s, practicing physicians faced a confusing plurality of hypertensions defined in therapeutic terms. For any patient with high blood pressure, the physician was first confronted with an etiologic question: was this patient's high blood pressure a symptom of some other potentially curable process—an adrenalin-secreting tumor, local pathology of the kidney, or perhaps primary aldosteronism—or was it a condition in its own right, "essential" hypertension? If the latter was true, and hypertension was the primary condition, the next question was one of temporality: did this patient's high blood pressure represent an *acute* event ("malignant hypertension," or a "hypertensive emergency"), or an insidious and *chronic* illness ("benign hypertension")? This last category—benign essential hypertension—was the largest group by far and the center of controversy. Depending on the mode of diagnosis, chronic hypertension could be classified as "severe," "moderate," or "mild"—a distinction that roughly correlated with the diagnostic presentation of symptom, sign, or number. In other words, "severe" hypertension was manifest enough to be *symptomatic* to the patient; "moderate" hypertension was insensible to the patient but manifest to the trained eye of the clinician through a series of subtle *signs*, such as retinal damage, which constituted material proof of pathological processes; while "mild" hypertension was imperceptible to both doctor and patient and visible only in the *number* of the sphygmomanometric reading.[68] By the late 1950s, hypertension as a treatable disease was largely limited to the symptomatic (malignant and severe benign forms only) and treated with highly toxic medications.[69] For the patient with no symptoms, there was no clear consensus as to how to proceed; indeed, many medical textbooks depicted uncomplicated asymptomatic high blood pressure as a *probability* of a disease rather than a disease in itself.[70]

Cast into this environment of therapeutic uncertainty, Diuril would prove a crucial catalyst in broadening the definition of treatable hypertension. It held immediate empirical and theoretical appeal to those disposed to treat the asymptomatic patient with measurably high blood pressure. Where all prior hypotensive agents had lowered blood pressures equally in hypertensive and normotensive patients, Diuril appeared to lower the blood pressure only in individuals with high blood pressure, suggesting that chlorothiazide was specifically active in the hypertensive state. MSD marketers encouraged researchers and clinicans to see Diuril as the first true *antihypertensive* drug; as one "Dear Doctor" letter from the company reminded physicians, "Diuril is the only hypotensive agent with 'specificity' of action, i.e., it reduces B.P. only in hypertensive patients."[71] Though the exact mechanism remained to be elucidated, the promise that Diuril held out—of a unifying mechanism legitimating the disease-status of essential hypertension—was swiftly adopted.There existed by 1958 a small camp of hypertension researchers who were already convinced that the broad development and use of antihypertensive drugs in mild and moderate cases of hypertension was itself a public health movement with self-evident merit. Many of these individuals—such as the Cleveland Clinic's Irvine Page, and Edward Freis of the Washington, D.C., Veterans' Association Hospital—were drawn from the network of researchers who had conducted initial clinical research on ganglionic blockers, hydralazine, and reserpine.[72] To these therapeutic enthusiasts, the safety profile of chlorothiazide immediately presented the grounds for a more expansive treatment program. With so little to risk, clinicians could *afford* to be more liberal with antihypertensive medications. Freis noted during a Merck, Sharp & Dohme symposium in early 1958 that Diuril's lack of toxicity made it worth using even if the benefit could not be quantified:

> While it may take 20 years to prove that reduction toward normal of elevated blood pressure in mild hypertension is beneficial, do it now using Diuril alone (rarely adequate) or in combination with reserpine, veratrum alkaloids or ganglionic blockers, and reduced sodium intake.[73]

A number of other hypertension specialists echoed Freis's optimism: with such minimal side effects and such potential gain, why *not* treat asymptomatic hypertension? Reviewing the prognostic data on existing drugs, Henry Schroeder suggested that "even though we don't have evidence at hand now which would validate the concept, mild hypertension should be rigorously treated or managed in whatever way is necessary to effect the desired result."[74] From a "philosophical position," A. C. Corcoran maintained, the current understanding of high blood pressure as a potentially reversible condition *demanded* early treatment.[75]

Expanding the Ranks of the Treatable

In the absence of data-driven consensus, prescribing physicians in the late 1950s and early 1960s were instead encouraged to feel comfortable with the broader use of antihypertensives through an empirical plea to "clinical experience" and a theoretical model of hypertension as an insidious and progressive illness in which early intervention would prevent later calamity. As early as 1959, the visual rhetoric of Diuril's advertising had shifted away from a thematics of novelty toward a reassuring trope of familiarity. Through its own surveys of physicians' responses to pharmaceutical advertisements, the pharmaceutical industry well understood the value of "reassurance symbols" for prescribing physicians and the importance of generating what they termed a "climate of believability about a new drug."[76] Diuril's one-year anniversary campaign utilized the clinical ubiquity of the Diuril Man to proclaim the "weight of evidence" behind Diuril's usage. Subsequent advertisements in the early 1960s continued this tone of familiarity, urging physicians to "start with what you know is right" when deciding whether a mildly hypertensive patient should be put on medications.

By 1960 Merck had become the leading advertiser in most medical journals, and in part the familiar figure of the Diuril Man was employed to help distinguish Diuril from the subsequent thiazides and other antihypertensives that emerged shortly afterward.[77] Within one year of Diuril's release, Ciba brought to market a competitor product, Esidrix (hydrochlorothiazide), which was ten times as potent as chlorothiazide; although this did not translate into any increased clinical efficacy or safety, Esidrix would have made for significant competition had Merck's Karl Beyer not submitted a patent for hydrochlorothiazide at roughly the same time. MSD's brand of hydrochlorothiazide, HydroDiuril, was the first extension of the Diuril brand line; subsequent combinations such as Diupres (Diuril mixed with reserpine) worked to further identify Merck and Diuril in the mind of the prescribing physician. As other competitors—such as Squibb's Naturetin (bendroflumethiazide),

Robins's NaClex (benzthiazide), and Geigy's Hygroton (chlorthalidone)—came to market, Merck's promotional efforts helped to keep Diuril's sales robust for the majority of the decade.

In addition to the shift in perceptual environment mediated through its promotional materials, chlorothiazide—along with the other antihypertensives—also had a material impact on the natural history of hypertensive disease. Over the course of the 1950s and 1960s, as more "severe" hypertensives were treated with these oral agents, the nature of hypertensive mortality had shifted from fatal processes internal to the disease, such as acute hypertensive crises and hypertensive kidney failure, to fatal processes external to the disease, such as heart attacks and strokes. By the late 1960s, the most common cause of death among hypertensives was coronary artery disease.[78] This shift in mortality burden altered the rationale by which therapeutic enthusiasts could argue for the value of early treatment. In the first half of the twentieth century, a deterministic model of hypertensive disease had maintained that the condition progressed along an irreversibly degenerative course; therapeutically, the best one could hope for was to slow progression from a twenty-year sentence to, say, a thirty-year sentence.[79] Over the course of the 1960s, however, arguments for preventive treatment began to shift from a fatalistic logic of degeneration to an activist logic of reversibility and prevention of secondary conditions.

Once Diuril had engendered a safe and efficacious oral therapy, large-scale placebo-controlled trials became feasible. What would be known in retrospect simply as "the VA Trial" began to admit research subjects in 1964: several hundred asymptomatic hypertensive patients, recruited from Veterans Administration (VA) hospitals across the country, were assigned to receive either active oral combination chlorothiazide-reserpine-hydralazine therapy or a placebo. By 1967, data indicated a statistically significant effect in the prevention of hypertensive complications in patients with diastolic pressures over 115 mm Hg, and by 1970 a significant difference was recorded for patients with diastolic pressures from 105 to 114 mm Hg.[80] The following year, the VA study would earn Freis the Lasker Award—American medicine's highest prize—with a citation recognizing the trial as "the definitive study and demonstration of the fact that even *moderate* hypertension is dangerous, and should, and *can* be treated successfully."[81]

Yet Diuril's involvement in the VA study should not be understood merely as the triumph of the RCT as a more powerful technique of therapeutic research: it also represents an early moment of realization—on the part of a pharmaceutical manufacturer—that large-scale postmarketing clinical research was a powerful and essential marketing tool. Eugene Kuryloski, then-director of marketing for MSD, recollects:

> Another thing that was done was to develop clinical studies all over the place. ... through our contacts with the government, we got them to agree to do a large five-year study on Diuril. We agreed to supply them all the Diuril and placebos they wanted. They were going to do cross-over studies, and it was going to be a long-range study. But it paid dividends.[82]

Consequently, Merck swiftly produced a set of advertisements promoting the results of the VA study as a justification for the early use of antihypertensives.[83]

The VA study would present more value to manufacturers of antihypertensive drugs than mere advertising copy. In his speech accepting the Lasker Award, Freis recommended that a national body be set up to make the increased detection and treatment of hypertension a public health priority.[84] Assisted by the efforts of the Lasker Foundation—and the considerable influence of Mary Lasker and Michael DeBakey on Capitol Hill, the National Institutes of Health, and the United States Public Health Service—the VA study became the central evidence justifying the creation of the National High Blood Pressure Education Program

(NHBPEP) in September 1972.[85] Among its other activities promoting the detection and treatment of the "silent epidemic" of hypertension, the NHBPEP convened a series of conferences that produced, in 1977, the first *Joint National Committee [JNC] Report on Detection, Evaluation, and Treatment of High Blood Pressure*—one of the first broadly binding sets of numerically based clinical guidelines in general medical practice. Over the course of the next three decades, the JNC would convene eight times, each time revising the thresholds of treatment to promote the broader definition of treatable hypertension. While each of these changes helped to place more hypertensives at lower risk for heart disease and stroke, each successive lowering of the threshold also generated substantial increases in the population of daily consumers of chronic pharmacotherapy.

Detaching "Diuril" from Hypertension

As the definition of who had treatable hypertension was diverted away from the immediacy of a patient's symptoms and toward a numerical threshold established by committee, "treatable hypertension" became a fluid and expansive category. Ironically, at the same time that the diagnosis of asymptomatic hypertension was becoming widespread, Diuril's role in the definition and treatment of hypertension was rapidly fading.

Merck had initially promoted Diuril as the first *specific* antihypertensive drug—a "magic bullet" for vascular tone. The very existence of this specificity of action held out the hope that somewhere in the mysteries of chlorothiazide's pharmacology lay a specific mechanism that could explain hypertension.[86] As this hope thinned, however, newer therapeutic agents that held out more promising molecular explanations and longer patent viability began to dominate both the research literature and promotional efforts. Already by 1960, the introduction of two centrally acting catecholamine blockers—Ciba's Ismelin (guanethidine) and Merck's Aldomet (alpha-methyl-dopa)—had begun to direct attention away from the kidney and toward the sympathetic nervous system; other agents soon followed. By 1968, as Diuril advertisements were casting chlorothiazide as an old and trusted companion to the practicing physician, these newer generations of antihypertensive drugs attempted to claim their own molecular insight into the fundamental mechanism of hypertension. Later decades would bring subsequent examples of rational drug design: beta-blockers, calcium-channel blockers, ACE-inhibitors, and angiotensin receptor blockers—each accompanied by an outpouring of promotional materials. As these newer drugs displaced Diuril and the other thiazides as first-line antihypertensive agents, they made use of precisely the same promotional tools that had earlier offered Diuril's message to the prescribing physician public: research symposia, journal articles, sales representatives, journal advertising, and public relations. Moreover, in the 1980s, competing pharmaceutical firms began to fund and promote studies suggesting that chlorothiazide and other generically available thiazide diuretics bore additional risks to patients—such as elevated blood cholesterol, cardiac arrhythmias, and diabetes mellitus—which the newer, on-patent antihypertensive medications did not.[87]

Ironically, the recent publication of the National Institutes of Health's Antihypertensive and Lipid Lowering Therapy to Reduce Heart Attacks Trial (ALLHAT) places us at a moment when thiazide diuretics have recently been demonstrated to be the most efficacious and appropriate first-line antihypertensive therapy for most patients, though their actual prescription rates now lag far behind those of newer, more heavily advertised drugs.[88] The examination of Diuril's career, then, leaves us with some unsatisfying ambivalence toward the drug-promotion process: while we might applaud the fact that Diuril was launched into the world so effectively, it is clear that the same efficient machine of promotion was instrumental in the subsequent decline and neglect of the thiazide diuretics once they ceased to be a financial priority for the industry. Grasping this irony is essential to understanding the dual nature of pharmaceutical promotion as a process rooted in both education and salesmanship, a process that is now fundamental to the circulation of the knowledge and changing practice of American medicine.

As the anthropologist Claude Lévi-Strauss has famously noted, objects often take on a cognitive importance that extends beyond their immediate utility, because they become "good to think with."[89] Diuril not only altered the options available for the treatment of hypertension, but also changed irreversibly the tools available to think "hypertension" with. By making antihypertensive therapy a sweeter pill to swallow, Diuril lowered the thresholds for the prescription and consumption of antihypertensive medications, enlarged the population of potential hypertensive patients in both clinical trials and clinical practice, and contributed to the consolidation of a single, mobile threshold for the definition of hypertension. Its oral tablet form enabled the expanded chronic pharmacology of the outpatient setting and was easily commensurate with the expanding practice of large-scale, multisite, randomized clinical trials for chronic conditions. Data produced by these trials engendered a "looping effect" that provided more physicians with additional confidence to diagnose hypertension and to enroll more patients in therapeutic programs and further clinical trials.[90] The category of hypertension after Diuril would be incommensurate with the hypertension that came before.

During the course of Diuril's development, an unforeseen interaction with hypertension launched Merck, Sharp & Dohme into the business of producing agents for the prevention of heart disease, reflective of a much broader shift in the primacy of daily chronic pharmacotherapy as the bread-and-butter underpinning of contemporary pharmaceutical and medical practice. At the same time, it is also evident that Diuril catalyzed the transformation of hypertension from a symptom-bound to a numerically defined disease that could be conceived and treated according to a logic of risk. Neither transformation was either immediate or complete; they were both, however, tightly contingent on the interaction between drug *and* disease in the multiple spaces of clinic, laboratory, and marketplace. The reshaping of hypertension around Diuril relates in microcosm a much larger therapeutic transition occurring in American medicine in the second half of the twentieth century, as the goals of public health shifted away from infectious-disease control and toward the widespread preventive pharmacotherapy of chronic conditions through branded products like Diuril. The story of hypertension and Diuril encapsulates the complex centrality of the pharmaceutical in the definition of disease in the contemporary period.

NOTES

1 Albert N. Brest, "Milestones in Clinical Pharmacology: Antihypertensive Drug Therapy: A 30-Year Retrospective," *Clin. Therapeut.*, 1992, *14* (1): 78–80, quotation on p. 78. Also see Marvin Moser, *The Treatment of Hypertension: A Story of Myths, Misconceptions, Controversies, and Heroics* (Darien, Conn.: Le Jacq Communications, 2002).

2 Chris Feudtner, "A Disease in Motion: Diabetes History and the New Paradigm of Transmuted Disease," Perspect. Biol. & Med., 1996, 39: 158–70; Keith Wailoo,"The Corporate 'Conquest' of Pernicious Anemia: Technology, Blood Researchers, and the Consumer," in Wailoo, Drawing Blood: Technology and Disease Identity in Twentieth-Century America (Baltimore: Johns Hopkins University Press, 1997), pp. 99–133.

3 Harry F. Dowling, *Medicines for Man: The Development, Regulation, and Use of Prescription Drugs* (New York: Knopf, 1970); Milton Silverman and Philip R. Lee, *Pills, Profits, and Politics* (Los Angeles: University of California Press, 1974).

4 W. D. McAdams, "Three Major Marketing Problems on the Desks of Pharmaceutical Management Today," *Proc. Amer. Pharmaceut. Manufact. Assoc. Midyear Mtg.*, 17 December 1947, pp. 272–80.

5 Richard G. Kedersha, ed., *Pharmaceutical Marketing Orientation Seminar* (New Brunswick, N.J.: Rutgers, the State University College of Pharmacy, 1959).

6 Harry F. Dowling, "The American Medical Association's Policy on Drugs in Recent Decades," in *Safeguarding the Public: Historical Aspects of Medicinal Drug Control*, ed. John B. Blake (Baltimore: Johns Hopkins Press, 1970), pp. 123–31.

7 Richard J. Hull, "Marketing Concepts," in *Workings and Philosophies of the Pharmaceutical Industry*, ed. Karl Reiser (New York: National Pharmaceutical Council, 1959), pp. 53–63, on pp. 53–56; Robert Bartels, "Influences on the Development of Marketing Thought, 1900–1923," *J. Marketing*, 1951, *16* (1): 1–17.

8 By 1957, Merck could boast six Nobel laureates among its network of in-house and externally supported researchers: see Max Tishler, "The Search for Better Drugs," 11 November 1957, folder 2, Diuril Papers (hereafter DP), R3-2.74, Public Affairs Subject Files, Merck Archives (hereafter MA), Whitehouse Station, N.J. See also Louis Galambos and Jeffrey Sturchio, *Values and Visions: A Merck Century* (Rahway, N.J.: Merck, 1991), pp. 27–28.

9 In the 1930s, 75% of all prescriptions were compounded by pharmacists; by 1970, only one out of every hundred prescriptions was compounded: Gregory J. Higby, "Evolution of Pharmacy," in *Remington: The Science and Practice of Pharmacy*, 20th ed., ed. Alfonso R. Gennaro (Philadelphia: Lippincott & Williams & Wilkins, 2000), pp. 7–18, on p. 14.

10 Robert E. Bedingfield, "Proposed Sharp & Dohme, Merck Merger Regarded as Deal of New, 'Encircling' Type," *New York Times*, 14 April 1953, pp. 37, 41).

11 "'Diuril': Confidential Product Summary," November 1959, pp. 3, 10, MA.

12 Morris Fishbein, "The Story of a New Drug," *Postgrad. Med.*, 1960, *27* (4): 553–54. Also see W. B. Schwartz, "The Effect of Sulfanilamide on Salt and Water Excretion in Congestive Heart Failure," *New England J. Med.*, 1949, *240:* 173–79.

13 See Milton Moskowitz, "Diuril Creates a New Market," *Drug & Cosmet. Indust.*, 1960, *87:* 841–47; Carroll Handley and John Moyer, *The Pharmacology and Clinical Use of Diuretics* (Springfield, Ill.: Thomas, 1959).

14 "'Diuril': Confidential Product Summary" (n. 14), pp. 14–17.

15 Ibid, pp. 18–19.

16 John H. Moyer, "Historical Aspects of the Development of Chlorothiazide," in *Decade of Diuril*, ed. Charles Lyght (Rahway, N.J.: Merck, Sharp & Dohme, 1968), pp. 8–9.

17 "New Drug Tested for Hypertension," *New York Times*, 15 October 1957, p. 38; "Hypertension, New Hope," *Newsweek*, 25 November 1957, p. 82.

18 Memorandum, "Resume of Meeting on Diuril," R. G. Denkewalter to Marketing Area, 14 May 1957, folder 3, DP.

19 George Schott to Beyer, Edmonston, Gibson, Heath, Horan, Jennings, Klodt, Krieger, Kuryloski, Novello, Sprague, and Thomas, memorandum attached to "Press Information on 'Diuril,'" 23 October 1957, folder 3, DP (emphasis added).

20 Ibid.

21 Leon Gortler and Jeffrey L. Sturchio, *Karl Henry Beyer Jr.: An Interview for the Merck Archives*, 1988, pp. 33–34, MA. The initial papers Beyer refers to, along with each team's subsequent publications in more prominent medical journals, are E. D. Freis, Annmarie Wanko, and I. M. Wilson, "Potentiating Effect of Chlorothiazide (Diuril) in Combination with Other Antihypertensive Agents: Preliminary Report," *Med. Ann. District of Columbia*, 1957, *26* (468): 516; R. W. Wilkins, "New Drugs for Hypertension with Special Reference to Chlorothiazide," *New England J. Med.*, 1957, *257:* 1026–30; E. D. Freis, A. Wanko, I. M. Wilson, and A. E. Parrish, "Treatment of Essential Hypertension with Cholorothiazide (Diuril)," *JAMA*, 1958, *166:* 137–40.

22 *Statistics from the U.S. National Health Survey: Heart Conditions and High Blood Pressure Reported in Interviews, July 1957–June 1958,* series B, no. 13, February 1960 (Washington, D.C.: U.S. Department of Health, Education, and Welfare, Public Health Service, 1960), p. 3.

23 Jeffrey L. Sturchio and Louis Galambos, *Gordon R. Klodt: An Interview for the Merck Archives*, 1988, MA.

24 Prior to the development of the thiazides, diuretic therapy was used primarily in the treatment of congestive heart failure, premenstrual edema, edema of pregnancy, nephritic syndrome, hepatic disease, and iatrogenic steroid edema: see Handley and Moyer, *Pharmacology* (n. 13), pp. 150–62.

25 See, e.g., Louis Bader and Sidney Picker, *Marketing Drugs and Cosmetics* (New York: Van Nostrand, 1947); and Paul Olsen, *Marketing Drug Products* (New Brunswick, N.J.: Rutgers University Press, 1948)—neither of which specifically mentions any relationship between marketing and clinical research.

26 Paul de Haen, *Development Schedule of New Drug Products* (New York: Romaine Pierson, 1949), p. 16.

27 Hull, "Marketing Concepts" (n. 7), pp. 53–54.

28 Jeffrey L. Sturchio and Louis Galambos, *John Lloyd Huck: An Interview for the Merck Archives*, 1990, p. 23, MA).

29 Economic Research Area, "Pre-Market Recognition and Usage of Chlorothiazide or 'Diuril,'" 15 January 1958, p. 10, folder 16, DP.

30 The study of the "influential" had become a prominent subject in sociological and marketing research journals by the 1950s. See, e.g., Elihu Katz and George Menzel, "Social Relations and Innovation in the Medical Profession: The Epidemiology of a New Drug," *Pub. Opin. Quart.*, Winter 1955, pp. 337–72; James Coleman, Herbert Menzel, and Elihu Katz, "Social Processes in Physicians' Adoption of a New Drug," *J. Chron. Dis.*, 1959, *9* (1): 1–19.

31 F. K. Heath, "Final 1957 Report on Diuril Promotional Program," folder 3, DP.

32 F. K. Heath, "Diuril Meetings" (n.d.), folder 3, DP.

33 "Resume of Meeting on Diuril" (n. 18).

34 Medical Publications Department, Merck, Sharp & Dohme, *Chlorothiazide & Hydrochlorothiazide Annotated Bibliography* (Rahway, N.J.: Merck, Sharp & Dohme Research Laboratories, 1970).

35 Freis, Wanko, and Wilson, "Potentiating Effect" (n. 21).

36 "'Diuril': Confidential Product Summary" (n. 14), p. 22.

37 C. Cray Williams, *The Pharmaceutical Manufacturers' Association: The First Thirty Years* (Washington, D.C.: Pharmaceutical Manufacturers' Association, 1989), p. 6.

38 Press releases, 30 January 1958, folders 9–10, DP.

39 American Pharmaceutical Manufacturers' Association, *Primer of Public Relations for the Pharmaceutical Industry* [Washington, D.C.: American Pharmaceutical Manufacturers' Association, 1953].

40 "Press Information on 'Diuril'" (n. 19), p. 2.

41 Ibid, p. 3.

42 Ibid.

43 G. R. Klodt to J. J. Horan, E. L. Kuryloski, and J. A. Wells, (n.d.), folder 13, DP: "Thank you for supplying me with the information regarding your recent meeting with Dr. de Kruif and Dr. Spies. It appears that an article on 'Diuril' will be published in the Readers Digest as we desire."

44 Paul de Kruif, "New Hope for Overloaded Hearts," *Reader's Digest*, April 1959, pp. 44–48.

45 Ben Pearse, "The Pill with the Built-In Surprise," *Saturday Evening Post*, 4 October 1958, pp. 26ff, quotation on p. 98.

46 Daniel Starch & Staff to John T. Connors, "Consumer Readership: 'The Pill With the Built-In Surprise,'" 26 November 1958, folder 13, DP.

47 *Reader's Digest* to John T. Connors, "1,500,000 Patients a Month Now Use Merck-Developed Diuril," (n.d.) 1959, ibid.

48 "Press Information on 'Diuril'" (n. 19), p. 3.

49 PMA, *Primer* (n. 39), p. 26.

50 *Diuril News Report*, no. 11, 27 June 1958, folder 7, DP. The article referred to is "A Triple-Threat Drug That Fights High Blood Pressure," *Coronet*, July 1958, pp. 45–48.

51 The pharmacist was also an important target for pharmaceutical marketing, but with the passage of the Durham-Humphrey Act in 1954 requiring prescriptions for the sale of ethical drugs, and the coincident shift in pharmaceutical manufacturing away from standardized chemicals and toward the marketing of precompounded pharmaceutical preparations and "specialty" drugs, pharmaceutical marketing came to focus more exclusively on the physician.

52 See Jonathan Liebenau, *Medical Science and Medical Industry* (Baltimore: Johns Hopkins University Press, 1987), p. 4.
53 Bader and Picker, *Marketing Drugs and Cosmetics* (n. 25), p. 234.
54 On the history of the detail man, see Arthur F. Peterson, "The Professional Care Pharmacist," *J. Amer. Pharmaceut. Assoc.*, 1951, *12* (4): 212–13, 251; Jeremy A. Greene, "Attention to Details: Etiquette and the Pharmaceutical Salesman in Postwar America," *Soc. Stud. Sci.*, 2004, *34* (2): 271–92.
55 Hull, "Marketing Concepts" (n. 7), p. 58.
56 Ibid., p. 57.
57 Ibid.
58 Economic Research Area, "Pre-Market Recognition" (n. 44).
59 Merck, Sharp & Dohme, Medical Publications Department, *Information for the Physician on Diuril (Chlorothiazide), a New Diuretic and Antihypertensive Agent* (Philadelphia: Merck, Sharp & Dohme, 1958). Merck's own market research indicated that direct mail was an effective way to reach a number of physicians; this finding would be substantiated by subsequent market research agencies. See Economic Research Area, "Pre-Market Recognition" (n. 29); Mark Kenyon Dresden, Jr., "Are Physicians Receptive to Pharmaceutical Promotion by Direct Mail?" (1959), box 11, Dowling Papers.
60 See Theodore Caplow and John J. Raymond, "Factors Influencing the Selection of Pharmaceutical Products," *J. Marketing*, 1954, *19:* 18–23; Robert Ferber and Hugh G. Wales, "The Effectiveness of Pharmaceutical Marketing: A Case Study," *J. Marketing*, 1956, *22* (4): 398–407; Ferber and Wales, *The Effectiveness of Pharmaceutical Promotion* (Urbana: University of Illinois, 1958); Coleman, Menzel, and Katz, "Social Processes" (n. 30).
61 Walter O. Wegner, "Trends in Pharmaceutical Advertising," *J. Marketing*, 1960, *24:* 65–67.
62 Moskowitz, "Diuril Creates a New Market" (n. 13).
63 "Telling the Diuril Story," *Merck Rev.*, 1958, *19:* 7, MA.
64 "A Story with Heart," *MSD Sales Dispatch*, April 1960, p. 10, MA.
65 Moskowitz, "Diuril Creates a New Market" (n. 13).
66 Ibid.
67 See Carsten Timmermann, "A Matter of Degree: The Normalization of Hypertension, circa 1940–2000," in *The Normal and the Abnormal*, ed. Waltraud Ernst (London: Routledge, forthcoming); "The Question of Norms: The Fallacy of the Dividing Line between the Normal and the Pathological," in Postel-Vinay, *Century of Arterial Hypertension* (n. 1), pp. 133–42.
68 Milton J. Chatton, S. Margen, and H. Brainerd, *Handbook of Medical Treatment*, 5th ed. [Los Altos, Calif.: Lange Medical Publications, 1956], pp. 159–60).
69 H. P. Dustan et al., "The Effectiveness of Long-Term Treatment of Malignant Hypertension," *Circulation*, 1958, *18:* 644–51; H. Mitchell Perry, Jr., and Henry A. Schroeder, "The Effect of Treatment on Mortality Rates in Severe Hypertension: A Comparison of Medical and Surgical Regimens," *Arch. Internal Med.*, 1958, *102:* 418–25.
70 Arthur M. Master, Charles I. Garfield, and Max B. Walter, *Normal Blood Pressure and Hypertension: New Definitions* [Philadelphia: Lea & Febiger, 1954], p. 124).
71 MDS, *Information for the Physician* (n. 59), p. 19.
72 E. D. Freis, "Should We Treat Hypertension Early?" *GP*, 1956, *14* [1]: 72–73, on p. 73.
73 Heath, "Diuril Meetings" (n. 32). The parenthetical "rarely adequate" refers to the more potent use of Diuril in combination with other antihypertensive medications.
74 Schroeder quoted in John H. Moyer, "Summary: Today's Recommendations for Drug Therapy of Hypertension," in *Hypertension*, ed. Moyer and John Raymond Beem (Philadelphia: Saunders, 1959), pp. 735–74, quotation on p. 737.
75 Ibid., p. 736.
76 Institute for Motivational Research, *Research Study on Pharmaceutical Advertising* (Croton-on-Hudson: Pharmaceutical Advertising Club, 1955).
77 Karl Beyer, "Chlorothiazide: How the Thiazides Evolved as Antihypertensive Therapy," *Hypertension*, 1993, *22:* 388–91, on p. 390.
78 Edward D. Freis, "Changing Outlook in Essential Hypertension," *Hypertens. Vasc. Dis.*, 1967, *1* (1): 280–85.

79 This shift from deterministic models of chronic diseases as degenerative processes to a more activist logic of chronic disease as preventable has been discussed by Merwyn Susser, "Epidemiology in the United States after World War II: The Evolution of Technique," *Epidemiol. Rev.*, 1985, *7:* 147–77; and by Robert Aronowitz, *Making Sense of Illness: Science, Society, and Disease* (New York: Cambridge University Press, 1998), pp. 111–44.

80 Veterans Administration Cooperative Study Group on Antihypertensive Agents: "Effects of Treatment on Morbidity in Hypertension: Results in Patients with Diastolic Blood Pressures Averaging 115 through 129 mm Hg," *JAMA,* 1967, *202* (11): 116–22; "Effects of Treatment on Morbidity in Hypertension: II. Results in Patients with Diastolic Blood Pressure Averaging 90 through 114 mm Hg," *JAMA,* 1970, *213* (7): 1143–52.

81 Excerpted from the Citation of the Clinical Research Award of the Albert and Mary Lasker Foundation, as recorded by Congressman Olin E. Teague in the *Congressional Record,* 17 November 1971 (Washington, D.C.: Government Printing Office, 1971), p. E 12340.

82 Jeffrey L. Sturchio and Louis Galambos, *Eugene L. Kuryloski: An Interview for the Merck Archives*, 1993, p. 44, MA.

83 "What Effect Does the Treatment of Essential Hypertension Have on Morbidity?" [proof copy of advertisement, 1972]; "When Is Blood Pressure High Enough for Drug Treatment?" [proof copy of advertisement, 1973], the latter accompanied by a memorandum from John P. Burns of MSD to Freis, 23 October 1973, all of the above found in bound correspondence files of Edward Freis, collected at the home of his daughter, Susan Freis, Bluemont, Va. (hereafter Freis Papers).

84 Jane E. Brody, "Drive on High Blood Pressure Urged," *New York Times,* 22 November 1971, p. 53.

85 Maier to Freis, 17 November 1971; Maier to Lasker, Fordyce, and Freis, 15 August 1972; Maier to Lasker, Fordyce, and Freis, 20 September 1972, Freis Papers. See also Claude Lenfant and Edward J. Roccella, "Beginnings," in *National High Blood Pressure Education Program: Twenty Years of Achievement* (Bethesda: National High Blood Pressure Education Program, 1992), pp. 3–6.

86 See Lawrence Galton, "The Amazing Drug That Helps High Blood Pressure," *Pageant,* April 1958, pp. 96–99.

87 M. Moser, M. D. Blaufox, E. Freis, et al., "Who Really Determines Your Patients' Prescriptions?" *JAMA*, 1991, *265:* 336–43.

88 Lawrence J. Appel, "The Verdict from ALLHAT: Thiazide Diuretics Are the Preferred Initial Treatment for Hypertension," *JAMA*, 2002, *288:* 3039–42.

89 Claude Lévi-Strauss, *Totemism* (Boston: Beacon Press, 1963), p. 89.

90 Ian Hacking's concept of the "looping effect" of nominal classifications is particularly useful here: see Ian Hacking, "The Looping Effect of Human Kinds," in *Causal Cognition: A Multidisciplinary Debate*, ed. Dan Sperber, David Premack, and Ann James Premack (New York: Oxford University Press, 1995), pp. 351–94.

5

Dep®ession and Consum♀tion: Psychopharmaceuticals, Branding, and New Identity Practices

Nathan Greenslit

As pharmaceuticals are moving from private patient–doctor conversations to public television and print advertisements, best-selling books, and top TV shows, as well as into everyday conversations around risk and illness, how people understand health, sickness, and their own identity is changing. This paper explores some of these changes by unpacking some of the social, political, and personal layers that are complicating the production and marketing of prescription drugs, and that are transforming the identity practices around contested illness. The paper focuses on Sarafem and premenstrual dysphoric disorder (the illness Sarafem was marketed for) as a case study.

Introduction

Fluoxetine hydrochloride, under the brand name Prozac, is white and green and was introduced as an antidepressant; fluoxetine hydrochloride, under the brand name Sarafem, is pink and lavender and is offered to women as a treatment for premenstrual dysphoric disorder (PMDD). Both are developed, manufactured, and marketed by the drug company Eli Lilly. "Sara*fem*" is homophonic with "seraphim," the borrowed Hebrew word meaning "angel" and targeted to *fem*ales. Through this kind of packaging, marketing, and targeting, pharmaceutical products take on changing symbolic lives and represent in new ways a constellation of cultural messages regarding illness.

Nathan Greenslit "Dep®ession and Consum♀tion: Psychopharmaceuticals, Branding, and New Identity Practices,"in Culture, Medicine and Psychiatry 29:4 (2005). pp. 477–502. Reproduced with permission from Springer Science+Business Media.

The circulation of pills as social signifiers happens as part of the evolution of certain psychiatric diagnostic categories. As I hope to show, the new "social lives of drugs"[1] can turn out to be a key dimension of the social histories of mental illnesses. The case of PMDD is particularly illuminating, since its evolution as a diagnosis has been markedly contentious both within and outside of psychiatry, instigating questions of gender and pathology, and has involved issues of professional boundaries, medical expertise, and scientific authority. Yet the story of PMDD can't be told without telling the story of Sarafem, whose very availability ended up diffusing authority that formerly had been centered in psychiatry.

Branded Identity and "Symbolic Mistakes": The New Social Lives of Pharmaceuticals

Social scientists are increasingly interested in questions about illness and agency (e.g., Dumit 2003; Epstein 1996): that is, on the one hand, about the use of illness and its institutions (medicine, psychiatry, pharmaceutical companies, insurance) to instigate social and political changes and, on the other hand, about how individuals come to make contested illnesses—illnesses whose "realities" are in question—meaningful for themselves. People fight to be ill (e.g., Vietnam veterans and post–traumatic stress disorder [PTSD; Young 1995]) and fight not to be ill (e.g., gays and homosexuality as a medical category [Bayer 1981]), and they forge collective identities along the way. Now more than ever these social formations are being complicated by the relationships that people can develop with pharmaceutical products. In the case of Sarafem, for instance, people on either side of the fence have made demands in the name of illness that are hard not to respond to:

> Has anyone seen the commercial for Sarafem [pink flavored Prozac;-)]? The commercial tries to pathologize the mood changes often associated with menstruation: "Think you have PMS? Think again! You may have PMDD, Premenstrual Dysphoric Disorder, a recognized medical condition." Medical condition my ass, do the words "dysphoria" and "disorder" sound familiar to the community? (From a listserv for transgendered people, soc.support.transgendered; posted March 15, 2001)

and

> I'm so glad to hear the good Sarafem is doing. All I can say is that it's about time they're treating PMS more seriously. (From an on-line discussion group on depression, www.depressionforums.com; posted May 31, 2002; translated from "e-speak")

In the first quote, Sarafem represents a medical/corporate intrusion into the gender politics that have formed around questions of menstruation and pathology; in the second quote Sarafem represents a long-overdue recognition of a medical condition that is uniquely female. Between these sides sits a new factor: the pharmaceutical product's *identity*. Sarafem and Prozac are chemically identical, but Eli Lilly (the company that manufactures and markets both) justifies the separate branding of Sarafem for PMDD as an ethical response to consumer demand:

> We asked women and physicians, and they told us that they wanted a treatment with its own identity. Women do not look at their symptoms as a depression, and PMDD is not depression but a separate clinical entity. Prozac is one of the more famous pharmaceutical trademarks and is closely associated with depression. (Laura Miller, marketing associate for Eli Lilly; quoted in Vedantam, *The Washington Post*, April 29, 2001: A01)

The pharmacology of a prescription drug alone does not provide consumers with new ways to understand what it means to treat illness: it is only in the context of a set of social explanations that the identity of a drug and an illness becomes crystallized. The new logic at work in the quote from Lilly is that the drug's branded identity itself can parse illness into separate and differently experienced diagnoses (here, depression and PMDD).

At times, these social lives of drugs can generate new anxieties around what it means to be ill:

> Last week, I saw 10 patients with PMS that had been prescribed Sarafem. Not one was told that she was taking Prozac. They were shocked and angry.[2]

This quote begs an important question: *Were* these patients taking Prozac? This doctor denies that Sarafem is anything but Prozac, and it is this sense of all of a sudden finding out what some drug is "for" that demands attention, since it points to the precariousness of keeping illnesses apart when their treatments are the same and highlights the fragility of how, in this context of rebranding, people can experience medical diagnoses.

Rebranding and symbolically recoding drugs is happening in the context of direct-to-consumer advertising (DTC), which, in its current form that includes print and broadcast advertisements and Web sites, was approved by the FDA in 1997. It is thus relatively recently that pharmaceutical companies have begun extending and differentiating products in a meaningful way to consumers, and it is within the context of DTC that a number of tactics for representing pills as brands have emerged. For instance, the Web site for Prozac contains specific sections for learning about *generic* fluoxetine hydrochloride, which nearly collapsed Prozac's share in the selective serotonin reuptake inhibitor (SSRI) market when it was first introduced (Scott-Levin 2002), under the heading "Generic or Brand Name? Are There Differences?"

> Can I still get brand name Prozac? The answer is "yes"... . We think it is important you know that Lilly will not manufacture generic fluoxetine... . Generic fluoxetine is not identical to brand name Prozac in appearance. The generic prescription you pick up at the pharmacy won't look like brand name Prozac. Receiving medication with a different color or shape may be unsettling or cause concern. (Originally accessed via www.prozac.com, 2000–2001)

About 50 years ago most pills were white and round (Hogshire 1999:51). But the language of the Prozac web site suggests that pharmaceutical companies have new struggles over how to represent pills as brands. Clearly Eli Lilly is tapping into and trying to generate anxiety around generic fluoxetine, exemplifying how pharmaceutical developers now carefully consider the sociomedical meanings of what Jean Baudrillard (1968: 142) critically referred to as the "inessentials" (e.g., color) of advertised commodities. Baudrillard called certain features inessential to separate them from functional aspects (you buy a dishwasher because it washes dishes, not because it's black—although its color sets it apart from a series of dishwashers and will probably play into your decision to purchase it) and argued that in the postindustrial world of consumption, personalization could only be achieved through the emphasis of such inessential aspects of a commodity.

Eli Lilly is not unique in this new preoccupation with surface appearances. A professor of drug marketing, quoted in a *Boston Globe* article (Wen 2001:D1), said, "You wouldn't make a pink Viagra."[3] The article went on to say that "designers propose colors for a particular medicine and help make sure there are no *symbolic mistakes*" (emphasis added).

Markets, Molecules and Meanings

Pharmaceutical companies are trying to convey to consumers that brands matter, but they cannot do so by making direct claims about clinical superiority to other brands, which would be in violation of FDA guidance on DTC advertising.

But branding and the social coding of drugs are situated within medical contexts: PMDD is different than depression, and so Sarafem "belongs" to it more than Prozac does. As the previous quotes showed us, this has been met with appreciation, and with derision. And, in addition to complicating consumers' relationships with prescription drugs, this attempt to make brands stick to illnesses invites a whole new set of tensions among pharmaceutical companies, health care providers, and insurance companies. Now that generic fluoxetine is commercially available, for instance, managed care providers—for whom "therapeutic equivalence"[4] and not brand name is key—typically refuse to cover the cost of Sarafem.[5] This suggests that, within these different institutional settings, the patient-consumer can encounter quite different ideas of how illnesses, bodies, and drugs go together.

Similarly, DTC interpellates patients into a relationship with prescription drugs that is different from how physicians are interpellated to prescribe them. The Web site for Sarafem, for instance, includes separate "physician information" and "patient information" sections, each of which describes in different ways the relationship of Sarafem to Prozac:

Physicians are told,

> Fluoxetine was initially developed and marketed as an antidepressant (Prozac[QR], fluoxetine hydrochloride). (Lilly 2002a)

Whereas patients are told,

> What is the active ingredient in Sarafem? Sarafem contains fluoxetine hydrochloride, the same active ingredient found in Prozac[QR]. (Lilly 2002b)

These two statements are both technically true, but socially they produce very different meanings. The differences in these descriptions are not those of technical expertise; the patient-directed description is not "simpler" than the physician- directed one. For physicians, the first statement allows that Sarafem and Prozac are the *same drug*, with different packages. The second statement, for patients, conveys that they are *different drugs*, with the same ingredient. And as patient advocacy is increasingly overlapping with consumer advocacy, these differences are not trivial: as some of the previous quotes suggest, we now live in a world where people can be "shocked and angry" that their prescription drug is chemically identical to another, whereas others welcome new brands as an important material-semiotic aspect of their health care.

Sarafem is not an antidepressant—not because of its chemical makeup, but because of its brand. Branding has functioned as a strategy to keep *certain* illnesses apart but not others. Unlike Prozac becoming Sarafem for PMDD, Pfizer's Zoloft, for instance, was originally marketed as an antidepressant but was *not* rebranded once it was approved to treat PTSD and OCD. The distance between depression and PMDD, or between depression and nicotine addiction, may thus be seen as a *symbolic incompatibility*. To rephrase the Lilly quote about Sarafem, some people just don't want PMDD and depression to be the same thing, which is exactly what might be achieved symbolically if they were treated by the same brand. The lesson here is that the marketing logic of rebranding does not simply dictate the cultural logic of how illnesses relate to each other, even though branding drugs differently can function as a way to sustain the conceptual separation of certain illnesses.

Sarafeminism?

> Many doctors counter that medicines such as Sarafem help women who suffer severe discomfort, irritability and tension every month. A simple matter of medicine, they say, has been complicated by gender politics, drug marketing and the future of Prozac. (From a Washington Post article on the Sarafem controversy, Vedantam 2001: A1)

Emily Martin (1988) has explored how medical and scientific ideas about menstruation have fit together with the historically contingent requirements of social and economic systems in the United States. Specifically, Martin points out that, after women began entering the workforce at the start of World War II, the periodic changes in energy and mood associated with menstrual cycles became understood in terms of losses of productivity.

It is interesting to read Martin (1988) alongside *Listening to Prozac* (1993), where Peter Kramer (1993) claims that, to the extent that antidepressants can put women in a position to be more motivated and active, "there is a sense in which antidepressants are feminist drugs, liberating and empowering" (40). This seems to be exactly what Eli Lilly *wants* to say about Sarafem but obviously is not in the right subject position to do so. The language of DTC advertising, however, is precisely about women "taking control" of their symptoms (the very opposite of the retrospective discourses of women and benzodiazepines—the "mother's little helpers" of the 1950s and 1960s, like Miltown and Valium—in which antidepressants and antianxiety drugs helped keep women "in their places"). For instance, the following is the voice-over from a Lilly TV commercial for PMDD, during a scene in which a woman is trying to find lost keys, growing increasingly frustrated:

> Think it's PMS? It could be PMDD, premenstrual dysphoric disorder. You know, those intense mood and physical symptoms the week before your period. Sound familiar? Call to get free information about PMDD and a treatment your doctor has to relieve its symptoms. Why put up with this another month? (Lilly 2001)

The subtext here is that severe premenstrual symptoms get in the way of a woman's personal and social functioning, and that it is the woman's responsibility to treat them—which in itself is a self-empowering act. A recent print advertisement for Sarafem (from the www.sarafem.com website, accessed 2000–2001, now defunct) included the altered text "~~irrit~~ability," which also says this through a different logic. What is conveyed graphically in this ad is that "ability" is embedded in the symptom of "irritability," and that deriving one from the other—that is, treating PMDD with Sarafem—*is* a feminist act. Whereas Martin (1988: 172) posed the question of whether menstrual capacities themselves could be seen "as powers, not liabilities," the message of the Sarafem ads is that power resides in the act of treating them.

DTC has influenced how consumers come to learn about illnesses and treatments (Kaiser Family Foundation 2001). DTC advertising therefore participates in (and, given the scale of pharmaceutical marketing,[6] even dominates) mental health care debates as a powerful new medium for circulating biological frameworks in which to understand something like depression or premenstrual symptoms. Similarly, DTC has influenced how people treat their mental disorders. For instance, since the mid-1990s, prescription rates for psychotropic drugs that have been advertised DTC have risen sharply, especially for mood stabilizers like SSRIs, to which Prozac, Zoloft, and Paxil belong (Kreling et al. 2001; Olfson et al. 1998).

Sarafem was one of the first prescription drugs to be introduced after the appearance of broadcast DTC advertising. It was marketed from the beginning with a large print and broadcast campaign, representing one of the first times a pharmaceutical company had spent more on DTC than physician-directed advertising in the first months of a drug's release. The Sarafem campaign, in particular, also played into a more general controversy around DTC advertising and its effects on pharmaceutical expenditures, prescription practices, and possible delays in bringing generic drugs to market. In Europe, for instance, DTC is not permitted, and opposition there has cited the Sarafem campaign as an example of the potentially deleterious effects of DTC (like the overprescription of antidepressants to women).[7] In the United States, the Sarafem campaign was quickly implicated in debates over advertising as a new space where people encounter ideas about health, illness, drugs, and selves, and DTC became a new site for social movements to instigate health care reforms. For instance, the National Women's Health Network (NWHN; *Our Bodies, Ourselves*) testified at public FDA hearings on DTC advertising, using Sarafem ads to critique more generally the practices of DTC, and suggested that pharmaceutical companies should fund independent consumer-run groups to evaluate drug commercials. The NWHN had then begun its own policy of monitoring DTC ads and contacting the FDA when it deemed them "inaccurate and incomplete" (NWHN 2001).

For all sides of the debate over DTC, the stake seems to be in establishing the gateways for participating in one's own health care. For instance, the pharmaceutical industry has met criticism about DTC with claims that this kind of advertising "empowers" consumers to participate in their own health care, "rather than remaining uninformed and relying entirely on health care professionals."[8] Along these lines, the pharmaceutical industry has also claimed that DTC doubles as "educational campaigns" about illness and treatments, inevitably making health care more democratic. It is somewhat ironic that it was the pharmaceutical industry that "answered the call," picking up on the very language of empowerment and democracy that women's groups were using to challenge DTC in the first place, especially the question of whether DTC might actually be *limiting* the kinds of ways in which people could learn about illness. (For instance, in pharmaceutical advertising learning about something like depression *can only mean* learning about Prozac or Zoloft—and not, say, psychotherapy.)[9] Either way, the controversy around DTC and the fact that social movements have been inserting themselves into health care policy debates suggest that a new form of medical citizenry has emerged, one in which informed patients must be savvy consumers and political activists, and that these new kinds of medical citizens are emerging at the same time that sites for health care reform are shifting.

The specific question of how women have been represented in psychopharmaceutical advertisements was enlivened in November 2000 when the FDA sent a warning letter to Lilly over its first DTC advertising campaign for Sarafem. The contested spots featured a frustrated woman trying to extract her shopping cart from others lined up in front of a supermarket, along with the voice-over, "Think it's PMS? Think again. It could be PMDD." The FDA claimed that "the imagery and the audio presentation in the advertisement never completely define or accurately illustrate [PMDD], and there is no clear distinction between premenstrual syndrome and PMDD communicated" and that the Sarafem spots "trivialized the seriousness of PMDD."[10,11]

But what was it that made possible the language of "trivialization"? How did the line for representing PMDD separately from PMS become so thin, and so contested? It turns out that the FDA's warning letter about the Sarafem campaign replicated the institutional struggles over PMDD, especially the insistence that PMDD be cleanly separated from PMS. What later became a key tension between the market reach for rebranded Prozac and the FDA's insistence that PMDD be discontinuous with PMS was originally a tension among psychiatry, gynecology, and women's advocacy groups over the "ownership" of PMS.[12]

Premenstrual Dysphoric Disorder in the Making

In the mid-1980s, the controversy around whether a premenstrual disorder should be included in the DSM-III-R (American Pyschiatric Association [APA] 1987) quickly polarized into two basic sides within the APA: some argued that the creation of PMDD would pathologize *all* premenstrual symptoms (and, therefore, in a sense pathologize all women), whereas others embraced the diagnosis as a long-overdue recognition of the uniqueness of female suffering.

Attempts to resolve the debates over the inclusion of a premenstrual disorder category in the DSM-III-R drew additional actors into the controversy. For instance, Jean Hamilton was a member of the "Premenstrual Advisory Committee" and led the opposition against any version of PMDD, eventually recruiting the APA's Committee on Women and outside women's health groups (including the National Coalition for Women's Mental Health and the American Psychological Association's own Committee on Women) to challenge the decision to include a premenstrual disorder in the DSM-III-R. In the end, PMDD (then called "late luteal phase dysphoric disorder") was assigned a code number that placed it under "Other and Unspecified Special Symptoms or Syndromes, Not Elsewhere Classified" and placed it in a special appendix in the DSM for areas "needing further research," which was created especially for it.

In the early 1990s, when the APA committees reconvened to plan for the next edition of the DSM (the DSM-IV), the question of the appropriateness of a premenstrual category was taken up again. A key figure in this controversy was Paula Caplan (a psychologist and member of the new PMDD Work Group), who renewed the opposition against a premenstrual category within the "science, not politics" framework, charging—and publicizing—that there was only "bad science" around PMS (1995: 146–151).

Prozac became commercially available in 1987—the same year in which the DSM-III-R was published—and added a new dimension to the controversy around a premenstrual category in the DSM-IV. Previously, the inclusion of a premenstrual disorder was contested partly because there were no established treatments for its symptoms; but now the commercial introduction of Prozac and its off-label usage to treat severe premenstrual symptoms provided a new way for psychiatrists to talk about how to distinguish PMDD from PMS (Figert 1996: 166). Proponents of PMDD argued that drugs that specifically targeted mood-based symptoms (and not somatic symptoms, like cramping) allowed for the identification of symptoms that are truly psychiatric.

A separate issue was that a diagnostic code for PMDD would open up the possibility of third-party reimbursement for drug treatment costs. This represented a new logic that some psychiatrists deployed to defend the inclusion of PMDD in the DSM-IV: if PMDD is not recognized and legitimated as a disorder, then the treatments for what count as its symptoms cannot be reimbursed. This health insurance logic had epistemological implications for the disorder: "If psychiatrists and physicians aren't knowledgeable about PMDD, women with the disorder won't be given therapy and/or antidepressants."[13] The very availability of antidepressants became part of an argument that the reality of PMDD should be disseminated to mental health care professionals and primary care physicians. In the end, PMDD was coded for these purposes, despite remaining in an appendix. But as part of the new DSM-IV coding schema, the reference to PMDD in the main text was changed to "Depressive Disorder, Not Otherwise Specified."

Of course, the new relevance of psychopharmacology in the PMDD debates did not evacuate the politics around women's health care. If anything, it demonstrated that science and medicine could not settle issues of inequality. Consider the following exchange of editorial comments in the *New England Journal of Medicine* after a study on the effects of fluoxetine on PMDD was published in 1995 (Steiner et al. 1995), one year after the DSM-IV was published:

> This study provides further evidence that science thinks it must rescue women from their bodies. And it gives more evidence of the negative view this culture holds of women and their physiology. (Prior et al. 1995)

The response:

> To deny these women effective treatment merely because our culture has negative views of female physiology is bad medicine. (Steiner 1995)

These quotations also invoke the relationship between medicine and "culture" in important ways. In the first quotation, medicine is complicit with a culture that demeans female physiology; in the second quotation, medicine is fighting against such a culture. And, as we've seen above, pharmaceutical advertising is newly implicated in precisely this question of what position medicine is in to connect illness and social categories in meaningful ways. Perhaps obviously, it is in the interest of pharmaceutical marketing to connect with presupposed social realities of specific illnesses. As the case of Prozac and Sarafem illustrates, however, this interaction between marketing and medicine can produce new contests over what counts as real.

Symbolic Side Effects

Prozac represented one of the so-called "blockbuster drugs"—defined by IMS-Health (a large market intelligence firm for the pharmaceutical and health care industries) as products with sales of $500 million or more. Blockbuster drugs have come to change how pharmaceutical companies think about their markets, specifically in terms of the short-term practicability of segmenting markets through existing products rather than developing new drug classes.[14] IMS-Health attributes the blockbuster drug phenomenon primarily to increases in FDA approval time and the bottom-line it takes to actually get a drug to market:

> To offset their substantial RD investments in new drugs, companies increasingly look to the revenue generated by blockbusters. To sustain growth and market share ... they are looking for ways to extend the life of their patents; to receive FDA approval for new indications of existing products; and to create new, improved versions of existing products. (IMS-Health 2000)

Accordingly, the launching of Sarafem was part of a strictly economic move, exemplifying new pressures in U.S. pharmaceutical markets to get drugs approved and marketed for multiple illnesses to extend their patent lives. In this case, as soon as generic fluoxetine was made available, it was added to 91% of managed care drug formularies, half of which immediately dropped their coverage of brand-name Prozac altogether (Scott-Levin 2002). And within a month after generic fluoxetine went public, Prozac lost two-thirds of its prescription volume, a collapse in market share that represented "an all-time speed record" for the pharmaceutical industry (Seiden 2002). Marketing journals at the time spoke of Sarafem as part of an attempt by Lilly to recoup inevitable losses from Prozac's patent expiration and the subsequent availability of generic fluoxetine (by getting FDA approval for an additional use under another brand name), and IMS-Health (2000) also anticipated the appearance of Sarafem as a tactic to "combat generic erosion."

When Sarafem was launched in 2000, the media picked up on the coincidence of Prozac's patent expiration. Much of the news coverage referred to PMDD as a "new" illness category and not infrequently raised the question of whether PMDD was in actuality created for the marketing of Sarafem:

> Irritability, sudden mood changes, bloating? Ladies, if you suffer from these nasty symptoms just before your monthly period, you could have Premenstrual Dysphoric Disorder. Sounds serious? Eli Lilly certainly hopes you think so. You may never have heard of PMDD, but the American drug company wants you to take a pill for it. (From "Marketing Madness," *The Economist*, July 21, 2001)

Anxiety over the creation of consumer demand for Sarafem was predicated on the uneasiness over PMDD as a legitimate illness category—but now the institutional genealogy of PMDD (including its footholds in psychiatry) was largely absent from the new discourses around Sarafem. Women's health care groups, feminist groups, and individuals participating in on-line discussion groups also focused on the timing of Sarafem with the patent expiration of Prozac, using language like "Prozac repackaged"[15] to describe the drug. When PMDD was debated by the APA, there were publicly expressed concerns about how psychiatry might medicalize premenstrual experiences; when Sarafem came on the market, these were made complex by concerns about how the pharmaceutical industry might capitalize on premenstrual experiences. But within both frameworks, public concerns about PMDD have always been about the extent to which it either reinvented or intruded on PMS. The following quotation, from a news wire service, makes even more complex these new tensions among Sarafem, Prozac, and PMDD:

> The popular antidepressant Prozac has just won a new use: to treat women suffering from a severe form of premenstrual tension. But if you use Prozac to treat "premenstrual dysphoric disorder," don't call it Prozac—the manufacturer has come up with a new name, Sarafem, to catch women's attention. It's the same drug, known chemically as fluoxetine, the U.S. Food and Drug Administration stressed. (From "Prozac for PMD," *The Daily Telegraph*, July 8, 2000: 25)

Unlike in the previous quotation, in which consuming Sarafem means consuming PMDD, here it is assumed that women might already be taking Prozac for PMDD and that Lilly has simply encouraged them to start calling it Sarafem. The (sarcastic) logic here is that women might instantaneously change their relationship to *the same drug*, rather than being prescribed a different drug or coming to learn about a new diagnosis through a new drug.

Sarafem rekindled the controversy around PMDD, but also restructured it. The pharmaceutical industry and the FDA took center stage, especially after Lilly's first round of DTC campaigning for Sarafem (the shopping cart ads), which became a target for women's health groups and, ultimately, the FDA. Also, the launching of Sarafem gave those who had been involved with the DSM working groups on premenstrual disorders a platform to renew (and sometimes subtly redefine) their positions on PMDD. For instance, Darrel Regier, director of the American Psychological Association's division of research, was quoted in *The Washington Post* as saying that PMDD was "the first indication for a drug that the FDA has approved for a nonofficial diagnosis" (Vedantam 2001: A1). The language of "nonofficial diagnosis" is noteworthy, since it both allows for the diagnosis and delegitimates it. Regier's comment is especially interesting when lined up with Paula Caplan's own statements about Sarafem and PMDD, for instance, that "the decision to accept Lilly's description of Sarafem as effective for 'PMDD' exacerbates the misleading and dangerous assumption that this condition even exists" (Caplan 2001: 16). Regier's and Caplan's statements about Sarafem revealed new grammatical splits among those who were politically aligned against PMDD when it was being debated within the APA: on the one hand, PMDD might exist but is not official (since it does not appear in the main text of the DSM and might require more compelling evidence to move it there); on the other hand, PMDD simply does not exist (and should never have been placed in the DSM to begin with).

Others welcomed Sarafem. Robert Spitzer (former chair of the work groups to revise the DSM-III and DSM-III-R), for example, defended Sarafem by appealing to women's suffering: "My own view—and the view of the people who originally proposed the category [of PMDD]—is that there is a small subset of women who suffer from this disorder, and the best thing you can do for these women is to recognize and develop effective treatments for it" (Osterweil 2001). For Spitzer, the development of drug treatments obviated the need for debates about the reality of PMDD. Here there is a subtle logic that reproduces a key argument supporting PMDD in the DSM-IV: the development of drug treatments for PMDD *is* simultaneously the decision that PMDD exists. This sentiment was shared by David Rubinow, clinical director at the National Institute of Mental Health (NIMH), also quoted in *The Washington Post* as saying that "concerns over the disorder are about politics, not science. If a woman was in distress and an effective treatment was available, common sense dictated that she should get help" (Vedantam 2001). What was never said outright, though, was that "politics, not science" now also translated debates over the marketing of Sarafem.

Marketing (and) Medical Turf: Symbolic Fallout

PMDD and Sarafem have also figured prominently in a turf battle between medical specialties—with ramifications for the epistemology and experience of PMS. A recent survey of fellows of the American College of Obstetricians and Gynecologists suggested that gynecologists consider PMDD to be one of their primary responsibilities but that major depressive disorder is not (Hill et al. 2001). That gynecologists feel PMDD is in an important sense theirs, and that a condition like depression is not, is due on the one hand to the lineage that gynecology has had with premenstrual symptomatologies—which have been conceptualized as somatic and hormonal, not mental. But, as we have seen, PMDD is a *psychiatric* category that the APA had to fight for in important ways. Carving out PMDD from PMS was simultaneously a response to concerns from women's groups about the boundaries between a supposedly psychiatric disorder like PMDD and PMS and to concerns from gynecologists about the proper boundaries between psychiatry and medicine.

Telling the story of PMDD as a history of interactions between psychiatry and women's medicine adds another layer to the amount of work it took to keep it apart—conceptually, clinically—from PMS. Gynecological authority over PMS generated tensions between the APA and women's medicine over the legitimacy of PMDD, intensifying reasons for it to be conceptualized mostly in terms of mood (whereas PMS was characterized more somatically in terms of fatigue, "bloating," etc.). This move was complicated by the fact that the DSM-III represented deliberate attempts to align psychiatry with medicine (again, to make the DSM "more scientific"). For instance, one of the main motivations behind the coding system in the DSM-III and subsequent editions was to make it more compatible with international diagnostic systems, especially those of the World Health Organization's *International Classification of Disease* (in 1986, the ICD-9-CM). But the ICD-9-CM included "premenstrual tension syndromes" under the category "Other Disorders of the Female Genital Tract," so the use of an analogous code number within the DSM would in effect have duplicated a *gynecological* category within a *psychiatric* nosology. This proposal led to conflict between psychiatrists and gynecologists, and this particular classification for PMDD was eventually rejected (Figert 1996: 76–79).

Once the marketing of Sarafem became the primary vehicle for the public to learn about PMDD, the conceptual distance between PMDD and PMS took on another dimension. While the clinical trials for fluoxetine in PMDD were meant to establish treatment efficacy (what the FDA requires), Lilly's marketing of Sarafem transformed claims about treatment *efficacy* into claims about premenstrual symptom *etiology*. The publicity around Prozac as a treatment for depression played a crucial role in circulating the language of "chemical imbalances," and the marketing for Sarafem—non-Prozac fluoxetine—also incorporated this framework to characterize PMDD. The Web site that Lilly maintains for information about Sarafem describes PMDD as "believed to be caused by an imbalance of a chemical in the body called serotonin" and states that "Sarafem taken daily helps to correct the imbalance of serotonin that many physicians believe contributes to PMDD" (Lilly 2000b). This framework locates the causes of PMDD in the brain and aligns it exactly with the neurobiological discourses for depression and anxiety. This represents a significant shift, because the language of hormones and abnormal menstrual cycles previously had dominated both scientific and popular discourses of premenstrual symptoms. For example:

> [Premenstrual tension comes from] a malfunction in the production of hormones during the menstrual cycle... . This upsets the normal working of the menstrual cycle and produces the unpleasant symptoms of [PMS]. (Lever 1981; quoted in Martin 1988)

NIMH researchers who coauthored the *Journal of Women's Health* article mentioned above have argued publicly that hormones should be downplayed in discussions of premenstrual symptomatology, characterizing them as "triggers" but not "causes" (Rubin 2000). But Lilly's "educational campaign" about PMDD extends this logic one step farther, characterizing hormones and hormonal activity as "normal," effectively moving the pathology of severe premenstrual symptoms *completely* to the brain:

> While PMDD is not fully understood, many doctors believe it is caused by an imbalance of a chemical in the body called serotonin. The normal cyclical changes in female hormones may interact with serotonin, and may result in the mood and physical symptoms of PMDD. (Lilly 2000b)

These statements do not allow that the premenstrual cycle is where PMDD originates. Moreover, these statements are part of the move to link *what fluoxetine does* to *what PMDD is*. The psychiatrist and historian of medicine David Healy (2003) has written about this phenomenon more generally, arguing that, historically, neuroscientific theories of drug action have been hijacked as marketing claims about the biological reality of mental illnesses. A relevant aside: the writer and producer of a number of television spots for Prozac and Sarafem told me that he assumed "*Sara*fem" alluded to *sero*tonin, the neurochemical whose activity fluoxetine specifically affects (personal interview, January 23, 2003).

In DTC advertising generally, mental illness is medical, not mental, and the promotional material for psychopharmaceuticals typically refers consumers to "doctors" or "physicians"—never psychiatry or psychiatrists. Accordingly, the Sarafem Web site includes a section entitled "treatment options" for PMDD, but there is no mention of psychiatrists or psychologists (Lilly 2000b). Perhaps ironically, the rhetoric of PMDD in contemporary DTC advertising for Sarafem is quite similar to the rhetoric of PMS in mid-1980s ads for over-the-counter drugs. In those ads, psychiatry was not too subtly maligned for making PMS mental:

"Premenstrual tension is not a psychological issue. It is a physical condition.... Premenstrual tension is not in your mind. It's in your body. Use your head—get to the physical source" (from an ad for PreMysyn PMS in *People Magazine*, June 30, 1986; cited in Figert 1996). The PreMysyn ad campaign also prominently featured recommendations from "leading OB/GYNs." This kind of challenge to psychiatry's claims to PMS resonates with contemporary DTC ads for Sarafem—which is a prescription-only drug for a psychiatric syndrome, but whose promotional materials never actually mention psychiatry. It is true that DTC ads for Sarafem do not mention gynecology explicitly either, but for many women the "talk to your doctor" refrain of this kind of advertising *means* talk to your OB/GYN. This also speaks to the fact that gynecologists feel that PMDD is one of their specific responsibilities.

DTC promotion of psychopharmaceuticals has also changed the way health care policy experts weigh in on mental illness:

> Perhaps more important than the side effect profile of SSRIs is how they have changed the perception of mental illness.... Depression can be viewed as a treatable medical event much like hypertension or high cholesterol. One needn't visit a psychiatrist to get better; even primary care physicians can help. (Cutler 2002)

The grammar here is that *the drugs themselves* have changed the social reality of mental illness. Indeed, once the pharmaceutical industry got its hands on PMDD, it became medical—in the sense of bodily (but not hormonal)—once again. In a series of complicated moves, the pharmaceutical industry went through psychiatry (mental) to get to the brain (physical) to produce ideas about premenstrual symptoms (which became neither psychiatric nor gynecological).

One implication here is that pharmaceutical products allow psychiatric diagnoses to travel into other medical fields—but not without transformation. In this case, Sarafem helped to redefine who should treat PMDD (any M.D.), and DTC advertising redirects where potential patient populations seek out their psychopharmaceuticals (any M.D.). So, on the one hand, the pharmacotherapy that DTC advocates leads to fewer women seeking specifically psychiatric care for severe PMS; but on the other hand, the contested psychiatric diagnosis of PMDD gets legitimated when deployed elsewhere, and informs practitioners in other fields. (The fact that PMDD is still in a special "needs further research" appendix in the DSM-IV doesn't matter when it is touted as a bona fide medical condition in pharmaceutical promotional materials in general practitioners' offices.) Here, one effect of pharmaceutical marketing is to decouple the authority to determine psychiatric categories from the authority to treat these categories.

PMDD is so socially manifold, so intertextual, because it lives in the APA's DSM-IV, yet gynecologists feel that in an important sense it is theirs. Because Eli Lilly was worried both about the stigma of psychiatric disorders and about the market reach for Sarafem, however, for them PMDD is simply "medical." Likewise, "officially" PMDD is a "Depressive Disorder, Not Otherwise Specified;" yet for the purposes of Eli Lilly's "educational campaign," PMDD and depression are symbolically incompatible.

As a final note, consider how the following ad interpellates women to participate in a clinical trial for PMDD treatments at a major Boston psychiatric research center:

> Do you feel moody, depressed, or anxious and irritable before your period? Do you suffer from severe PMS or PMDD (premenstrual dysphoric disorder)? (Posted in a Boston subway car; February 2003)

Here PMDD bleeds back into PMS: "severe PMS *or* PMDD" identifies separate kinds of premenstrual categories, but only for the purpose of collapsing them in a clinical trial population. "Severe PMS" is not a diagnostic category; on the contrary, it points to the spectrum of PMS that fights in the APA over establishing a diagnostic category were about. So I also want to understand this alongside the rhetorical question that Eli Lilly asks of its DTC viewership: "Think it's PMS? It could be PMDD." This is worth exploring in a couple of directions. First, the APA and the pharmaceutical industry have tried to make PMDD uncontroversial by arguing that it is a different creature altogether from PMS, but here is a clinical trial that solicits women with PMDD *or* with "severe PMS," as if the differences were *only* grammatical—as if the different grammars didn't betray anything other than etiological sameness. Second, it is important to note that we live in a world in which solicitations for clinical trials can function as a form of advertising for a syndrome that has been called "nonexistent" and "nonofficial." Here we have a situation in which compensation for participating in a clinical trial is pharmacological treatment for a psychiatric syndrome that is socially contested.

With this in mind, let us return to where we started and hear again those voices that are hard not to respond to:

> Medical condition my ass, do the words "dysphoria" and "disorder" sound familiar to the community?

and

> I'm so glad to hear the good Sarafem is doing. All I can say is that it's about time they're treating PMS more seriously.

Now we can understand these statements as being about boundaries, too. On the one hand, PMDD is a medical condition that constrains social communities by rigidly defining them; on the other hand, the perceived commercial success of Sarafem is a way to spread out recognition that *PMS* is no longer a trivial matter. The little word "or" in "PMDD or severe PMS" makes the clinical trial flyer something good to think with. By understanding some of the complicated ways that such an object is historically and socially situated, we can understand how the coproduction of illness categories and pharmaceutical treatments can offer up ways for people to speak about themselves as medical objects and experience themselves as subjects of medical discourses.

Conclusions

> *We all know someone who is on Prozac, or think about going on it ourselves, or see it seep into our communities in ways both alarming and amusing. Prozac, for these reasons alone, is a remarkable drug. It is perhaps the only drug to have seeped so far out of its plastic shell, to have been absorbed by the bloodstreams of so very many, even those who have never had any tactile relationship with it. I would go so far as to say we are all "on" Prozac, in that we all must grapple with its presence, its meaning, and its implications for our lives.* (From *Prozac Diary* (Slater 1999: 9, appendix))

Prescription drugs are medical technologies that are taking on new social lives through marketing, and we need to account for how this might be changing the ways in which people experience and identify with illness. Patient identity can become branded identity, and knowing which brands belong with which illnesses can complicate experiences with medications. For example, if you were taking Prozac and left your pills at home, would you take your friend's Sarafem? What about your friend's generic fluoxetine? How are we interpellated to consume prescription drugs? How do the new ways in which pills are designed and marketed affect our consumption practices and guide our experience of medical diagnoses?

The "identity practices" that I refer to in the title of this paper turn out to be ambiguous. Identity practices refer to how individuals and social movements, including professional organizations, participate and position themselves in sociomedical discourses; but it also refers to the pills themselves, and how marketers and doctors and patients and regulators have come to think about how a pharmaceutical product's identity—including the illness that it is associated with—can be represented in the space of DTC advertising. This is part of the power of DTC; these advertisements provide rich and lively material for cultural criticism precisely because their purpose is to represent and act out the symptoms of mental illness in such a way that these illnesses connect with viewers. Advertising, like pharmaceutical products, is about the structure of desire, and within this context, the phenomenology of the pill itself is intended to act like a therapeutic intervention. So we need to decide whether Baudrillard gets to have the last word. It is getting harder and harder to confidently demarcate the "essential" from the "inessential" aspects of psychopharmaceuticals. Chemicals matter; but so do colors.

Indeed, the question of how we experience illness through social categories must simultaneously be a question of how we encounter ideas about illness, drugs, and brains in the first place (cf. Dumit 2003). Especially since the advent of DTC, prescription drugs are being produced not only as chemicals consumed by bodies, but as texts that have to be consumed socially, culturally, and personally. This is not to say that pharmaceutical consumption in a postmodern world is any "more" cultural or social or personal than it has been during any other time in the history of medicine but, rather, that, more and more, these are the levels that constitute how consumers, doctors, drug developers, and marketers assume, worry about, or get excited over how we (should) relate to our pharmaceuticals. Apropos of that, we could ask what kind of world must exist in order for a science journalist to produce the statement "symbolic mistake" to refer to a not-quite- medical interaction between a drug and an illness. I began this paper with an exploration of the symbolic life of Sarafem with this level of analysis in mind, and was continually surprised. Who would have thought that the color of a prescription drug could be read backward in time to reveal institutional and social struggles over a diagnosis, and then read forward as a new component of a contemporary technology of self?

NOTES

1 This phrase comes from Kopytoff (1988).

2 Kramer called this "diagnostic bracket creep."

3 Viagra is manufactured by Pfizer.

4 "Drug products evaluated as 'therapeutically equivalent' can be expected to have equal effect and no difference when substituted for the brand name product. The FDA considers drug products to be substitutable if they meet the criteria of therapeutic equivalence, even though the generic drug may differ in certain other characteristics (e.g., shape, flavor, or preservatives)" (http://www.fda.gov/cder/about/faq/default.htm#3; accessed March 2002).

5 For example, Aetna's coverage policy will only cover Sarafem if patients can document contraindications for the generic equivalent (http://www.aetna.com/products/rx/data/sarafemcpb.html). Likewise, Blue Cross/ Blue Shield does not cover Sarafem (http://www.bcbsma.com/pharmacy/enUS/pharmacyIndex.jsp ; accessed March 2002).

6 DTC is the fastest-growing area of pharmaceutical advertising. Between 1994 and 2000, DTC expenditures have increased ninefold, from $266 million to $2.5 billion (Frank et al. 2002).

7 "U.K. Consumers Reject Direct Advertising to Patients by Drug Industry" (British Medical Journal 324:1416, 2002). "Providing Prescription Medicine Information to Consumers: Is There a Role for Direct-to-Consumer Promotion?" (Health Action In- ternational Europe symposium report, 2002). The full proceedings are available at http://www.haiweb.org/campaign/DTCA/symposium reports.html.

8 From the Pharmaceutical Manufacturers of America's web page: http://www.phrma.org/publica tions/documents/backgrounders/2000-11-05.189.phtml (accessed March 2002).

9 Hailing women simultaneously as sufferers of PMDD and as an empowered consumer demographic has important implications for the evolving relationships between medicine and marketing. For one thing, the kinds of mental illness that the public comes to learn about through DTC in part turn on the kinds of audiences that are expected to engage in consumerist behavior. There is a large market for antipsychotic drugs, for example, but to date there have been no DTC ads for them. The effectiveness of DTC as a medium for disseminating neuroscientific understandings of mental illness depends in part on the kinds of people pharmaceutical companies expect to be watching their ads. Mental illness turns out to have a demographic complexity too.

10 The entire letter is available at http://www.fda.gov/cder/warn/nov2000/dd9523.pdf.

11 Lilly complied with the FDA's request, immediately pulling the contested Sarafem commercials.

12 This metaphor is taken from *Women and the Ownership of PMS* (Figert 1996).

13 Judith Gold, chair of the APA's PMDD Work Group, quoted in Figert 1996: 161.

14 In fact, about a third of the pharmaceutical industry's research and development budget goes toward such "line extensions" (Frank et al. 2002).

15 For instance, from a zine on sexuality: http://www.theposition.com/coverstories/cover1/00/11/27/pmdd/default.shtm. The American Psychological Association has adopted this language as well: http://www.apa.org/monitor/oct02/pmdd.html (accessed October 2002).

REFERENCES

American Psychiatric Association.

1987. *The Diagnostic and Statistical Manual of Mental Disorders*. 3rd edition. Rev. Washington, DC: APA.

1994. *The Diagnostic and Statistical Manual of Mental Disorders*. 4th Edition.Washington, DC: APA.

Baudrillard, Jean.

1968. *The System of Objects*. New York: Verso.

Bayer, R.

1981. *Homosexuality and American Psychiatry: The Politics of Diagnosis*. New York: Basic Books.

Caplan, Paula.

1995. *They Say You're Crazy: How the World's Most Powerful Psychiatrists Decide Who's Normal*. Reading, MA: Addison Wesley.

2001. Expert Decries Diagnosis for Pathologizing Women. *Journal of Addiction and Mental Health* 4(5): 16.

Cutler, D. M.

2002. The Power of the Pill: Prozac and the Revolution in Mental Health Care. Unpublished MS.

Daily Telegraph.

2000. Prozac for PMD. *The Daily Telegraph*. Washington, DC. July 8: 25.

Dumit, Joseph.

2003. Is It Me or My Brain? Depression and Neuroscientific Facts. *Journal of Medical Humanities* 24(1/2).

Economist.

2001. Marketing Madness. *The Economist*, July 21.

Epstein, Steven.

1996. *Impure Science: AIDS, Activism, and the Politics of Knowledge*. Berkeley: University of California Press.

Figert, A. E.
1996. Women and the Ownership of PMS. Chicago: Aldine de Gruyter.
Frank, R. E., Ernst R. Berndt, Julie Donohue, A. Epstein, Meredith Rosenthal.
2002. Trends in Direct-to-Consumer Advertising of Prescription Drugs. Kaiser Family Foundation. Washington, DC.
Healy, David.
2003. The Creation of Psychopharmacology. Cambridge, MA: Harvard University Press.
Hill, L. D., B. D. Greenberg, G. B. Holzman, and J. Schulkin.
2001. Obstetrician-Gynecologists' Attitudes towards Premenstrual Dysphoric Disorder and Major Depressive Disorder. Journal of Psychosomatic Obstetrics and Gyne-cology 22(4).
Hogshire, J.
1999. Pills-A-Go-Go: A Fiendish Investigation into Pill Marketing, Art, *History and Consumption*. Venice, CA: Feral House.
IMS-Health
2000. Life After Prozac. Electronic document, http://www.imsglobal.com/insight/newsstory/0009/newsstory000925.htm.
Kaiser Family Foundation
2001. New Kaiser Family Foundation Reports Highlight Influence of Direct-to-Consumer Ads on Prescribed Drugs. Electronic document, http://www.kaisernetwork.org/daily reports/repindex.cfm?hint=3&DROD=8307, accessed August 2001.
Kopytoff, I.
1988. The Cultural Biography of Things: Commoditization as Process. *In* The Social Life of Things: Commodities in Cultural Perspective. Arjun Appadurai, ed., pp. 64–93. Cambridge: Cambridge University Press.
Kramer, Peter
1993. Listening to Prozac: A Psychiatrist Explores Antidepressant Drugs and the Re- making of the Self. New York: Penguin Books.
Kreling, D. H., David A. Mott, and Joseph B. Wiederholt
2001. Prescription Drug Trends: A Chartbook Update. Washington, DC: Kaiser Family Foundation.
Lever, J., and M. G. Brush
1981. Pre-menstrual Tension. New York: Bantam Books.
Lilly, Eli
2000a. Prozac website, www.prozac.com. Electronic document, now defunct, originally accessed 2000–2001.
2000b. Sarafem website, www.sarafem.com. Electronic document, now defunct. Original text can be found at http://www.webmd.com/content/article/40/3312 242.
2001. Sarafem television commercial. Aired February 2001.
2002a. SarafemTM: Fluoxetine Hydrochloride.Electronic document, http://pi.lilly.com/us/sarafem.pdf.
2002b. Information for the Patient: SarafemTM, Fluoxetine Hydrochloride. Electronic document, http://pi.lilly.com/us/sarafem-ppi.pdf.
Martin, Emily
1988. Premenstrual Syndrome, Work Discipline, and Anger in Late Industrial Societies. *In* Blood Magic: New Perspectives in the Anthropology of Menstruation. Thomas Buckley and Alma Gottleib, eds., pp. 161–186. Berkeley: University of California Press.
National Women's Health Network (NWHN)
2001. NWHN Consumer Protection Advocacy. Electronic document, http://www.womenshealthnetwork.org/advocacy/cpa.htm, accessed 2001.
Olfson, M., S. C. Marcus, H. A. Pincus, J. M. Zito, J. W. Thompson, and D. A. Zarin
1998. Antidepressant Prescribing Practices of Outpatient Psychiatrists. Archives of General Psychiatry 55(4): 310–316.
Osterweil, Neil
2001. Women Behaving Badly? Female Troubles. June 18. Electronic document, http://www.medicinenet.com/script/main/art.asp?articlekey=51284, originally accessed 2001, again January 9, 2006.

Prior, J. C., K. Gill, and Y. M. Vigna

1995. Fluoxetine for Premenstrual Dysphoria. *New England Journal of Medicine* 333(17): 1152.

Rubin, Rita

2000. PMS Women No Longer Must Accept Agony. USA Today. February 18: D9.

Scott-Levin

2002. Managed Care Formulary Drug Audit. Electronic document, http://www.quintiles.com/productsandservices/informatics/scottlevin/pressreleases/pressrelease/printfriendly/1,1255,359,00.html.

Seiden, C.

2002. Even without Prozac, Lilly Won't Suffer Depression. Medical Marketing and Media 37(3).

Slater, Lauren

1999. Prozac Diary. New York: Penguin Books.

Steiner, M.

1995. Fluoxetine for Premenstrual Dysphoria. New England Journal of Medicine 333(17): 1153.

Steiner, M., S. Steinberg, D. Stewart, D. Carter, C. Berger, R. Reid, D. Grover, D. Streiner

1995. Fluoxetine in the Treatment of Premenstrual Dysphoria. New England Journal of Medicine 332(23): 1529–1534.

Vedantam, Shankar

2001. Renamed Prozac Fuels Women's Health Debate. Washington Post, April 29: A1.

Wen, Patricia

2001. Pills that Pop: Prescription Drugs are Getting the Designer Touch, With A Consumer's Subconscious in Mind. Boston Globe, May 20: D1.

Young, Allan

1995. The Harmony of Illusions: Inventing Post-Traumatic Stress Disorder. Princeton, NJ: Princeton University Press.

6

BiDil: Medicating the Intersection of Race and Heart Failure

Anne Pollock

When it won the FDA's approval in 2005, BiDil became the first drug ever approved for use in a specific race, bearing the indication for "heart failure in self-identified black patients." The blatancy of its racialization has attracted considerable scholarly critique, and yet much of the critique has leaned too heavily on old arguments about race and genetics on the one hand, or about blockbuster drugs on the other. Neither of these lines of critique is up to the task of deconstructing a drug that is simultaneously effective in treating symptoms and delaying death, supported by diverse epistemologically eclectic actors, and commercially unsuccessful. This chapter highlights the divergent goals of the various actors that aligned around BiDil's approval. For the Association of Black Cardiologists, the FDA, and the pharmaceutical company NitroMed, BiDil was a means to address different problems, and these actors should not be analytically collapsed. The chapter argues that BiDil has undecidabilities: the drug is irredeemably *pharmakon* (remedy and poison), and it is material-semiotic. Attempts by some of those mobilized for and against the drug to purge either side of those undecidabilities are unsuccessful. Drugs, like race, are both material and semiotic, and there is an inescapable polyvalence of a "black drug" in this current historical moment.

The scene was a two-day conference in April, 2006, that had played a part in organizing with MIT's Center for the Study of Diversity in Science, Technology and Medicine. The conference, titled "Race, Pharmaceuticals and Medical Technology"[1] took place just months after the launch of BiDil, a new pill that combined two older drugs, hydralazine and isosorbide dinitrate. When it was approved by the U.S. Food and Drug Administration in

Anne Pollock, Medicating Race: Heart Disease and Durable Preoccupations with Difference. Durham, NC: Duke University Press, 2012. pp. 155–179. Republished with permission from Duke University Press.

The Pharmaceutical Studies Reader, First Edition. Edited by Sergio Sismondo and Jeremy A. Greene.

2006 for "heart failure in self-identified black patients," BiDil became the first drug ever to bear a racial indication. The explicitness of its racialization had attracted much critique from scholars, especially among the social scientists and historians of race and medicine who made up most of the conference attendees.

The critical race theorist and legal scholar Dorothy Roberts had just presented her paper on the diverse responses of African Americans to racial therapeutics such as BiDil, outlining frameworks that could foster or inhibit African American support for the drug.[2] After the talk, one questioner stood up. He identified himself as Juan Cofield, the president of the New England Area Conference of the National Association for the Advancement of Colored People, a major American civil rights organization. Cofield then declared: "There is consensus in the black community that this drug is good for black people." Roberts, after a beat, said: "There isn't consensus among the black people *in this room*."

It was an exchange that would resonate through the rest of the conference.[3] It would seem in a formal logical sense that the disagreement among the African Americans who spoke at the conference would be enough to prove the lack of African American consensus generally. But, as the chair of the session, David Jones, would note in his closing remarks, it turned out to be more complicated than that.

Cofield's statement provides an opportunity to consider a few common rhetorical moves in the BiDil debates. First, he represented his moral stakes as exceeding those of himself as an individual conference participant. This rendered his intervention both more important and more explosive. In this move, he claimed an authority that both included (some of the) conference participants and exceeded them, opening questions of accountability both of himself and of all of us. Second, his intervention denied the polyvalence of BiDil. Framing BiDil as pure salve, Cofield sought to dismiss many of the conference participants' concerns about the dangers of using racial categories in medicine. Third, he moved – unsuccessfully – to close the debate.

Claiming consensus in medicine – or anywhere – is never a practice of observation, but always a rhetorical strategy. If there had been consensus, this tense conference would have been a bland affair. As the theorist Chantal Mouffe highlights, in the politics of deconstruction, it is precisely the impossibility of consensus that renders democratic debate lively.[4] Chaos underlies a provisional stabilization of consensus. This provides, in Derrida's terms, both a risk and a chance.[5] Many of the conference attendees spoke of the risk of racial reification, and Cofield was responding to another kind of risk: he was worried that any doubts about BiDil might hinder its distribution. But there was also a *chance* here in this debate, to make interlocutors' stakes in debates in race and medicine more explicit, and to mine BiDil as a new site for both academic analysis and political engagement.

I argue that BiDil is irredeemably a *pharmakon* – a remedy and a poison. The pill is also irredeemably both material (stuff) and semiotic (meaning). Grappling with the polyvalence at this intersection of the material-semiotic categories of race and pharmaceuticals is key to understanding the simultaneous appeals and unpalatabilities of BiDil.

Considering Heart Failure as a Disease Category

BiDil's indication is for heart failure in "self-identified black patients," but discourse around it has been so overwhelmingly focused on the final words of that phrase that many observers inaccurately describe it as a drug for hypertension or vaguely define it as a drug for heart disease. On one level, this makes sense: although it is impossible to have an opinion about BiDil without having an opinion about race (even if that opinion is a disavowal), heart failure as a disease category does not operate that way. Just as it is possible to have an opinion about Vioxx without having an opinion about arthritis, it is possible to have an opinion about BiDil without having an opinion about heart failure. Critiques of BiDil have taken scant account of the particularities of heart failure. However, ignoring the specificities of heart failure is a missed opportunity to understand the drug's full context. What does it mean for hearts to fail?

The heart is emblematically responsive to load. It changes its rate and volume according to the demands of the body and beyond it. It generally cannot grow new cells in order to repair itself – this is why heart cancer is so extraordinarily rare – and so its cells enlarge and "remodel" to accomplish more work.[6] For example, if blockages in the vessels or high peripheral pressure make it harder to circulate the blood, the heart's cells will increase in size – like any other muscle worked hard – and the capacity will also increase. But this is a temporary fix, called compensation. As soon as this cellular remodeling and hypertrophy starts, it's a sign of problems to come. Compensation is a symptom-free prelude to *de*compensation. Decompensation means that after the temporary respite offered by the heart's compensatory efforts, the success starts to break down. Either not enough blood can be accommodated by the chambers within the heart's now bulky muscle, or not enough can be expelled from the enlarged chambers, and insufficient oxygenization of the peripheral body leads to shortness of breath and fatigue, first with activity and then even at rest.

The diagnostic category "heart failure" has a contingent, technologically-dependent history. That is, like myocardial infarction or hypertension, its clinical definition is confirmed on the basis of diagnostic tests and arbitrary dividing lines. For example, scans can show compensatory shape change in the left ventricle, and "ejection fraction." Whereas normally a well-functioning heart relaxes to allow in fresh blood and has an ejection fraction of over 50%, a heart that either does not relax enough to fill or has an ejection fraction of less than 40% is considered failing.[7] These processes and fractions can only be determined through visualization technologies in a doctor's office.

Uncontrolled hypertension can cause heart failure, and so in some real sense heart failure can be considered to be the end of a line drawn from that starting point. Where hypertension is a way of understanding pre-heart-disease, heart failure is a way of characterizing its conclusion. As the National Heart Lung and Blood Institute fact sheet on the topic puts it: heart failure "is often the end stage of cardiac disease."[8] However, unlike the stages of hypertension, the stages of heart failure are not determined numerically. Rather, symptoms define the stages: Classes I and II are defined by whether symptoms such as shortness of breath, palpitation, and fatigue cause no limitation on physical activity or slight limitation on physical activity respectively. Classes III and IV are based on whether those symptoms occur only during normal physical activity or whether they are present even at rest.[9] Thus heart failure as a disease category is both a technical construct and a consciously embodied reality.

Consider how we might "make sense of" this illness in Robert Aronowitz's terms.[10] Aronowitz describes the tensions and interplay between *ontological* notions of disease rooted in doctor's expertise in identifying abstract disease categories, and *holistic* notions of disease rooted in the patient's idiosyncratic experience. Whereas hypertension is mainly ontological, heart failure is predominantly holistic. Heart failure is not (in Aronowitz's terms) as dominantly a "doctor's disease" as hypertension is; it is also a "patient's illness."

This difference in the holistic embodied reality of the conditions that they treat is one thing that makes BiDil very different from risk-averting drugs such as thiazide diuretics. This matters for each drug's racialization: staking claims on abstract disease categories is different from doing so on experienced suffering. It also matters for each drug's role in contemporary pharmaceutical economies. Like thiazide diuretics, BiDil is imagined to be taken for the rest of a person's life, yet the prognosis for the length of that life is quite short. And unlike thiazides, lifestyle drugs, or potential future drugs for combinatorial categories of risk such as metabolic syndrome,[11] BiDil does not expand the category of the illness it seeks to treat. It is a drug for people who are sick, not for an infinitely expandable category of those at risk for becoming so.[12] It also often does make them feel better in the short term, and has impacts on prevention of hospitalization and death that can be on a scale that a patient can experience as a real improvement.

A drug for heart failure in blacks could never reach the scale of a blockbuster drug. Even if every single self-identified black patient with heart failure in the United States took the drug, the estimated 750,000 prescriptions would be a tenth of a percent of the 60 million annual prescriptions in this country for leading brand of statin at the time, Lipitor (or for that matter the tens of millions of prescriptions for thiazide diuretics).[13] Even if the racial indication were ignored, and every person with heart failure in the United States took BiDil, that would still be a relatively tiny market of 5.8 million.[14] Moreover, more than half of those diagnosed with heart failure will die within five years, and 80% will die within eight to twelve years.[15] Although the prevalence of heart failure as a diagnosis is growing, the potential for growth of the heart failure treatment market is hindered by the poor longevity of its sufferers (even with BiDil). The heart failure market is much more limited in terms of total patient-days of consumption than the market for "lifelong" drugs for young healthy people. Market expansion happens with antihypertensives and statins because more people become diagnosed with the risk factors than die with the diagnosis. But market expansion happens much more slowly with heart failure because time between diagnosis and death is limited. In order to increase the total number of patients living with the diagnosis, the increase in newly diagnosed patients would have to be of greater scale than those who die of the diagnosis. As it is, heart failure remains far from the scale of the pre-heart-diseases such as hypertension and high cholesterol, which have become sites of blockbusters.

Of course, there is much money to be made in small markets and on what I have called elsewhere "drugs for short lives,"[16] but BiDil is also a poor fit for a niche model. It is not only easy to copy, it is a copy – a methods patent on combining two already existing generic drugs for new indication. This is not to suggest that cheap ingredients should necessarily yield little revenue. Much is made of the high production cost of cancer biologics, but that is not actually the reason that they are so expensive. Prices are set not only by production costs, but by willingness to pay – and our willingness to pay has been extraordinarily high for remarkably ineffective end-stage cancer drugs. So why was it not for BiDil?

BiDil's Contingent History: V-HeIT to A-HeIT

BiDil's emergence did not follow a path typical for either blockbusters or niche drugs. It took the drug combination that would become BiDil a long time to get a trial that could show its success. Since the 1970s, the University of Minnesota cardiology professor Jay Cohn has believed for elegant physiological reasons that the combination of isosorbide dinitrate and hydralazine (I/H) – generic drugs already in wide use for other indications – would be highly beneficial for heart failure. He collaborated with Veterans Affairs, the U.S. government agency that provides health benefits to military veterans, to put his combination to the test in two cooperative studies between 1980 and 1991, called the Vasodilator in Heart Failure Trials (V-HeFT) I and II.[17] In the first trial, Cohn's combo did better than the placebo and the other agent, but not statistically significantly. In the second, the combo was not quite as effective as the ACE (angiotensin-converting-enzyme) inhibitor with which it was put head to head.

Like many scientists confronted with evidence that fails to support their hypothesis, Cohn still believed that his idea worked.[18] He started to think that perhaps the combination of ACE inhibitors and his combo would provide the long-sought benefit, but could not find the commercial or governmental support to test his idea. A pharmaceutical benefit management company called Medco – a third party administrator of prescription drug provision then owned by Merck, as it experimented with vertical integration[19] – secured property rights from Cohn and trademarked the drug combination as BiDil in 1995. Cohn went with Medco representatives to the FDA to seek a new drug application based on the data from the V-HeFT trials. But the FDA was not supportive of a new drug application based on the data amassed, especially since the components of the new drug were available generically, and it rejected the application.[20] Medco left the picture.[21]

But by the late 1990s, a time when focus on health disparities was growing at the FDA and beyond, two things had changed: ACE inhibitors were widely argued to be less effective in blacks, and Cohn and a colleague conducted a retrospective analysis of the few blacks in the V-HeFT trials. That analysis seemed to suggest that Cohn's combo showed a stronger benefit for them.[22] Cohn got a new methods patent for BiDil, this time for the race-specific benefit of the combination, and licensed it to a small biotech company called NitroMed. NitroMed had never developed or marketed drugs, but teamed up with Cohn's longtime colleagues at the Association of Black Cardiologists (ABC) to design a trial.[23] The FDA was supportive of the idea of a trial that would focus on this poorly served population. Thus emerged the trial that would lead to BiDil's approval: the African American Heart Failure Trial (A-HeFT).

A-HeFT began in 2001 with a cohort of 1,050 self-identified black patients with class III or IV heart failure. [24] It added BiDil or placebo to the current standard-of-care, which now included those ACE inhibitors that BiDil had gone head to head against in V-HeFT II. This combination proved to be very potent. By the time that the trial was ended two years later, in 2004, (early, because of the strength of the results), 43% fewer in the standard + BiDil group had died compared with the standard + placebo group, while 39% fewer had been hospitalized, and those in the treatment arm also reported better quality of life.[25]

The mechanism of BiDil is not completely understood. No one knows why BiDil was so much more effective in A-HeFT than it had been in the V-HeFT trials. Perhaps it was because of the synergistic effects of ACE inhibitors, with which it had not been previously combined.[26] Perhaps the synergy of drugs was even more comprehensive, by adding a fourth mechanism (nitrous oxide enhancement) to the mechanisms addressed by the standard of care, as several A-HeFT investigators have suggested.[27] Perhaps it had to do with other differences between the V-HeFT and A-HeFT populations: more hypertensive etiology, a younger cohort, the inclusion of women. But though there are questions, there seem to be few who contest the general efficacy of the drug combination.

In the A-HeFT trial, stakeholders who were not necessarily previously aligned came together around a practical project. The "pragmatism" here is like that which Joan Fujimura has theorized. To put this case Fujimura's terms, heart failure in African Americans was a problem that was "ripe," or "both intellectually interesting and doable."[28] As she points out, the doability does not rest only on the technical. Whether the A-HeFT trial was an optimal way to get at efficacy or not, it had been a way to make a "doable problem" out of a conundrum. Or perhaps three conundrums: a federal agency grappling with health disparities, a cardiologist and a pharmaceutical company salvaging a drug, and a professional organization of African American cardiologists with particular professional needs and patient populations. A-HeFT is an "articulation," of both problems and potential solutions. What made African American heart failure "ripe" for the FDA, NitroMed, and ABC was rising interest in health disparities, the deluge of data around African-American responses to ACE inhibitors, and increasing cardiologists to do clinical trials.

The debate at the FDA hearing on BiDil's approval covered many questions about the study design and the role that the V-HeFT trials could play in approval based on the small A-HeFT trial, but discord focused not on whether BiDil should be approved, but squarely on whether it should receive the racially specific indication NitroMed desired.[29] That specification would allow a longer patent for the drug – since that indication was patented for later than the non-race-specific one.[30] Moreover, in the hearings, it became clear that the cardiologist Steven Nissen, the chair of the FDA committee, wanted to go on the record as doing something specifically for blacks to round out his tenure at the FDA.

In the lead-up to BiDil, there was alignment of interests by NitroMed and ABC, but they were not necessarily seeing BiDil as a solution to the same problem. For NitroMed, the principal problem was how to get approval for the drug combination in a way that would be profitable. They thought that the longer patent life of the race-specific indication would lead to that. For ABC, the problem was and is more diffuse: how to get the funding to run trials and thus participate in the production of evidence-based medicine, and how to find solutions for black morbidity and mortality from heart failure. In these senses, ABC is very much in the tradition of black practitioners in the early twentieth century who sought access to research hospitals. A-HeFT becomes a way for African American practitioners to participate in cutting-edge research and contribute to the communities that they serve at the same time.

Many critics of BiDil highlighted – and as it turned out greatly exaggerated – the money that investigators stood to make, not quite claiming that it led to biased results per se, but suggesting that financial interests distorted the trajectory of the research.[31] This kind of implication is one that has fostered ill will in the debate, triggering doctors' defensiveness about whether the money they receive colors their expert judgment. Physicians often respond to critiques of their participation in gift-exchange with pharmaceutical companies with righteous indignation, that *they* would never be swayed by such things. But what makes the gifts powerful is precisely this space: they might well believe, or they might not. Critics of BiDil often address ABC as if they are simply paid ventriloquists for NitroMed – in the account of the legal scholar and prominent BiDil critic Jonathan Kahn, ABC, the NAACP, the National Minority Health Month Foundation, and the Congressional Black Caucus are all evacuated of agency; they are portrayed simply as "able surrogates on hand to do the job for" NitroMed, and who "put a 'black face' on BiDil as it went before the FDA" and, later, promoted off-label use.[32]

But gifts are more complicated than that. There should be room for some conceptual space here between being bought off and, in a limited way and with an independent voice, buying in. This is not to diminish the power of the gifts circulating here, but rather to capture the way that the gifts' power is actually more interesting than a simple purchase of support. Marcel Mauss taught us that there are no free gifts,[33] and funding for the physicians' organization that supports a drug trial comes at a cost for its recipient as well as for its giver. This critique applies not just to BiDil and ABC, but to the more general alliance of pharmaceutical funding (or government funding), clinician-scientists, and social justice organizations that campaign around health. For both physicians and their patients, the power of gifts is salient: the gift is something that should be received, yet is dangerous to take. When NitroMed and ABC align, the force of the objects of giving is both practical and mystical. More than mere utility circulates, and obligation and liberty intermingle.

Like the physicians engaged in contract research who are tracked by the sociologist Jill Fisher, ABC's role in A-HeFT straddles two distinct identities: "entrepreneurial agent" and "pharmaceutical emissary." If we pay attention only to the latter element, we lose sight of the organization's agency. At the same time, because of the distinct role of African American cardiologists in advocating for African American patients, these ABC physicians also take on the role of what Alondra Nelson has called "bio-cultural brokers," deploying "authentic expertise" "available to them as both minorities and community-minded professionals to forge consensus in and between biomedicine, scientific domains, policy circles, and the public."[34]

The FDA approved BiDil in June 2005. Its package insert describes its indications:

> BiDil is indicated for the treatment of heart failure as an adjunct to standard therapy in self-identified black patients to improve survival, to prolong time to hospitalization for heart failure, and to improve patient-reported functional status.

Just because the population studied was "self-identified black patients," that did not necessarily mean that the indication had to be limited to that group. Consider a contrasting case of drugs believed to be more effective in whites: ACE inhibitors and angiotensin receptor blockers (ARBS) often include in their package inserts that their benefits have not been proven in black patients,[35] or are less effective in black patients.[36] This grammar is slightly but crucially different from that of BiDil. BiDil could have, like ACES and ARBS, been approved for everyone while being accompanied by a package insert indicating that "this drug's benefit has not been proven in non-black patients." Instead, absence of evidence in nonblack patients was treated as tantamount to evidence of absence. The blackness of the subjects on whom the drug was tested could not be detached from the drug – neither for the FDA, nor for BiDil's critics.

Many have criticized the use of the unreliable category of race rather than sound medical indications in the design of the trial,[37] but Cohn has responded to criticisms that race is an arbitrary category by saying that age and presence/absence of ventricular abnormalities are arbitrary, too, but that does not mean that a study cannot be constructed around them.[38] But just because it is easier to target a drug this way does not mean that the enterprise is easy. The year after BiDil's release, a tiny percentage of eligible patients were taking the drug,[39] and NitroMed's stock had fallen by an order of magnitude from its high (from $27 per share to $2.50).[40] Critics of BiDil had not only reported its hype, but had also fueled it, using the highest possible estimates of projected revenue.[41] Real challenges confront a small pharma player in a Big Pharma field, and the polyvalence of the intersection of race and drugs exceeds NitroMed's control. The study around which the ABC, NitroMed and the FDA intersected is not the complete articulation of BiDil, and BiDil's poor success may be connected to difficulties in articulating BiDil to broader publics.

Too High a Price?

If the power and meaning of gifts is not simple, neither is the power of price. Many critics took for granted that NitroMed could receive any price it demanded, even long after it became clear that BiDil was a commercial failure.[42] Critics used asking price as a straightforward stand-in for patient cost. For example, the anthropologist and historian of science Duana Fullwiley has put BiDil into a framework of pharmacogenomics: "In its first instance (the African American heart medication called BiDil), race-tailored therapy has dramatically increased cost for the racial group it claims to benefit."[43] But although the FDA hailed BiDil as a step toward "personalized medicine," and many analysts have situated their critique in terms of pharmacogenomics, BiDil is not a pharmacogenomic drug,[44] and the members of the "racial group it claims to benefit" are overwhelmingly not receiving the drug at all, at any price.

The conventional wisdom on the commercial failure of BiDil is that it was priced too aggressively, especially since its components are available as generics.[45] But why was BiDil not able to command ten dollars per day? That is a bargain compared to hospitalization,[46] and orders of magnitude below the price point of the niche biotech drugs that are a primary source of profit for the pharmaceutical industry today. High price might have even added to the allure of the drug, since commodity fetishism often results in more value being imputed to that which is more expensive. The market's willingness to pay is up for debate, and could change in response to political pressure. But the pharmaceutical company's sponsorship of physicians and civil rights organizations turned out not to be able to buy sufficient political pressure to force insurers and government to pay.

NitroMed did try to prop up BiDil's high price by using a common technique: having a drug donation program for patients who could not afford the drug called "NitroMed Cares." As Stefan Ecks has shown in his analysis of Glivec in India, drug donation programs should be understood as part of "a global pricing strategy" that "should not be disguised through a rhetoric of good citizenship." Yet this drug donation strategy has been ineffective in BiDil's case, either in propping up price or in widely distributing the drug. A key element that NitroMed's drug donation program ignored is something that anthropologists of pharmaceuticals in the Global South have pointed out: even when the drug is fixed, the place of labor in the distribution of drug donations is complex. Since BiDil's patient population is already often under-served by overstreteched doctors, it is unrealistic to expect those doctors to take the uncompensated time to do the paperwork necessary to get patients free drugs.

Even if the brand's value-added over the generic is not deemed to be worth it, BiDil's failure does not even end there. As of 2006, not only was just a small percentage of the African American heart failure population receiving BiDil, only 6% of patients were receiving the combination of isosorbide dinitrate and hydralazine at all, including generic equivalents.[47] If physicians' reluctance to prescribe BiDil had been due only to its price, they would have been adopting generics in droves. That they have not done so suggests that there are resistances unaccounted for by price.

Resistances to BiDil certainly do come from willingness to pay – by the complicated regimes of payers we have in the United States, and by consumers themselves. But one of the lessons of BiDil is that catering to a well-defined market of first-world consumers is not always enough to secure a high price. The assumption made by both BiDil's makers and its critics that patients would hear the publicity about BiDil and successfully demand it from their physicians suggests that they underestimate how structurally underserved the population treated by BiDil is. The *Wall Street Journal* wrote: "The drug's unavailability, say some medical experts, may also be symptomatic of a deeper problem in the health-care system, where issues affecting minorities and the poor sometimes fall through the cracks."[48]

Neither BiDil's proponents nor its opponents seemed to grasp that a drug "for heart failure in self-identified black patients" is a poor fit for consumerist logics developed for iconic lifestyle drugs. Given the wide range of physicians who deal with heart failure with already intensive drug regimens, it has not been easy for BiDil to find its way in this terrain. Most general practice physicians keep their patients on whichever drugs they were prescribed in the hospital where their heart failure diagnosis was most likely received, meaning that advertising to hospitals is particularly important. But for a tiny company like NitroMed, getting hospitals and insurance formularies to change their practices was a huge challenge.

And as it happened, although BiDil generated a good deal of publicity, it generated very little advertising that could have provided patients with scripts for making demands on doctors.[49] Its patient and provider education website mobilized some of the typical grammars of pharmaceutical websites, with the evocative URL – www.hearthealthheritage.com – but

NitroMed was slow to focus on "elite" cardiovascular experts, health plans, and medical centers.[50] These experts are normally the first line of marketing for any drug, since sales generated by direct-to-consumer advertising are small as a percentage of investment (even if still profitable for blockbusters). This traditional approach might be more in tune with who actually has more determining power in the prescribing patterns of African Americans. A limitation of relying on this website, direct-to-consumer ads in black newspapers, and community education in black churches is that they rest on the assumption that doctors listen to their black patients in the same way that they do their white patients, that "patient empowerment" to demand drugs works whether the patient in question is imagined to be a "compliant" one or a "drug-seeking" one. The challenge of configuring a "typical black patient" within grammars of an unmarked "typical patient" applies as much here as it did treating coronary disease or hypertension.

Pharmakon

The meanings of any drug exceed that given by its marketers or medical experts.[51] In the case of BiDil, the meanings that have circulated around the drug have been polarized and volatile. This situation is not, of course, unique to BiDil. As Asha Persson has pointed out, "For all their innocuous appearance, every pill is a potent fusion of ingredients, including scientific practices, political agendas and commercial interests, along with social activism and media spin."[52] She turns to the concept of *pharmakon,* to understand not "misuse" of drugs – in her case antiretrovirals – but precisely on how "correctly" used drugs "have the capacity to be beneficial and detrimental *to the same person at the same time.*" The pharmakon is also a useful theoretical tool for considering BiDil.

Derrida, writing about the polyvalent meanings of the Greek term *pharmakon,* criticizes the translation of it as "remedy," with its sense of inherent beneficience.[53] He argues, rather, that the pharmakon cannot be so constrained. The word "*remedy*" excludes what he characterizes as "the magic virtues of a force whose effects are hard to master, a dynamics that constantly surprises the one who tries to manipulate it."[54] But hard-to-master forces and surprising dynamics are key to understanding BiDil.

BiDil has promised remedy on (at least) three registers: survival and quality of life benefit of the pill for individual patients, a potential mechanism in progress toward the alleviation of health disparities, and as a path toward pharmacogenomics. Similarly, the danger associated with BiDil has been on (at least) three registers: that of potential literal toxicity of the pill, that of harm to the cause of antiracism in medicine and society, and that of profits for amoral drug companies at the expense of suffering patients. A good deal of discursive boundary work has gone into trying to address BiDil's remedy and harm separately. For example, commentators such Jonathan Kahn want to accept the physical benefit of the pill for individual patients while arguing that its racial indication leads away from progress in race relations and medicine. Perhaps part of the reason that Kahn so often gets criticized for wanting to deny the pill to patients in need is that these registers cannot quite be separated.

The potential unpalatability of a black drug was not predicted by many critics of proponents of BiDil, even though warnings about the risk of unpredictable market acceptance and potential difficulty of convincing third-party payers to accept BiDil was already present in NitroMed's 2004 financial disclosures.[55] Right from the early stages of the A-HeFT trial, the prominent sociologist of race and medicine Troy Duster lamented in the popular press that although "it is difficult to bring anti-discrimination to the market," BiDil showed that the future of drug development was about "population aggregates that become the target market."[56] In 2005, the sociologist George Ellison characterized the drug's racial specification as "highly palatable" in that political and market context:

> There is a political demand for treatments for African Americans in America that makes the production of an ethnic drug for African Americans a highly palatable political event. At the same time, as we're well aware within our racialised societies, African Americans have a social and political identity that makes them a powerful lobbying group and a powerful market in their own right. So it's possible to develop a drug for African Americans because we can identify them, we can market to them, we can sell it to them, we can justify it to them, and that makes it a commercially sensitive commercially successful enterprise.[57]

Yet, as its poor market performance should alert us, BiDil's "palatability" is not so overdetermined.

Associations between blackness and drugs are overwhelmingly illicit. Black drugs connote black markets. In the context of Tuskegee and rumors that crack was a government invention to suppress Black Power, there is a sinister connotation to "a drug for black people." All of this inhibits palatability. Moreover, black patients are stigmatized in medical literature for their distrust,[58] and noncompliant and refractory nature,[59] so drugs for black people bear a taint. We even have the peculiar situation in which a drug that combines two banal old generics to treat a disease with high morbidity and mortality generates references, especially in black media, to doubts about whether BiDil is "safe."[60] All of this suggests that there may actually be, in Nathan Greenslit's terms, a "symbolic mistake"[61] in targeting drugs at African Americans.

Approval by the FDA does not by itself determine drug palatability in a differentiated society. We might read FDA approval as certification of credibility, albeit one not always trusted. Yet credibility alone does not determine what is "good to eat", which as we learned from Claude Levi-Strauss is inextricable from what is "good to think."[62] It is not altogether clear, a priori, whether evidence of discrimination is to be found in greater access to drugs – as it is in the distribution of crack sales, or in excessive prescriptions for the antipsychotic drug Haldol[63] – or in less access to drugs is, as is generally understood in medical disparities literature. Indeed, both kinds of access can operate together: less access to antihypertensives and statins leads to more heart failure – and hence, potentially a role for BiDil. Although BiDil was "good to think" from the perspective of turn-of-the-millennium biotech investors and the FDA, not many rushed to swallow the black pill.

This is not to suggest that these dangerous connotations themselves explain BiDil's failure. The inability of a pharmakon to shed its toxic aspects does not always impede its spread. Sense of toxicity can add to the appeal of a pharmakon. The dangers pointed to in raising the specter of race and drugs together are not necessarily understood as a counterindication for a racial drug. When Kahn describes the ABC and Congressional Black Caucus support for the "purportedly benign" use of race as biology in BiDil, he operates on the assumption that if its malignance were known it would be rejected.[64] But many leaders of the ABC were concerned from the outset about the dangers of racial profiling in medicine, and participated anyway because of their commitment to serving the immediate needs of their very sick patients.[65]

Moreover, the poison that is part of the pharmakon is not separate from its efficacy, but immanent with it. This helps to understand why a low side-effect profile does not guarantee that a drug will be taken. Indeed, as we saw with thiazides, a low side-effect profile for a drug for an asymptomatic condition can inhibit compliance. If a drug causes no harm, it may not have any effect at all. Side effects, then, can either inhibit or inspire compliance. We can see a lateral but evocative parallel with antiretrovirals, as described by Persson:[66] for some people the evidence of the drug's toxicity on their bodies was evidence of its effectiveness against an otherwise invisible virus.

The relationship between a drug and its side effects is analogous to the relationship between BiDil as a pill and its location in debates about race. Sense of toxicity can add to the appeal of a pharmakon. The toxicity of the connection between drugs and blackness suggests, for some, that the unease must be worth it. Some of the calls to tackle fear and pursue racial medicine come across like disingenuous right-wing arguments,[67] but others do seem genuinely interested in keeping the focus on black well-being. [68] The problem of black disease is widely recognized as serious, and yet hard to get a handle on. If the problem is considered intractable, a risky discursive intervention can hold a powerful appeal.

Even though the poles of the pharmakon are inseparable, many of BiDil's supporters shared the sense of Juan Cofield in the opening vignette at the start of this chapter, to ignore or deny dissent. Many supporters have expressed anxiety that social science and other critiques of the drug would make people afraid of it, and thus prevent access to the remedy it offers. They wanted to suppress expression of the poison aspects of this pharmakon. This rhetorical strategy suggests that the danger comes not from the drug itself, but from the lack of consensus about its unqualified beneficence.

The Material-semiotic

There is a second, interrelated undecidable in addition to the pharmakon: the material-semiotic. Drugs are a clear case for Haraway's "material-semiotic": they are generally accepted as having both physical and social aspects. They are a ready example of the capacity of objects to carry both matter and meaning. Moreover, their ability to move between the material and the semiotic renders drugs appealing objects for boundary work with regard to other categories on that divide. Just as arguments over the "reality" of mental illness are sometimes staked out in terms of antidepressants, the "reality" of race has been staked out in terms of BiDil. Yet the attempt to use BiDil to put race onto one side or the other of a material/semiotic divide ultimately fails because both BiDil and race keep their dual aspect. Critique of BiDil's role in the "biological basis" of race is insufficient; we should attend to the productive work it is doing at the social-biological boundary.

Pharmaceutical-centered medicine is an excellent site for critique of race because it intervenes on the boundaries between the social and the biological, the material and the semiotic. Race operates on precisely these boundaries. Racial difference in heart disease is material: early mortality of African Americans relative to whites takes place in actual bodies in the world and, despite caveats about the trickiness of data and etiology, death is a material event and the terrain is necessarily in part about biology. Yet racial difference in heart disease is also semiotic: the data cannot be extricated from lenses of difference-oriented preoccupations, and arguments about race and disease become ways to articulate difference in other aspects of society and individual identity.

If black heart failure is to be "fixed" through this pharmacological intervention, it is in at least three ways: by rendering race identifiably stable, by focusing attention upon it, and by promising easy repair. Pharmaceuticals are mobilized not only on the basis of existing biological categories, but also on their capacity for changing biology. One aspect of this process is that race is a difference that is imagined to be fixed enough for action, but that is at the same time potentially able to be medically mitigated. This is a key to understanding the support for BiDil from such antiracist actors as the Association of Black Cardiologists. Pharmaceuticals can provide a basis for argument not only for essential racial difference, but also for mutability. As the anthropologist Jonathan Xavier Inda has argued, part of BiDil's potent appeal was its ability to "materialize hope."[69]

Several critics have responded to BiDil by advocating regulatory efforts to separate material from semiotic categories in race research, for example through guidelines that would require distinguishing between "race as a sociopolitical category" and "race as a biological and/or explicitly genetic category." [70] But as Latour teaches us, modern science is not capable of creating pure categories without creating hybrids, and analysts are in error if we take modernism at its reductionist word.[71] When BiDil's critics want to make a choice for social justice against biology, they are solidifying the validity of that boundary in the sense that, as Nancy Krieger points out, "the notion that scientific thinking and work must somehow 'choose' between social justice and biology is itself an ideological stance."[72] Trying to separate out that nexus of race as a social/biological and material/semiotic will not lead to a better account of race in medicine or the world, and the undecidabilities will remain. Scientific medicine is not even capable of fully purifying and rationalizing its objects of study into piles of genes – the human organisms that are the necessary intersection between genes and society continually get in the way.

It is BiDil's critics, not NitroMed or ABC, who reduce race-as-biological to race-as-genetic.[73] Although much criticism has debunked BiDil on the lack of a genetic basis of disparity, this is not actually a direct engagement with NitroMed or ABC. Paul Underwood, former president of ABC, responded to Kahn categorically: "I think there's no implication at all that genetics has anything to do with BiDil's mechanism of action. In fact, there's no claim that there's genetics at all. I believe that race in the United States is a social construct, not really a genetic construct." [74] This disconnect over the stakes of the debate should alert us that we have more work to do than simply, repeatedly and in each case reiterating that "race is not genetic." Only a few scholars have taken seriously why the drug was supported by many antiracist actors who explicitly reject race as a genetically deterministic category. Many in the ABC have a deeper engagement with the complexly material-semiotic character of race than do their critics. To grapple with the alliance of ABC and NitroMed, we should not assume that "value" and "values" are necessarily in opposition, and should instead seize the opportunity for "transcending dichotomies between the economic and the moral."

Pharmaceutical research is a central project of American medicine, and pharmaceutical consumption an important site of American biological citizenship. This renders problematic critics' complaints that BiDil "not only that it biologizes race but also ... create[s] the impression that the best way to address health disparities is through drug development." [75] Kahn, for example, makes drug development sound preposterously easy, suggesting that "the appeal of taking a predominantly biomedical approach to addressing health disparities is undeniable—instead of fixing social inequality you simply fix molecules."[76] There should be conceptual space between drug development as "a way" to address disparities and drug development as "the best way" to do so. If we assume that conducting clinical trials is generally an endeavor in which diverse researchers should be involved, A-HeFT was not in vain: it did build capacity among members of the Association of Black Cardiologists to conduct clinical trials, a capacity that continues even after the drug's promise of profit recedes.

Conclusion

Efforts to close down the heterogeneous meanings of BiDil opened this chapter, and BiDil's critics' efforts to segregate BiDil's acceptable molecules from its unacceptable meanings bring it to an end if not a close. Both are attempts to pin down the slipperiness of BiDil and race in order to make a clear embrace or denunciation on one register. If the NAACP's Juan

Cofield wanted the only thing at stake to be African American access to drugs as remedies, many of BiDil's critics wanted the only thing at stake to be the purging of race from drug development and marketing. But BiDil retains what we can characterize in Derrida's terms as undecidability. The goal of critical scholars should not be to claim the decision, but to engage with the tenacity of undecidabilities.

The poor economic performance of BiDil has been explained away too quickly with reference to structural and market aspects (availability of generic versions, resistances from formularies, too small a marketing force), as well as tactical errors (price, too little marketing to hospitals). If we let these explanations rest, we miss an opportunity to use BiDil to extend not only critical scholarship of race but also of pharmaceuticals. Exploring the case of BiDil, then, is an opportunity to open up the contingency of pharmaceuticals more generally. Drugs do not always reach their markets, and we can use analysis of BiDil to destabilize notions of the inevitability of drugs' capacity for infinite expansion. Where much scholarship has attended to the expansive potential of drugs, this chapter seeks to understand what sites of resistance might impede complete saturation of American publics with drugs.

BiDil's racialization has attracted considerable scholarly critique, but this has almost all been reluctant to grapple with why prominent civil rights and black health actors have backed the drug, typically resorting to the implicit suggestions that they have been bought off. Yet the involvement of organizations long critical of the genetic reification of race should spur further analysis. Engaging those who invoke racialized pharmaceuticals to indict injustices and articulate aspirations can disrupt assumptions of the superiority of "natural" bodies over pharmaceutically-enrolled ones, and the privileging of the sameness of "natural" bodies over lived inequalities. The NAACP and ABC articulate a sense of the racialized diseased body as the site not only of genetics, but also of history—and of both hope and hype.[77]

Considering race to be fixed enough for action is one part of the process we could call "medicating race." Yet since pharmaceuticals are mobilized not only on the basis of existing biological categories, but also on their capacity for changing biology, we can see their appeal for those with a stake in the very malleability of race. At the same time, the commercial failure of BiDil can allow us to reflect upon how both BiDil's proponents and its opponents overestimated the ease of drugs reaching their markets and underestimated the unpalatability of a "black drug" in the current historical moment.

NOTES

1 "Race, Pharmaceuticals, and Medical Technology," Massachusetts Institute of Technology Center for the Study of Diversity in Science, Technology and Medicine, April 7-8, 2006.
2 Her paper was among several of those from the conference published in a special issue of the *Journal of Law, Medicine and Ethics*: Roberts, "Is Race-Based Medicine Good for Us?"
3 Roberts has written about the exchange in her article "Race and the New Biocitizen," 269.
4 Mouffe, "Deconstruction, Pragmatism, and the Politics of Democracy," 9.
5 Derrida, "Remarks on Deconstruction and Pragmatism," 77-88.
6 Dyer and Lilly, "Heart Failure."
7 Dyer and Lilly, "Heart Failure."
8 National Heart, Lung and Blood Institute, "Data Fact Sheet: Congestive Heart Failure in the United States: A New Epidemic," September 1996, accessed March 5, 2011, at http://www.vidyya.com/2pdfs/dfschf.pdf.
9 Dyer and Lilly, "Heart Failure."
10 Aronowitz, *Making Sense of Illness*.
11 See Hatch, *The Politics of Metabolism*.

12 This is not to say that BiDil did not have the potential to transform into a larger preventative drug: the compensation stage may be that eventually we will all be defined as having pre-heart-failure, which is in any case analogous to (and could even be synonymous with) our status as having "high" cholesterol and hypertension as well as "abnormalities" that appear on visual diagnostic technologies. We might be imagined to be all "compensating" for the pathologies unknown to us, ready to decompensate unless we are protected by pharmaceuticals. If this had happened, BiDil would have fallen into the "dependent normality" along the lines described by Dumit, "Drugs for Life."

13 An estimated 63,219,000 Lipitor prescriptions were dispensed in the US in 2005, and 42,757,000 for the top thiazide (hydrochlorothiazide) as well as many more for other thiazides. http://www.rxlist.com/top200.htm

14 The American Heart Association, *American Heart Disease and Stroke Statistics*.

15 NHLBI Congestive Heart Failure Fact Sheet. http://library.thinkquest.org/27533/facts.html.

16 Pollock, "Transforming the Critique of Big Pharma."

17 Cohn, et al. "Effect of vasodilator therapy on mortality in chronic congestive heart failure"; Cohn, et al. "A comparison of enalapril with hydralazine-isosorbide dinitrate in the treatment of chronic congestive heart failure."

18 After BiDil's approval, Cohn said: "This has been 30 years. I have to feel that I am finally vindicated" (as quoted in Pollack "Drug Approved for Heart Failure in Black Patients"). Cohn's belief remains that the combination works (period) as he always predicted, rather than just for a smaller group: "Dr. Cohn said that despite any flaws in the first studies, the similar findings in the new trial suggest the original data was accurate. 'The replication gives me confidence that this combination is more likely to be effective in people who call themselves black than in people who call themselves white,' he said. 'Do I believe this drug should work in whites? Biology would tell me it should.'" (Saul, "U.S. to Review Heart Drug Intended for One Race").

19 Bloomberg Business News, "Merck Profits Were Higher in Second Quarter"; Harvard Business School, "Merck-Medco: Vertical Integration in the Pharmaceutical Industry."

20 "Panel Recommends FDA Reject BiDil Application," *Wall Street Journal*, February 28, 1997, p. 3.

21 Pollack, "Drug Approved for Heart Failure in Black Patients."

22 Carson, Ziesche, Johnson, and Cohn. "Racial differences in response to therapy for heart failure."

23 Cohn is among the couple of white physicians whose hand-painted portraits are included in the portrait gallery of dozens of notable cardiologists at the Association of Black Cardiologists headquarters in suburban Atlanta.

24 Taylor, Ziesche, Yancy, Carson, D'Agostino, Ferdinand, Taylor, Adams, Sabolinski, Worcel, Cohn; the African-American Heart Failure Trial Investigators. "Combination of isosorbide dinitrate and hydralazine in blacks with heart failure."

25 Taylor, Ziesche, Yancy, Carson, D'Agostino, Ferdinand, Taylor, Adams, Sabolinski, Worcel, Cohn; the African-American Heart Failure Trial Investigators. "Combination of isosorbide dinitrate and hydralazine in blacks with heart failure."

26 Bloche, "Race-Based Therapeutics."

27 Ghali, Tam, Sabolinski, Taylor, Lindenfeld, Cohn, Worcel, "Exploring the Potential Synergistic Action of Spironolactone on Nitric Oxide-Enhancing Therapy."

28 Fujimura, "Constructing 'Do-Able' Problems in Cancer Research."

29 Department of Health and Human Services Food and Drug Administration Center for Drug Evaluation and Research, 2005. "Cardiovascular and Renal Drugs Advisory Committee, Volume II," Gaithersberg, MD, June 16, 2005. Transcript available at http://www.fda.gov/ohrms/dockets/ac/05/transcripts/2005-4145T2.pdf.

30 Kahn, "How a Drug Becomes 'Ethnic'."

31 Kahn and Sankar, "BiDil: Race Medicine or Race Marketing?"

32 Kahn, "Exploiting Race in Drug Development," 750-751.

33 Mauss, *The Gift*.

34 Nelson, "Inclusion-and-Difference Paradox," 742-43. See also Nelson, "The Factness of Diaspora."

35 For example, the patient product information for the ARB COZAAR suggests that one reason to prescribe it may not apply to blacks: "to lower the chance of stroke in patients with high blood

pressure and a heart problem called left ventricular hypertrophy. COZAAR may not help Black patients with this problem." http://www.merck.com/product/usa/pi_circulars/c/cozaar/cozaar_ppi.pdf.

36 For example, the package insert of the ACE-Inhibitor ALTACE notes that "Although ALTACE was antihypertensive in all races studied, black hypertensive patients (usually a low-renin hypertensive population) had a smaller average response to monotherapy than non-black patients;" and "In considering use of ALTACE, it should be noted that in controlled trials ACE inhibitors have an effect on blood pressure that is less in black patients than in non-blacks. In addition, ACE inhibitors (for which adequate data are available) cause a higher rate of angioedema in black than in non-black patients." http://www.altace.com/altace/pdf/PI.pdf

37 Hoffman, "Racially-Tailored Medicine Unravelled."

38 Cohn, "The Use of Race and Ethnicity in Medicine."

39 Westphal, "Tough Prescription."

40 Syre, "NitroMed's Challenge."

41 The most glaring example of this is Kahn and Sankar, "BiDil: Race Medicine or Race Marketing?", 458. Kahn and Sankar not only uncritically quote the sales projections of $1 billion from NitroMed's CEO, but use the price once released to ratchet up the projection to $3 billion.

42 Kahn has continued to use the highest possible projections of revenue – in order to decry their egregiousness – long after it was clear that BiDil was a commercial failure. Jonathan Kahn, "Exploiting Race in Drug Development," 754.

43 Fullwiley, "The Molecularization of Race," 2-3.

44 That is, unlike drugs like Herceptin and Gleevec, it is not targeted according to protein or biogenetic markers. See Haga and Ginsburg, "Prescribing BiDil," 12-13.

45 "BiDil Flops," 2008. *Nature Biotechnology* Vol. 26, No. 3 (March 2008): 252.

46 Angus, "Heart Failure; Study finds that African-American heart failure drug is cost effective," 84.

47 Devine "NAACP Goes to the Grassroots for BiDil."

48 Westphal, "Tough Prescription."

49 Even within the category of "patient education" marketing by NitroMed, most of the resources have targeted black churches and communities on a low-budget grassroots level. There was a print advertisement that appeared in black newspapers in Houston, Detroit, and the District of Columbia in October and November 2006, that looked like a copy-cat of major pharmaceutical campaigns, made on the cheap. The half-page advertisement is dominated by a photograph of an old man and a young girl, smiling together. They appear to be grandfather and granddaughter, which resonates with the campaign by the Association of Black Cardiologists, framing the importance of heart health around "Children Should Know Their Grandparents." The large print ad copy under the picture reads "Live longer…Live Better." Also in prominent typeface is "BiDil®" and underneath is its chemical name "isosorbide dinitrate/hydralazine HCI" and the slogan "More Life to Live." The basic promise of the ad is indistinguishable from one for arthritis or some other condition – "Life is made for living. And you deserve to enjoy every moment of it" – before discussing specifics. There was also a radio ad that played in black stations in Houston, DC, and Detroit, that dramatized the potential need for BiDil in a conversation in which a grandfather was too tired to play. See Jewell, "Ad campaign for blacks-only heart drug touches lightly on race."

50 Devine, "Heart pill maker slashes sales staff."

51 Pollock, "Pharmaceutical Meaning Making"

52 Persson, "Incorporating *Pharmakon*," 46.

53 Derrida, "Plato's Pharmacy." There are even more definitions than Derrida fully explores. The pharmakon is also, according to the Tufts *Greek-English Lexicon*: (1) drug, whether healing or noxious; (2) healing remedy, medicine; (3) enchanted potion, philter, hence charm, spell; (4) poison; (5) lye for laundering; II generally remedy, cure; (2) means of producing something; (3) remedy or consolation in; III. Dye, paint, color; IV chemical reagent used by tanners.

54 Derrida, "Plato's Pharmacy," 97.

55 See Tutton, "Promising Pessimism."

56 Duster, "Medicine and People of Color," B7.

57 George Ellison on Kenan Malik, "A Colour Coded Prescription."

58 Byrd and Linda, *An American Health Dilemma: Vol. 1.*
59 Smith, *Health Care Divided.*
60 Chepesiuk and Jones, "Are Race-Specific Drugs Unethical?", 37; Kimberly, "Rx for Black Hearts," http://www.blackcommentator.com/143/143_freedom_rider_rx.html.
61 Greenslit, "Dep®ession and Consumჹtion," 478.
62 Claude Levi-Stauss, *Totemism*, trans. Rodney Needham, (Boston: Beacon Press, 1963).
63 For a compelling account of racism in antipsychotic prescribing practices, see Metzl, *Protest Psychosis.*
64 Kahn, "How a Drug Becomes 'Ethnic'."
65 Charles Curry, quoted in Wheelwright, "Human, Study Thyself," http://discovermagazine.com/2005/mar/human-study-thyself.
66 Persson, "Incorporating Pharmakon."
67 Sailer, "Race Flat-Earthers Dangerous To Everyone's Health," http://www.vdare.com/sailer/medicine_and_race.htm. See also Carlson, "The Case of BiDil." These are among the many of the race-embracers that narrate what Dunklee, Reardon and Wentworth, in "Race and Crisis," describe as "Galilean victimization narrative in which a small vanguard group or individual is cast as being persecuted by the powerful Orthodox forces for their/his allegiance to the Truth."
68 Sammons, "Racial Profiling," 4.
69 Inda, "Materializing Hope."
70 Kahn, "How a Drug Becomes 'Ethnic,' 44.
71 Latour, *We Have Never Been Modern.*
72 Krieger, "Stormy Weather," 2155.
73 The most categorical equations of biology with genetics go so far as to say that any race-based medical claim fails unless "each individually-defined or self-declared race would have to be a 100% pure and homogenous gene pool," (Hoover, "There is No Scientific Rationale for Race-Based Research." Harriet Washington puts her discussion of BiDil into a chapter called "Genetic Perdition: The Rise of Molecular Bias" (Washington, *Medical Apartheid*). In equating race-as-biological with race-as-genetic, BiDil's critics are like BiDil's right-wing fans rather than like the ABC.
74 Goodman, "The FDA Approves a Race-Specific Drug for the First Time in History."
75 Kahn and Sankar, "BiDil: Race Medicine or Race Marketing?", 462.
76 Kahn, "How a Drug Becomes 'Ethnic'," 7.
77 This alliterative framing was used by Tavis Smiley, "Dr. Ian Smith: Race-Specific Drugs," *NPR: The Tavis Smiley Show*, November 17, 2004.

WORKS CITED

Angus, Derek. "Heart Failure; Study finds that African-American heart failure drug is cost effective," *Heart Disease Weekly, Jan* 8, 2006, p. 84.

Aronowitz, Robert A. *Making Sense of Illness: Science, Society and Disease*. Cambridge: Cambridge University Press, 1998.

Bibbins-Domingo, Kirsten, and Alicia Fernandez. "BiDil Flops," 2008. *Nature Biotechnology* 26.3 (March 2008): 252.

Bloche, M. Gregg. "Race-Based Therapeutics," *New England Journal of Medicine*, 351 (November 11, 2004): 2035–2037.

Bloomberg Business News, "Merck Profits Were Higher in Second Quarter," *New York Times, July* 19, 1996.

Byrd, W. Michael, and Linda A. Clayton. *An American Health Dilemma: A Medical History of African Americans and the Problem of Race, Beginnings to 1900*. New York: Routledge, 2000.

Byrd, W. Michael, and Linda A. Clayton. *An American Health Dilemma : Volume II : Race, Medicine, and Health Care in the United States 1900-2000*. New York: Routledge, 2002.

Carson, P., S. Ziesche, G. Johnson, and J.N. Cohn. "Racial differences in response to therapy for heart failure: analysis of the vasodilator-heart failure trials. Vasodilator-Heart Failure Trial Study Group," *Journal of Cardiac Failure* 5 (1999): 178–187.

Chepesiuk, Ron, and Joyce Jones, "Are Race-Specific Drugs Unethical?" *Black Enterprise, Nov.* 2005, 37.

Cohn, Jay. "The Use of Race and Ethnicity in Medicine: Lessons from the African American Heart Failure Trial," *Journal of Law, Medicine and Ethics*, 34 (Fall 2006): 552–554.

Cohn, J.N., et al. "Effect of vasodilator therapy on mortality in chronic congestive heart failure. Results of a Veterans Administration Cooperative Study," *New England Journal of Medicine* 314 (1986): 1547–1552.

Department of Health and Human Services Food and Drug Administration Center for Drug Evaluation and Research, 2005. "Cardiovascular and Renal Drugs Advisory Committee, Volume II," Gaithersberg, MD, June 16, 2005. Transcript available at http://www.fda.gov/ohrms/dockets/ac/05/transcripts/2005-4145T2.pdf.

Derrida, Jacques. "Remarks on Deconstruction and Pragmatism," in *Deconstruction and Pragmatism, ed.* Chantal Mouffe, New York: Routledge, 1997, 77–88.

Derrida, Jacques. "Plato's Pharmacy." In: *Dissemination*. Translated by Barbara Johnson. Chicago: University of Chicago Press, 1981.

Devine, Dan. "NAACP goes to the grassroots for BiDil," *Bay State Banner, Oct* 5, 2006, p. 7.

Devine, Dan. "Heart pill maker slashes sales staff," *Bay State Banner, October* 19, 2006.

Dumit, Joseph. "Drugs for Life," *Molecular Interventions* 2.3(2002): 124–127.

Duster, Troy. "Medicine and People of Color: Unlikely Mix – Race, Biology, and Drugs," *San Francisco Chronicle, Monday, March* 17, 2003, p. B7.

Dyer, George S.M. and Leonard S. Lilly, "Heart Failure," in Leonard S. Lilly, ed., *Pathophysiology of Heart Disease: A Collaborative Project of Medical Students and Faculty* (3rd Edition), Philadelphia: Lippinicott Williams & Wilkins, 2003, 211–236.

Fujimura, Joan. "Constructing 'Do-Able' Problems in Cancer Research: Articulating Alignment," *Social Studies of Science*, 17 (May 1987): 257–293.

Fullwiley, Duana. "The Molecularization of Race: Institutionalizing Human Difference in Pharmacogenetics Practice," *Science As Culture* 16.1 (March 2007): 1–30.

Ghali, J.K., S.W. Tam, M.L. Sabolinski, A.L. Taylor, J. Lindenfeld, J.N.Cohn, M. Worcel, "Exploring the Potential Synergistic Action of Spironolactone on Nitric Oxide-Enhancing Therapy: Insights from the African-American Heart Failure Trial," *Journal of Cardiac Failure* 4 (2008):718–723.

Goodman, Amy. "The FDA Approves a Race-Specific Drug for the First Time in History. Will it Address the Real Health Issues Facing African-Americans?" *Democracy Now!*, Monday, August 1st, 2005.

Greenslit, Nathan. "Dep®ession and Consum♀tion: Psychopharmaceuticals, Branding, and New Identity Practices," *Culture, Medicine and Psychiatry* 29(2005): 477–502.

Haga, Susanne B., and Geoffrey S. Ginsburg, "Prescribing BiDil: Is it Black and White?" *Journal of the American College of Cardiology* 48.1 (2006): 12–13.

Hatch, Anthony. *The Politics of Metabolism: The Metabolic Syndrome and the Reproduction of Race and Racism*, PhD Dissertation, College Park, MD: University of Maryland Department of Sociology, 2009.

Hoffman, Sharona. "Racially-Tailored Medicine Unravelled," *American University Law Review* 55 (2005): 396–452.

Hoover, Eddie L. "There is No Scientific Rationale for Race-Based Research," *Journal of the National Medical Association* 99.6(June 2007): 690–692.

Inda, Jonathan Xavier. "Materializing Hope: Racial Pharmaceuticals, Suffering Bodies, and Biological Citizenship," in Monica Casper, ed., *Corpus: An Interdisciplinary Reader on Bodies and Knowledge* (Palgrave-MacMillan, forthcoming).

Jewell, Mark. "Ad campaign for blacks-only heart drug touches lightly on race," *Associated Press, September* 1, 2006.

Kahn, Jonathan. "Exploiting Race in Drug Development: BiDil's Interim Model of Pharmacogenomics," *Social Studies of Science* 38.5(October 2008): 737–758.

Kahn, Jonathan, and Pamela Sankar, "BiDil: Race Medicine or Race Marketing?" *Health Affairs* 24 (Jul-Dec 2005): 455–463.

Kahn, Jonathan. 2004. "How a Drug Becomes "Ethnic": Law, Commerce, and the Production of Racial Categories," *Yale Journal of Health Policy, Law, and Ethics* 4: 1–46.

Krieger, Nancy. "Stormy Weather: *Race*, Gene Expression, and the Science of Health Disparities," *American Journal of Public Health* 95 (December 2005): 2155–2160.

Latour, Bruno. *We Have Never Been Modern*, trans. Catherine Porter. Cambridge, MA: Harvard University Press, 1993.

Levi-Stauss, Claude. *Totemism*. Trans. Rodney Needham, Boston: Beacon Press, 1963.

Malik, Kenan. "A Colour Coded Prescription," BBC Radio 4, November 17, 2005. http://www.kenanmalik.com/tv/analysis_race+medicine.html (accessed March 10, 2011).

Mauss, Marcel. *The Gift: Forms and Functions of Exchange in Primitive Societies*. Glencoe Ill: Free Press, 1954.

Metzl, Jonathan, *Protest Psychosis: How Schizophrenia Became a Black Disease*, Boston: Beacon Press, 2010.

Mouffe, Chantal. "Deconstruction, Pragmatism, and the Politics of Democracy," in *Deconstruction and Pragmatism*, ed. Chantal Mouffe, New York: Routledge, 1997, 1–12.

National Heart, Lung and Blood Institute, "Data Fact Sheet: Congestive Heart Failure in the United States: A New Epidemic," September 1996, accessed March 5, 2011, at http://www.vidyya.com/2pdfs/dfschf.pdf.

Nelson, Alondra. "The Inclusion-and-Difference Paradox: A Review of Inclusion: The Politics of Difference in Medical Research by Steven Epstein," *Social Identities* 15 (2009): 741–43.

Nelson, Alondra. "The Factness of Diaspora," in Eds. Barbara Koenig, Sandra Soo-Jin Lee, and Sarah Richardson. *Revisiting Race in a Genomic Age*. New Brunswick, NJ: Rutgers University Press, 2008.

NHLBI Congestive Heart Failure Fact Sheet. http://library.thinkquest.org/27533/facts.html. "Panel Recommends FDA Reject BiDil Application," *Wall Street Journal*, February 28, 1997, p. 3.

Persson, Asha. "Incorporating Pharmakon: HIV, Medicine, and Body Shape Change," *Body and Society* 10 (2004): 45–67.

Pollack, Andrew. "Drug Approved for Heart Failure in Black Patients," *New York Times, July* 20, 2004.

Pollock, Anne. "Pharmaceutical Meaning Making Beyond Marketing: Racialized Subjects of Generic Thiazide." *The Journal of Law, Medicine, & Ethics* 36.3 (September 2008): 530–536.

Pollock, Anne. "Transforming the Critique of Big Pharma," *BioSocieties* 6.1 (March 2011): 106–118.

Roberts, Dorothy. *Killing the Black Body: Race, Reproduction, and the Meaning of Liberty*. Pantheon Books, 1997.

Roberts, Dorothy. "Race and the New Biocitizen," in *What's the Use of Race?: Modern Governance and the Biology of Difference*, Eds. Ian Whitmarsh and David S. Jones. Cambridge, MA: MIT Press, 2010, pp. 259–276.

Sailer, Steve. "Race Flat-Earthers Dangerous To Everyone's Health," http://www.vdare.com/sailer/medicine_and_race.htm.

Sammons, Leah. "Racial Profiling: Not Always a Bad Thing," *The Jacksonville Free Press*, Feb 16-Feb 23, 2006, p. 4.

Saul, Stephanie. "U.S. to Review Heart Drug Intended for One Race," *New York Times, June* 13, 2005.

Smiley, Tavis.

"Dr. Ian Smith: Race-Specific Drugs," *NPR: The Tavis Smiley Show, November* 17, 2004.

Smith, David Barton. *Health Care Divided: Race and Healing a Nation*. Ann Arbor: University of Michigan Press, 1999.

Syre, Steven. "NitroMed's Challenge." Knight Ridder Tribune Business News, *Boston Globe*, Aug 10, 2006, pg. 1.

Taylor, AL, S Ziesche, C Yancy, P Carson, R D'Agostino Jr, K Ferdinand, M Taylor K Adams, M Sabolinski, M Worcel, JN Cohn; the African-American Heart Failure Trial Investigators. "Combination of isosorbide dinitrate and hydralazine in blacks with heart failure," *New England Journal of Medicine* 351 (2004): 2049–2057.

Tutton, Richard. "Promising Pessimism: Reading the Futures to be Avoided in Biotech," *Social Studies of Science* (Advance Online Publication, February 21, 2011, DOI: 10.1177/0306312710397398).

Washington, Harriet A. *Medical Apartheid: The Dark History of Experimentation on Black Americans from Colonial Times to the Present*. New York: Double Day, 2006.

Westphal, Sylvia Pagan. "Tough Prescription: Heart Medication Approved for Blacks Faces Uphill Battle; As Insurers Debate Costs And Generics Loom, BiDil Fails to Reach Needy; The Role of Medicare Part D," *Wall Street Journal, Oct* 16, 2006, p. A.1.

Wheelwright, Jeff. "Human, Study Thyself : Learning Series: Genes, Race, and Medicine," *Discover* 26. 3 (March 2005). http://discovermagazine.com/2005/mar/human-study-thyself.

7

Manufacturing Desire: The Commodification of Female Sexual Dysfunction

Jennifer R. Fishman

The process of bringing new drugs to market interweaves commercialism, science, clinical medicine, and governmental regulation. Through their authority and public persona as medical experts, academic clinical trial researchers studying these pharmaceuticals are integral to this process, serving as mediators between producers (the pharmaceutical companies) and consumers (clinicians and patients) of new drugs through a complex set of exchange networks. Using examples from ethnographic research on the search for pharmaceuticals to treat what has become known as female sexual dysfunction, this paper explores the links academic researchers make with drug manufacturers and consumer markets. Academic researchers have become an integral aspect of drug development, not only by conducting clinical trial research, but also by participating in a number of other activities that assist pharmaceutical companies in identifying and creating new markets. This paper examines how researchers attend professional meetings where they present clinical trial data, lecture at continuing medical education conferences, and offer themselves as 'experts' to raise awareness about disorders and their treatments. Modifying a sociology of technology approach, this paper focuses on the actors in the social network who mediate the junctions between technological producers and consumers. This extends work in this area through theorizing the linkages between exchange networks, commodification techniques, and technoscientific developments.

New pharmaceuticals to treat life's problems have attained a type of cachet in popular and medical culture, both as commodities and as objects of enormous popular interest. The process of bringing new drugs to market interweaves commercialism, science, clinical medicine, and governmental regulation. Through their authority and public persona as medical

Jennifer R. Fishman, "Manufacturing Desire: The Commodification of Female Sexual Dysfunction," in Social Studies of Science 34 (2004): 187–218. Reproduced by permission of SAGE.

The Pharmaceutical Studies Reader, First Edition. Edited by Sergio Sismondo and Jeremy A. Greene.

experts, academic clinical trial researchers studying these pharmaceuticals are integral to this process, serving as mediators between producers (the pharmaceutical companies) and consumers (clinicians and patients) of new drugs through a complex set of exchange networks. Using examples from my ethnographic research on the search for pharmaceuticals to treat what has become known as female sexual dysfunction (FSD),[1] this paper explores the links academic researchers make with drug manufacturers and consumer markets. Clinical trial researchers play integral and often purposeful roles in bringing new sexual dysfunction drugs to market, by making them publicly acceptable and by legitimating their clinical uses. In this capacity, researchers often position themselves as mediators between pharmaceutical companies and regulatory agencies, the professional medical community, and potential consumers of new drugs. Researchers thus contribute to the commodification of new drugs and diseases, while promoting and marketing their own medical expertise and legitimacy. This paper demonstrates the 'infungibility' of the processes of production and distribution of medico-scientific knowledge, pharmaceutical innovation, and commercial marketing in contemporary biomedical practices.

In the wake of Viagra's success as a treatment for erectile dysfunction,[2] attention turned to finding equally effective drugs to treat women's sexual problems, labeling this 'new' condition female sexual dysfunction (FSD).[3] At the time of writing, there are no US Food and Drug Administration (FDA)-approved prescription drugs available for the treatment of FSD,[4] but a number of compounds are in clinical trials and several, Viagra included, are used 'off-label'. Clinical trial researchers of sexual dysfunction drugs are typically physicians or clinical psychologists with academic appointments in medical schools. With the increasing privatization and commercialization of biomedicine and biomedical research, the pharmaceutical industry has become an important funding stream for academic health centers and their researchers. Conversely, academic researchers have become an integral aspect of drug development, not only by conducting clinical research trials, but also by participating in a number of other activities that assist pharmaceutical companies in identifying and creating new markets.

Because pharmaceutical companies must simultaneously produce medico-scientific knowledge when bringing new compounds to market as commercial drugs, they direct their internal scientific research and the external research they sponsor toward the development of marketable drugs and marketable diagnoses. Drug development and marketing have come to resemble the development of other commodified products in a competitive marketplace. This is especially true in the USA, where prescription drugs are now advertised directly to consumers through print advertisements and television commercials. However, unlike many other commodities, pharmaceuticals have the advantages and disadvantages of being dependent upon the biomedical sciences for legitimation and approval. This works in favor of the marketing of pharmaceuticals, because drugs can be promoted through scientific claims about the medical benefit, efficacy, and necessity supposedly revealed by objective clinical research. On the other hand, pharmaceutical companies are also subject to regulatory controls that limit their direct marketing of products to consumers. Researchers, by mediating drug development, can circumvent many of these restrictions because of their perceived autonomy, expertise, and objectivity. These mediated performances are effective for marketing drugs largely because of cultural idealizations that presume separations between scientific research and politics, economics, and commerce.

New Diagnoses for New Drugs: Creating a Market

The process of bringing a new pharmaceutical to market is a privatized and profit-driven venture, yet it is also one that relies on the acquisition of 'objective' scientific data in order to obtain federal drug approval. Academic medical researchers are integral to the collection of clinical trial data and the verification of the clinical applicability of a drug under investigation. Moreover, within the drug development process, they are often charged with establishing the variables of both a disease diagnosis that will warrant a drug's prescription and the 'patient population' for which a new drug is deemed appropriate. Thus, they mediate and facilitate pharmaceutical company relationships with regulatory agencies such as the US FDA, which oversees this process. So-called lifestyle drugs, such as sexuo-pharmaceuticals, have raised questions about how pharmaceutical companies can meet the approval guidelines for new drugs given their questionable status for treating 'diseases'. Such drugs will only be approved if they treat an established 'disease', and lifestyle issues or even 'quality of life' issues have not traditionally fallen into this category. Hence, the biomedicalization of a condition (Clarke et al., 2003) is in fact necessary for a lifestyle drug to gain approval. By contributing to the commodification of a disease category and its concomitant 'diseased' population, an academic researcher participates in the commodification of the category through the creation of a consumer market for a new pharmaceutical (Fosket, 2004).[5] This process begins at the earliest stages of drug development, interlocking clinical trial research with pharmaceutical drug commodification.

For example, one of the products currently in development for the treatment of FSD is a testosterone-replacement patch for women.[6] In development by Procter and Gamble Pharmaceuticals in conjunction with Watson Pharmaceuticals, Inc., the testosterone patch was tested on women who have undergone an oophorectomy and hysterectomy, and whose primary sexual complaint is 'low sexual desire'.[7] The Phase II trials of the patch were conducted in 1999 and 2000, and a paper reporting these results appeared in the *New England Journal of Medicine* in September 2000 (Shifren et al., 2000). These results indicated that, despite an 'appreciable' placebo response, when the 75 women were given a 300 μg testosterone patch they reported greater frequency of sexual activity and orgasm when compared with placebo.

Soon after these results appeared in print, an announcement was circulated for a conference, sponsored by the University of Medicine and Dentistry of New Jersey and the Robert Wood Johnson Medical School, entitled 'Androgen Deficiency in Women: Definition, Diagnosis, and Classification' to take place in summer 2001 in Princeton (NJ, USA). The conference was organized by three of the authors of the *New England Journal of Medicine* paper who had participated in collecting data for the trial of the testosterone patch.[8] It was funded through unrestricted educational grants by a number of pharmaceutical companies, each of which had a testosterone product in development, including the patch, gels, and a pill. Although the title seems to presume the existence and known contours of the disorder, the purpose of the conference was to develop a 'consensus statement' on the definition, diagnosis, and classification of an 'androgen deficiency syndrome in women'. On the first day of the conference, data were presented by a list of 'international experts' to discuss the possible existence of a female androgen deficiency, with symptoms including low libido, low energy, and fatigue. Presenters included endocrinologists, obstetrician-gynaecologists, urologists, psychologists, and psychiatrists, who described research data about the effects of androgens on women and especially about the decreasing levels of testosterone in aging and postmenopausal women.[9] In addition to presenting their data to one another, these experts also presented to a larger audience, including other researchers, pharmaceutical company representatives, and clinicians, who received continuing medical education (CME) credits for attending.

The presenters met the following day behind closed doors to develop a consensus document. This appeared in the journal *Fertility and Sterility* in April 2002 (Bachmann et al., 2002). Five of the 19 researchers who contributed to the consensus document were authors of the earlier *New England Journal of Medicine* paper detailing the trial results for the testosterone patch. Most of the other presenters were working with other testosterone compounds currently in clinical trial through other pharmaceutical companies.[10] Neither of the journals required the authors of the two papers to disclose financial arrangements with any pharmaceutical companies.

Studies in the social construction of technology often look at the ways in which technologies and their users are co-constituted.[11] However, my point is somewhat different, in that it specifically indicates the creation and configuration of a 'market' of potential users rather than individual users in the production of a technology. Furthermore, it also identifies processes through which individuals are transformed into *consumers*, in addition to users, of new drugs and in new markets. This is an attempt to bring technoscience studies to bear on consumption studies.[12]

The creation of new drugs with new markets has been documented in a number of other cases, including the changing nomenclature for attention deficit disorder in connection with the availability of Ritalin (Conrad & Potter, 2000; Lakoff, 2000), the 'new' diagnostic category of premenstrual dysphoric disorder in conjunction with the repackaging of Prozac under the new brand name Sarafem (Greenslit, 2002), and the promotion of social anxiety disorder in order to boost sales of Paxil (Healy, 2001). David Healy (1997) argues, moreover, that the availability of selective serotonin reuptake inhibitors (SSRI), such as Prozac and Paxil, has led to a rise in depression diagnoses, indicating that the SSRI market has contributed to an expansion (and commodification) of the disease. Peter Kramer (1993: 15) refers to this phenomenon as 'diagnostic bracket creep – the expansion of categories to match the scope of relevant medications'.

Similar trends are occurring with the present and future availability of sexuopharmaceuticals, such as Viagra, raising questions about what constitutes a 'disease', especially as both the diagnosis and the market for a treatment expand simultaneously.[13] In particular, a consensus conference similar to the one discussed earlier was convened in 1998 in order to develop a classification schema for sub-types of FSD (Basson et al., 2000).[14] The four disorders within the larger rubric of FSD were identified as: female sexual desire disorder, female sexual arousal disorder, female orgasmic disorder, and female sexual pain disorder (Basson et al., 2000). With the delineation of the symptoms of a disorder, a consensus document also (often explicitly) identifies clinical trial outcome measurements. The FDA uses documents like this, produced by experts in the field, to provide authoritative definitions of the disorder, despite the contradiction that the disorders were often identified on the bases of the symptoms that a new drug can help alleviate.

Therefore, such classification guidelines are co-produced, with the clinical trial endpoints already chosen, for a new drug under investigation. In turn, consensus conferences and expanding diagnostic definitions can legitimize a clinical trial protocol, easing a new drug's path through the FDA approval process and promoting the drug's necessity and effectiveness to the FDA. For example, one of the speakers at the 'Androgen Deficiency in Women' conference was an FDA official who evaluates new drug approval applications. His presentation focused on the clinical trial endpoints that would be acceptable to the FDA to show 'efficacy' of a drug to treat female androgen deficiency. There is a clear linkage here between development of the disease category, the purported purpose of the conference, and FDA approval of a new drug to treat that disease.

Sexual dysfunction researchers position themselves as experts in their field of study, thereby acting as mediators among a pharmaceutical company (which needs their expertise to establish a new drug's clinical necessity), patients in the clinical trials, and the FDA (which relies on the researchers' expertise in order to approve new drugs). By helping to create official scientific documents that become part of the drug regulatory process, researchers establish a necessary path through which a pharmaceutical technology must traverse in order to enter the consumer market as a legitimate treatment, and they also construct themselves as indispensable guides.[15] This mandatory process simultaneously shapes the contours of a new pharmaceutical user and the parameters of a consumer market.

The Commodification of Continuing Medical Education

In addition to mediating the creation of new markets, sexual dysfunction researchers also position themselves as mediators between pharmaceutical companies and other clinicians. After a potential treatment for sexual dysfunction begins to make its way through clinical trial, sexual dysfunction researchers often engage in another related activity – serving as faculty at CME conferences, which clinicians attend as part of their professional license renewal requirements. CME conferences are 1–3-day meetings including a number of scheduled lectures. Lecturers, typically academic researchers with medical school faculty appointments, present the latest clinical trial data for drugs in development. Other lectures might focus on the diagnostic criteria (for example, the results of consensus conferences such as the one described earlier), epidemiological data, and/or more general research and clinical data on the disorder in question.

The conferences are sponsored by pharmaceutical companies through 'unrestricted educational grants'. This type of grant stipulates that the conference organizers are given money for the conference without any input from the pharmaceutical company on how the money is spent. Recently, these types of grants have come under increased scrutiny. In April 2003, the Office of the Inspector General of the US Department of Health and Human Services released its final guidelines for managing pharmaceutical manufacturer–physician relations, in an attempt to help manufacturers avoid violating anti-kickback statutes (Office of Inspector General, 2003). The guidelines target the use of educational grants for sponsoring lunches, lectures, and workshops at hospitals and medical schools, labeling these activities a 'key area of potential risk' of violation (2003: 16), where there might be explicit or implicit expectations of eventual repayment through increased prescription of the manufacturer's drugs.

As a policy already in place by medical schools, it attempts to ensure that conference organizers and participants are independent from industry underwriters, and to show that lecture content and materials are not beholden to the companies. This conceptualization, however, underestimates the multi-leveled and integrated relationships between pharmaceutical companies and academic medicine, and between the science of drug development and the marketing of pharmaceuticals. Indeed, the notion that it is possible (and even desirable) to clearly delineate biomedical knowledge dissemination from medical commerce assumes that science can be separate from its publics and medicine from its politico-economic context.

The nebulous definitions of 'medical education', the multiple roles of the clinical trial researcher, and the lack of regulatory oversight of these conferences combine to create complicated and ethically ambiguous scenarios. Educating clinicians about new developments in medical treatment is intertwined with pharmaceutical promotion and marketing. It becomes difficult to distinguish education from advertising in these instances. While some may argue that it is an important educational task to make clinicians aware of the latest drug developments, this can also be construed as a means to promote commercial products to clinicians who will prescribe them.

Although the ultimate end-users of a drug are the patients, clinicians must first be made aware of the existence of a new drug as a treatment option. CME conferences are venues where clinicians are educated about new drug developments. By sponsoring CME conferences and enabling researchers to present data on new in-trial drugs, pharmaceutical companies, in conjunction with academic researchers, are able to promote and 'brand' their drugs to clinicians *before* the FDA has granted approval for the drug's release. The market is thus 'pre-organized'.

The following examples highlight the ways in which a mythology about scientific autonomy and objectivity continues to dictate regulatory practices, ironically making it difficult to regulate the work practices of researchers in these situations. To illustrate these relationships in action at CME conferences, I will use examples taken from my ethnographic observations and interviews at seven such conferences on female sexual (dys)function in the period between October 2000 and December 2002. My analysis of these meetings reveals the intricate exchange networks formed between academic researchers and pharmaceutical companies. These networks and the academic researchers' multiple roles within these collaborations ultimately assist in the marketing of new drugs to clinicians. Researchers once again serve as mediators between pharmaceutical companies and their markets, facilitating a new 'consumption junction' between a new drug and its consumers.

CME conferences display an intricate orchestration in the performances of academic researchers as marketers/educators. The intricacy arises in large part due to the ethical codes and regulatory restrictions placed on pharmaceutical companies for their involvement in these conferences. In 1991, the American Medical Association House of Delegates adopted a resolution regarding guidelines for assuring high-quality CME programs. The guidelines address physicians directly, advising them how to attend a CME conference and also how to act as faculty at one:

> Physicians serving as presenters, moderators, or other faculty at a CME conference should ensure that (a) research findings and therapeutic recommendations are based on scientifically accurate, up-to-date information and are presented in a balanced, objective manner; (b) the content of their presentation is not modified or influenced by representatives of industry or other financial contributors, and they do not employ materials whose content is shaped by industry. Faculty may, however, use scientific data generated from industry-sponsored research, and they may also accept technical assistance from industry in preparing slides or other presentation materials, as long as this assistance is of only nominal monetary value and the company has no input in the actual content of the material. (American Medical Association, 1996)

Within these guidelines, the discourse assumes the autonomy of the faculty member and a clear separation between 'industry' and 'physicians'.[16] The instruction to not use materials whose 'content is shaped by industry' further implies a discrete distinction between academic and industry research. However, the faculty (and organizers) at CME conferences for sexual dysfunction are the same researchers who conduct industry-sponsored research on Viagra for women and on testosterone therapies. Although the guidelines permit faculty to present data based on industry-sponsored research, this research is also clearly 'shaped by' industry employees who work *in collaboration* with academic researchers.

In another attempt to regulate the ethics of CME conferences, faculty members are required to disclose any financial arrangements that they have with private industry. They are still permitted to speak, so long as their relationship with industry is revealed. Dana and Loewenstein (2003), researchers in the decision sciences, demonstrate that even when subjects are told about someone's explicit bias, they do not think that they will be affected by it. Yet research has shown that physicians are influenced by financial relationships with pharmaceutical companies in terms of their prescribing practices (Wazana, 2000). Dana and Loewenstein conclude that although prescribing physicians are consciously trying to do good work, they underestimate the ways in which marketing practices may affect them. In fact, other empirical research has shown that when someone with a conflict of interest does disclose a conflict, they are likely to act in even *more* self-serving ways, as if given dispensation to be biased due to 'full disclosure' (Bazerman et al., 2002). Although the content of these speakers' lectures may not have been shaped by industry, their participation in the CME conference itself is due to their industry involvement. The research network engaged in presenting data on new drugs and disorders – the very organization of CME itself – can thus be viewed as a technique for commodification.

Recently, questions have been raised within the medical community about the ethics and validity of presenting data on drugs that have not yet received approval and on the 'off-label' uses of available drugs. Physicians have long been permitted to prescribe drugs for uses other than those approved by the FDA. This was an early strategy of the FDA to preserve physician autonomy and clinical discretion, thus gaining physician support for state regulation of pharmaceutical safety and efficacy.

However, recent debate has focused on whether a pharmaceutical company can provide unsolicited information to physicians about the potential off-label uses of a particular drug. This is especially important in the case of FSD treatments, for which there are as yet no FDA-approved pharmaceutical therapies. Because Viagra and testosterone therapies are approved for men, they are thus available as off-label prescriptions for women. All of the CME conferences on sexual dysfunction that I attended discussed the off-label uses of these drugs for women. In the past, the FDA had limited the discussion of off-label drug use and non-approved drugs at medical conferences. However, the restrictions were still somewhat strict, now permitting discussion of off-label prescription drug use at CME conferences, but only if a company gained advance approval from the FDA by meeting a series of stringent criteria and by agreeing to conduct the clinical studies necessary to gain approval for the indication involved.

CME conferences, as technologies of knowledge distribution, thus rely on the activities of these researchers to mediate data to clinicians. The speakers' bureau members are well paid for their travel time and appearances, and become linked as scientists to the chemical compounds they study and promote as pharmaceuticals when they travel from city to city lecturing on their potential effectiveness for treating sexual dysfunctions. Their mediated roles in this capacity allow them to interact with clinicians nationally and internationally, augmenting their reputations in their own research fields.

The researchers' roles here strongly resemble those of pharmaceutical detail men in previous eras, yet researchers have the added legitimacy conferred by medical degrees and academic appointments. With the rise of physician as pharmaceutical spokesperson, this dream of the professionalization of pharmaceutical representatives is finally realized.

The Celebrity of the 'Sex Expert': Media and the Commodification of Female Sexual Dysfunction

In addition to mediating relationships between the pharmaceutical industry and clinicians, many sexual dysfunction researchers also engage directly and indirectly with the 'lay public'. Commodifying themselves as experts, such researchers promote themselves and the drugs they research to a consuming public. In this capacity, a researcher establishes a media-driven relationship with potential consumers of new pharmaceutical drugs. They relate to patients/consumers not in their capacities as clinicians seeing patients on a one-on-one basis, but rather through mass media communication channels: television, the Internet, print newspapers, magazines, and journals.

Information on health and illness is proliferating in many kinds of media, especially newspapers, on the Internet, in popular magazines, and through direct-to-consumer prescription and over-the-counter drug advertising. In fact, biomedicine has become a fundamental element of mass culture, so much so, Martin Bauer (1998) suggests, that its constant presence in popular media points to the medicalization of both the science news and of society more generally:

> [O]ur evidence of the dominance of health news is an empirical indicator of the advent of a medicalized society. ... [The] medicalization of science news is a correlate of these larger changes in society, celebrating the successes of medical sciences, anticipating breakthroughs on the health front, and mobilizing an ever greater demand for medication and services. (Bauer, 1998: 747)

The particular exchange relations between medicine and the media at this historical moment are predicated on at least three concurrent trends in contemporary US culture: (1) the availability of direct-to-consumer advertising of pharmaceutical drugs; (2) the commercialization of self-help and consumer movements (Tomes, 2001); and (3) the rising popularity of media, including the Internet as sources of health information (Bauer, 1998). Embedded within each of these trends is the assumption that it is both the responsibility and the entitlement of the consumer/patient to find paths to better health (and in this case, better sex) through information gathering and through responsible consumption practices (Bunton et al., 1995; Tomes, 2001). While the researcher–physician as public expert has become somewhat commonplace in mainstream media, this shift has been especially available for sex researchers due to Viagra's popularity and the well-known commercial appeal of sexual topics in media venues.[17] Sexuo-pharmaceuticals are fetishized commodities *par excellence*, imbued with promises of better sex, better intimate relationships, youthfulness, and fulfillment of one's desires (sexual and otherwise) (Mamo & Fishman, 2001). Researchers of these commodities too become fetishized as their expertise and access to knowledge about these drugs are commodified, exoticized, mystified, and revered. The symbolic capital of their expert status and the social capital of their medical authority are commodities for exchange within the channels of mass media. The coalescence of these factors has led to the sexual dysfunction clinical trial researcher as media celebrity.

The quintessential case of this is two prominent FSD researchers – Drs Jennifer and Laura Berman. Jennifer Berman is a urologist and Laura Berman is a clinical psychologist. These sisters are co-directors of the University of California at Los Angeles Female Sexual Medicine Center, where they treat patients and conduct research on FSD and its treatments. They are prominent figures in FSD research, conducting industry-sponsored research for Pfizer on Viagra's effects on women, as well as on a number of other pharmacological therapies and medical devices (Billups et al., 2001), organizing professional conferences, and publishing papers in peer-reviewed journals.

In February 2001, the Berman sisters appeared twice on the Oprah Winfrey television show (the first time on Valentine's Day) as experts in the field of FSD, to promote their new book *For Women Only: A Revolutionary Guide to Overcoming Sexual Dysfunction and Reclaiming Your Sex Life* (Berman & Berman, 2001). After their appearance on Oprah, their book rose to number one on the sales chart of Amazon.com. For each hour-long show, they were the 'experts' asked to address questions about 'why women don't want to have sex' and how new medical research can help women have satisfying sex lives. These shows generated more posts on Oprah's online message board than any other show until that point.

The publication of clinical trial data, brought to the 'public' by the researchers themselves, demonstrates the larger changes in access and availability of biomedical information for consumer/patients (Clarke et al., 2003). Moreover, it signals new types of relationships among medical researchers, pharmaceutical companies, potential consumers, and various media technologies. Researchers in the act of promoting themselves to broad audiences also help to create anticipatory market bases through which to promote new prescription drugs. As such, researchers act as mediators between potential consumers and pharmaceutical companies, facilitating the marketing of prescription drugs on the Internet without violating any FDA regulations. The Bermans' website is just one mediated technology that accomplishes this; others include television news segments reporting the results of medical studies, and health magazines that feature summaries of recent health studies. The information on the website is further legitimated as 'medical knowledge' because of its source: it comes from medical experts rather than a pharmaceutical company itself. The information presented in the form of a clinical research paper carries with it the authority of medico-scientific knowledge seemingly devoid of commercial or marketing intent. While many Web users may not interpret the Bermans' efforts as purely educational and altruistic, they may welcome the presentation of this information as a public entitlement to medical information. The democratic distribution of knowledge is, at least in part, a marketing strategy.

Robust Pipelines[18]

The relations among clinical trial design, clinical diagnostic criteria development, the dissemination of scientific knowledge about pharmaceuticals, and the promotion of new drugs for new disorders are overlapping and interwoven. Contemporary professional and everyday work activities of researchers are also pathways for the promotion of pharmaceutical drugs and the creation of new markets. For present purposes, I am reading researchers' activities *as* marketing in order to underscore how researchers' activities mediate and contribute to the consumption of pharmaceuticals. A set of exchange relations is set up between academic researchers, pharmaceutical companies, journalists, clinicians, and prospective patients such that researchers' involvement with the development of new drugs is necessarily a process in which a number of 'goods' become commodified. In this paper, I have demonstrated the ways in which drugs, diseases, biomedical knowledge, expertise, and the researchers themselves become commodified as they mediate the marketing of new drugs to treat FSD.

The case of the promotion of FSD indicates a process in which a specific commodity was produced by, circulated among, and consumed by a specific set of actors with particular purposes. Following the activities of sexual dysfunction researchers complicates our understanding of the practices of mediation, dissolving the convenient distinctions between science and culture, knowledge dissemination and drug promotion, education and marketing, basic and applied science, academic science and private industry, and production and consumption. These are the distinctions upon which conventional interpretations of science, the media, and pharmaceutical drug regulation rest. As FSD was exchanged between different networks of production and consumption, it became a cultural commodity.

With the privatization and commercialization of biomedicine and medical care in the USA (Estes & Linkins, 1997), it is unsurprising that pharmaceutical drug development looks like and is big business, exercising strategies that will help promote sales of prescription drugs. The activities that would simply be labeled 'good marketing' in other industries are still seen very differently within the field of biomedicine, which historically has maintained different ethical standards of practice and relations between suppliers and consumers in an attempt to set itself apart from commerce. In what Nancy Tomes identifies as 'medical exceptionalism', physicians and patients in the 'golden age' of US medicine did not behave as 'normal' consumers and suppliers. Patients relied on the professional credentialing process and the code of medical ethics, which explicitly put the patient's welfare before a physician's own profits. In another example, medical services were not priced based on supply–demand logics. From this, the medical marketplace was considered exceptional and did not conform to the conventions and practices of other markets. This, however, was not an inevitable development within medicine, but rather it had to be manufactured and defended (Tomes, 2001).

This idealization of medicine, medical practice, and the medical marketplace remains intact and even lionized despite the erosion of both the exceptional practices themselves and the ideologies that undergird these practices. As a result of the patients' rights and consumer movements of the 1970s and the managed care revolution of the 1990s, medicine's commercial practices have changed markedly. Physicians and managed-care organizations now have to compete for patients, disclose information about the costs of their services, and use cost-benefit analyses to decide which type of health care is most appropriate. Although some read this as yet a different corruption tale of the ethos of the medical professional and of healthcare more generally, this has also been a deliberate attempt to reverse the exceptionalism granted to medicine, in an attempt to allow it to work in favor of the consumer.

The language of consumerism now associated with clinical practice and medical research seems to endorse a market logic that many find odious. The irony of the current situation is that the institutional arrangements, regulatory policies, and individual physicians' self-images as ethical and autonomous were carefully orchestrated by physicians in order to promote this exceptionalism. It is the legacy of and continued adherence to these policies, practices, and norms that allow the current practices – a move away from medical exceptionalism – to occur.

With the increasing public-private arrangements being brokered between industry and academia, these ethical issues only become more entangled. Conventional medical ethics is unequipped to deal with these questions. Business ethics is likewise unable to accommodate the particular responsibilities of the biomedical project. The chasm left in between is where the academic researcher now treads, guided only by professional conventions and a growing entrepreneurialism and commercialism in medicine.

Clinical trial researchers have elaborated new pathways between pharmaceutical companies and consumers through their activities in different fields of action within drug development and marketing. Researchers' relations with different actors can be understood as a network of exchange relations. Therefore, rather than describing a one-way model of an actor enrolling others (for example, other scientists, regulatory bodies, the press, and so on), I have attempted to show the ways in which this process is multi-directional and located within the drives toward the commodification of goods and services and consumer culture. Extending the framework of technology studies, my analysis examines how the production of medical technologies, as social and cultural products which configure users, are also interwoven with the production of commercial *markets* and marketing practices, disrupting conventional assumptions about drug development, technology diffusion, and knowledge dissemination.

NOTES

1 The materials used in this paper have been collected since 2000 through in-depth interviews, ethnographic fieldwork at scientific and medical conferences on female sexual dysfunction, and content analysis of articles in both popular media venues and medical journals.

2 Since its release in March 1998, more than 17 million prescriptions have been written for Viagra worldwide. Pfizer reported US$1.74 billion in Viagra sales worldwide in 2002 (Pfizer, Inc., 2002). Pfizer further claims that there are nine Viagra pills dispensed *every second* (<www.viagra.com>, accessed 17 August 2003).

3 This is arguably not a 'new' condition at all. Sexual dysfunction disorders were listed in the 4th edition of the *Diagnostic and Statistical Manual of the American Psychiatric Association* (1994) (DSM-IV) as psychological conditions before Viagra's appearance. In addition, they also appear in the *International Classification of Diseases* (ICD-10) in similar ways. However, a new classification of these disorders, under the broad category of 'female sexual dysfunction', was developed in order

to help conceptualize FSD as a medical disorder (Basson et al., 2000). For critiques of this 're-invention' see Tiefer (2000), Moynihan (2003), and Fishman (2003). This is not a unique phenomenon. Other scholars have long analyzed the production of new disorders within biomedicine (Becker & Nachtigall, 1992; Klasen, 2000).

4 The only FDA-approved technology for FSD is a mechanical device called The EROS – a hand-held battery-operated device with a suction cup placed on the clitoris that works as a vacuum to enhance blood flow. For an analysis of this device vis-a-vis Viagra, see Fishman & Mamo (2002).

5 Although I wish they had elaborated it further, Bowker & Star (1999: 3) refer to (some) categories as 'commodified, elaborate, expensive ones generated by medical diagnoses, government regulatory bodies, and pharmaceutical firms'.

6 This product is expected to receive FDA approval in 2004. The name Intrinsa has already been trademarked for the patch.

7 Oophorectomy is removal of the ovaries.

8 I registered for and attended this conference as a participant. The data in this section are from my fieldnotes, July 2001.

9 These presentations were published as articles in a special edited volume of *Fertility and Sterility* in April 2002. See Rosen et al. (2002).

10 At the conference, presenters' financial conflicts of interest were presented in the conference handbook that all attendees received. Researchers' activities included receiving research grants from pharmaceutical companies, serving as consultants for companies, and being on pharmaceutical companies' speakers' bureaus.

11 See for example, Akrich (1992), Bijker et al. (1987), Clarke & Montini (1993), Cockburn & Furst-Dilic (1994), Mamo & Fishman (2001), Oudshoorn (1999), and Woolgar (1991).

12 On technologies and consumption, see for example de Grazia (1996), Hogshire (1999), Horowitz & Mohun (1998).

13 The results of a sex survey that appeared in the *Journal of the American Medical Association* (Laumann et al., 1999) further contributed to perceptions of a huge market of potential consumers of sexuopharmaceuticals. The oft-cited statistic from this study that 43% of women suffer from some form of sexual dysfunction, can be read not only as an epidemiologic figure, but also as a potential marketing figure. In fact, this statistic often appears in a pharmaceutical company's promotional products as a way of encouraging potential investors' interest in the company.

14 These had already been part of the 4th edition of the *Diagnostic and Statistical Manual* of the American Psychiatric Association, but this 'new' schema was intended as a means of including *medical* aspects of sexual dysfunctions within the diagnoses.

15 This is what Latour (1988) posits as an 'obligatory passage point'. For example, he argues that Pasteur enlisted other actors through convincing them that they needed to pass through his laboratory in order to solve society's problems.

16 These guidelines also reflect a lack of awareness about the psychological characteristics of 'bias'. In a paper appearing recently in the *Journal of the American Medical Association*, Dana & Lowenstein (2003) posit that the guidelines for managing issues in conflicts of interest between pharmaceutical manufacturers and physicians depend upon a false notion of bias as intentional. Instead, they demonstrate through a review of the literature on psychological bias that individuals are not aware of their own biases. Furthermore, they found that the size of the remuneration did not correlate with the degree of bias.

17 Nicholas King's (2001) analysis of the relationship between science and the mass media relies on theories of exchange relations in which social capital in the field of science is transformed into 'value' in the field of the media. In his empirical example of the transformation of 'emerging diseases' into a commodity, he concludes that 'novelty was a singularly effective lubricant in these exchange networks' (King, 2001). In the analysis of the commodification of FSD presented here, 'sex' is the effective lubricant between the fields of medicine and the media.

18 'Robust pipelines' was a 'term of the month' on the Cambridge Healthtech Institute's 'Genomic Glossaries: Evolving Terminology for Emerging Technologies' Webpage in April 2003.

REFERENCES

Abbasi, Kamran & Richard Smith (2003) 'No More Free Lunches', *British Medical Journal* 326 (31 May): 1155–56.

Adams, Vincanne (2002) 'Randomized Controlled Crime: Indirect Criminalization of Alternative Medicine in the United States', *Social Studies of Science* 32(5/6): 659–90.

Akrich, Madeleine (1992) 'The De-Scription of Technical Objects', in W. Bijker and J. Law (eds), *Shaping Technology/Building Society* (Cambridge, MA: MIT Press): 205–24.

American Medical Association (1996) *Ethical Issues in CME*, American Medical Association: <*www.ama-assn.org/ama/pub/category/2934.html*> (accessed 18 January 2003).

American Psychiatric Association (1994) *Diagnostic and Statistical Manual of Mental Disorders: DSM-IV*, 4th edn (Washington, DC: American Psychiatric Association).

Applbaum, Kalman (2000) 'Marketing and Commodification', *Social Analysis* 44: 106–28.

Bachmann, Gloria, John Bancroft, Glenn Braunstein, Henry Burger, Susan Davis, Lorraine Dennerstein, Irwin Goldstein, Andre Guay, Sandra Leiblum, Rogerio Lobo, Morris Notelovitz, Raymond Rosen, Philip Sarrel, Barbara Sherwin, James Simon, Evan Simpson, Jan Shifren, Richard Spark & Abdul Traish (2002) 'Female Androgen Insufficiency: The Princeton Consensus Statement on Definition, Classification, and Assessment', *Fertility and Sterility* 77(4): 660–65.

Baird, Patricia, Jocelyn Downie & Jon Thompson (2002) 'Clinical Trials and Industry', *Science* 297(5590): 2211.

Basson, Rosemary, Jennifer Berman, Arthur Burnett, Leonard Derogatis, David Ferguson, Jean Fourcroy, Irwin Goldstein, Alessandra Graziottin, Julia Heiman, Ellen Laan, Sandra Leiblum, Harin Padma-Nathan, Raymond Rosen, Kathleen Segraves, R. Taylor Segraves, Ridwan Shabsigh, Marcalee Sipski, Gorm Wagner & Beverly Whipple (2000) 'Report of the International Consensus Development Conference on Female Sexual Dysfunction: Definitions and Classifications', *Journal of Urology* 163(3): 888–93.

Bauer, Martin (1998) 'The Medicalization of Science News – from the "Rocket-Scalpel" to the "Gene-Meteorite" Complex', *Social Science Information* 37(4): 731–51.

Bazerman, M.H., G. Loewenstein & D.A. Moore (2002) 'Why Good Accountants Do Bad Audits', *Harvard Business Review* 80(11): 96–100.

Beck, James M. & Elizabeth D. Azari (1998) 'FDA, Off-Label Use, and Informed Consent: Debunking Myths and Misconceptions', *Food and Drug Law Journal* 53(1): 71–104.

Becker, Gay (2000) 'Selling Hope: Marketing and Consuming the New Reproductive Technologies in the United States', *Sciences Sociales et Santé* 18(4):105–25.

Becker, Gay & Robert D. Nachtigall (1992) 'Eager for Medicalization: The Social Production of Infertility as a Disease', *Sociology of Health and Illness* 14(4): 456–71.

Berman, Jennifer & Laura Berman (2001) *For Women Only: A Revolutionary Guide to Overcoming Sexual Dysfunction and Reclaiming Your Sex Life* (New York: Henry Holt and Company).

Berman, Jennifer & Laura Berman (2002) *Welcome!* Vibrance Associates, LLC. (cited 10 November 2002).

Berman, Jennifer R., Laura A. Berman, Steven M. Toler, Jennifer Gill, Scott Haughie, Groton Pfizer Global Research and Development, CT, and Sandwich Pfizer Global Research and Development, UK (2002) *Study of Viagra in Post-Menopausal Women Shows Promising Results*, Vibrance Associates, LLC (cited 29 October 2002) (<*www.newshe.com/articles/viagrawomen9.25.shtml*>).

Berman, Laura, Jennifer Berman, Stan Felder, Dan Pollets, Sachin Chhabra, Marie Miles & Jennifer Ann Powell (2003) 'Seeking Help for Sexual Function Complaints: What Gynecologists Need to Know About the Female Patient's Experience', *Fertility and Sterility* 79(3): 572–76.

Biagioli, Mario (1993) *Galileo, Courtier* (Chicago, IL: University of Chicago Press).

Bijker, Wiebe E., Thomas Hughes & Trevor J. Pinch (eds) (1987) *The Social Construction of Technological Systems* (Cambridge and London: MIT Press).

Billups, K.L., L. Berman, J. Berman, M.E. Metz, M.E. Glennon & I. Goldstein (2001) 'Vacuum-Induced Clitoral Engorgement for Treatment of Female Sexual Dysfunction', *Journal of Sex and Marital Therapy* 27(5): 435–41.

Bodenheimer, Thomas (2000) 'Uneasy Alliance – Clinical Investigators and the Pharmaceutical Industry', *New England Journal of Medicine* 342: 1621–26.

Bowker, Geoffrey C. & Susan Leigh Star (1999) *Sorting Things Out: Classification and Its Consequences* (Cambridge, MA: MIT Press).

Bunton, Robin, Sarah Nettleton & Roger Burrows (eds) (1995) *The Sociology of Health Promotion: Health, Risk, and Consumption under Late Modernity* (London: Routledge).

Burnham, John C. (1987) *How Superstition Won and Science Lost: Popularizing Science and Health in the U.S.* (New Brunswick, NJ: Rutgers University Press).

Chen, Joanne (2003) 'The Pleasure Principle', *Vogue* (February): 196–203.

Clarke, Adele E. (1991) 'Social Worlds/Arenas Theory as Organizational Theory', in D.R. Maines (ed), *Social Organization and Social Process: Essays in Honor of Anselm Strauss* (New York: Aldine De Gruyter): 128–35.

Clarke, Adele E. & Theresa Montini (1993) 'The Many Faces of RU486: Tales of Situated Knowledges and Technological Contestations', Science, *Technology and Human Values* 18(1): 42–78.

Clarke, Adele E., Janet K. Shim, Laura Mamo, Jennifer Ruth Fosket & Jennifer R. Fishman (2003) 'Biomedicalization: Technoscientific Transformations of Health, Illness, and U.S. Biomedicine', *American Sociological Review* 68: 161–94.

Cockburn, Cynthia & Ruza Furst-Dilic (eds) (1994) *Bringing Technology Home: Gender and Technology in a Changing Europe* (Buckingham, Bucks: Open University Press).

Collier, Stephen & Andrew Lakoff (2004) 'On Regimes of Living', in S. Collier & A. Ong (eds), *Global Assemblages: Technology, Rationality, Ethics* (Oxford, UK and Malden, MA: Blackwell) (in press).

Conrad, Peter & Deborah Potter (2000) 'From Hyperactive Children to ADHD Adults: Observations on the Expansion of Medical Categories', *Social Problems* 47(4): 559–82.

Cowan, Ruth Schwartz (1987) 'The Consumption Junction: A Proposal for Research Strategies in the Sociology of Technology', in W.E. Bijker, T. Hughes and T. Pinch (eds), *The Social Construction of Technological Systems* (Cambridge: MIT Press): 261–80.

Dana, Jason & George Loewenstein (2003) 'A Social Science Perspective on Gifts to Physicians from Industry', *Journal of the American Medical Association* 290(2): 252–55.

de Grazia, Victoria (ed.) (1996) *The Sex of Things: Gender and Consumption in Historical Perspectives* (Berkeley and Los Angeles, CA: University of California Press).

Dewey, John (1916) *Democracy and Education: An Introduction to the Philosophy of Education* (New York, NY: Macmillan).

Downey, Gary Lee, Joseph Dumit & Sharon Traweek (1997) 'Corridor Talk', in G.L. Downey and J. Dumit (eds), *Cyborgs and Citadels: Anthropological Interventions in Emerging Sciences, Technologies and Medicines* (Santa Fe, NM: School of American Research Press): 1–25.

Duenwald, Mary (2003) 'Effort to Make Sex Drug for Women Challenges Experts', *The New York Times* (25 March): 5F.

Dumit, Joseph (2003) 'A Pharmaceutical Grammar: Drugs for Life and Direct-to-Consumer Advertising in an Era of Surplus Health', paper presented at the *Exchange Networks in Biomedical Science Workshop*, University of California, San Francisco.

Estes, Carroll L. & Karen W. Linkins (1997) 'Devolution and Aging Policy: Racing to the Bottom of Long Term Care?', *International Journal of Health Services* 27(3): 427–42.

Evans, Rory (2003) 'Sexual Advances', *Allure* (January): 105–08.

Fishman, Jennifer R. (2003) *Desire for Profit: Viagra and the Remaking of Sexual Dysfunction.* PhD Thesis, University of California, San Francisco.

Fishman, Jennifer R. & Laura Mamo (2002) 'What's in a Disorder? Descripting the Medical and Pharmaceutical Constructions of Male and Female Sexual Dysfunction', *Women and Therapy* 24(2): 179–93.

Fosket, Jennifer Ruth (2002) *Breast Cancer Risk and the Politics of Prevention: Analysis of a Clinical Trial.* PhD Thesis, University of California, San Francisco.

Fosket, Jennifer Ruth (2004) 'Constructing "High Risk" Women: The Development and Standardization of a Breast Cancer Risk Assessment Tool', *Science, Technology & Human Values* 29(3): 291–313.

Greene, Jeremy (2004) '"Attention to Details": Medicine, Marketing, and the Emergence of the Pharmaceutical Representative', *Social Studies of Science* 34: 271–292.

Greenslit, Nathan (2002) 'Pharmaceutical Branding: Identity, Individuality, and Illness', *Molecular Interventions* 2(6): 342–45.

Hagstrom, Warren O. (1982) 'Gift Giving as an Organising Principle in Science', in B. Barnes and D. Edge (eds), *Science in Context: Readings in the Sociology of Science* (Buckingham, Bucks.: Open University Press): 21–34.

Healy, David (1997) *The Antidepressant Era* (Cambridge, MA and London: Harvard University Press).

Healy, David (2001) 'Have Drug Companies Hyped Social Anxiety Disorder to Increase Sales? Yes: Marketing Hinders Discovery of Long-Term Solutions', *Western Journal of Medicine* 175: 364.

Hitt, Jack (2000) 'The Second Sexual Revolution', *The New York Times* (20 February): 34–37.

Hogle, Linda F. (2002) 'Claims and Disclaimers: Whose Expertise Counts?', *Medical Anthropology* 21: 275–306.

Hogshire, Jim (1999) *Pills-a-Go-Go: A Fiendish Investigation into Pill Marketing, Art, History, and Consumption* (Venice, CA: Feral House).

Horowitz, Roger & Arwen Mohun (eds) (1998) *His and Hers: Gender, Consumption, and Technology* (Charlottesville, VA, & London: University Press of Virginia).

Hubbard, William K. (1994) 'Citizen Petition Regarding the Food and Drug Administration's Policy on Promotion of Unapproved Uses of Approved Drugs and Devices; Request for Comments' (Washington, DC: Department of Health and Human Services).

King, Nicholas B. (2001) *Infectious Disease in a World of Goods*. PhD Thesis, Harvard University.

Klasen, Henrikje (2000) 'A Name, What's in a Name? The Medicalization of Hyperactivity, Revisited', *Harvard Review of Psychiatry* 7(6): 334–44.

Klinenberg, Eric Martin (2000) *Dying Alone: A Social Autopsy of the 1995 Chicago Heat Wave*. PhD Thesis, University of California, Berkeley.

Kohler, Robert E. (1999) 'Moral Economy, Material Culture, and Community in *Drosophilia* Genetics', in M. Biagioli (ed), *The Science Studies Reader* (New York & London: Routledge): 243–57.

Kowalczyk, Liz (2003) 'Hospital, Drug Firm Relations Probed', *The Boston Globe* (29 June): 1.

Kramer, Peter (1993) *Listening to Prozac* (New York: Viking).

Lakoff, Andrew (2000) 'Adaptive Will: The Evolution of Attention Deficit Disorder', *Journal of the History of the Behavioral Sciences* 36(2): 149–69.

Latour, Bruno (1988) *The Pasteurization of France* (Cambridge, MA: Harvard University Press).

Laumann, Edward O., Anthony Paik & Raymond C. Rosen (1999) 'Sexual Dysfunction in the United States', *Journal of the American Medical Association* 281(6): 537–44.

Maines, Rachel P. (1999) *The Technology of Orgasm: 'Hysteria', the Vibrator, and Women's Sexual Satisfaction* (Baltimore, MD, & London: Johns Hopkins University Press).

Malone, Ruth, Elizabeth Boyd & Lisa A. Bero (2000) 'Science in the News: Journalists Constructions of Passive Smoking as a Social Problem', *Social Studies of Science* 30(5): 713–35.

Mamo, Laura & Jennifer Fishman (2001) 'Potency in All the Right Places: Viagra as a Technology of the Gendered Body', *Body and Society* 7(4): 13–35.

Merton, Robert K. (1973) 'The Normative Structure of Science', in R.K. Merton, *The Sociology of Science: Theoretical and Empirical Investigations* (Chicago, IL: University of Chicago Press): 267–78.

Moynihan, Ray (2003) 'The Making of a Disease: Female Sexual Dysfunction', *British Medical Journal* 326 (4 January): 45–47.

Nelkin, Dorothy (1987) *Selling Science: How the Press Covers Science and Technology* (New York: W.H. Freeman).

Office of Inspector General (2003) *Compliance Program Guidelines for Pharmaceutical Manufacturers* (Washington, DC: US Department of Health and Human Services): 1–56.

Oudshoorn, Nelly (1999) 'On Masculinities, Technologies and Pain: The Testing of Male Contraceptives in the Clinic and the Media', Science, *Technology and Human Values* 24(2): 265–89.

Pfizer, Inc. (2002) *Annual Report 2001*. Pfizer, Inc.: *<www.pfizer.com/pfizerinc/investing/annual/2001/p2001ar16.html>* (accessed 2 October 2002).

Rabinow, Paul (1996) *Making PCR: A Story of Biotechnology* (Chicago, IL: University of Chicago Press).

Relman, Arnold S. (2001) 'Separating Continuing Medical Education from Pharmaceutical Marketing', *Journal of the American Medical Association* 285(15): 2009–12.

Rose, Nikolas (1996) *Inventing Our Selves: Psychology, Power, and Personhood* (Cambridge & New York: Cambridge University Press).

Rose, Nikolas (1999) *Powers of Freedom: Reframing Political Thought* (New York: Cambridge University Press).

Rose, Nikolas (2001) 'The Politics of Life Itself', *Theory, Culture, and Society* 18: 1–30.

Rosen, Raymond, Gloria Bachmann, Sandra Leiblum & Irwin Goldstein (2002) 'Editors' Introduction', *Fertility and Sterility* 77(4) Suppl.: S2.

Rosin, Hanna (2003) 'The Pink Viagra', *The Washington Post* (18 January): 23.

Schudson, Michael (1995) *The Power of News* (Cambridge, MA: Harvard University Press).

Shifren, Jan L., Glenn D. Braunstein, J.A. Simon, P.R. Casson, J.E. Buster, G.P. Redmond, R.E. Burki, E.S. Ginsburg, Raymond C. Rosen, Sandra R. Leiblum, K.E. Caramelli & N.A. Mazer (2000) 'Transdermal Testosterone Treatment in Women with Impaired Sexual Function after Oophorectomy', *New England Journal of Medicine* 343(10): 682–88.

Smith, Michael L. (1994) 'Recourses of Empire: Landscapes of Progress in Technological America', in L. Marx & M.R. Smith (eds), *Does Technology Drive History? The Dilemma of Technological Determinism* (Cambridge, MA: MIT Press): 37–52.

Strauss, Anselm L. (1978) 'Social Worlds', *Studies in Symbolic Interactionism* 1: 119–28.

Swann, John P. (1988) *Academic Scientists and the Pharmaceutical Industry* (Baltimore, MA, & London: Johns Hopkins University Press).

Tiefer, Leonore (2000) 'Sexology and the Pharmaceutical Industry: The Threat of Co-Optation', *Journal of Sex Research* 37(3): 273–83.

Tiefer, Leonore (2001) 'The Selling of "Female Sexual Dysfunction"', *Journal of Sex and Marital Therapy* 27(5): 625–28.

Tomes, Nancy (2001) 'Merchants of Health: Medicine and Consumer Culture in the United States, 1900–1940', *Journal of American History* 88(2): 519–47.

United States General Accounting Office (2000) *Commercial Activities in Schools* (Washington, DC: United States General Accounting Office): 1–54.

Vos, Rein (1991) *Drugs Looking for Diseases: Innovative Drug Research and the Development of the Beta Blockers and the Calcium Antagonists* (Dordrecht: Kluwer).

Wailoo, Keith (1997) *Drawing Blood: Technology and Disease Identity in Twentieth-Century America* (Baltimore, MA: Johns Hopkins University Press).

Wazana, A. (2000) 'Physicians and the Pharmaceutical Industry: Is a Gift Ever Just a Gift?', *Journal of the American Medical Association* 283: 373–80.

Weber, Max (1946) 'Science as a Vocation', in H. Gerth and C.W. Mills (eds), *From Max Weber* (Oxford: Oxford University Press): 196–244.

Willems, Dick (1998) 'Inhaling Drugs and Making Worlds', in M. Berg and A. Mol (eds), *Differences in Medicine: Unraveling Practices, Techniques, and Bodies* (Durham, NC: Duke University Press): 110–18.

Woolgar, Steve (1991) 'Configuring the User: The Case of Usability Trials', in J. Law (ed.), *A Sociology of Monsters: Essays on Power, Technology, and Domination* (New York: Routledge): 57–101.

Part III

Drugs and the Circulation of Medical Knowledge

The Pharmaceutical Studies Reader, First Edition. Edited by Sergio Sismondo and Jeremy A. Greene.

As pharmaceuticals move through local and global markets, their production, circulation, and consumption are intimately bound up with the production, circulation, and consumption of knowledge claims. Entire markets can be made, and unmade, on the circulation of a new piece of information related to the safety or efficacy of a given product. The chapters of this section each attends to different nodes in the circulation of pharmaceutical knowledge. Adriane Fugh-Berman, a former family practice physician, and Shahram Ahari, a former pharmaceutical sales representative, describe in Chapter 8 several strategies used by pharmaceutical sales representatives to affect physicians' prescribing decisions. Their account of the role of person-to-person salesmanship in the circulation of pharmaceutical knowledge emphasizes the role of physician profiling and market research to target specific sales messages to specific kinds of prescribers. Pharmaceutical companies put considerable effort into creating knowledge about physicians and patients as well as drugs and diseases. The result looks a little like a game of strategy in which the sales representatives see one move further than the doctors, and even doctors' efforts to remain uninfluenced simply lead to different sales maneuvers.

The marketing that anthropologist Kalman Applbaum and philosopher Sergio Sismondo describe in Chapters 9 and 10 (as well as Chapters 3 and 7 by Joseph Dumit and Jennifer Fishman, respectively) explicitly concerns knowledge production and circulation. Applbaum, drawing on internal documents from Eli Lilly's campaign for its antipsychotic drug Zyprexa, shows how the company created opportunities by developing lateral forms of evidence around original FDA approval for schizophrenia and convincing doctors that the drug could also treat a "growth market" of bipolar disease—if physicians were willing to reclassify some types of patients as bipolar rather than depressive. The result was an integrated plan for promoting the drug, depending on making different convincing arguments to various different actors, and aligning them all in a single channel. Sismondo's chapter focuses on the publication of medical journal articles. Drug companies produce and sponsor a considerable amount of medical research, and publication of this research presents opportunities to make an impact that is simultaneously scientific and marketing, feeding into the strategies described by Fugh-Berman and Ahari, on the one hand, and Applbaum, on the other. Sismondo draws on his attendance of meetings of "publication planners," who hire ghostwriters to create successive drafts of manuscripts, find medical researchers and doctors to serve as authors, and shepherd the manuscripts to publication.

In Chapter 11, Jongyoung Kim charts an alternate geography of pharmaceutical knowledge production and circulation that focuses on cultural translation. Kim tells the story of recent efforts to make traditional Korean medicine more globally accessible by translating it into a set of pharmaceutical or essentially pharmaceutical products. This particular translation is based in a supposedly hybrid science that produces products that are simultaneously biomedical and recognizable as part of traditional Korean medicine. This hybridity provides a novel basis for expansion into new markets, especially in the United States.

8

Following the Script: How Drug Reps Make Friends and Influence Doctors

Adriane Fugh-Berman and Shahram Ahari

Pharmaceutical companies spend billions of dollars annually to ensure that physicians most susceptible to marketing prescribe the most expensive, most promoted drugs to the most people possible. The foundation of this influence is a sales force of drug reps that provides rationed doses of samples, gifts, services, and flattery to a subset of physicians. In this chapter, a former pharmaceutical sales representative (SA) and a physician who researches pharmaceutical marketing (AFB) explore the strategies used by reps to manipulate physician prescribing. In particular, they describe how doctors are classified and then matched up with appropriate sales strategies.

It's my job to figure out what a physician's price is. For some it's dinner at the finest restaurants, for others it's enough convincing data to let them prescribe confidently and for others it's my attention and friendship ... but at the most basic level, everything is for sale and everything is an exchange.

—Shahram Ahari

You are absolutely buying love.

—James Reidy [1]

In 2000, pharmaceutical companies spent more than 15.7 billion dollars on promoting prescription drugs in the United States [2]. More than 4.8 billion dollars was spent on detailing, the one-on-one promotion of drugs to doctors by pharmaceutical sales representatives,

Adriane Fugh-Berman and Shahram Ahari, "Following the Script: How Drug Reps Make Friends and Influence Doctors," PLoS Med 4(4): e150. doi:10.1371/journal.pmed.0040151.

The Pharmaceutical Studies Reader, First Edition. Edited by Sergio Sismondo and Jeremy A. Greene.

commonly called drug reps. The average sales force expenditure for pharmaceutical companies is $875 million annually [3].

Unlike the door-to-door vendors of cosmetics and vacuum cleaners, drug reps do not sell their product directly to buyers. Consumers pay for prescription drugs, but physicians control access. Drug reps increase drug sales by influencing physicians, and they do so with finely titrated doses of friendship. This article, which grew out of conversations between a former drug rep (SA) and a physician who researches pharmaceutical marketing (AFB), reveals the strategies used by reps to manipulate physician prescribing.

Better than You Know Yourself

> *During training, I was told, when you're out to dinner with a doctor, "The physician is eating with a friend. You are eating with a client."*
>
> —*Shahram Ahari*

Reps may be genuinely friendly, but they are not genuine friends. Drug reps are selected for their presentability and outgoing natures, and are trained to be observant, personable, and helpful. They are also trained to assess physicians' personalities, practice styles, and preferences, and to relay this information back to the company. Personal information may be more important than prescribing preferences. Reps ask for and remember details about a physician's family life, professional interests, and recreational pursuits. A photo on a desk presents an opportunity to inquire about family members and memorize whatever tidbits are offered (including names, birthdays, and interests); these are usually typed into a database after the encounter. Reps scour a doctor's office for objects—a tennis racquet, Russian novels, seventies rock music, fashion magazines, travel mementos, or cultural or religious symbols—that can be used to establish a personal connection with the doctor.

Good details are dynamic; the best reps tailor their messages constantly according to their client's reaction. A friendly physician makes the rep's job easy, because the rep can use the "friendship" to request favors, in the form of prescriptions. Physicians who view the relationship as a straightforward goods-for-prescriptions exchange are dealt with in a businesslike manner. Skeptical doctors who favor evidence over charm are approached respectfully, supplied with reprints from the medical literature, and wooed as teachers. Physicians who refuse to see reps are detailed by proxy; their staff is dined and flattered in hopes that they will act as emissaries for a rep's messages. (See Table 8.1 for specific tactics used to manipulate physicians.)

Gifts create both expectation and obligation. "The importance of developing loyalty through gifting cannot be overstated," writes Michael Oldani, an anthropologist and former drug rep [4]. Pharmaceutical gifting, however, involves carefully calibrated generosity. Many prescribers receive pens, notepads, and coffee mugs, all items kept close at hand, ensuring that a targeted drug's name stays uppermost in a physician's subconscious mind. High prescribers receive higher-end presents, for example, silk ties or golf bags. As Oldani states, "The essence of pharmaceutical gifting ... is 'bribes that aren't considered bribes'" [1].

Reps also recruit and audition "thought leaders" (physicians respected by their peers) to groom for the speaking circuit. Physicians invited and paid by a rep to speak to their peers may express their gratitude in increased prescriptions (see Table 8.1). Anything that improves the relationship between the rep and the client usually leads to improved market share.

Table 8.1 Tactics for Manipulating Physicians

Physician Category	Technique	How It Sells Drugs	Comments
Friendly and outgoing	I frame everything as a gesture of friendship. I give them free samples not because it's my job, but because I like them so much. I provide office lunches because visiting them is such a pleasant relief from all the other docs. My drugs rarely get mentioned by me during our dinners.	Just being friends with most of my docs seemed to have some natural basic effect on their prescribing habits. When the time is ripe, I lean on my "friendship" to leverage more patients to my drugs… say, because it'll help me meet quota or it will impress my manager, or it's crucial for my career.	Outgoing, friendly physicians are every rep's favorite because cultivating friendship is a mutual aim. While this may be genuine behavior on the doctor's side, it is usually calculated on the part of the rep.
Aloof and skeptical	I visit the office with journal articles that specifically counter the doctor's perceptions of the shortcoming of my drug. Armed with the articles and having hopefully scheduled a 20 minute appointment (so the doc can't escape), I play dumb and have the doc explain to me the significance of my article.	The only thing that remains is for me to be just aggressive enough to ask the doc to try my drug in situations that wouldn't have been considered before, based on the physician's own explanation.	Humility is a common approach to physicians who pride themselves on practicing evidence-based medicine. These docs are tough to persuade but not impossible. Typically, attempts at geniality are only marginally effective.
Mercenary	The best mercenary docs are typically found further down the prescribing power scale. There are plenty of 6's, 7's, and 8's [lower prescribing doctors] who are eagerly mercenary but simply don't have the attention they desire fawned on them. I pick a handful out and make them feel special enough with an eye towards the projected demand on my limited resources in mind. Basically, the common motif to docs whom you want to "buy out" is to closely associate your resource expenditure with an expectation—e.g., "So, doc, you'll choose Drug X for the next 5 patients who are depressed and with low energy? Oh, and don't forget dinner at Nobu next month. I'd love to meet your wife."	This is the closest drug-repping comes to a commercial exchange. Delivering such closely associated messages crudely would be deemed insulting for most docs so a rep really has to feel comfortable about their mercenary nature and have a natural tone when making such suggestions.	Drug reps usually feel more camaraderie with competing reps than they do with their clients. Thus, when a doctor fails to fulfill their end of the prescriptions-for-dinners bargain, news gets around and other reps are less likely to invest resources in them.

(*Continued*)

Table 8.1 (*cont'd*)

Physician Category	Technique	How It Sells Drugs	Comments
High-prescribers	I rely on making a strong personal connection to those docs, something to make me stand out from the crowd.	Friendship sells. The highest prescribers (9's and 10's) are every rep's sugar mommies and daddies. It's the equivalent of spitting in the ocean to try to buy these docs out because, chances are, every other rep is falling head over heels to do so.	The highest prescribers receive better presents. Some reps said their 10's might receive unrestricted "educational" grants so loosely restricted that they were the equivalent of a cash gift, although I did not personally provide any grants.
Prefers a competing drug	The first thing I want to understand is why they're using another drug as opposed to mine. If it's a question of attention, then I commit myself to lavishing them with it until they're bought. If they are convinced that the competitor drug works better in some patient populations, I frame my drug to either capture another market niche or, if I feel my drug would fare well in a comparison, I hammer its superiority over the competing drug.	If, during the course of conversations, the doctors say something that may contradict their limited usage of our products, then the reps will badger them to justify that contradiction. This quickly transforms the rep from a welcomed reprieve to a nuisance, which can be useful in limited circumstances. We force the doctors to constantly explain their prescribing rationale, which is tiresome. Our intent is to engage in discourse but also to wear down the doc until he or she simply agrees to try the product for specific instances (we almost always argue for a specific patient profile for our drugs).	For reps this is a core function of our job. We're trained to do this in as benign a way as possible. No doc likes to be told their judgment is wrong so the latter method typically requires some discretion.
Acquiescent docs	Most docs think that if they simply agree with what the rep says, they'll outsmart the rep by avoiding any conflict or commitment, getting the samples and gifts they want, and finishing the encounter quickly. Nothing could be further from the truth. The old adage is true, especially in pharmaceutical sales: there is no such thing as a free lunch.	From the outset of my training, I've been taught to frame every conversation to ultimately derive commitments from my clients. With every acquiescent nod to statements of my drug's superiority I build the case for them to increase their usage of my product. They may offer me false promises but I'll know when they're lying: the prescribing data is sufficiently detailed in my computer to confirm their behavior. Doctors who fail to honor their commitments, no matter how casually made, convert the rep into a badgering nuisance. The docs are often corralled into a conversational corner where they have to justify their previous acquiescence.	Gifts are used to enhance guilt and social pressure. Reps know that gifts create a subconscious obligation to reciprocate. New reps who doubt this phenomenon need only see their doctors' prescribing data trending upwards to be convinced. Of course, most of these doctors think themselves immune to such influence. This is an illusion reps try to maintain.

No-see/ No-time (hard-to-see docs)	Occasionally docs refuse to see reps. Some do it for ethical reasons, but most simply lack the time. Even when I don't manage to see the doctor, I can still make a successful call by detailing the staff. Although they're on the doc's side for the most part, it's amazing how much trouble one can rile up when the staff are lavished with food and gifts during a credible sounding presentation and then asked to discuss the usage of a drug on their patients.	It's a victory for me just to learn from the staff about which drugs are preferred, and why. That info provides powerful ammunition to debate the docs with on the rare occasions that I might see them. However, it's a greater success when the staff discusses my meds with the doc after I leave. Because while a message delivered by a rep gets discounted, a detail delivered by a co-worker slips undetected and unfiltered under the guise of a conversation. And the response is usually better then what I might accomplish.	One's marketing success in a particular office can be strongly correlated to one's success in providing good food for the staff. Goodwill from the staff provides me with critical information, access, and an advocate for me and my drug when I'm not there.
Thought leaders	As a rep, I was always in pursuit of friendly "thought leaders" to groom for the speaking circuit. Once selected, a physician would give lectures around the district. I would carefully watch for tell-tale signs of their allegiance. This includes how they handled questions that criticized our product, how their prescribing habits fluctuated, or simply how eager they were to give their next lecture.	The main target of these gatherings is the speaker, whose appreciation may be reflected in increased prescribing of a company's products. Local speaking gigs are also auditions. Speakers with charisma, credentials, and an aura of integrity were elevated to the national circuit and, occasionally, given satellite telecast programs that offered CMEs.	Subtle and tactful spokespersons were the ideal candidates. I politely dismissed doctors who would play cheerleader for any drug … at the right price, of course.

These descriptions are based on SA's experience working for Eli Lilly and testimony in IMS Heath Inc. v. Ayotte, US District Court, New Hampshire. Actual tactics may vary. doi:10.1371/journal.pmed.0040150.t001

Script Tracking

An official job description for a pharmaceutical sales rep would read: Provide health-care professionals with product information, answer their questions on the use of products, and deliver product samples. An unofficial, and more accurate, description would have been: Change the prescribing habits of physicians.

—*James Reidy* [5]

Pharmaceutical companies monitor the return on investment of detailing—and all promotional efforts—by prescription tracking. Information distribution companies, also called health information organizations (including IMS Health, Dendrite, Verispan, and Wolters Kluwer), purchase prescription records from pharmacies. The majority of pharmacies sell these records; IMS Health, the largest information distribution company, procures records on about 70% of prescriptions filled in community pharmacies. Patient names are not included, and physicians may be identified only by state license number, Drug Enforcement Administration number, or a pharmacy-specific identifier [6]. Data that identify physicians only by numbers are linked to physician names through licensing agreements with the American Medical Association (AMA), which maintains the Physician Masterfile, a database containing demographic information on all US. physicians (living or dead, member or non-member, licensed or non-licensed). In 2005, database product sales, including an unknown amount from licensing Masterfile information, provided more than $44 million to the AMA [5].

Pharmaceutical companies are the primary customers for prescribing data, which are used both to identify "high-prescribers" and to track the effects of promotion. Physicians are ranked on a scale from one to ten based on how many prescriptions they write. Reps lavish high-prescribers with attention, gifts, and unrestricted "educational" grants (Table 8.1). Cardiologists and other specialists write relatively few prescriptions, but are targeted because specialist prescriptions are perpetuated for years by primary care physicians, thus affecting market share.

Reps use prescribing data to see how many of a physician's patients receive specific drugs, how many prescriptions the physician writes for targeted and competing drugs, and how a physician's prescribing habits change over time. One training guide states that an "individual market share report for each physician... pinpoints a prescriber's current habits" and is "used to identify which products are currently in favor with the physician in order to develop a strategy to change those prescriptions into Merck prescriptions" [7].

A *Pharmaceutical Executive* article states, "A physician's prescribing value is a function of the opportunity to prescribe, plus his or her attitude toward prescribing, along with outside influences. By building these multiple dimensions into physicians' profiles, it is possible to understand the 'why' behind the 'what' and 'how' of their behavior." [8] To this end, some companies combine data sources. For example, Medical Marketing Service "enhances the AMA Masterfile with non-AMA data from a variety of sources to not only include demographic selections, but also behavioral and psychographic selections that help you to better target your perfect prospects" [9].

The goal of this demographic slicing and dicing is to identify physicians who are most susceptible to marketing efforts. One industry article suggests categorizing physicians as "hidden gems": "Initially considered 'low value' because they are low prescribers, these physicians can change their prescribing habits after targeted, effective marketing." "Growers" are "Physicians who are early adopters of a brand. Pharmaceutical companies employ retention strategies to continue to reinforce their growth behavior." Physicians are considered "low value" "due to low category share and prescribing level" [10].

In an interview with *Pharmaceutical Representative*, Fred Marshall, president of Quantum Learning, explained, "One type might be called 'the spreader' who uses a little bit of everybody's product. The second type might be a 'loyalist', who's very loyal to one particular product and uses it for most patient types. Another physician might be a 'niche' physician, who reserves our product only for a very narrowly defined patient type. And the idea in physician segmentation would be to have a different messaging strategy for each of those physician segments " [11].

In *Pharmaceutical Executive*, Ron Brand of IMS Consulting writes "... integrated segmentation analyzes individual prescribing behaviors, demographics, and psychographics (attitudes, beliefs, and values) to fine-tune sales targets. For a particular product, for example, one segment might consist of price-sensitive physicians, another might include doctors loyal to a given manufacturers brand, and a third may include those unfriendly towards reps" [12].

In recent years, physicians have become aware of—and dismayed by—script tracking. In July 2006, the AMA launched the Prescribing Data Restriction Program (see http://www.ama-assn.org/ama/pub/category/12054.html), which allows physicians the opportunity to withhold most prescribing information from reps and their supervisors (anyone above that level, however, has full access to all data). According to an article in *Pharmaceutical Executive*, "Reps and direct managers can view the physician's prescribing volume quantiled at the therapeutic class level" and can still view aggregated or segmented data including "categories into which the prescriber falls, such as an early-adopter of drugs, for example ...."[13]. The pharmaceutical industry supports the Prescribing Data Restriction Program, which is seen as a less onerous alternative to, for example, state legislation passed in New Hampshire forbidding the sale of prescription data to commercial entities [14].

The Value of Samples

The purpose of supplying drug samples is to gain entry into doctors' offices, and to habituate physicians to prescribing targeted drugs. Physicians appreciate samples, which can be used to start therapy immediately, test tolerance to a new drug, or reduce the total cost of a prescription. Even physicians who refuse to see drug reps usually want samples (these docs are denigrated as "sample-grabbers"). Patients like samples too; it's nice to get a little present from the doctor. Samples also double as unacknowledged gifts to physicians and their staff. The convenience of an in-house pharmacy increases loyalty to both the reps and the drugs they represent.

Some physicians use samples to provide drugs to indigent patients [15,16]. Using samples for an entire course of treatment is anathema to pharmaceutical companies because this "cannibalizes" sales. Among the aims of one industry sample-tracking program are to "reallocate samples to high-opportunity prescribers most receptive to sampling as a promotional vehicle" and "identify prescribers who were oversampled and take corrective action immediately" [17].

Studies consistently show that samples influence prescribing choices [15,16,18]. Reps provide samples only of the most promoted, usually most expensive, drugs, and patients given a sample for part of a course of treatment almost always receive a prescription for the same drug.

Funding Friendship

While it's the doctors' job to treat patients and not to justify their actions, it's my job to constantly sway the doctors. It's a job I'm paid and trained to do. Doctors are neither trained nor paid to negotiate. Most of the time they don't even realize that's what they're doing...

—Shahram Ahari

Drug costs now account for 10.7% of health-care expenditures in the US [19]. In 2004, spending for prescription drugs was $188.5 billion, almost five times as much as what was spent in 1990 [20]. Between 1995 and 2005, the number of drug reps in the US increased from 38,000 to 100,000 [21], about one for every six physicians. The actual ratio is close to one drug rep per 2.5 targeted doctors [22], because not all physicians practice, and not all practicing physicians are detailed. Low-prescribers are ignored by drug reps.

Physicians view drug information provided by reps as a convenient, if not entirely reliable, educational service. An industry survey found that more than half of "high-prescribing" doctors cited drug reps as their main source of information about new drugs [23]. In another study, three quarters of 2,608 practicing physicians found information provided by reps "very useful" (15%) or "somewhat useful" (59%) [24]. However, only 9% agreed that the information was "very accurate"; 72% thought the information was "somewhat accurate"; and 14% said that it was "not very" or "not at all" accurate.

Whether or not physicians believe in the accuracy of information provided, detailing is extremely effective at changing prescribing behavior, which is why it is worth its substantial expense. The average annual income for a drug rep is $81,700, which includes $62,400 in base salary plus $19,300 in bonuses. The average cost of recruiting, hiring, and training a new rep is estimated to be $89,000 [25]. When expenses are added to income and training, pharmaceutical companies spend $150,000 annually per primary care sales representative and $330,000 per specialty sales representative [25]. An industry article states, "The pharmaceutical industry averages $31.9 million in annual sales spending per primary-care drug.... Sales spending for specialty drugs that treat a narrowed population segment average $25.3 million per product across the industry" [26].

Conclusion

As one of us (SA) explained in testimony in the litigation over New Hampshire's new ban on the commercial sale of prescription data, the concept that reps provide necessary services to physicians and patients is a fiction. Pharmaceutical companies spend billions of dollars annually to ensure that physicians most susceptible to marketing prescribe the most expensive, most promoted drugs to the most people possible. The foundation of this influence is a sales force of 100,000 drug reps that provides rationed doses of samples, gifts, services, and flattery to a subset of physicians. If detailing were an educational service, it would be provided to all physicians, not just those who affect market share.

Physicians are susceptible to corporate influence because they are overworked, overwhelmed with information and paperwork, and feel underappreciated. Cheerful and charming, bearing food and gifts, drug reps provide respite and sympathy; they appreciate how hard doctor's lives are, and seem only to want to ease their burdens. But, as SA's New Hampshire testimony reflects, every word, every courtesy, every gift, and every piece of information provided is carefully crafted, not to assist doctors or patients, but to increase market share for targeted drugs (see Table 8.1). In the interests of patients, physicians must reject the false friendship provided by reps. Physicians must rely on information on drugs from unconflicted sources, and seek friends among those who are not paid to be friends.

REFERENCES

1. Elliott C (2006) The drug pushers. Atlantic Monthly (April): 2–13.
2. Rosenthal MB, Berndt ER, Donohue JM, Epstein AM, Frank RG (2003) Demand effects of recent changes in prescription drug promotion. Henry J Kaiser Family Foundation. Available: http://www.kff.org/rxdrugs/6085-index.cfm. Accessed 23 March 2007.
3. Niles S (2005) Sales force effectiveness (the third in a series of articles that examine problems and solutions of detailing to physicians). Med Ad News 24: 1.
4. Oldani MJ (2004) Thick prescriptions: Toward an interpretation of pharmaceutical sales practices. Med Anthropol Q 18: 328–356.
5. Reidy J (2005) Hard sell: The evolution of a Viagra salesman. Kansas City: Andrews McMeel Publishing. 210 p.
6. Steinbrook R (2006) For sale: Physicians' prescribing data. New Engl J Med 354: 2745–2747.
7. Merck (2002) Basic training participant guide. Available: http://oversight.house.gov/features/vioxx/documents.asp. Accessed 23 March 2007.
8. Nickum C, Kelly T (2005) Missing the mark(et). Pharmaceutical Executive. Available: http://www.pharmexec.com/pharmexec/article/articleDetail.jsp?id = 177968. Accessed 23 March 2007.
9. Medical Marketing Services (2007) American Medical Association list. Available: http://www.mmslists.com/category_drilldown.asp?nav = category&headingID = 1&itemID = 1. Accessed 23 March 2007.
10. Hogg JJ (2006) Marketing to professionals: Diagnosing MD behavior. Pharmaceutical Executive: 168. Available: http://www.pharmexec.com/pharmexec/article/articleDetail.jsp?id = 162039. Accessed 23 March 2007.
11. Hradecky G (2004) Breaking point. Pharmaceutical Representative. Available: http://www.pharmrep.com/pharmrep/article/articleDetail.jsp?id=102324. Accessed 23 March 2007.
12. Brand R, Kumar P (2003) Detailing gets personal: Integrated segmentation may be pharma's key to "repersonalizing" the selling process. Pharmaceutical Executive. Available: http://www.pharmexec.com/pharmexec/article/articleDetail.jsp?id = 64071. Accessed 23 March 2007.
13. Alonso J, Menzies D (2006) Just what the doctor ordered. Pharmaceutical Executive: 14–16. Available: http://www.pharmexec.com/pharmexec/article/articleDetail.jsp?id = 323314. Accessed 23 March 2007.
14. Remus PC (2006 November 10) First-in-the-nation law pits NH against drug industry. New Hampshire Business Review. Available: http://www.nh.com/apps/pbcs.dll/article?AID=/20061110/BUSINESSREVIEW05/61108030/1/BUSINESSREVIEW. Accessed 23 March 2007.
15. Chew LD, O'Young TS, Hazlet TK, Bradley KA, Maynard C,et al. (2000) A physician survey of the effect of drug sample availability on physicians' behavior. J Gen Intern Med 15: 478–483.
16. Groves KEM, Sketris I, Tett SE (2003) Prescription drug samples—Does this marketing strategy counteract policies for quality use of medicines? J Clin Pharm Ther 28: 259–271.
17. Sadek H, Henderson Z (2004) It's all in the details: Delivering the right information to the right rep at the right time can greatly increase sales force effectiveness. Pharmaceutical Executive. Available: http://www.pharmexec.com/pharmexec/article/articleDetail.jsp?id = 129291. Accessed 23 March 2007.
18. Adair RF, Holmgren LR (2005) Do drug samples influence resident prescribing behavior? A randomized controlled trial. Am J Med 118: 881–884.
19. United States Government Accountability Office (2006) Prescription drugs: Price trends for frequently used brand and generic drugs from 2000 through 2004. Available: http://www.gao.gov/new.items/d05779.pdf. Accessed 23 March 2007.
20. Kaiser Family Foundation (2006a) Prescription drug trends. Available: http://www.kff.org/rxdrugs/3057.cfm. Accessed 23 March 2007.

21. Marshall PC (2005) Rep tide: Pulling back in magnitude, pushing forward efficiency: Recent talk of pharma companies restructuring or even paring back their sales forces is the first acknowledgement that efficiency, and not noise, is the key to effective detailing. Med Market Media 40: 96.
22. Goldberg M, Davenport B, Mortellito T (2004) PE's annual sales and marketing employment survey: The big squeeze. Pharmaceutical Executive 24: 40–45. Available: http://www.pharmexec.com/pharmexec/article/articleDetail.jsp?id = 80921. Accessed 23 March 2007.
23. Millenson ML (2003) Getting doctors to say yes to drugs: The cost and quality of impact of drug company marketing to physicians. Blue Cross Blue Shield Association. Available: http://www.bcbs.com/betterknowledge/cost/getting-doctors-to-say-yes.html. Accessed 23 March 2007.
24. Kaiser Family Foundation (2006b) National survey of physicians. Available: http://www.kff.org/rxdrugs/upload/3057-05.pdf. Accessed 23 March 2007.
25. Goldberg M, Davenport B (2005) In sales we trust. Pharmaceutical Executive. Available: www.pharmexec.com/pharmexec/article/articleDetail.jsp?id = 146596. Accessed 23 March 2007.
26. [No authors listed] (2004) Hard sell: As expanding the sales force becomes a less attractive option, pharmaceutical companies are reevaluating their sales strategies. Med Ad News 23: 1.

Funding: This work was supported by a grant from the Attorney General Prescriber and Consumer Education Grant Program, created as part of a 2004 settlement between Warner-Lambert, a division of Pfizer, and the Attorneys General of 50 States and the District of Columbia, to settle allegations that Warner-Lambert conducted an unlawful marketing campaign for the drug Neurontin (gabapentin) that violated state consumer protection laws.

Competing Interests: Shahram Ahari is a former pharmaceutical sales representative for Eli Lilly, and the primary findings of this paper summarize points he made in testimony as a paid expert witness on the defendant's side in litigation against a New Hampshire law prohibiting the sale of prescription data. Adriane Fugh-Berman has accepted payment as an expert witness on the plaintiff's side in litigation regarding menopausal hormone therapy.

9

Getting to Yes: Corporate Power and the Creation of a Psychopharmaceutical Blockbuster

Kalman Applbaum

This paper analyzes documentary evidence from a pharmaceutical company's strategic marketing campaign to expand the sale of an antipsychotic medication beyond its conventional market. It focuses on the role of the managerial function known as channel marketing, the task of which is to minimize friction, achieve coordination and add value in the distribution of the company's products. However, the path to achieving these objectives is challenged because members of the marketing channel, or intermediaries, may not be contractual members of the channel; in fact they may have widely divergent goals or may even be hostile to the manufacturer's efforts at control. This can be construed to be the case for physicians and others who are in the pharmaceutical manufacturer's distribution channel but not of it. Their views and actions must somehow be brought into alignment with the manufacturer's goals. This paper seeks to show part of the process from the manufacturer's strategic standpoint, in which potential dissenters are incorporated into the pharmaceutical company distribution channel. The routinization of this incorporation results in the diminishment of psychiatry's professional autonomy by means of what is—paradoxically to them, but not to a student of marketing—a competitive threat. The paper concludes with a discussion of corporate power.

The greatest of human powers is that which is compounded of the powers of most men, united by consent, in one person, natural or civil, that has the use of all their powers depending on his will; such is the power of a Commonwealth.

—*Thomas Hobbes (1998:Chap. X)*

Kalman Applbaum, "Getting to Yes: Corporate Power and the Creation of a Psychopharmaceutical Blockbuster," Culture, Medicine, and Psychiatry 33 (2009). pp. 185–215. Reproduced with permission from Springer Science+Business Media.

The Pharmaceutical Studies Reader, First Edition. Edited by Sergio Sismondo and Jeremy A. Greene.

> *How, then, can a 'channel captain' implement the optimal channel design in the face of interdependence among channel partners, not all of whom have the incentive to cooperate in the performance of their designated channel flows? The answer lies in the possession and use of channel power.*
>
> —*Coughlan and Stern (2001:259)*

As the normative framework for how people interface with health-care services has shifted from that of patient to that of consumer, the agency of each member of the chain from pharmaceutical/insurer/health industry actors to health-care givers and then to individual recipients of service has been transformed. For the pharmaceutical industry, the consumer paradigm for health-care utilization authorizes an unambiguous call to action: consumers have unmet needs to be determined by (and sold to by) means of the tools of marketing. How marketers discover "unmet needs" that they subsequently "sell to" consumers is an intricate procedure that will be partly evinced in the case material below (see Applbaum (2003) and Healy (2008) for more inclusive discussions).

We can begin with a more basic challenge facing prescription pharmaceutical marketers, namely, "Who is the consumer?" This question is less straightforward than it might seem. Before one can reach the end user of a drug, one must penetrate a mesh of other choice-makers. These typically include prescribing physicians, hospitals, payers (insurers, Medicare/Medicaid, private prescription benefit providers, etc.), pharmacists and, in some cases, those who surround and influence the end user, such as case workers and family members. An article in the *Market Leader* explains:

> The customer landscape for pharmaceutical companies is complex. Consider how medication is prescribed. Unlike most markets where consumers make their own brand choice and purchase decision, patients (end-consumers) pass their brand choice to a qualified healthcare professional, who diagnoses the condition and writes a prescription for a drug. The act of handing over the decision to external parties (co-dependent choice) is a defining characteristic of the pharmaceutical industry .... In the pharmaceutical industry, there is still further complexity. A doctor's choice of medication depends not only on his or her knowledge of the range of available treatments, but also on prescription guidelines developed by the healthcare authorities. These guidelines shortlist recommended drugs suitable for treatment of conditions and are aimed at controlling the cost of healthcare. (Cleland et al. 2004:51)

As we will see, the above list of "codependent choice makers" are marketed to *as* consumers, with all that implies in terms of sales and marketing practices. However, insofar as all these are conduits to the end user, their roles must equally be described as intermediaries or, in marketing terms, "members of the distribution channel" for the product. If marketers typically seek to persuade consumers with communicational instruments such as brands, advertisements and sales pitches, distribution channel members are subject to the exercise of what marketing theorists call "channel power." This power may be friendly, consisting of incentives and emoluments to trade. However, in the case of pharmaceutical channels, the power exercised is more often agonistic, even while it is never "hard" or threatening.

The inevitability of this logic can be understood from the context of pharmaceutical distribution itself. In most industries, distribution channel members are contractual partners in the trade. In the case of prescription pharmaceuticals, physicians, payers, etc., may be unavoidable members in the distribution channel between the manufacturer and the end user, but they are mostly not contractual members *of* the channel. Indeed, these actors may have widely divergent stakes and goals or may even be hostile to the manufacturer's efforts at control. Each group of intermediaries has a compelling and distinct investment in organizing its activities in accordance with profession- or group-specific criteria. Management theorists refer to this situation of divergent purposes as "goal conflict." The means to resolving goal conflict, as suggested in the second epigraph above, may be the employment of power, persuasive or coercive, by the "channel captain," which refers simply to the most dominant participant in the chain. The goal is channel coordination, as the same authors specify. "When the disparate members of the channel are brought together to advance the goals of the channel, rather than their own independent (and likely conflicting) goals, the channel is said to be coordinated.... Coordination is the end goal of the entire channel management process" (Coughlan and Stern 2001:261).

While textbook treatments of channel conflict typically stress the pecuniary interests of the various channel members, to be resolved either by financial threat by or mollification ("motivational programs"), the practical requirements of coordination often go much beyond economics. Coordination campaigns often entail bringing the moral and perceptual dimensions of the various actors into alignment. This may be particularly characteristic of international channel marketing because there one encounters what marketers call "cultural obstacles" (Applbaum 2000a). The example I bring here is mainly domestic in the United States, but is still ideal for demonstrating the procedure of seeking moral-cultural alignment so that passage can occur. The cultural obstacle, in this case, is the barrier dividing conventions in medical research and practice with marketing objectives.

In this sense, the combined consumers/intermediaries en route to the end user are, and are perceived to be, *gatekeepers*. The strategic goal becomes how to convert them from potential obstacles to compliant facilitators. The word gatekeeper calls to mind the prospect that it is not just doctors, hospital formulary-makers and insurers who are targets of marketing action, but regulatory agencies such as the FDA, treatment guideline commissions and patient advocacy groups such as NAMI (National Association for the Mentally Ill).

Figure 9.1 shows a network map of "key players" in the U.S. antipsychotic market used by Eli Lilly & Co. in their marketing program for their antipsychotic medication, Zyprexa. The key players map identifies the people who are in or who influence the marketing channel for the drug. Each needs to be influenced and brought into conformity.

The Zyprexa case is typical of contemporary pharmaceutical marketing. I therefore cast my analysis not in terms of violations, but in terms of normative marketing channel management and a cultural theory of corporate power. In the absence of a systematic investigation of pharmaceutical marketing initiatives along commercial and cultural dimensions, we will fail to comprehend contemporary market forces in health care.

I begin by focusing not on the weak or strong impact of marketing, so as to try to measure the power behind its strategies and tactics, but on how the context of its professional practice corresponds to a specific iteration of power. I propose to theorize marketing power as distinct from the coercive or oppositional power that informs most anthropological analyses. The term I use to describe corporate power comes from their own lexicon: synergistic power. Synergy is the means by which firms seek to synthesize "a whole that multiplies the value of the parts" (Kanter 1989).

This paper analyzes the strategies Eli Lilly & Co employed in its highly successful campaign to expand the sale of its antipsychotic medication, Zyprexa, beyond its conventional market and, in so doing, create a pharmaceutical blockbuster. I focus on the movement of an antipsychotic medication as it traverses several intermediaries in a distribution channel, with some emphasis on physicians, whose cooperation is necessary to the circulation of the drugs.

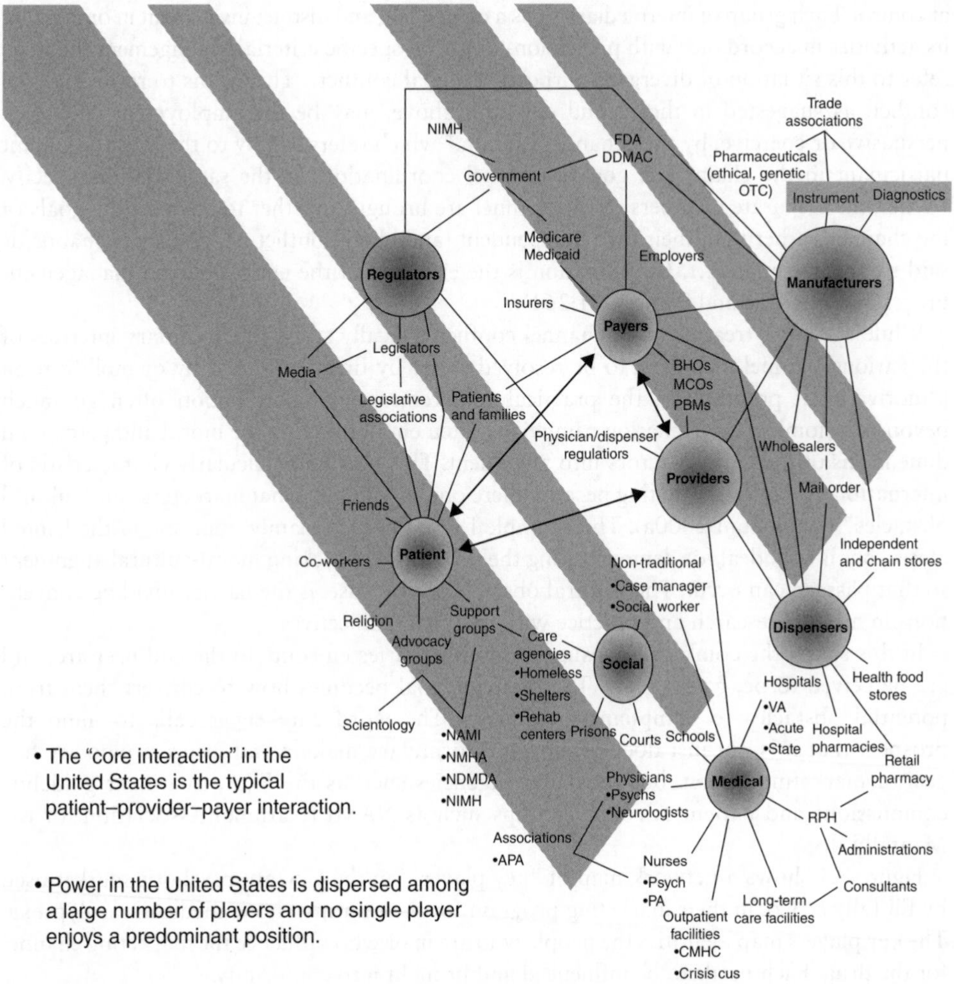

Figure 9.1 Key players in the US antipsychotic marketplace

From Schizophrenia to Complicated Moods: The Evolution of Zyprexa

Zyprexa PCP Vision: Expand our market by redefining how primary care physicians identify, diagnose and treat complicated mood disorders (i.e., Bipolar Disorder).

—*Eli Lilly document*[1]

I open this section with this report because the medication I am about to describe, whose uses have been intentionally "blurred" so as to expand its application as widely as possible into the general population, is Zyprexa (generic olanzapine), an antipsychotic approved in 1996 for treating schizophrenia. The drug belongs to a next-generation class of antipsychotics called "atypicals," which, it was hoped, would be more efficacious than their predecessors and would carry fewer side effects. The short version of the history of the new antipsychotics, according to the results of a $42 million NIMH study involving more than 1400 research subjects, is that they turn out to be rather more typical than atypical. The hope of greater efficacy was not realized, and tolerability improved only slightly with some of the medicines. The side effects of all the medications remain severe (Lieberman et al. 2005).

Several of the atypical antipsychotic manufacturers, including Bristol-Myers Squibb, Pfizer, Janssen, AstraZeneca and Eli Lilly, have been brought up on charges for related violations in the past several years. As regards Eli Lilly and Zyprexa, many of the lawsuits have resulted from corporate cover-ups of the drug's tendency to cause hyperglycemia, weight gain, hypercholesterolemia and other metabolic conditions that can lead to diabetes, stroke and heart disease. Thus far, the company has settled with 28,500 individuals, for an ongoing tally of $1.2 billion (Berenson 2007). Another category of suit successfully brought against Lilly (and other companies) has been for promoting off-label use of the drug (i.e., for conditions or populations other than those for which the drug is approved). Finally, states are suing Lilly in connection with using illegal influence to obtain status for Zyprexa on state hospital formularies. Several workers unions are suing Lilly for its funding of the patient advocacy group NAMI to lobby state and federal governments to increase spending on Zyprexa.[2]

The number of smoking cannons uncovered across the industry suggests not isolated instances of corruption, but a systemically embedded set of practices attributable to the adoption of a marketing-driven protocol for developing and purveying the drugs. Among the evidentiary documents used in the Zyprexa litigations are dozens that reveal the marketing process in naked detail. For want of space, I select only a few key practices, with the aim of abstracting some general principles of practice.

Disease state prioritization

Shortly after Zyprexa was approved for use in schizophrenia in 1997, a strategy document was prepared at Lilly to consider future priorities for the drug. The "strategic intent" was declared as follows: "Zyprexa will be the world's number one neuroscience pharmaceutical in history."[3] The document material warned, "The ability of Eli Lilly to remain independent [i.e., and not be bought out by another company in a consolidating industry] and emerge as the fastest growing pharma company of the decade depends solely on our ability to achieve *world class commercialization of Zyprexa*" (original emphasis). This early plan was dominated by the goal to "prioritize disease state opportunities to pursue new indications based on prevalence of the disorder, unmet medical need and probability of technical success (market opportunity)." This disease state focus would maximize the product life cycle value because, with each new approved indication, the drug's patent would be extended.

In one exhibit, priority disease states were sorted into four columns. The first, labeled "highest priority," listed bipolar disorder, dementia with psychosis, depression with psychotic features, dysthmia, personality disorder with treatment associated psychosis, schizoaffective, schizophrenia and unipolar depression. Column two, labeled "second priority," listed substance-related disorders, anxiety disorders, borderline/schizotypal personality disorders, aggression, anorexia, delirium with psychotic features, psychotic disorders of low prevalence and schizophreniform. The origin of these diagnostic terms is the DSM-IV.

The first step for expanding the use of Zyprexa was to obtain scientific evidence. In a slide entitled, "Venture Team: Generate the New Data Required to Grow," various trial protocols and their descriptions were listed. The basic idea was to test the efficacy of Zyprexa against any condition of psychosis, but also to test it for the vaguely contiguous illness domains of dementia, autism and Parkinson's disease. The trial-everything approach to drug discovery is meant to capitalize on comorbidities. The mechanism of action for virtually every aspect of these drugs is poorly understood: in which case, the best product strategy is to throw as much mud as possible at the wall and see what sticks.

The use of Zyprexa for bipolar disorder was the first and most successful exploit of the disease-state expansion strategy. Unlike schizophrenia, which has an invariable incidence of about 1% in the population, diagnoses of bipolar disorder, newly renamed from manic-depression, were growing by leaps and bounds, in no small way because of the disease promotion activities of Lilly and its peers. Between the early 1980s and the mid-1990s, the diagnosis of bipolar disorder increased more than 50-fold. This coincided with the emergence of a suborder of diagnoses that included bipolar II, cyclothamia and bipolar disorder NOS (not otherwise specified). These diagnoses differed from the earlier manic-depression (now bipolar I) in that previously a diagnosis involved an episode of hospitalization for mania. The new bipolar disorder is mainly "community based," in David Healy's term (2006b), and may be evolving still into a "spectrum disorder [that] can be recognized in as much as 50% of the population" (Cookson 2003). The expansion of bipolar diagnoses into the pediatric population—an increase of 4000% between 1994 and 2002 (Moreno et al. 2007), accounting for even infant diagnoses—has added yet another layer of profitability to the annual US$18 billion and 10.9% growth market for atypical antipsychotics.

While the majority of initial testing for Zyprexa and its competitors-in-arms in the treatment of bipolar disorder used subject populations with acute mania (i.e., bipolar I subjects) to gain approval, the real target population appears to have been the rapidly growing segment under the new diagnoses. This became evident through the promotional strategies used in primary care settings, where acute mania is not generally seen, and in the staged approval-seeking process for use of Zyprexa not as a short-term medicine for acute (i.e., psychotic) episodes of mania, but as a prophylactic for all bipolar disorder.

The strategy to wield influence over the primary care setting is doubly germane because it can be seen as a marketing channel strategy that fulfills both strategic criteria of the discipline. First, it facilitates movement of product through the channel and widens distribution access. Second, it adds value during the distribution, not in the usual manner, with service add-ons, but by contributing to the growing diagnostic base of the disorder. As the company would have learned from the Prozac experience, and is generally understood by health-care researchers, the more medical care there is, the more demand grows to meet it. PCPs are a key site for inciting the process further.

Donna: A case study in sales-force power

A slide in the 1997 Strategic Intent reads:

Our Challenge:

- PCPs have not been trained to recognize this patient … some afraid of the "B" [bipolar] word.
- PCPs have traditionally not treated this patient.
  - Lack of comfort with the disease state.
  - Lack of comfort with the meds due primarily to safety concerns.

We can change their paradigm….

In the pharmaceutical industry the bottom line of all value is the patent. Patents are the geese that lay golden eggs. They are the equivalent of brands in other consumer products. Take away the name Coca-Cola, and the company is worth the real estate it sits on. For the pharmaceutical industry the patent is what counts most—only, instead of its being invested in a single named drug, such as Cymbalta or Zyprexa, the value rolls from one patent-protected entity to the next. When the patent for a popular drug expires, the product becomes what in commercial lingo is called a commodity—an object without a name, equivalent to any copy, and priced low accordingly. "Commoditization" is the mortal enemy of marketing (Applbaum 2000b).

Of the strategies a company can employ to retain value in the transition, the most secure one is to transfer the consumers themselves into the product loyalty sphere of the next patented drug. With SSRI antidepressants coming off patent, Lilly might have determined that one way to retain at least a percentage of those customers was to transfer the consumers either to Cymbalta or to Zyprexa, both of which remained under patent protection. While there is no explicit strategic statement to this effect, in the context of the phenomenal new industry-sponsored research attention being given to bipolar disorder, the notion gained currency that those patients who were receiving no benefit from SSRIs were in this position not because SSRIs are imperfect drugs, but because of an erroneous diagnosis. They were not unipolar after all, but bipolar: "...When you look at patients who are already being treated or diagnosed with depressive disorders, as many as 30% may actually be bipolar." The solution was to put them on Zyprexa.[4]

Moving product through the physician's hands into the end user's medicine cabinet requires blurring physicians' status as experts with their status as channel members and consumers. They are consumers insofar as they themselves have to be convinced about the usefulness and safety of the drugs. Drug reps are trained to exude knowledgeability and confidence about the medications, and they are trained to be able to respond to doubts by marshalling scientific and epidemiological data on drug effects that doctors themselves do not have the time to investigate. At the same time, drug reps collect and feed back to headquarters information from the field about common physician concerns regarding the drugs and, also, what patient experiences are like. This information becomes the basis for the next round of sales-force training (Oldani 2006).

For example, a common "area of concern" for PCPs in the use of antipsychotics was the presentation of extrapyramidal symptoms (EPSs). EPSs include a long list of horrible side effects such as Parkinsonism, akithesia (distressing body restlessness) and a potentially fatal alteration of breathing and heart rate (neuroleptic malignant syndrome). The most common and feared—because it is sometimes irreversible—side effect is tardive dyskinesia (TD), involuntary movement of the mouth, lips and tongue. More than 60% of patients taking conventional antipsychotics face one or more EPS. The atypical antipsychotics have had a better track record with these particular side effects, but PCPs were familiar with these first and were understandably concerned about encountering them in their general practice. Here is a sample sell tactic:

[MD]:	I am concerned about EPS/TD.
CUSHION:	I understand your concern regarding EPS/TD.
CLARIFY:	Can you clarify your concern regarding EPS?
ADDRESS AOC	[area of concern] (go to Favorable Safety page):
EPS:	Zyprexa has a low risk of EPS, and in a study using the most exacting measurements, the Simpson Angus Scale, Zyprexa's rate of EPS was comparable to placebo across all dose ranges (page 6)....
TD:	Zyprexa has a minimal risk for Tardive Dyskinesia (TD). In a clinical trial vs. Haldol, the incidence of TD was .52% with Zyprexa vs. 7.45% with Haldol over a 1-year period
CHECK FOR AGREEMENT:	How do you feel about this safety data?
GET BACK TO SELLING.	

Similar sales scripts were written to allay physicians' concerns over sedation, weight gain and diabetes, common side effects of the atypicals. The scripted responses for side effects common to the atypicals would naturally be more evasive because the real data are damning.

Pharmaceutical companies are shrewd not to overestimate the sophistication of the average doctor. Lilly based their bipolar sales pitch on hypothetical patient profiles, perhaps harking back to Freud's case studies—Anna O., Dora, Little Hans, etc. The most commonly referred-to patient profile, and Zyprexa's sweet spot patient, is Donna.

> Donna is a single mom in her mid-30s, appearing in your office in drab clothing and seeming somewhat ill at ease. Her chief complaint is, "I feel so anxious and irritable lately." Today, she says she's been sleeping more than usual and has trouble concentrating at work and home. However, several appointments earlier, she was talkative, elated, and reported little need for sleep. You have treated her with various medications including antidepressants with little success.

After the usual sales rigmarole of awarding the physician due respect by listening to his answers to open-ended questions, you reassure him, "You will be able to assure Donna that ZYPREXA is safe and that it will help to relieve the symptoms she is struggling with." Once this is apparently taken in, the salesman is encouraged to "cash in your chips":

> Doctor, today you agreed that ZYPREXA's reliability can help you meet your therapeutic needs for your patients with complicated mood symptoms because … (recap the doctor's statements in regards to ZYPREXA's efficacy). Based on your confidence in ZYPREXA's efficacy and safety, will you try ZYPREXA in a patient like Donna?

Share of voice and the goal of maintenance status

In March 2000, Zyprexa was approved for short-term use in acute bipolar mania. That same month, the rollout for projects "Clinical Management of the Bipolar Spectrum for the New Millennium" and "Restoring Balance: Long-Term Mood Stabilization in the Bipolar Patient" were propounded in a number of strategic documents. To be provided in coming months were catered psychiatric conferences and continuing medical education "satellite symposiums" led by big-name psychiatrists for an audience of 6,000 MDs and 8,000 treatment team members from 1000 facilities; 15 bipolar dinner meetings, with 150 to 400 MDs per dinner; distribution of sell sheets to 30,000 MDs and 95,000 pharmacists; 30 regional psychosis/bipolar weekend symposia; and so on. These policy sheets were followed by others entitled "Use of antipsychotics in geriatric populations" and "The interface of neuropsychiatric disorders in the elderly," to be similarly supported by faculty presentations and other direct-to-physician (DTP) initiatives to "build the Zyprexa 'New Opportunities' LTC [long-term care] business."[5]

The Integrated Product Plan for 2001 similarly promoted uses of the drug not or not yet approved, suggesting violation of the no-off-label marketing rules. Note the initiatives on the plan (Fig.9.2).[6] The first goal under "Support initiatives to maximize olanzapine's [Zyprexa] *commercial* value," reads: "Establish share of voice (SOV) leadership with psychiatrists as a corporate priority." This is particularly pertinent to our discussion. "Share of voice" is a concept that will enable the corporation to accomplish two objectives necessary to removing friction and uncertainty from the distribution channel.

The first objective is straightforwardly to compete with psychiatrists over whose expert voice will be heard by the public when the subject of bipolar disorder is raised. The ways in which this can be accomplished are by advertising directly to the public, by successfully transferring prescription responsibilities to PCPs, who receive most of their education about Zyprexa from MRs, and by creating an infrastructure of shadow experts, scientists and psychiatrists in the company's employ who will drown out the voices of independent investigators.

2.0 Charter

***2.1 In Scope-funded* (*content approved by PMC*):**

- **Olanzapine *compound* support**

- Hyperglycemia, weight gain, CIB, Annual Report, Alerts, other safety responses as necessary to address customer/regulatory inquiries, (e.g., triglycerides and cholesterol)

- **Support the schizophrenia and bipolar *franchises* woldwide**

- New studies, publications, presentations, rapid response to worldwide regulatory questions, rapid response to customer, affiliate, and promotional inquiries/challenges.
- Bipolar depression (Q4/Q3)and maintenance (Q2/04) indications (i.e., mood stabilization)
- Increased physician support for presentations at conferences and to key and to key customers.
- ZydisIV elotab (launched 4/00), rapid-acting IM (RAIM) (7/01), long-acting (depot) injectible (Q2/05), granules for Japan (Q2/02).
- Meet FDAMA pediatric requirements for additional exclusivity
- Redifining expectations of efficacy through existing databases and novel studies

- **Support initiatives to maximize olanzapine's *commercial* value**

- Establish share-of-voice (SOV) leadership with psychiatists as a corporate priority
- Continuous review of pricing strategy versus Ziprasidone~sperda 1/Seroquel/Depakote
- Market research to define our future — where we will compete and where we will not
- Marketing plan maintenance and dessage evolution
- Optimal use of novel communication/promotion opportunities (e.g., E-commerce)

- **Support the use of olanzapine in patients with *Alzheimer's disease***

- Widespread publication/presentation of existing data
Pursuit of a psychosis in Alzheimer's claim in the United States and EU (registration decision 7/01)
Behavioral disturbances in elderly patients (EUIType I) (registration decision 7/01)

***2.2 Currently Out of Scope — requesting funding*:**
Obtain efficacy and safety data above 20mg for patients needing enhanced efficacy
- Borderline personality disorder, post-traumatic stress disorder, and emesis subject to unique headcount requirements for dedicated subteams

Figure 9.2 2001 integrated product plan (abridged)

This last strategy is accomplished through funding and publicizing research—often ghost-written by the company—that supports company interests, sponsoring journal supplements that will publish these findings exclusively, and so on (Antonuccio et al. 2003; Healy 2006c; Moffatt and Elliott 2007; Sismondo 2007).

These activities effectively pitch medical scientific and commercial expertise into direct competition, thereby enabling the blurring and eventual conversion of the former into the latter. This is the ultimate objective, because it coordinates and integrates the distribution channel along solidly commercial lines. The independent, noncommercial goals and ideas of psychiatrists and psychiatric researchers continually threaten to obstruct the distribution channel with what, I have noted earlier, is known to channel marketers as "goal conflict." Establishing superior share of voice—a term bearing family resemblance to the consumer product marketing concepts of market share and "share of mind," which refers to the space inside the consumer's head that one strives to have devoted to one's product—is a competitive project (Applbaum 2003)—only here, the competition is not with other atypical antipsychotics, but with the opinions of non-company-aligned scientific persons and entities. The battlefields for share of voice might include, for example, academic journal space, doctor's

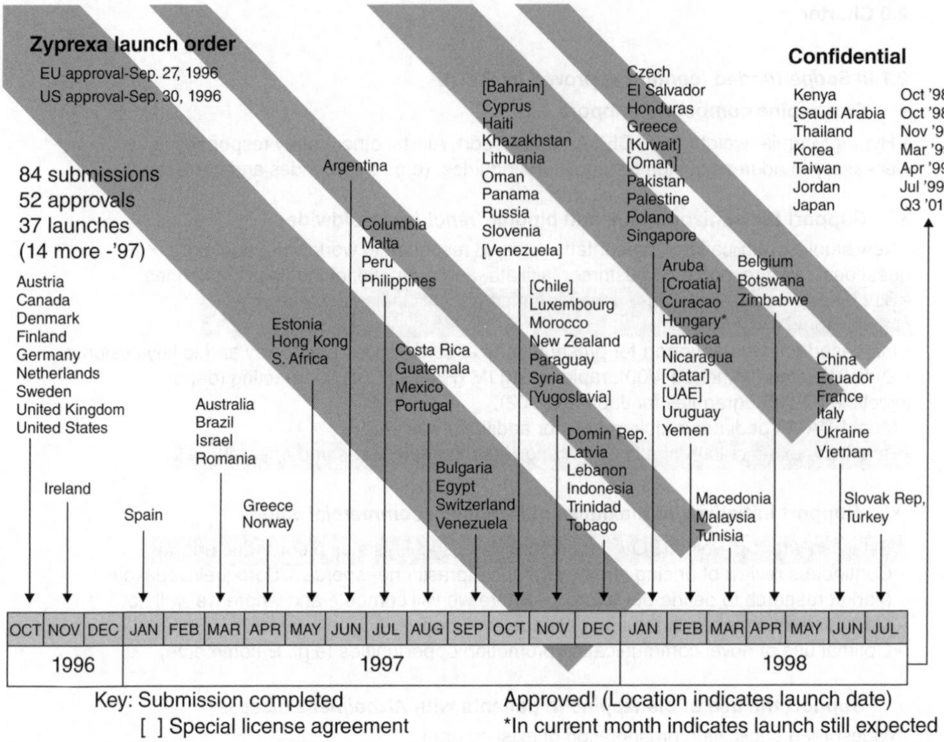

Figure 9.3 Zyprexa global rollout

office brochures, NAMI endorsements, government guidelines for treatment, media reports and scientific programming at psychiatry conferences. All of this is merely spadework to prepare the persuasion of numerous other channel members such as regulators, payers, social agencies, patient friends and family, etc., and before "ask your doctor" and other direct-to-consumer campaigns are introduced.

The procedure is repeated for each new possible off-label indication, and is reproduced in some localized version in every accessible foreign market, so that profits can have a global base (see Fig 9.3).

Marketing Channels and Synergistic Power: Conclusion

In the second epigraph at the beginning of this paper, I cited a marketing channels expert to the effect that the "channel captain" has at its disposal something called "channel power" to apply to wayward members of the channel. I have not yet explained the nature and scope of what sort of power it is that can achieve the goal of channel coordination. Here I refer again to synergistic power as the key to how independent and potentially reluctant channel members are brought willingly into the channel so the smooth flow of product can be maintained. Synergistic power relies on consensus building across interest or institutional barriers. A term often used in business to describe this process as a strategic proposition is "getting to yes." *Getting to Yes* is the title of a perennially best-selling management how-to book written by a lawyer, a psychologist and a one-time anthropology graduate student (Fisher et al. 1991). The book is hugely acclaimed, as is its most famous expression: a "win–win situation." Win–win is when both sides of a negotiation believe that they are benefiting, and even getting the better of their opponent. Nobody loses. In this case, it is not consensus that is being built, but eagerness on the part of all concerned to participate or to "get onboard and move forward."

The application of getting to yes as a managerial cultural process lies in the way managers are able to create the consciousness for everyone in a channel that they are on the same team and are absorbed in achieving the same ends. Initially one finds a range of views regarding any subject, such as contradictory epidemiological opinion about the prevalence of a disorder or the cost-effectiveness of a proposed solution. Getting to yes does not rely on everyone having the same point of view, only on their reaching the understanding that they are all pursuing allied goals and participating in the same universe of meaning. The agonistic consensus that the pharmaceutical industry systematically orchestrates through "collaborative competitorship" (Hamel et al. 2002) results in the ability to pull all those disparate strings so that it looks likes there is a consensus firming up from multiple locations, and hence it is not manipulated, cannot *possibly* be manipulated. One of the reasons the manipulation is obscure to us is that it seems as if they are not supervising the process at every step, because their hands are off the process so much of the time—And how, anyway, could they control the entire system?

I offer as the final illustration an abstracted sketch of the rise of the mega-blockbuster SSRIs. In the 1990s everyone in mental health care could relate to the tragic reality of individuals who, untreated for depression, ended up committing suicide. There is no doubt that this occurred commonly, and continues to. It was natural for all concerned to strive for a future in which this would never occur.

The two-part solution offered by the drug companies, who were already the de facto channel captains for mental health care, was as follows. First, an antidepressant pill to cure depression and prevent suicidal outcomes to the disease was created or designated. At this point, the question of whether the drugs were to be approved on the basis of murky, marginal, bogus or, for that matter, sterling efficacy was immaterial to the company—one should not be particular about the distinction; it is just business (Hart 2005). Second, following this, working in parallel but also in concert with each other, the companies endeavored to disseminate the pill as widely as possible, with the irreproachable aim of ushering in a future in which afflicted but potentially undiagnosed individuals would no longer slip through the cracks. The language of prevention, which by that point had gained ground in other areas of medicine, helped harness the public shoulder to the wheel. Professional consensus affirming that the industry's wildest dreams were also the public's was not so much argued as kindled by some of the marketing methods outlined above: combined marketing and R&D divisions created and publicized research to demonstrate the efficacy of the drug; obtained academic "key opinion leader" (KOL) endorsements for professional audiences (people whose careers and pocketbooks improved simultaneously); aired celebrity spokespeople and advertising to educate the lay public about the disease; lavishly funded antistigma campaigns; promoted among family doctors the use of abridged depression questionnaires and educated, and thus empowered, these doctors (and eventually their non-MD assistants) to look for telltale signs of depression and treat it; enrolled (in some cases, also bankrolled) the support of patient advocacy groups and solicited testimonials from among them; generated certified guidelines formulated and endorsed by psychiatrists in the employ of industry, to be adopted by hospital formularies and public insurance programs; took a lead role in determining the curriculum and scientific programs at continuing medical education programs and professional congresses; designed Web sites with diagnostic self-tests encouraging consumers along the path from self-diagnosis to the request for medication at the doctor's office—a request most often honored; dispatched the MR brigades; and so on (e.g., Antonuccio et al. 2003; Healy 2003, 2004, 2006a; Applbaum 2004, 2006b; Medawar and Hardon 2004; Moynihan 2004;

Conrad 2005). The result was a phenomenal increase in the diagnosis of conditions for which a prescription of an SSRI ensued. Between 1994 and 2002, there were some 6 million to 8 million new prescriptions *per year* in the United States for Prozac, Zoloft and Paxil alone (Healy and Aldred 2005).

The entire process may begin with a pill that actually does decisively ameliorate suffering, or it may begin with a pill that beats placebo only by a hair. It may begin with a pill that was approved not by reason of efficacy, but because its clinical trials were manipulated to show a lower side effect profile than its competitor or its generic predecessor—exactly the history of Zyprexa's first approval (Healy 2006b). By the time the entire marketing edifice has been built and the profits from billions of dollars in annual sales are surging into company coffers, the original questions of how or how well the pill actually works (Kirsch and Sapirstein 1998; Moncrieff and Cohen 2006), whether it creates dependency, causes mania (Breggin 2003), or triggers suicide more often than it prevents it (Beasley et al. 1991; Medawar and Hardon 2004)—none of which have been put to bed—no longer matter. The highly abstracted initial idea that brought all the channel members "onboard"—the shared commitment to reduce suffering—has receded beyond the horizon.

Getting-to-yes is the means whereby pharmaceutical corporations fuse the divergent positions of market intermediaries under the banner of a more abstract, univocal and often ethical purpose, drawing even on the energy of those intermediaries to construct a singly directed force propelling them toward company objectives. Getting-to-yes means avoiding conflict, bringing everyone to agreement, to the feeling that they are all pursuing the same goal. It does not, however—as in the distribution channel literature cited above, or even as regards the firm's interactions with consumers—eliminate power from the equation. It merely *conceals* the exercise of power. The truth of this concealment of power is more difficult to fathom vis-à-vis the health-care channel, which is filled with devoted, educated individuals who pledge the public good and would seem to have enough self-determination and awareness not to be duped or to be persuaded of things that are either untrue or inimical to their constituents, their ethical charter or their own professional autonomy.

The corporation is able to devote its state-sized resources single-mindedly and efficiently. To consumers it offers a slice of the good life, undivided by particular positionality. Even people with less personal agency, such as children, the elderly or the severely mentally ill, can be bounteous consumers of pharmaceutical products—so long as the people around them who will approve prescribe and pay for the medicines are adequately incorporated into the channel. The dreams of perfect health and self-realization through the exercise of free choice in the market, of modern style and progress, are not difficult to sell. In a consumer society, as I pointed out earlier, it seems hard to justify a hegemonic theory of power. This seems to be particularly so for the leading proponents of Cultural Anthropology today, for whom the agency of individuals has come to be conflated with their identity as consumers. In this scheme, handing too much determinative agency to corporations is not easily countenanced.[7] A rudderless raft of complicated, stylish theories has thus been devised to prove that corporations are unable, hard as they may try, to deny agency to the consumer. One can outdo these too-subtle arguments: we willingly buy the goods, we subscribe to the ideology of prosperity through stuff and some of us even become shareholders or get MBAs and, thereby, become two parts more the corporation ourselves. In the end, at least in the industrialized world, Toys R not Them, but Us.

Or so it would seem, if all we had to say was, "We are all consumers now." The consumers-have-the-power model rests on the idea that commodities are just ordinary things that people can use to construct whatever identities they choose. How does it differ when we discover that the pharmaceutical company treats physicians as consumers who are to be drawn into the channel unwittingly, even while it stands to cause them to violate their professional oath? What might we learn about the power exercised toward consumers in general when the statement "We are all consumers now" is indistinguishable from "We are all members of the distribution channel now"?

The motivational logic of marketing channels is not really as it seems, perhaps even from the above discussion: that a product is created at place A and you have to get it to place F, convincing B, C, D and E along the way to sanction or improve the flow. Channels themselves are the new objects of control. In marketing channels one finds all manner of bits and shreds of life that do not fly the company logo: laws, knowledge, organizations, infrastructure, disease categories, physicians, lifestyles, social relations and even common language. We fail to notice this vast net of semiownership because we continue to be caught up in the idea that commodities are solid, isolated entities, identities (consider all the people who say not, "I have bipolar disorder," but, "I am bipolar" [Martin 2007]) that can or have been isolated and forged far away from corporate boardrooms.

Pharmaceutical manufacturers, like other marketing-driven enterprises, have realized that it is less in the product, the brand or even the patent where their fortunes lie, but in the stream, the marketing channel. Once you control the channel, you can insert any product you like into it, no matter how useless or dangerous. The trick is to cut a large swathe and to run it through other institutions without their noticing that they have become victims of compulsory purchase (eminent domain). This is a structural (and structurally violent) facet of pharmaceuticalization that calls for our investigation.

Corporations, in their superior capacity to manage complexity, will be remembered as the champions of our age. Like all forms of power, corporate power is culturally constituted. Its mode of communication—commercialization and, well we might add, pharmaceuticalization and strategic medicalization—is contagious to other domains, perhaps as Durkheim (1995) reported of the tendency of the sacred in religious society. The contagious effect of corporate power is hardly limited to markets and marketplaces. It extends as concretely into politics, into the habits and worldviews of people—consumers, now, who conform as much to commodity-differentiated lifestyles as to cultures—and, in the case of pharmaceuticals, into the veinal and neural pathways of humanity, increasingly through channels forged globally. Until we have revealed both theoretically and ethnographically how corporate power feels like truth instead of like force, we will neither comprehend it nor stand to harness its mighty power for the good of humanity.

NOTES

1 Eli Lilly Document: "Managed Care-June 2002." Available at: http://www.furiousseasons.com/zyprexa%20documents/ZY200083405.pdf. Accessed December 14, 2007.

2 See: http://www.psychsearch.net/documents/tmap/sheet.pdf. Accessed November 27, 2008. See also: http://www.psychsearch.net/lawsuits.html. Accessed November 27, 2007.

3 Eli Lilly Document: "Zyprexa Product Team: Four Column Summary." Available at: http://www.furiousseasons.com/zyprexa%20documents/ZY200270343.pdf. Accessed December 14, 2007.

4 The same process may be at work in the case of the vastly overdiagnosed ADHD (attention deficit/hyperactivity disorder). A growing percentage of all those millions of children who are failing to show improvement on a class of drugs quickly falling from patent are being diagnosed with pediatric bipolar disorder (Healy and Le Noury 2007).

5 Eli Lilly Document: "Zyprexa Launch March 2000." Available at: http://www.furiousseasons.com/zyprexa%20documents/ZY201448094.pdf. Accessed December 14, 2007.

6 Eli Lilly Document: "2001 Integrated Plan Zyprexa Product Team." Available at: http://www.furiousseasons.com/zyprexa%20documents/ZY200061996.pdf. Accessed December 14, 2007.

7 I do not mean to suggest that corporate power is omnipotent, or that informal outlets for economic engagement or interpretive action are weak agencies. However, in their pragmatic intercourse with consumers—in which physicians and their patients become indistinguishable except by the technique with which they are engaged—pharmaceutical corporations are *somehow* managing to incorporate their opposer's positions and to make it seem like everyone is running in the same direction. The *somehow* is what I am calling—not entirely as an objectivist proposition, since it is their own term—synergistic power.

I believe that health care is a special case. Not because marketers operate according to a unique scheme in that field—quite the opposite—but because health care is the ultimate arena in the struggle between human need and corporate power. "What drives suffering?" Farmer (2003) asks. He advocates the notion of structural violence to explain what drives suffering in public health in the developing world. I think he is utterly correct. Let us call what I am identifying in this paper "corporate structural violence," and let us analyze it as a social process, with all the good intentions gone awry included.

REFERENCES

Aneesh, A.
2006 *Virtual Migration*. Durham, NC: Duke University Press.
Antonuccio, D.O., W.G. Danton, and T.M. McClanahan
2003 Psychology in the Prescription Era: Building a Firewall between Marketing and Science. American Psychologist 58: 1028–1043.
Applbaum, Kalman
2000 Crossing Borders: Globalization as Myth and Charter in American Transnational Consumer Marketing. American Ethnologist 27(2): 257–282.
2000 Marketing and Commoditization. Social Analysis 44: 106–128.
2003 *The Marketing Era: From Professional Practice to Global Provisioning*. London: Routledge.
2004 How to Organize a Psychiatric Congress. Anthropological Quarterly 77: 303–310.
2005 Directions in the Anthropology of Markets. *In* Handbook of Economic Anthropology. Carrier James, ed., pp. 275–289. London: Edward Elgar.
2006a Educating for Global Mental Health: American Pharmaceutical Companies and the Adoption of SSRIs in Japan. *In* Pharmaceuticals and Globalization: Ethics, Markets, Practices. Kleinman, Arthur, Andrew Lakoff, and Adriana Petryna, eds., pp. 85–110. Durham, NC: Duke University Press.
2006b Pharmaceutical Marketing and the Invention of the Medical Consumer. PLoS Med 3(4): e189. doi:10.1371/journal.pmed.0030189.
2009 Consumers Are Patients!: Shared Decision Making and Treatment Non-compliance as Business Opportunity. Transcultural Psychiatry 46(1): 107–130. doi:10.1177/1363461509102290.
Barry, P.
2000 What's Behind High Drug Prices in the U.S.? AARP Bulletin 4: 4–10.
Beasley, C., B. Dornseif, J. Bosomworth, M. Sayler, A. Rampey, and J. Heiligenstein
1991 Fluoxetine and Suicide: A Meta-analysis of Controlled Trials of Treatment for Depression. British Medical Journal 303: 685–692.
Berenson, Alex
2006 Eli Lilly Said to Play Down Risk of Top Pill. The New York Times, December 17.
2007 Lilly Settles with 18,000 Over Zyprexa. The New York Times, January 5.
Biehl, Joao
2007 Pharmaceuticalization: AIDS Treatment and Global Health Politics. Anthropological Quarterly 80: 1083–1126.
Breggin, Peter R.
2003 Suicidality, Violence and Mania Caused by Selective Serotonin Reuptake Inhibitors (SSRIs): A Review and Analysis. International Journal of Risk and Safety in Medicine 16: 31–49.
Brown, S., H. Inskip, and B. Barraclough

2000 Causes of the Excess Mortality of Schizophrenia. British Journal of Psychiatry 177: 212–217.
Castels, Manuel
1996 The Rise of the Network Society. London: Blackwell.
Cleland, Robin, Lars Finskud, and Vittorio Raimundi
2004 Nine Prescriptions for Brand Health. Market Leader Spring: 50–55.
Conrad, Peter
2005 The Shifting Engines of Medicalization. Journal of Health and Social Behavior 46: 3–14.
Cookson, J.C.
2003 Review of Bipolar Disorder. British Journal of Psychiatry 183: 268–269.
Coughlan, Anne, and Louis Stern
2000 Market Channel Design and Management. *In* Kellogg on Marketing. Dawn Iacobucci, ed. New York: Wiley.
Coughlan, Anne, Erin Anderson, Louis W. Stern, and Adel I. El-Ansary
2006 Marketing Channels. 7th Edition. New York: Prentice-Hall.
Cowley, Geoffrey
1994 The Culture of Prozac. Newsweek, February, pp. 41–42.
Dannhaeuser, Norbert
1989 Marketing in Developing Urban Areas. *In* Economic Anthropology. S. Plattner, ed. Stanford: Stanford University Press.
Durkheim, Emile
1995 Elementary Forms of the Religious Life. New York: Free Press.
Eaton, Margaret L., and Mark Xu
2005 Developing and Marketing a Blockbuster Drug: Lessons from Eli Lilly's Experience with Prozac. Cambridge, MA: Harvard Business School.
Elliott, Carl
2006 The Drug Pushers. Atlantic Monthly, April, pp. 2–13.
Farmer, Paul
2003 Pathologies of Power: Health, Human Rights, and the New War on the Poor. Berkeley: University of California Press.
Faunce, Thomas
2007 Who Owns Your Health? Medical Professionalism and the Market State. Baltimore, MD: Johns Hopkins University Press.
First, Michael B.
2005 Mutually Exclusive Versus Co-occurring Diagnostic Categories: The Challenge of Diagnostic Comorbidity. Psychopathology 38: 206–210.
Fisher, Roger, William Ury, and Bruce Patton
1991 *Getting to Yes*. New York: Penguin.
Fugh-Berman, A., and S. Ahari
2007 Following the Script: How Drug Reps Make Friends and Influence Doctors. PLoS Med 4(4): e150. doi:10.1371/journal.pmed.0040150.
Gagnon, M. A., and J. Lexchin
2008 The Cost of Pushing Pills: A New Estimate of Pharmaceutical Promotion Expenditures in the United States. PLoS Med 5(1): e1. doi:10.1371/journal.pmed.0050001.
Hamel, Gary, Yves L. Doz, and C. K. Prahalad
2002 Collaborate with Your Competitors—and Win. *In* Harvard Business Review on Strategic Alliances. Boston: Harvard Business School Press.
Hart, Keith
2005 The Hit Man's Dilemma: Or Business, Personal and Impersonal. Chicago: Prickly Paradigm Press.
Healy, David
2003 *Let Them Eat Prozac*. Toronto: James Lorimer.
2004 Shaping the Intimate: Influences on the Experience of Everyday Nerves. Social Studies of Science 34: 219–245.
2006a Manufacturing Consensus. Culture, Medicine and Psychiatry 30: 135–156.

2006b The Latest Mania: Selling Bipolar Disorder. PLoS Med 3(4): e185. doi:10.1371/journal.pmed.0030185.
2006c The New Medical Oikumene. *In Global Pharmaceuticals: Ethics, Markets, Practices*. A. Petryna, A. Lakoff, and A. Kleinman, eds., pp. 61–84. Durham, NC: Duke University Press.
2007 The Engineers of Human Souls and Academia. Epidemiologia e Psichiatria Sociale 16(3): 206.
2008 *Mania: A Short History of Bipolar Disorder*. Baltimore: Johns Hopkins University Press.
Healy, David, and Graham Aldred
2005 Antidepressant Drug Use and the Risk of Suicide. International Review of Psychiatry 17: 163–172.
Healy, David, and Joanna Le Noury
2007 Pediatric Bipolar Disorder: An Object of Study in the Creation of an Illness. International Journal of Risk and Safety in Medicine 19: 209–221.
Hisey, Terry
2004 The Big Squeeze: The Simple Answer to Pharma's Pipeline Crisis? Get More Value Out of the Products You Already Have. Pharmaceutical Executive. Available at: http://www.pharmexec.com/pharmexec/article/articleDetail.jsp?id=129292.
Hobbes, Thomas
1998 Leviathan. Oxford: Oxford University Press.
Joukamaa, M., M. Heliovaara, and P. Knekt, et al.
2006 Schizophrenia, Neuroleptic Medication, and Mortality. British Journal of Psychiatry 188: 122–127.
Kanter, Rosabeth M.
1989 When Giants Learn to Dance: Mastering the Challenges of Strategy, Management, and Careers in the 1990s. New York: Simon and Schuster.
Kirsch, Irving, and Guy Saperstein
1998 Listening to Prozac but Hearing Placebo: A Meta-analysis of Antidepressant Medication. Prevention and Treatment, June 26, article 00002a.
Lacasse, J. R., and J. Leo
2005 Serotonin and Depression: A Disconnect between the Advertisements and the Scientific Literature. PLoS Med 2(12): e392. doi:10.1371/journal.pmed.0020392.
Lane, Christoper
2007 Shyness: How Normal Behavior Became a Sickness. New Haven, CT: Yale University Press.
Lieberman, Jeffrey A., T. Scott Stroup, Joseph P. McEvoy, Marvin S. Swartz, Robert A. Rosenheck, Diana O. Perkins, Richard S.E. Keefe, Sonia M. Davis, Clarence E. Davis, Barry D. Lebowitz, Joanne Severe, and John K. Hsiao
2005 Effectiveness of Antipsychotic Drugs in Patients with Chronic Schizophrenia.New England Journal of Medicine 353: 1209–1223.
Marcus, George E., ed.
1998 Corporate Futures: The Diffusion of the Culturally Sensitive Corporate Form. Chicago: University of Chicago Press.
Martin, Emily
2007 Bipolar Expeditions: Mania and Depression in American Culture. Princeton, NJ: Princeton University Press.
Medawar, Charles, and Anita Hardon
2004 Medicines Out of Control? Antidepressants and the Conspiracy of Goodwill. Amsterdam: Aksant Academic.
Moffatt, B., and C. Elliott
2007 Ghost Marketing: Pharmaceutical Companies and Ghostwritten Journal Articles. Perspectives in Biological Medicine 50: 18–31.
Mol, Annemarie
2008 The Logic of Care: Health and the Problem of Patient Choice. New York: Routledge.
Moncrieff, J., and D. Cohen
2006 Do Antidepressants Cure or Create Abnormal Brain States? PLoS Med 3(7): e240. doi:10.1371/journal.pmed.0030240.

Moreno, Carmen, Gonzalo Laje, Carlos Blanco, Huiping Jiang, Andrew B. Schmidt, and Mark Olfson
2007 National Trends in the Outpatient Diagnosis and Treatment of Bipolar Disorder in Youth. Archives of General Psychiatry 64: 1032–1039.
Moynihan, Raymond
2004 The Intangible Magic of Celebrity Marketing. PLoS Med 1(2): e42. doi:10.1371/journal.pmed.0010042.
Moynihan, Raymond, and A. Cassels
2005 *Selling Sickness*. New York: Nation Books.
Moynihan, Ray, and David Henry
2006 PloS Medicine Special Issue: Disease Mongering. PloS 3(4): e191–e213.
Ofek, Elie
2007 Eli Lilly: Developing Cymbalta. Cambridge, MA: Harvard Business School.
Oldani, Michael
2004 Thick Prescriptions: Toward an Interpretation of Pharmaceutical Sales Practices. Medical Anthropology Quarterly 18: 325–356.
2006 Filling Scripts: A Multisited Ethnography of Pharmaceutical Sales, Psychiatric Prescribing and Phamily Life in North America. Ph.D. dissertation. Princeton University.
Parry, Vince
2003 The Art of Branding a Condition. Med Mark Media 38: 43–49.
Rangan, Kasturi V.
1994 Reorienting Channels of Distribution. Cambridge, MA: Harvard Business School.
Sahlins, Marshall
1961 The Segmentary Lineage: An Organization of Predatory Expansion. American Anthropologist 63: 322–345.
Shorter, Edward
1997 A History of Psychiatry: From the Era of the Asylum to the Age of Prozac. New York: John Wiley & Sons.
Sismondo, Sergio
2007 Ghost Management: How Much of the Medical Literature Is Shaped Behind the Scenes by the Pharmaceutical Industry? PLoS Med 4(9): e286. doi:10.1371/journal.pmed.0040286.
Tuttle, E., A. Parece, and A. Hector
2004 Your Patent Is About to Expire: What Now? Pharmaceutical Executive, November.

10

Pushing Knowledge in the Drug Industry: Ghost-Managed Science[1]

Sergio Sismondo

The pharmaceutical industry produces an abundance of special-purpose knowledge, and floods the knowledge markets in which it has the most interests. This paper describes some key processes and contexts of that knowledge production. To gain the largest scientific impact and market value from scientific research, drug company articles are often written under the names of independent medical researchers. Pharmaceutical company statisticians, reviewers from a diverse array of company departments, medical writers, and publication planners are only rarely acknowledged in journal publications, and company scientists only sometimes acknowledged. The public knowledge that results from this ghost-managed research and publication provides bases for continuing medical education, buttresses sales pitches, and contributes to medical common sense and further research. In the pharmaceutical industry, knowledge is a resource to be accumulated, shaped, and deployed to best effect.

Introduction

Pharmaceutical companies perform and sponsor significant amounts of medical research and analysis, especially clinical trials, but also meta-analyses, reviews, epidemiology, laboratory science, and health economics research. While pharmaceutical companies have long recognized the value of scientific journal articles that report their research (e.g. Rasmussen, 2005), since the 1980s companies have increased efforts to *systematically* treat research as a resource, one that needs to be carefully developed and deployed to affect the opinions of researchers and practitioners. Although most published articles associated with industry-sponsored research are 'authored' by academic researchers, authors mostly provide visible authority; most of the work to shape, produce, analyze and write up research is done by

Sergio Sismondo, "Pushing knowledge in the drug industry: Ghost-managed science". Manuscript.

The Pharmaceutical Studies Reader, First Edition. Edited by Sergio Sismondo and Jeremy A. Greene.

actors who are largely invisible. I call the whole process the 'ghost management' of pharmaceutical research and publication. Ghost management represents a massive intervention in the production and dissemination of pharmaceutical knowledge, one that is markedly different from traditional scientific and academic research and publishing activities. Ghost management has brought clinical research into the 'marketing era' (Applbaum, 2004).

Publication of pharmaceutical company sponsored research in medical journals, and its presentation at conferences and meetings, is governed by 'publication plans', created and implemented by 'publication planners'. In this article I describe publication planning in some depth. I draw primarily on detailed notes from three conferences on publication planning, though also on a number of documentary sources and interviews. In addition to describing publication planning, I argue that it is part of a new, corporatized, mode of scientific research. This new mode is *scientific* in the sense that it generally bears all the hallmarks of good medical science, defensibly constructing evidence and bringing it to bear on medical issues. Yet it is *corporatized* both in how it is organized and how it is used to support specific company goals. Our main concerns about this new mode of science, I argue, should be focused on how it is designed to find certain truths and further certain interests.

It is worth quoting at length one publication plan's description of planning itself:

> Strategic publication planning provides the tactical recommendations necessary to develop a scientific platform within the biomedical literature to support the market positioning of an established product or the launch of a new product. The process of publication planning includes:
>
> - An analysis of the characteristics of the market into which the product will be launched
> - An analysis of competitive issues
> - The expected product profile
> - Identification of issues relevant to the disease state or primary indication for the product
> - Development of a series of key communication messages addressing the major issues
> - The availability of clinical and preclinical data to support the key communication messages
> - Recognition of appropriate target audiences for each of the recommended publication tactics
> - Recommendations for publication vehicles (e.g., journals, meetings, congresses, etc.) for each publication activity. (Wyeth, 2002)

How much medical literature is ghost managed? From the limited number of cases where we have hard data, it appears that roughly 40% of medical journal articles mentioning recently patented drugs are parts of individual publication plans on the drugs. A legal action gave psychiatrist David Healy access to a document listing 85 articles on the drug sertraline (Zoloft or Lustral), many of them written by medical writers and then authored by academics, being handled by a public relations firm, Current Medical Directions, for Pfizer (Healy & Cattell, 2003). Lawsuits about rofecoxib (Vioxx) led to a systematic study identifying 96 published articles (24 on clinical trials and 72 review articles) on which Merck had worked prior to their publication, and which were later published mostly under the names of academic first authors (Ross et al., 2008). 40% is a very substantial amount, certainly allowing a company to attract interest in a drug and shape the perception of it, mostly under the names of apparently independent authors.

Various facts make it plausible that thousands of articles per year are ghost managed. First, pharmaceutical companies sponsor some 70% of all clinical trials of drugs, and 70-75% of those are outsourced to contract research organizations that have no interest in publishing the results under their own names—they produce data that is wholly owned by their sponsors (Mirowski and van Horne, 2005; Fisher, 2009). Thus, pharmaceutical companies have control over roughly half of all clinical trial data. Second, more than 50 agencies advertise publication planning on the Internet. Some boast of having hundreds of employees who handle many hundreds of manuscripts per year. The industry is large enough that there are two competing international associations of publication planners. One of those associations, the International Society of Medical Planning Professionals (ISMPP), has over 1000 members. Both ISMPP and its smaller competing association, The International Publication Planning Association (TIPPA), hold annual conferences, and the latter hosts various regional conferences. ISMPP runs broader educational and accreditation activities than TIPPA, and creates guidelines for ethical and best practices. Planners handle dozens of manuscripts per year, and one told me that she was in charge of a campaign involving more than a hundred manuscripts and conference presentations.

A Sample Manuscript

We start, though, by following an individual manuscript through its early phases. 'PC(2)' was the label for one manuscript in the drug company Wyeth's 2002 publication plan for its Premarin/trimegestone hormone therapies. Apparently responding to the Women's Health Initiative trial that challenged the safety of much hormone therapy (Writing Group, 2002), the plan was entitled 'Achieving Clarity, Renewing Confidence'. As a result of a lawsuit, many documents related to that plan have become publicly available. [2]

The first draft of manuscript PC(2) – which investigated the hormone therapy sold as 'Totelle' in a number countries – was ready on August 16, 2002. Jean Wright, a member of the team working for the British medical education and communication company (MECC) and publisher Parthenon Publishing, contacted a group of Wyeth employees. 'Please find attached the first draft of PC(2)', she wrote. This manuscript, based on data coming from a clinical trial performed for Wyeth, had the unwieldy title 'A 2-year comparison of the effects of continuous combined regimens of 1 mg 17ß-estradiol and trimegestone with regimens containing estradiol and norethisterone acetate upon endometrial bleeding and safety in postmenopausal women'. Just under the title of that draft was written: 'Author: to be determined'.

Between August of 2002 and April of 2003, the manuscript underwent several rounds of comments by Wyeth employees and subsequent revisions at Parthenon, all recorded on monthly tracking reports. Through all those revisions it remained authorless. It was moving towards its final shape, however, and in April 2003, three authors finally appeared on the tracking report, Wyeth's Daniele Spielmann being the third. A note on the author list read 'Need to contact', perhaps suggesting that the first two had not yet been consulted. By June 6, 2003, the manuscript had clear authors: 'Bouchard P, Addo S, Spielmann D, and the Trimegestone 301 Study Group'. The first two of these are independent researchers, and the last is the name for a long list of physicians who had provided patients for the Wyeth trial. The manuscript continued through another few rounds of comments by Wyeth employees, and subsequent revisions.

Sometime in September 2003 the authors changed. They became 'Bouchard P, De Cicco-Nardone F, Spielmann D, Garcea N, and the Trimegestone 301 Study Group'. What had happened? An email by Spielmann explained: 'The 2 italian authors agree with the paper and replace ADDO woho [sic] went to our competitors.' Another email, from Jean Wright, clarified: 'Please note that S. Addo has been deleted from the author list for PC(2). Daniele was doubtful whether she should be included because she now has connections with Organon.'

Even though every internal round of reviews and revisions was carefully tracked by the agencies handling the manuscript—for example, a tracking report showed that in July

Parthenon updated the manuscript before it was sent out to external authors for their final review—there is no indication on any report that the external authors made any input. A later version of the article was eventually published in the journal *Gynecological Endocrinology*.

Publication Planning 101/201: An Insider View of the Field

For the most part, this paper reports on three meetings, one of the ISMPP in 2007, and two of TIPPA, both in 2011. I refer to the speakers at these public meetings by initials—not their own. I am taking the views of most of these speakers as representative of publication planners more generally, so there is no need to highlight their identities. I maintain that naming convention even when the speakers are invited outsiders. The paper also draws on interviews with publication planners and on publicly available sources, such as websites.

Almost all attendees of the ISMPP and TIPPA meetings were publication planners, some working for independent agencies and some directly for pharmaceutical companies. The non-planners were mostly invited speakers, including journal editors, ethicists, and consultants to the industry.

I registered in Publication Planning 101/201 preceding the 2007 ISMPP meeting; this provided 'an interactive and instructive introduction to the world of strategic publication planning', for those either new to it, working as support to publication planning, or working in connected areas. The program for Publication Planning 101/201 began with a history of the field given by HK, a senior member of the field and the CEO of a medium-sized agency. No doubt artificially, HK pinpoints to 1984 the origins of publication planning, when three employees of Pfizer realized that the company had extensive data on the drug amlodipine (Norvasc, a calcium antagonist), and wondered where they should publish it. To do this rationally, they had to gather information about all of the trials to which Pfizer had access, information on other publications, sort it all, and decide how to publish it in credible journals for non-overlapping global audiences. Pfizer had to greatly increase its internal communication to achieve this. Even by 1988 publication planning was not well established within Pfizer; HK quoted an internal memo: 'Please ... return details of any new trials, new plans for publication of existing trials, or missing details.' He made it clear that this sounds quaint today, because of close tracking of all trials from their conception onward, and top-down guidance of their publication. 'Today, if you go to a meeting, you know pretty much what is going to be presented.'

CI, a planner working within a pharmaceutical company, starts her presentation by saying,

> This is what utopia looks like from an industry perspective. We have agreement and alignment on a plan, not even just a publication, a full plan, investigators on board, agencies lined up, everybody ready to play and we're going to get this done in a timely way, in an orderly fashion, and things work like clockwork.

Ideally, a plan sets out an orderly performance of research and rolling out of presentations and publications; appendices give the relevant data for each of the meetings and journals to which abstracts and papers will be submitted—the audiences they reach, their impact factors, their rejection rates, and publication lead times (e.g. Complete Healthcare Communication, 2006). Tactical recommendations are for specific submissions, based on strategic considerations, parceling out data for different target audiences, time and resource considerations, and the sequence in which one wants the data to roll out. A plan also may describe other communication opportunities, such as symposia and roundtables, journal supplements, advisory board meetings, and more.

The publication planning team should be put in place early, says seminar leader FD, 'before too much data has gone unpublished'. Although planners' focus is on publications, they believe that ideally they would be involved in research design. This is especially important if there is 'need to create [a] market' or create an 'understanding of unmet need'. In the terms of critics, creating a market generally takes the form of 'disease mongering' or 'selling sickness' (Moynihan & Henry, 2006; Moynihan & Cassels, 2005). Publication planning probably plays important roles in this: Healy (2004) connects the dramatic expansion of depression to publication planning campaigns; Jennifer Fishman (2004) describes what amounted to a campaign to establish Female Sexual Dysfunction as a disease.

The publication planning team might be formed at various stages in a product's development cycle, and the team tightly manages knowledge flow: Planner MS advises that articles from Phase I (pilot trials typically on healthy subjects) should be written early, so that Phase II (small clinical trials to guide Phase III ones) articles can refer to them; MH says that the number of articles should peak at about the time that the product launches, for maximum effect. The right knowledge flow should lead to increased presence in the medical imagination and the commercial market.

Marketing

Marketing occupies an uncomfortable position within publication planning. On the one hand, all of the actors recognize that pharmaceutical companies publish scientific results in part to sell drugs. Websites of publication planning firms promote their work on that basis. 'Data generated from clinical trials programs are the most powerful marketing tools available to a pharmaceutical company', writes one (Envision Pharma, 2006). Another advertises that its 'mission is to ensure that your messages reach and energize your target customers', including through 'hardcore scientific writing' (Watermeadow Medical, 2007). And 'Adis Communications works in partnership with clients to position their products at the right place, at the right time through: Hundreds of well-respected, and high-impact factor journals ...' (Adis Communications, 2006).

New publication planners are told to pay attention to marketing. Seminar leader MH says that publication plans should identify 'target audiences', should lay out key 'scientific & clinical communication points', should do 'competitor publication & gap analyses', and need to outline 'top-line tactics' and 'critical timing'. Clearly, these analyses are parts of the apparatus of interested intervention, not disinterested diffusion of results. Company planner CD speaks about how marketing messages come from the top:

> At the beginning of the year, we kind of have a scientific strategy for every product, saying, y'know, these are the key messages that we're hoping to get out, depending on what clinical data we have available. We'll look at all the points that the upper management folks would like us to try and see if we have the data to address, and then we'll go through it point by point and try to see.

Ultimately, publication planning needs to generate revenue by providing information that increases sales.

Yet there is another side to planning's standard self-presentation: it should be, though isn't always, independent of marketing. It should be in the service of scientific knowledge about results: 'We really do like to stress that the publication planning company is not an advertising agency, is not a PR [public relations] agency, even though it might look like one', says NF. Planners understand that they are in a sensitive position.

Revelations of ghostwritten medical journal articles have caused scandals and have resulted in coverage in prominent newspapers (Mathews, 2005; Barnett, 2003; Berenson, 2005). On a number of occasions, audience members at ISMPP and TIPPA conferences were reminded to watch what was written down or entered into databases, because their documents and databases could become public through lawsuits or otherwise. MH suggested, for example, that planners talk about 'communication points' rather than 'messages', because critics see the latter as driven by marketers. In addition, 'A publication plan might be made public, might appear on the front page of the *Wall Street Journal*. So you don't want to make it appear that you don't have authors. This is verboten today.'

Though they appear inconsistent, planners are not merely being duplicitous when they distance themselves from marketers. They understand that their work has marketing value, but they see a clear distinction between what they do and what marketing departments do. Marketers, as planners portray them, would consistently ride roughshod over scientific standards, would be relatively unconcerned with what the scientific data can support. To be compliant with 'Good Publication Practice,' says MH, a publication plan is a basis for dissemination of scientific and clinical data, and is 'not a marketing communications plan'. The marketing department, NF said, is considered lucky to have one place on a publication team—it does typically retain that one place, because 'they're probably paying the bill'. Publication planning negotiates between marketing and science, implies FD, to avoid 'bottlenecks' and 'delays', but also to avoid publications from being 'cherry-picked'.

Scientific standards are doubly important. First, meeting them constitutes part of what is considered ethical behavior, and so underpins the distinction between doing publication planning and public relations. Second, publication planners can only succeed if their work displays high standards, so that their articles will be published to best advantage. Medical journals have high rejection rates, as high as 94% in the case of such journals as *Journal of the American Medical Association* and *British Medical Journal* (McCook, 2006). It is only by stifling the marketing department's efforts to hype the product that publication planners can do effective marketing to scientific audiences. At least some of the time, marketing is best done if it is invisible.

Publications address many audiences, and these sometimes create conflicting pressures. Presentations and articles in key meetings and journals may reach the general public via press releases (Ham, Jun, & Lee, 2008). Publications reach some researchers and clinicians directly, and are often distributed to clinicians by sales representatives. Says RS, an industry consultant and an expert on US regulatory issues, 'Folks, they're dying for your work, by the way. Field reps are dying every day for more of your work. You know that, right? Because that's what doctors are going to see.' Hank McKinnell, former CEO of Pfizer, says of pharmaceutical sales representatives: 'We call it a sales force, but our sales force doesn't sell. It transmits knowledge' (quoted in Petersen, 2008: 321).

There are other vectors for the dissemination of reprints. In addition to sales representatives, large companies also employ 'medical science liaisons', whose job it is to provide physicians with information without engaging in promotion, says ethics seminar leader FJ: The medical sales liaison is to the sales representative as the publication planner is to the marketer. Unlike sales representatives, medical science liaisons have advanced degrees in relevant sciences, and do not have prescription quotas they are expected to meet. Communications between these professionals and physicians are deemed to fall under the scientific 'safe harbor', as long as they do not involve promotion.

Given these different routes to physicians, with their different regulatory frameworks, publication planners have to understand the purposes of manuscripts before they are written. Again, this places their work in the context of broad communication strategies.

Medical Journals

Invited to address each ISMPP and TIPPA meeting are editors of a few of the best-regarded medical journals, medical publishers, and journal editors' organizations. Publishers and editors are seen as having very different attitudes toward planners. BC, the head of a publication planning firm, says, 'From publishers we often get quite a strong sell, engagement and willingness to work with. And from editors we often get very much a hands-off and keep your distance.' Though BC wishes that journals could iron out this difference, he understands its origins: 'We understand and recognize that tension. To me it actually mirrors very closely the relationship between medical and marketing within the pharmaceutical industry.... And it's about the relationship between commercial needs and the integrity of the science.'

Several publication planning firms are divisions of major publishing houses. For example, Carus Clinical Communications offers publication planning services 'supported by the unmatched depth and breadth of Elsevier's worldwide medical publication resources' (Carus Clinical Communications, 2007). Thomson Scientific Connexions, owned by the publisher Thomson, will develop 'a publications strategy and recommendations for coordinated and targeted data dissemination through medical meetings, journal articles, and other communication vehicles to educate clinicians and build a foundation for clinical acceptance' (Thomson Scientific Connexions, 2006). The connections may improve planners' access to their publishers' journals, and may improve access to key opinion leaders.

A key opinion leader or KOL is a well-known physician, highly regarded by peers, who has experience with the product and, in the words of publisher RB, 'can influence other physicians'. Thus a KOL is defined by being able to act as a intermediaries in the path from companies to physicians. In practice, the term is only applied to people who are already enmeshed in relationships with pharmaceutical companies, not to fully independent influential physicians (Sismondo, 2014).

Publishers and journal editors have reasons to encourage submissions of industry-sponsored articles. Some of these articles report on well-funded, well-constructed clinical trials. Given that clinical trials are the most valued sources of medical data, these articles are likely to be highly regarded and cited, even without publication planners working to cite their own articles—of the most highly cited recent articles reporting clinical trials, the majority are funded by the pharmaceutical industry (Patsopoulos et al., 2006). Some medical journals allow companies to sponsor supplements on special topics, at rates that help to subsidize the journal as a whole. In addition, reprints of the articles may represent a significant source of revenue for journals. Representatives take reprints of their articles to physicians' offices to back up their claims, and reprints can be distributed at conferences and in other ways. Richard Smith, former editor of the *British Medical Journal*, claims that Merck bought 900,000 copies of a *New England Journal of Medicine* article reporting a large trial of Vioxx. (Smith, 2006). Though that number is an outlier, when I requested a quote on an order of 10,000 reprints of an eight-page article in black and white, the *New England Journal of Medicine* emailed me within hours—US$15,974.

Speaking at publication planning conferences, most journal editors express a concern to safeguard scientific integrity, insisting on performing clinical trials well, reporting them honestly and in an unbiased fashion, and following rules for writing and disclosing support. Theirs is a transactional view of scientific publishing that does not distinguish between pharmaceutical company-sponsored trials and other trials so long as the 'rules' of science and of medical publishing are followed. Editor SG says, 'The way to get an article published easily, which is what our goal is and yours, is to avoid practices that are going to slow things up and slow the period of time before you can start enjoying the acclaim and the revenue that comes with successful publication in a big journal.' MD, a former editor of a very well regarded journal, emphasizes issues of trial design in a simplified manner, as does SG. LB, an associate editor, emphasizes procedural matters of disclosure and authorship; ME, a senior editor at a top medical journal, similarly gives a simple overview of issues of integrity in publishing, in the context of the history of the journal's conflict of interest policy. While some editors explicitly condemned ghostwriting, there was also appreciation of medical writers, who improve manuscripts. 'We appreciate [medical writing] as editors because we have to read a lot of papers and we can tell which ones have had expert writers participate in their development', says LB.

There are different sets of criteria for authorship of medical papers, but the most important is that of the International Committee of Medical Journal Editors' (ICMJE), adopted by most journals. According to these criteria,

> Authorship credit should be based on 1) substantial contributions to conception and design, or acquisition of data, or analysis and interpretation of data; 2) drafting the article or revising it critically for important intellectual content; and 3) final approval of the version to be published. Authors should meet conditions 1, 2, and 3. (ICMJE, 2005)

These criteria are an attempt to enforce traditional notions of authorship: tying credit to intellectual responsibility, which begets moral responsibility (Biagioli, 2003). LB, speaking to an audience of publication planners, describes what *authors* need to do to make sure that medical writers don't become ghostwriters: 'An academic researcher needs to insist on early active involvement in the research project. They should decline any offers to sign off on already-written manuscripts, particularly in review articles. They should insist that the article reflects their own interpretation of the evidence. They have to be adamant about full disclosure ....' The burden is placed on academic authors who, by implication, sometimes fail at one or more of these junctures.

These journal editors thus treat planners as full and legitimate participants in, and valued contributors to, medical research and publishing. They can address an audience of 400 publication planners, warn them against ghostwriting and the inappropriate manipulation of data, and then solicit their business. As do medical journal editors as a whole, these editors welcome industry-sponsored manuscripts, even cater to them, but describe a set of rules of conduct and reporting intended to safeguard scientific integrity and authorial function. Although they know that the science involved involves careful interpretive work and depends heavily on expertise, they treat it as formulaic and try to make it more so. Although some editors and editors' organizations have taken strong stances against the pharmaceutical industry's research and publication practices, they are probably too dependent on the industry for material and revenue to refuse industry manuscripts. One editor interviewed, who has been active in setting high standards to combat ghostwriting, said that until economic structures of medicine and medical research change, the pharmaceutical industry will have a major presence in medical journals. Medical publishing has normalized ties with the pharmaceutical industry.

Authorship and its Limits

The *visible* experts who serve as the prominent authors on ghost managed research, without whom the publications would have much less value, stand in front of a number of other people who have likely done the bulk of the intellectual and organizational work. Visible experts are needed not for the contents of their expertise, but for their apparent independence and consequent authority. The ghost management of medical research has thus rehabilitated the connection of authors to authority: academic authors are valued almost entirely for their authority.

Undoubtedly, authors of industry manuscripts contribute to those manuscripts in varying degrees, but their contributions are often quite limited—they typically range from supplying some of the patients for a clinical trial, to editing the manuscript, to simply signing off on the final draft. As a result, authorship problems represent a major ethical concern voiced at publication planning conferences. Planners have difficulties dealing with ICMJE criteria for authorship because their position involves coordinating work by people who they (typically) do not want to become authors, such as company statisticians, company and agency researchers, and medical writers. These hidden contributors would not often meet the bar for authorship, in part because the ICMJE's concept of authorship does not apply well to corporate production of manuscripts. Nonetheless, research as managed by publication planners directly opposes the ICMJE's implicit ethical stance.

Meanwhile, planners do want KOLs to appear as legitimate authors in order to provide the credibility that is essential for publications. Especially since their work is driven by deadlines, these KOLs often do not meet ICMJE criteria. In addition, relations with them can be severely damaged if their names are removed from manuscripts late in the process. Therefore, it is best if planners can work to create authors out of KOLs.

Although they are recognized as crucial, KOL authors are often portrayed as lazy and greedy. As depicted by planners, KOLs typically make few substantial contributions to the manuscripts, are slow to respond and miss deadlines. They expect prominence in authorship order, and sometimes demand money for their contributions. (Payment to a KOL author contravenes guidelines of good publication practice, and a lawyer speaking at one meeting strongly cautioned against it, because it might be seen as a kickback, and as part of an attempt to manipulate prescribers.) KOL authors even try to violate planners' attempts to meet their ethical standards, for example by trying to remove acknowledgement of medical writers.

To satisfy good publication practice guidelines, authors need to contribute to manuscripts. Publication planners have techniques for managing this process. Planner CZ recommends very specific questions as a way of eliciting a contribution: 'You can actually guide them to where you want feedback. So don't just say, "Here's a first draft, and can I have your comment." Say, "Here's a first draft, and I've tried to figure out the methodology, to fit within the word requirement. However, I feel, could you pay some attention to this, and have I picked up the right point?"' CZ tries to create authors in ICMJE's sense (though adopting a broad interpretation of the criteria), by giving KOLs very specific writing responsibilities. In this context, even the author's complete non-contribution becomes a kind of contribution, seen as a tacit endorsement of the manuscript.

While planners complain about deadbeat authors, they create the conditions for those deadbeats. According to speaker BJ's estimate, 50% of companies show only the penultimate manuscript to authors, to solicit their input. It is likely that authors will have little to add to a well-crafted penultimate manuscript, especially if they are given tight deadlines. Medical researcher BB remarks that he received ghostwritten abstracts only after they were submitted (and accepted) for meetings, and authors receive manuscripts only days before the planners' deadlines for journal submission. Tightly managed schedules mean that authors are likely to contribute little.

The concept of ghostwriting presumes old-fashioned norms of authorship, which are then violated; in prototypical cases of ghostwriting, a single author's writing is done by a single ghostwriter. However, much medical writing, and especially pharmaceutical company sponsored writing, is part of a larger process of the corporate production of knowledge, of which authors are only one link. Articles are produced by teams, perhaps no one member of which meets requirements for authorship. In this largely unseen process, companies initiate and fund the planning, research, analysis, writing, and the placing of articles, and typically maintain control of data throughout. In the corporate production of knowledge, medical writers perform their functions, just as planners, company scientists and statisticians ... and authors do.

Creating Knowledge Through Mediation

Publication planners are both outsiders and insiders to the clinical research world. They are outsiders because they are not physicians or statisticians, who would normally be thought to contribute most to clinical research, and do not play a visible role in knowledge production. They are insiders because they often have detailed knowledge about clinical research, pharmacology, and medicine—in conversations I had with planners, they appeared fluent in the areas in which they were currently working. More importantly, they contribute to an enormous amount of research. A typical active planner is involved with many more research publications than are most medical researchers.

Clinical research and publication is unusual, in that acceptable methods have been very precisely spelled out, and these have been widely accepted. Over the past half-century, distrust of individual physicians' clinical experience and advocacy by statisticians and medical reformers have led to the randomized, controlled trial becoming the 'gold standard' of clinical research for both researchers and physicians (Marks, 1997; Timmermans and Berg, 2003). Reports of clinical trials are relatively formulaic and constrained, as journals demand tightly structured articles, and are increasingly demanding structured abstracts. Though there are many choices behind any article reporting a clinical trial, there are fewer choices about their format or the language they employ.

It may appear, then, that at least for clinical trials the work of planners and writers is relatively mechanical. However, there is abundant evidence that designing, analyzing, and writing up results from trials involves extensive decision-making. Certainly, planners do not represent their own work as mechanical. Speaking without apparent humor, BC tries to present agency concerns to those working in pharmaceutical companies: 'My plea here is to think again about attempting to commoditize something [publication planning and medical writing] that is actually a highly tailored service, a professional skill. I believe that commoditization undermines the value of medical writing. You're not buying widgets.' Despite appearances, one cannot commission manuscripts by the gross—by the dozen perhaps, but even then each article is individually crafted.

In addition to making their own contributions, planners facilitate their teams' work, keeping in contact with medical writers, making sure that all documents produced are consistent with the plan, managing information, and reconciling divergent demands and suggestions. The work of the planner is creative mediation, using the insights of the many people who come into contact with data and drafts to develop manuscripts that will fare better in peer review, and will have an impact.

Pharmaceutical companies, like all large companies, are complicated organizations. From the outside we might be tempted to see them as consistently organized around producing their usual huge profits. However, they are split into divisions that develop their own proximate goals, often conflicting with the company's overall goal and the goals of other divisions. The clinical trials department may be trying to increase the number of trials it performs, and to thereby increase its budget and importance. That department may be permeated with values other than strict market values, including imported scientific values that emphasize rigor and caution. Thus, says FD, 'publications reflect the work of several functions and matter to several functions.'

The overall publication planning team, says FD, 'ensures buy-in from all stakeholders,' because those stakeholders have input into the process and result. The multiplication of contributors multiplies the knowledge. Pharmaceutical company planner CI says:

> Involving folks early works. The sooner you involve them before you have data available the easier it is. Much, much easier. You go from having one manuscript to having eight from a pivotal program. Which is phenomenal. And it's not data-mining, it's just things that are relevant to the clinical practice in that area.

Of course, many of these actors may give a manuscript only a cursory review, and may have little or no positive input into it. MH notes, 'All the people on the [manuscript development] team have input. But if 3 or 4 can get together and work things out' it will be a lot more efficient.

Changing Trajectories?

In recent years, ISMPP has adopted a code of ethics (2010) and a revised standard of 'good publication practice' (2009). According to these standards, authors must be involved from the earliest stages of drafting a manuscript. It is unclear to what extent these codes are followed. More likely to be followed are individual corporate integrity agreements, which typically stem from the settlement of legal cases involving the U.S. Federal Government. Some of these agreements establish strict procedures for industry publication practices, and the corporations involved appear to enforce the new procedures rigorously, for fear of running afoul of the U.S. Government. Of course, procedures can be followed while their spirit is violated: authors may be involved in publications from the beginning while being subtly discouraged from being too closely involved.

Allowing authors access to study data provides a case in point. In an about-face, recent codes of ethics have accepted that authors need to have access to data. For example, in 2009 the U.S. industry association and lobby group PhRMA (Pharmaceutical Research and Manufacturers of America) published principles on the conduct and communication of clinical trials, which state that '[i]nvestigators who are authors of study-related manuscripts will be given all study data needed to support the publication' (PhRMA, 2009). However, the companies themselves can decide what access authors need to support the publication, and whether data consists of hand-written patient records, electronic versions of those records, already-analyzed reports, or even statistics based on them.

Without rich access to data, authors are unlikely to make major contributions to the analysis or writing of an article. They are shown well-crafted manuscripts that have been reviewed by many scientists, writers, and marketers. They are given only limited access to the data. They are asked their views on very specific points. They are given short deadlines. Thus, authors of industry manuscripts are largely sidelined from the process of analyzing, writing, and publishing research.

Even as standards are changing—at least as seen in new codes of ethics, new guidelines and new operating procedures—there remains a central conflict in the publication of pharmaceutical industry research. The companies want to maintain as much control as possible over the shape and content of publications, in order to best market products. They also want the names of independent authors at the tops of those publications, to increase their credibility, again to best market products. But industry control is incompatible with independent authorship, and so the new codes and procedures do not solve this central conflict.

Discussion

Publication planning aims to maximize the value of pharmaceutical companies' research, in terms that are simultaneously commercial and scientific. Planners' activities—building on the work of a diverse array of actors that include company scientists and statisticians, contract research organizations, multiple reviewers and medical writers—produce manuscripts that establish positive and consistent profiles for drugs. These articles, generally published in good medical journals under the names of independent authors, contribute to accepted scientific opinions. The circumstances of their production, though, are largely invisible.

Implicit in many of the exposés of ghostwriting in the medical science and popular literature is an assumption that ghostwritten science is formally inferior. Leemon McHenry (2009) writes, for example: 'If the results of industry-sponsored clinical trials were reported honestly, then aside from the question of deception and plagiarism, ghostwriting would not present a serious concern for advancing knowledge.' Certainly there have been some egregious cases of industry-sponsored dishonesty. However, given the very high acceptance rates of ghost managed articles, the assumption that the research is inferior is questionable in general, though it may be right about important cases (Psaty & Kronmal, 2008). Industry funded trials, and I would claim that the majority of these are ghost-managed to some extent, score as well as or better than independent trials on standardized methodological tests (e.g. Lundh et al., 2012). Moreover, publication planners are keenly attentive to scientific norms, because it is only by meeting those norms that they can distinguish themselves from marketers, and in so doing achieve their marketing goals; their job, after all, is to persuade without appearing to persuade.

Pharmaceutical company research, analysis, and writing result in knowledge. Companies and their agents make decisions in the running of clinical trials, in interpretations of data and established medical science, in the messages they convey in articles and presentations, and in the timing and location of publications. Decisions by themselves, however, do not make company-produced knowledge different than other knowledge. This point is straightforwardly suggested by the longstanding commitment to symmetry in Science and Technology Studies, which prods us to explain beliefs using the same set of tools whether those beliefs are considered true or false (Bloor, 1976). It is justified by the results of canonical studies that have shown how science is choice-laden (e.g. Knorr Cetina, 1981; Pickering, 1984; Collins, 1991). Thus, the work of pharmaceutical companies to produce research and prominently place it in medical journals is not merely a corporate use of the patina of science. It is science, though done in a new, corporate mode.

However, commercially driven science is different from academic science in the narrowness of interests that drive it and the kinds of choices that produces. Unlike most independent researchers, pharmaceutical companies have clear and strong interests in particular kinds of research, questions and outcomes: ones that will increase markets and sales. If almost every decision in the research and publication process pushes the research even subtly in a consistent direction, then that is the direction in which the research will go. We can reasonably expect, and there is abundant evidence to support this, that the industry makes its choices to support its commercial interests.

That pharmaceutical companies' research produces *results* that favor its products has been repeatedly demonstrated (e.g. Lundh et al., 2012). We might care equally about the more nebulous issues of *kinds of research* and *questions*. To see why, let us take the extreme case of made-to-order journals. In the early 2000s, the publisher Elsevier produced an entire line of medical journals in order to place articles marketing drugs (Grant, 2009). The publication planning firm Excerpta Medica, an arm of Elsevier, had brokered the deals and provided the imprint for the journals; these included *The Australasian Journal of Bone and Joint Medicine* (*AJBJM*), produced to market two of Merck's drugs. (This is not an isolated event; for example, the publisher Wiley advertises on its website that it can produce 'custom books and journals' for the healthcare industry (Wiley, 2009)). Even if these journals all reported results honestly, we should still want to know about the commercial interests behind them.

The articles placed in *AJBJM* were presumably chosen for their commercially valuable messages. They were probably written with those messages in mind. The studies on which they are based were probably designed to maximize the chance of Merck-friendly results. Some of the original studies may even have been performed precisely for their public relations value. The result is a publication bias that covertly advertises particular drugs, supports them scientifically, and sets agendas for diagnosis and treatment. All of this affects prescriptions.

In the ghost management of medical research by pharmaceutical companies, we have a new mode of science. This is corporate science, done by many unseen workers, performed for marketing purposes, and drawing its authority from traditional academic science. The high commercial stakes mean that all of the parties connected with this new science can find reasons or be induced to participate, support, and steadily normalize it. It is likely here to stay for a while. We might then ask, with a widely circulating joke, is medical science for sale? No, its current owners are perfectly happy with it.

NOTES

1 Earlier versions of some elements of this article appeared in *Academic Matters* (May 2009: 8-12), *Learned Publishing* 25 (2012): 7-15), and *Bulletin of Science and Technology Studies* 31(2011): 482-492, and *Social Studies of Science* 39 (2009): 171-198. I would like to thank Jason Millar for his help in structuring this paper, Elliot Ross for research assistance, and Khadija Coxon for both her research assistance and for her excellent editorial work.

2 Documents related to Wyeth's campaign and PC (2) can be found in Prempro Products Liability Litigation, *Drug Industry Document Archive*. Available at http://dida.library.ucsf.edu (accessed 7 July, 2011).

REFERENCES

Adis Communications (2006) http://www.pharmalive.com/content/supplements/gpms/2004/adis.cfm (Accessed Dec. 20, 2006).

Applbaum, Kalman (2004) '*The Marketing Era: From Professional Practice to Global Provisioning*'. New York: Routledge.

Barnett, Antony (2003.) 'Revealed: How Drug Firms 'Hoodwink' Medical Journals', *The Observer* (Dec. 7, 2003).

Berenson, Alex (2005) 'Evidence in Vioxx Suits Shows Intervention by Merck Officials', *The New York Times* (April 24, 2005): A–1.

Biagioli, Mario (2003) 'Rights or Rewards? Changing Frameworks of Scientific Authorship'. In: Mario Biagioli and Peter Galison (eds) *Scientific Authorship: Credit and Intellectual Property in Science.* New York: Routledge, 253–279.

Bloor, David (1976) *Knowledge and Social Imagery*. London: Routledge & Kegan Paul.

Carus Clinical Communications (2007) http://www.carusclinical.com (Accessed Nov. 29, 2007).

Collins, H. M. (1991) *Changing Order: Replication and Induction in Scientific Practice* (Chicago: Chicago University Press).

Complete Healthcare Communication (2006) http://www.chcinc.com/ (Accessed Dec. 20, 2006).

Envision Pharma (2006) http://www.envisionpharma.com/publicationsPlanning/ (Accessed December 20, 2006).

Fisher, Jill (2009) *Medical Research for Hire: The Political Economy of Pharmaceutical Clinical Trials.* New Brunswick, NJ: Rutgers University Press.

Fishman, Jennifer (2004) 'Manufacturing Desire: The Commodification of Female Sexual Dysfunction'. *Social Studies of Science* 34(2): 187–218.

Grant, Bob (2009) 'Elsevier Published 6 Fake Journals'. *The Scientist.com* (7 May). http://www.the-scientist.com/templates/trackable/display/blog.jsp?type=blog&o_url=blog/display/55679&id=55679 (accessed 19 July 2009).

Ham, Chang Dae, Jong Woo Jun & Hyung-Seok Lee, (2008) 'How to Reach Consumers in a Market where DTC is Not Allowed'. *Journal of Medical Marketing* 8(2): 159–168.

Healy, David (2004) 'Shaping the Intimate: Influences on the Experience of Everyday Nerves'. *Social Studies of Science* 34(2): 219–245.

Healy, David, & Dinah Cattell (2003) 'Interface between Authorship, Industry and Science in the Domain of Therapeutics'. *British Journal of Psychiatry* 183: 22–27.

ICMJE (2005) 'International Committee of Medical Journal Editors Uniform Requirments for Manuscripts Submitted to Biomedical Journals'. http://www.icjme.org (Accessed April 30, 2008).

Knorr Cetina, Karin D. (1981) *The Manufacture of Knowledge: An Essay on the Constructivist and Contextual Nature of Science* (Oxford: Pergamon Press).

Lundh, Andreas, Sergio Sismondo, Joel Lexchin, Octavian Busuioc, and Lisa Bero (2012) 'Industry sponsorship and research outcome'. Cochrane Database of Systematic Reviews 2012, 12.

Marks, Harry M. (1997) *The Progress of Experiment: Science and Therapeutic Reform in the United States, 1900-1990* (Cambridge: Cambridge University Press).

Mathews, Anna Wilde (2005) 'Ghost Story: At Medical Journals, Writers Paid by Industry Play Big Role; Articles Appear Under Name Of Academic Researchers, But They Often Get Help; J&J Receives a Positive 'Spin''. *Wall Street Journal* (Dec.13, 2005: A1).

McCook, Alison (2006) 'Is Peer Review Broken?' *The Scientist* 20(2): 26–35.

McHenry, Leemon (2006) 'Ghosts in the Machine: Comment on Sismondo'. *Social Studies of Science* 39(6): 943–947.

Mirowski, Philip, & Robert Van Horn (2005) 'The Contract Research Organization and the Commercialization of Scientific Research'. *Social Studies of Science* 35: 503–534.

Moynihan, Ray, & Alan Cassels (2005) *Selling Sickness: How the World's Biggest Pharmaceutical Companies are Turning Us All into Patients* (Vancouver: Greystone Books).

Moynihan, Ray, & David Henry (2006) 'The Fight against Disease Mongering: Generating Knowledge for Action'. *PLOS Medicine* 3(4): e191.

Patsopoulos, Nikolaos, John P.A. Ioannidis, A. Analatos Apostolow (2006) 'Origin and funding of the most frequently cited papers in medicine: database analysis'. *British Medical Journal* 332: 1061–1064.

Petersen, Melody (2008) *Our Daily Meds: How the Pharmaceutical Companies Transformed Themselves into Slick Marketing Machines and Hooked the Nation on Prescription Drugs.* (New York: Farrar, Straus & Giroux)

PhRMA. 2009. 'Principles on Conduct of Clinical Trials, Communication of Clinical Trial Results'. Available at http://www.phrma.org/about/principles-guidelines/clinical-trials (accessed 7 July, 2011).

Pickering, Andrew (1984) *Constructing Quarks: A Sociological History of Particle Physics* (Chicago: University of Chicago Press).

Psaty, Bruce M., & Richard A. Kronmal (2008) 'Reporting Mortality Findings in Trials of Rofecoxib for Alzheimer Disease or Cognitive Impairment'. *Journal of the American Medical Association* 299(15): 1813–1317.

Rasmussen, Nicolas (2005) 'The Drug Industry and Clinical Research in Interwar America: Three Types of Physician Collaborator'. *Bulletin of the History of Medicine* 79: 50–80.

Ross, Joseph S., Kevin P. Hill, David S. Egilman, & Harlan M. Krumholz (2008) 'Guest Authorship and Ghostwriting in Publications Related to Rofecoxib: A Case Study of Industry Documents From Rofecoxib Litigation'. *Journal of the American Medical Association* 299(15): 1800–1812.

Sismondo, Sergio (2014) 'Key opinion leaders: valuing independence and conflict of interest in the medical sciences'. In: Isabelle Dussauge, Claes-Fredrik Helgesson, and Francis Lee (eds), *Value Practices in the Life Sciences*. Oxford: Oxford University Press, 36–55.

Smith, Richard (2006) 'Lapses at the New England Journal of Medicine'. *Journal of the Royal Society of Medicine* 99(8): 380–382.

Thomson Scientific Connexions (2006) http://www.sciconnex.com/ (Accessed Dec. 14, 2006).

Timmermans, Stefan, & Marc Berg (2003) *The Gold Standard: The Challenge of Evidence-Based Medicine and Standardization in Health Care* (Philadelphia: Temple University Press).

Turner, Erick H., Annette M. Matthews, Eftihia Linardatos, Robert A. Tell & Robert Rosenthal (2008) 'Selective Publication of Antidepressant Trials and Its Influence on Apparent Efficacy'. *New England Journal of Medicine* 358(3): 252–260.

Watermeadow Medical (2007) http://www.watermeadowmedical.com/ (Accessed Nov. 29, 2007).

Wiley Publishing (2009) 'Wiley Resources for the Healthcare Industry', http://eu.wiley.com/WileyCDA/Section/id-310320.html (accessed 19 July 2009).

Writing Group for the Women's Health Initiative Investigators. 'Risks and benefits of estrogen plus progestin in healthy postmenopausal women: principal results from the Women's Health Initiative randomized controlled trial'. *Journal of the American Medical Association* 288.3 (2002): 321–333.

Wyeth (2002) Publication Plan 2002 – Premarin/Trimegestone HRT Working Draft. Available at http://dida.library.ucsf.edu/tid/awb37b10 (accessed 19 August, 2013).

11

Transcultural Medicine: A Multi-Sited Ethnography on the Scientific-Industrial Networking of Korean Medicine

Jongyoung Kim

Through a multi-sited ethnography of three different types of organization—a traditional medical clinic, two laboratories, and a biotech company—this article examines how Korean medicine (KM) scientizes, globalizes, and industrializes its clinical knowledge. By tracing the complex networking process among multiple places, the article aims to understand how KM reinvents its knowledge, identity, and boundaries in a global situation. In particular, it pays attention to how this process involves multiple dimensions of power relations, economic interests, and scientific authorities. It concludes that heterogeneous and unequal encounters between KM, science, and industry lead to simultaneous productions of new culture.

In this article, I explore how a group of KM doctors, scientists, and businesspersons transform KM clinical knowledge in connection with science and industry in transcultural and global contexts. In 1999, two laboratory directors in the College of Oriental Medicine at Kyung Hee University suggested their laboratories and the Ye Oriental Clinic work together for the scientific verification of KM treatments on the one hand and the establishment of a new biotech company for the industrialization of the KM treatments on the other hand. In the clinic, three KM doctors would conduct modernized and hybrid medical practices, combining traditional medicine with several techniques and theories of biomedicine. After considering this suggestion for several months, the doctors finally agreed to the directors' original plan. In 2000, the directors and the doctors formed a biotech company called "Purimed" to scientize and industrialize KM, thereby expanding KM's existing boundary.

Jongyoung Kim, "Transcultural Medicine: A Multi-Sited Ethnography on the Scientific-Industrial Networking of Korean Medicine," in Medical Anthropology 28 (2009). pp. 31–64. Reproduced with permission from Taylor & Francis.

The Pharmaceutical Studies Reader, First Edition. Edited by Sergio Sismondo and Jeremy A. Greene.

I interpret this networking as a power-laden tuning process through which heterogeneous social and technical elements are newly connected in multiple social, political, and economic negotiations and conflicts. In this regard, my analysis engages critically with actor-network theory (ANT) in science and technology studies as well as postcolonial and transnational studies of Asian medicines. According to ANT (Callon and Law 1989; Latour 1987, 1988; Law and Hassard 1999), science and technology are constructed through actors' ongoing "association" or "enrollment" of various social and technical elements such as machines, personnel, statistics, natural objects, and other elements. In this process, the social and the techno-scientific are newly linked, generating a powerful "sociotechnical" network or assemblage. ANT's best strategy for understanding an emerging techno-scientific culture is to follow actors' association practices and the continuous transformation of the sociotechnical network itself.

However, ANT tends to depict the network as "a seamless terrain" stabilized by scientists' interpretive, material, and social practices. Although ANT successfully bridges the divide between science, nature, and society on an abstract level, it fails to recognize how multiple terrains such as economy, science, and politics interact in global knowledge-making on an empirical level. For instance, KM's networking with science and industry generates unprecedented events "without forging a stabilized network," leading to a continuous dialectic oscillation between the stabilization and destabilization of knowledge. In other words, while ANT focuses on the closure of scientific networking, KM's networking process shows continuous frictions, tensions, and destabilizations generated by heterogeneous and unequal interactions among multiple terrains: the global terrain of developed country-developing country, the knowledge-making terrain of traditional medicine-science, and the industrial terrain of small biotech venture—big pharmaceutical company.

ANT also fails to recognize the actor's positionality in a global field of knowledge-making. As some scholars argue (Martin 1997; Star 1991; Zhan 2001), ANT tends to depict the scientist as "a masculinist Eurocentric subject privileged to travel freely and forge strategic translocal networks" (Zhan 2001: 461). My ethnographic study describes KM's paradox, the simultaneous picture of KM doctors' inventive networking, and the limitations imposed on this networking by the global scientific regime and market capitalism. KM professionals lack scientific knowledge and skills at the levels required by the scientific community. More seriously, they still suffer from ongoing scientism and medical exclusion exerted by biomedical professionals. Consequently, ANT is not sensitive to knowledge-makers' huge affective investment in the wake of their positionality. While scientists in ANT are portrayed as cool talents, the KM professionals in my study, who are "scientifically subjugated but economically wealthy people," display a range of shifting and sometimes petty emotions, including anger, despair, aspiration, and competitiveness.

I conducted fieldwork mainly in three different places directly involved in the association process[1]: the Ye Oriental Clinic, the Physiology Lab and the Korean Medicine Lab in the College of Oriental Medicine at Kyung Hee University, and the Purimed Company.[2] I also traveled to Los Angeles, where a branch of the company sells its commodities to Korean Americans. Furthermore, I visited government organizations, university facilities, other hospitals, and medical industries related to the association. By following people and tracing artifacts, monies, and stories, I was able to identify emergent, unexpected trajectories and links in the association process.

To understand the current transformation of KM, my description starts with KM's brief modern history, concentrating on its political economy. The next part describes the KM professionals' global encounters with sciences and biomedicine. By following their biographies, I illuminate how these actors representing a national elite react to a global hierarchy of knowledge production. Then, I examine three sites where different types of knowledge and skills are produced and transformed through clinical, scientific, and business practices respectively. In doing so, I delve into how the KM professionals construct their networking in an open-ended way; how they negotiate and struggle with various actors; how the doctors reconstruct KM's identity and image; what kinds of ideologies and power structures are involved in the networking process; and how doctors take advantage of the transnational network. Finally, I argue that KM's scientific-industrial networking is an inventive but power-laden tuning process through which KM professionals intend to build a strong network, coping and negotiating with diverse ideologies and multiple forces.

A Brief Modern History of Korean Medicine and its Transformation

KM, which was imported from China around the sixth century, shares cosmological tenets and practices with Chinese medicine. While KM practitioners have regarded Chinese medicine as their own East Asian cultural heritage, they have also developed KM's unique clinical skills, such as Sasang constitution medicine and palm acupuncture. After Japan's colonization of Korea in 1910, the Japanese colonial government declared KM illegal and shut down its schools and professional organizations. Korea's liberation from Japan in 1945 opened a new possibility for KM armed with a strong nationalism. KM was finally legalized in 1951, and for the next several decades a series of new KM schools were founded. KM experienced a surge in popularity in the 1970s and 1980s, when the Korean economy achieved one of the fastest growth rates in the world. The Korean people, enjoying an increased income, could now consume the relatively expensive tonic medicines prescribed by KM practitioners.

In 2000, a total of 136 KM hospitals and 7243 KM clinics furnished medical service to the Korean people, who spent 18.4% of their total health costs on Korean medicine (Lim, 2001: 8, 56). In 1988, KM also joined a national medical insurance system, further increasing its popularity and availability. During this long period of expansion, KM doctors achieved the occupational status and economic success similar to that enjoyed by biomedical doctors in Korea. Wealthy KM doctors, like those I studied in Ye Oriental Clinic, can be found throughout South Korea.

However, KM has had to defend itself against biomedical professionals' continuous attacks, some of whom sought to maintain a monopoly of the medical market. On the one hand, biomedical professionals attempting to unify a bipartite medical system have argued that KM lacks scientific validity and thus harms people's health. On the other hand, biomedical professionals, especially pharmacists, wanted to gain profits from the herbal medicine market: their efforts culminated in the "Herbal Medicine Dispute" between KM professionals and pharmacists, which started in 1993 and was eventually resolved in 1996 (Cho 2000). While pharmacists sought legal permission to dispense herbal drugs, KM professionals resisted the legal change. Attacking KM as an unscientific medicine, pharmacists eventually succeeded in selling herbal medicine. Therefore, biomedicine's scientism and its encroachment on the KM market functioned as a massive driving force for KM professionals to transform, i.e. scientize, industrialize, and globalize KM knowledge since the 1990s.

One revolutionary event, Korea's unexpected financial crisis in 1997, changed the entire social terrain and should be mentioned to explain KM's industrialization and globalization. The Korean government, which was almost forced to declare a debt moratorium, eventually relied on an International Monetary Fund (IMF) bailout program, the largest financing package in IMF history (Coe and Kim 2002). For political and strategic reasons, the Korean government installed major economic policies supporting venture companies with relatively modest capital outlays. The government offered research funding, tax benefits, research personnel, and favorable regulation changes to KM companies.

The association among KM, science, and industry, therefore, is composed of multiple and heterogeneous forces, and the actors' strategic ripostes, in the 1990s (Kim 2006a). These forces and KM's responses include scientism that prevailed and operated against KM, the KM doctors' co-optation of science, and the KM researchers' reorientation of knowledge in response to the 1997 economic crisis. In the next section, I present KM doctors' personal narratives of KM's marginal position in the field of medicine and the global hierarchy of medical practitioners in order to understand their personal motivations for creating alliances among KM, science, and industry.

KM Doctors' Global Experiences: Biographical Accounts

The Purimed members' life stories illuminate why and how they are involved in reinventing KM. While their past experiences shaped the motivations for the association—directing concrete plans on how to combine different practices—their accumulated past knowledge, skills, and social capital, acquired as necessities of association among Ye Clinic, the two laboratories, and Purimed company, also grounded the actual process of reinventing KM. KM doctors display their marginalized experiences in relation to global science. Seeking "recognition" in scientific fields and the public, they aim to expand KM's network and influence in society.

Prof. Bae, the director of the Physiology Lab, is a KM doctor and scientist. He is one of the few KM professionals who earned a doctoral degree in a scientific field. In addition, his doctoral degree and research experience from the United States hold significant meaning in the KM community. He holds the same scientific qualification as other "serious" scientists, most of whom have derided KM researchers' lack of scientific competence.

His experience in the United States is critical to understanding his motivation for the association. In an interview, Prof. Bae described discrimination he experienced from his colleagues and teachers during his first year in the Physiology Department at the University of Illinois at Chicago. They considered Bae strange because he majored in Korean medicine; his colleagues in the department majored in the sciences or biomedicine. Many people doubted Bae's ability to study science and biomedicine due to his background even though he learned scientific methods in his KM and master's degree courses. One example of the discrimination concerned academic support. While all other doctoral students in his cohort received financial aid the first year, he alone was denied funding. He explained to me that scientists in the West do not recognize the existence of KM because KM practitioners have not published their research in international journals, the authoritative medium of communication and recognition among Western scientists. Prof. Bae attempted to gain recognition from his colleagues by explaining that KM students are recruited from the brightest students in South Korea, and that a KM doctor belongs to an elite class in South Korea. He realized soon that this effort was useless.

> Prof. Bae: In the eyes of American scientists, Korean medicine does not have serious scientific foundation. In Korea, people place Korean traditional doctors in top social positions. But, when I studied in the U.S., I felt myself situated at the bottom.

Even though Prof. Bae has double degrees, in KM and biomedical science, he strongly identified himself as a KM professional rather than a scientist. He also placed great importance on the infrastructure of research and the mutual dependence of money, science, and social recognition in both KM and Western medicine.

> Prof. Bae: We are living in a capitalistic system. To enlarge the field of Korean medicine, we need to channel markets and to associate with industry. If Korean traditional doctors are just satisfied

> with Korean medicine's current situation and if they do not try to widen its field, Korean medicine will never develop. Especially, Korean medicine must be industrialized to gain social recognition so that it can contribute to the Korean economy.

When Dr. Lee, the CEO of Purimed, narrates his professional biography, he points to his global encounter with alternative medical doctors and researchers in the United States. After graduating from the College of Oriental Medicine at Kyung Hee University, he entered the Korea Sport Science Institute, where he was involved in projects to understand herbal medicines' effects on athletes' performances. As an active member of the Association of Korean Oriental Medicine (AKOM), he was also elected the director of foreign affairs.

> As the director of foreign affairs, he had an opportunity to form social networks. Dr. Lee revealed that his global experience changed his view of KM. Through international travels and meetings with other alternative medical professionals, he found, and resented, a global hierarchy among alternative doctors based on nationality, professional recognition, and institutional affiliation. Alternative medical scholars in the West, especially those in the United States, occupy dominant positions in the field of international alternative medicine even though, according to Dr. Lee, their alternative medicine training is not superior to that of scholars in East Asia.Dr. Lee: Even though I possess excellent knowledge and skills in Korean medicine, they would be useless unless I have a network to *represent* them. If a scholar of the Center for Alternative Medicine at Harvard Medical School says something, it has a significant impact. Korean traditional doctors are like country bumpkins in the eyes of Americans. Who knows about Korean medicine? (Italics: Dr. Lee's emphasis.)

He lamented that KM has no global influence in the field of complementary and alternative medicine. It is evident that the field of alternative medicine is already global, where many practitioners compete with each other in the global market and scholarly fields. The scientization, globalization, and industrialization of KM also aim at enhancing the recognition of KM and enlarging the KM network to compete with other practitioners who practice alternative medicines.

Sharing common visions and goals, the two directors of the labs and three doctors of the clinic established Purimed Company in 2000. The basic relations among the three organizations are as follows. The research committee, the company, and the three doctors first decide which KM treatments should be industrialized in terms of market conditions, research potential, and the efficacy of a treatment under consideration.

After deciding to commercialize a treatment, the company estimates the necessary research funds, which it provides for the lab. Scientists design and conduct experiments to verify the efficacy of each treatment. In this process, the effectiveness of a given treatment is standardized and objectified in the laboratory. If the experiment succeeds in proving the targeted treatment, the laboratory sends the result to the clinic and the company. In the next section, I will show the transcultural construction of KM in each site, describing a full development of the association process.

Hybrid and Modernized Practice: The Production of Hybrid KM Treatments in the KM Clinic

The location and architecture of the Ye Oriental Clinic demonstrate how the doctors strove to create a new, modern image of KM. The clinic is placed in the so-called Kangnam area, which literally means the southern area of Han River in Seoul. The wealthy, upper-middle, and professional classes live in this area, which represents wealth and success to many

Koreans. In addition, the clinic is located in the Teheran Valley of Kangnam, regarded as the center of Korean venture industries. The clinic rented half of the 19th floor of a 20-story, gorgeous, modern building, which provides a breathtaking view of the middle of the metropolitan area.

Ye Oriental Clinic differs from a typical KM clinic, which generally consists of a consulting room and reception area. The typical scene includes herbal cabinets, a floor covered with laminated paper, a hanging calendar, a table, and chairs. Most KM doctors wear reformed Korean traditional costumes. The furnishings of a typical consulting room, where Chinese calligraphies and Oriental paintings are displayed, are not lavish. But unlike the typical KM clinic, the interior of Ye Oriental Clinic, mainly composed of marble walls and dark brown wood floors, creates modern, refined, and luxurious views. The clinic space is compartmentalized into specialized clinic rooms, meditation rooms, massage rooms, a dressing room, an examination center, a reception area, patient consulting rooms, doctors' offices, and a business management office. The examination center houses various diagnostic devices including a fat measurement machine, skin detection devices, a pulse-taking machine, and a liver diagnostic machine. The KM doctors in the clinic synthesize KM's typical clinical method, "syndrome differentiation and therapy determination," with those results from machinery devices. One cannot see the cabinets that contain herbs in the reception area, which symbolize the classic image of KM clinic. Instead, luxurious sofas and tables occupy the space. On the walls of the corridors and clinic rooms hang paintings by famous Korean artists. Because the clinic created a totally new image of a KM clinic—differing from the classical, traditional image—many patients report their impressions that "this clinic is not like a KM clinic."

Although the KM doctors provide typical KM treatments such as acupuncture, tonic medicines, and moxibustion, the Ye Oriental Clinic is famous for its weight-loss program and skin therapy. I will concentrate on these two programs for two reasons. First, around 80% of all patients visit this clinic for these programs, and these clinical specialties helped the doctors develop secret treatments that other KM doctors do not know and cannot harness. Second, the lab and the company eventually industrialized these therapies by making two commodities based upon these treatments: a skin soap and a weight-loss supplement. By demonstrating how the doctors developed these therapies, I will reveal complex connections between KM, biomedicine, and cosmetic skills.

The diet food industry and diet medical treatments started to develop in South Korea in the late 1980s. From the mid 1990s, cosmetic surgery has become increasingly popular and the whole industry has dramatically grown. Now the combined market size of the diet and cosmetic industries exceeds $1.5 billion in the country. The KM doctors I am studying appropriated this opportunity by accommodating the patients' desire and developing new herbal therapies. Many patients visit KM clinics to cure diseases of the musculoskeletal system and connective tissues. The doctors of Ye Clinic have also practiced acupuncture to treat patients who suffer from arthritis, gout, spondylosis, etc. Some patients, however, continued to take acupuncture without having any significant improvement. Dr. Lee, suggested a group study to understand these types of diseases. the doctors realized that arthritis, their patients' most common frequent complaint, is related to the patients' excess weight. The doctors advised the patients to lose weight for a more effective cure, but in reality the patients had neither specific programs nor guidance for losing weight. The doctors decided to develop a weight loss program by using herbal medicine and referred to heterogeneous medical resources to find suitable treatments for obesity. Herbal therapies they gathered from their KM colleagues significantly contributed to the development of therapy. In addition, they read articles by Chinese doctors on obesity and herbal treatments.

Their most important source for curing obesity, however, was Je-Ma Lee's constitutional medicine. Je-Ma Lee was a legendary KM doctor in Korea in the 19th century who created a new KM tradition called Sasang Medicine. From their colleagues' information and their own medical experiences, the doctors started to develop diet programs by using and modifying Lee's KM treatments. In addition, they hired a nutrition professional in the course of development and learned about nutritional science.

Combining various methods, treatments, and their own medical experiences, the doctors succeeded in treating obesity and achieved fame with many overweight patients. Because the diet program they coined requires several months of treatment, the doctors were able to make longitudinal observations of patients' bodily conditions. In this process, the patients who followed the diet program reported that their skin condition became much better than before they started the program. Patients who had acne, dermatitis, pigmentation, and keratosis were surprised that the diet program was also effective on their skin conditions. The doctors discovered an unexpected opportunity to practice a novel skin therapy by using traditional medicine. After this discovery, they also devoted time to studying KM classics that provide diverse treatment for skin diseases.

Even though they found many valuable treatments in the KM classics, they were not satisfied with them. KM methods are based on the traditional Ŭmyang (Yinyang in Chinese) and Ohaeng (Wuxing in Chinese) cosmologies, which do not explain how skin diseases actually occur in terms of physiological standpoints. Thus, the doctors started to learn dermatology from the biomedical point of view and gained a semi-professional knowledge of it. Furthermore, Dr. Son, one of the three doctors, apprenticed a couple of cosmetologists to learn practical treatments for skin improvement. Through Dr. Son's determined efforts and many skills, the doctors finally installed a skin therapy program.

The messy and irregular connections of the therapies made me curious about the doctors' identities as traditional doctors. I asked if Dr. Son, as a KM doctor, feels any contradictions and discomfort when he uses other medical skills and knowledge.

> Dr. Son: I don't think that I am a defender of tradition knowledge. I just want to pull out good and useful resources from traditional medicine in order to cure acne. I mix up traditional methods with preexisting biomedical and nutritional sciences.

Dr. Son challenges the dichotomy and boundary between biomedicine and KM, regarding both of them as "resources" for his valuable therapies. Paradoxically, at the same time, his hybrid identity and pragmatism weaken his professional identity as a "KM" doctor. The three doctors frequently call themselves "doctors" without the prefix "Korean medical." As in Jean Langford's (2002) observation of Ayruvedic doctors, the KM doctors "mimic" biomedical doctors, "the model" to which they aspire, while challenging the biomedical boundary and system. Moreover, the KM doctors mark the prestige of their profession by making the KM therapies a tool of class distinction. Most of their patients are high or upper-middle class females who can afford to consume modernized KM treatments at great expense. Advertising a cosmopolitan aura and catering to class tastes, the KM therapies become highly profitable commodities and achieve meanings radically different from the image of "traditional" medicine. The odd couplings among various medical traditions, consumerism, and desires for ideal bodies have created a new hybrid, transcultural medicine.

Laboratory Practice and the Scientization of Herbal Therapies

The two directors involved in the association process lead the Physiology Lab and the Laboratory of Korean medicine (LKM) in the College of Oriental Medicine at Kyung Hee University. Because their instruments and laboratory environments do not accommodate diversely designed experiments, the two laboratories collaborate with other laboratories. For example, the Purimed Company solicited a research team at Korea University to conduct a psychological experiment using an herbal treatment because no experts or facilities for psychological experiments exist in the two labs. The collaboration includes laboratories in the United States as well as those in Korea. Because the two directors received their Ph.D. degrees in North America and became researchers after graduating, they maintain connections with several labs in the United States.

The experiments aim to objectify the doctors' herbal treatments that had been verified before only in their clinical experiences. The material practices in the lab transform the embodied and unverbalized clinical treatments into visible "scientific facts"[3] that demonstrate self-evident cause-effect relations. By resituating herbal medicine in laboratory settings, the objectifying practices forge a new sociotechnical network among herbal medicine, material devices, experimental skills, statistics, and scientific representation. The subjective dimension of treatment detaches from its concrete situation and achieves depersonalized meaning (Porter 1999).

In addition to forming a new network between herbal therapy and laboratory science, KM researchers attempt to redefine the concept of science in relation to KM. A KM professional in the Physiology Lab argues that "Korean medicine is a science in its way," because KM has its own "systematic theory and understanding" of the body and the world. According to him, KM theories should be understood in the clinical context of KM, where those theories convincingly explain bodily phenomena. Meanwhile, a scientist in the Laboratory of Korean Medicine claims, "Korean medicine is absolutely not a medicine of miracle or mystery. It is not a miracle but a science." Unlike the KM professional, this scientist emphasizes the "replicable" application of herbal medicine to the same symptom more than KM's systematic theory. Therefore, he denies KM as a miracle, regarding it as science because its therapies are based on consistent and normalized "empirical efficacy and rationality." Prof. Bae himself newly defines KM as "practical knowledge or know-how" to treat illness and promote health, claiming that "it is almost impossible to scientize Korean medical theories." According to him, KM's practicality and empiricism deserve the category of science. Furthermore, Prof. Bae criticizes the dualistic perception of science and KM, articulating a transcultural and historical point of view.

> Prof. Bae: Korean medicine is not the opposite of science. Basically, medicine is art, not science. Before Western medicine was grafted with science, Korean medicine was superior to Western medicine. But Western medicine has dramatically developed since it embraced science. As such, we [KM researchers] can develop Korean medicine by embracing scientific methods.

In this remark, Prof. Bae neutralizes the term "science" by defining both Korean medicine and Western medicine as arts. This strategy intends to subvert the dichotomy between "scientific" biomedicine and "traditional" KM by equalizing them as arts.

A major paradox in the scientization of herbal medicine is that scientists and KM researchers do not pay attention to the conceptual and cosmological aspects of given therapies (Kim 2007). In the KM clinical setting, the herbal treatment is mostly based upon unique theories such as meridian affinity, flavor theory, Ŭmyang (Yinyang in Chinese), and Five Phase theories. On the contrary, KM researchers in the labs are interested only in whether X treatment or herb can be effective on Y symptom causally and statistically. Therefore, the "scientization" of KM causes the dissociation of herbal medicine from its KM theories. The "scientization" of KM mobilizes laboratory science, statistical reduction, and the visibility of herbal therapies, overtly emphasizing its empirical aspect while dropping its classical theories and concepts. In the end, herbs in the labs become only natural substances, emptied of any of KM's clinical meaning.[4]

In contradiction of ANT's main point, the encounter between KM and science does not stabilize the network. Although it forms a new assemblage, it destabilizes KM, creating frictions and contradictions. The mechanical application of laboratory skills and KM's disaggregation between theory and empirical effect in the scientization of KM produce multiple but contradictory political effects. Because KM researchers adopt laboratory science as a legitimate tool for judging KM's efficacy, KM succumbs to a global scientific hegemony that limits KM researchers' range of possible actions. For instance, KM researchers told me that KM concepts and theories are not allowed in scientific journals. Consequently, the researchers deliberately efface traditional concepts to publish their experiments. Despite this asymmetrical power relation between KM and science, the scientific verification of herbal medicine has enhanced the scientific legitimacy and recognition of KM. For example, the Korean Broadcasting System (KBS), the most influential broadcasting company in South Korea, has televised the successes of the experiments. A commodity based upon the skin therapy technology also won the Bronze Medal of the Grand Korea Patents Meeting. Within the university, Prof. Bae has come to be regarded as a leading scientist and KM researcher for achieving the school's goal of pursuing the scientization and globalization of KM. By publishing the experimental results of herbal medicine, Prof. Bae demonstrated the excellent quality of KM to Western scientists as well as Korean biomedical professionals. As a result, the KM college provided him with more funds, devices, and facilities. In addition, as expected, the three doctors advertised these scientific results to patients and the public. Dr. Choi delightedly said to me that "I don't need to explain the treatment to patients. The only thing I have to do is just to say: look at the data." However, the transformation of scientific facts into medical commodities became the most difficult task the members confronted, as I will explain in the next section.

Network of Networks: Industrialization Process of Herbal Medicine in the Purimed Company

Almost all the people in my study reported that the most difficult aspect in the association process is to make commodities to sell to consumers. The businessmen of Purimed move across multiple sites, forging allies beyond the network of the three organizations. As they move beyond clinical and scientific practices into the economic realm, the association's activities become increasingly messier, more contingent, and more destabilized.

As a first step, the company imported herbal materials from Taiwan. The researchers and the traditional doctors were well aware that Korean raw materials lack good quality control, since they are produced not by a factory system but by farmers, which leads to substantial variance in the potency of herbs. The Purimed Company contracted with a large Taiwanese herbal company with a long production history in the field of herbal medicine.

However, the final products are not "drugs" in a medical sense, but rather supplements and functional foods because of the specific sociotechnical relations of herbal medicine. The manufacture of medical commodities from Purimed Company concentrates on the production of supplements and functional foods that do not require stringent and complex experiments, and are not subject to equally stringent regulations. The technical process and the legal system sanction the nature of herbal commodities.

While most company profits come from the Korean market, the company's global networking and business also grew to be an important activity. Purimed established two branches in the United States and is now attempting to expand its market in Japan and China. The U.S. market attracted the company for several reasons. First, laws and regulations on supplements and functional foods in the United States are less rigid than in Korea, which allows the company to produce targeted commodities. For instance, Lycii Fuctus, a main component of a Purimed herbal commodity, is banned from production as an herbal supplement in Korea. This limitation led the company to produce the item in the United States, where the herb can be a major part of supplements. Second, because the United States has the largest Korean population abroad (1.08 million according to the United States 2000 census), the company can target a niche market where Korean-Americans might purchase the company's commodities. Purimed's two branches are in Los Angeles and New York, areas with the largest Korean-American populations in the United States. Finally, Purimed managers speculated that successful business in the United States could increase Purimed's credibility with Korean consumers. By improving the global image of KM and by earning profits from other countries, the company thrives by communicating double messages to Koreans: the superiority of Korean "national" culture and its "global" outlook and expansion.

Purimed depends heavily on advertisements to make Korean-Americans recognize its products. Its advertisements mainly appeal to the "Koreanness" of the herbal product, the scientific excellence of herbal supplements, and the researchers' affiliation with Kyung Hee University, which is known as the capital of KM. These double meanings—the scientific excellence of KM and the Koreanness of Purimed products—appeal to Korean-American's cultural desire to be connected with "Koreanness." A sales person reported to me that elderly Korean-Americans particularly like Purimed products. Most of them place deep trust in Korean medicine's scientificity and Kyung Hee University's symbolic prestige. Park's (1994) statistical research on Korean-Americans' usage of KM in the United States also shows that Korean-Americans strongly believe in the efficacy and the excellence of KM.

However, the fact that its products are sold mostly to Korean-Americans becomes a major limitation in the expansion of Purimed. Mr. Kim, the director of the Purimed L.A. branch, told me that it is very difficult to expand the Purimed market to reach other ethnic groups. Unable to create a major market, Purimed instead looks for a niche market. While this strategy may seem to be a compromise in local terms, it reaps symbolic benefits at another local site, in that Purimed advertises its global image to South Koreans by emphasizing its business activities in the United States.

In summary, Purimed's business practices involve the most extensive external networks and agents. The businessmen continuously mobilize, strategize, and negotiate with any available personal and social networks. In this networking process, business activities transform multiple agents and sites into an intertwined and mingled association beyond confined territories and reified categories. Now I turn to the final discussion of the networking process among the three organizations, which shows the multi-stranded and socio-technical dynamics among national culture, market capitalism, power asymmetry, and KM's scientific position.

Transcultural Medicine and Emergence of New Medical Assemblage in Global Power Relations

KM's network process involves multiple scientific, economic, and political dimensions, forming a "global assemblage" (Collier and Ong 2005: 4) through the formation and reformation of heterogeneous elements. The KM professionals orchestrate diverse conceptual, material, and social elements as they negotiate and struggle with the Korean government, Western scientists, and alternative medical professionals, biomedical professionals, and businessmen with diverse logics in different places. KM as a transcultural medicine challenges various dichotomies such as East/West, social/technical, local/global, and micro/macro. Conflating with Aihwa Ong's concept of transnationality (1999: 4), transcultural medicine in my study denotes the movement and rearrangement of KM elements to science and industry across space as well as KM's changed nature in the hybridization process. Forming an in-between and modernized identity, KM doctors developed effective skin and weight-loss therapies in Ye Clinic. In laboratories, herbal treatments turn into "scientific objects" that experimental devices and systems objectify as herbal efficacy. Then, the herbal treatments are commercialized as functional foods and supplements through Purimed's business operation. Depending on each site's socio-technical relations, Korean medicine is defined differently: it is a hybrid medicine in the clinic, a scientific object in the laboratory, and a functional food and supplement in the industry. My point is that KM's "multiplicity of becoming" arises with the emergence of each new medical network or assemblage.

Here, unlike the focus of actor-network theory (ANT) on the unifying and stabilizing process around a single center, i.e., the laboratory, the KM story shows how multiple centers destabilize and restabilize KM knowledge and skills, generating diverse forms of Korean medicine such as skin and weight-loss therapies, scientific facts on herbal treatments, and KM supplements. This polycenteredness and open-endedness of KM networking generates continuous frictions, tensions, and destabilization. In ANT, the laboratory functions as an obligatory passage point where scientists tinker with heterogeneous elements for the construction of scientific fact, focusing on the closure of experiment. On the contrary, rather than a single obligatory passage point, KM's networking hosts continuous reconfigurations among Ye Clinic, the two laboratories, and Purimed Company, and generates unprecedented and dialectic oscillation between the stabilization and destabilization of knowledge. ANT is especially insufficient for explanations of the networking between science and industry in the age of global capitalism because the development of science and technology is now heavily dependent upon intensive capital investment. Though ANT as a theory for the global-scale making of science is still relevant, it pays insufficient attention to capitalism and industry as the driving force shaping experimental practices, especially in the medical field (Petryna, Lakoff, and Kleinman 2006; Rajan 2006; van der Geest 2006). For instance, like other biotech companies, Purimed Company selects only the most profitable herbal treatments for experimentation, and selectively represents the experimental results to promote sales.

With regard to traditional medicine's political relation to Western science and industry, comparing my account with Vincanne Adams' study (2002) might be illuminating. In the transcultural encounter between biomedical research and Tibetan medicine, Adams shows that Tibetan medical practitioners were criminalized because they did not follow the state-sanctioned rule of randomized, controlled, double-blind testing. Paradoxically, Western pharmaceutical companies have usurped intellectual ownership from Tibetan medical practitioners, making and selling standardized Tibetan medicine to Westerners who want to consume the cultural and spiritual benefit of Tibetan medicine. In this process, Tibetan doctors are doubly discriminated against by biomedical researchers and pharmaceutical industries. In my study, on the contrary, KM professionals mobilized science and industry by themselves, and at the same time they began to gain the Korean government's financial and policy support, such as $2 million of research funding and favorable regulation changes. The experiments in the lab follow the controlled double-blind testing standard, verifying the herbal medicines' effects in a scientific way. The value of Purimed Company increased from $1.5 million in 2000 to $8 million in 2005, producing more profits. Unlike Adams' story of Tibetan medicine, KM's reinvention seems to succeed in forging a better and bigger network.

Furthermore, those power relations exert real forces that mold KM's reinvention process in a particular way. In laboratories, the scientific hegemony allows herbal medicine to be expressed as a cause-effect mechanism, but forces effacement of its theoretical foundations. In the pharmaceutical industry, a KM commodity cannot join the mainstream drug market because it cannot satisfy the legal requirements for drug manufacture. Although my study of KM's transformation seems to be much more optimistic than other postcolonial studies of Asian medicine, KM still faces obstacles. The simultaneity of opportunities and barriers is the exact reason why KM professionals negotiate various actors, rules, and ideologies at different levels on the one hand, and deliberately display subtle and contradictory strategies on the other hand: networking science and industry, subverting the dichotomy between KM and science/biomedicine, emulating laboratory science and biomedicine, following scientific methods and market logic, fashioning their own globalization, constructing KM as a high-class medicine, and reformulating its cultural identity. In sum, the heterogeneous and unequal encounters between KM, science, and industry lead to simultaneous productions of new culture and power without reducing them to a single logic and a center in a global age.

Conclusion

This article demonstrates how KM reinvents its knowledge, identity, and boundaries in connection with science and industry. The networking process of KM showcases unpredictable combinations and interplay among a national culture, the global market, and the politics of knowledge-making in transcultural and transnational situations. By showing how multiple and heterogeneous forces and dimensions are irregularly interacting in KM's scientific-industrial networking, this case study has challenged the great divides between East and West, traditional medicine and science, the local and the global, and the micro and the macro. However, the power asymmetry between science and Korean medicine and KM doctors' marginal positions also influenced the unique process of KM's reconfiguration. Therefore, I have interpreted KM's networking process as a power-laden tuning process through which a new socio-technical assemblage emerges, producing new types of medicine, science, and commodities.

NOTES

1 My fieldwork focused on the contemporary transformation of Korean medicine. This case study is a major part of my field research conducted for 22 months during a five-year span (1999–2003). For the entire project, I interviewed 76 people, including KM professionals, scientists, patients, and businesspersons. I also conducted several rounds of in-depth interviews with key players like Professor Bae, the three doctors, the CEO of Purimed, the managerial staffs of Purimed, and the scientists in the two laboratories.

2 I reveal the real names of institutions by permission of the laboratory directors, the three traditional doctors, the CEO of Purimed, and my informants and interviewees.

3 For the construction of scientific fact, see Latour and Woolgar (1986) and Knorr-Cetina (1999).

4 In this article, I do not pay attention to KM epistemology in detail. What I am arguing is that despite its new combination, synthesizing KM with science is an unequal process in which KM epistemology is disregarded. As Scheid argues (2002: 54), the synthesis of different medical and scientific elements involves "simultaneous emerging and disappearing." Also, it should be noted that epistemology does not have priority in the making of science and medicine (Kim 2006b; Pickering 1995; Galison 1997). Rather, material practices, epistemology, and social elements are mutually resisted and accommodated in the making of transcultural science and medicine without recourse to a single dimension.

REFERENCES

Adams, V.
2002 Randomized Controlled Crime: Postcolonial Sciences in Alternative Medicine Research. Social Studies of Science 32(5–6):659–690.
Callon, M. and J. Law
1989 On the Construction of Sociotechnical Networks: Content and Context Revisited. *In* Knowledge and Society. John Law, ed. Pp. 57–83. Greenwich, CT: JAI Press.
Cho, H. J.
2000 Traditional Medicine, Professional Monopoly and Structural Interests: A Korean Case. Social Science & Medicine 50:123–135.
Coe, D. and S. Kim
2002 Korean Crisis and Recovery. Seoul: International Monetary Fund.
Collier, S. and A. Ong
2005 Global Assemblages, Anthropological Problems. *In* Global Assemblages: Technology, Politics and Ethics as Anthropological Problems. Aihwa Ong and Stephen Collier, eds. Pp. 3–21. Oxford, UK: Blackwell Publishing.
Galison, P.
1997 Image and Logic: A Material Culture of Microphysics. Chicago: The University of Chicago Press.
Kim, J.
2006a Korean Medicine's Globalization Project and Its Powerscapes. Journal of Korean Studies 11(1):69–92.
2006b Beyond Paradigm: Making Transcultural Connections in a Scientific Translation of Acupuncture. Social Science & Medicine 62(12):2960–2972.
2007 Alternative Medicine's Encounter with Laboratory Science: The Scientific Construction of Korean Medicine in a Global Age. Social Studies of Science 37(6):855–880.
Knorr-Cetina, K.
1999 Epistemic Cultures: *How the Sciences Make Knowledge*. Cambridge, MA: Harvard University Press.
Langford, J.
2002 Fluent Bodies: Ayurvedic Remedies for Postcolonial Imbalance. Durham, NC: Duke University Press.
Langwick, S.
2007 Devils, Parasites, and Fierce Needles: Healing and the Politics of Translation in Southern Tanzania. Science, Technology, & Human Values 32(1):88–117.
Latour, B.
1986 Powers of Association. *In* Power, Action, and Belief: A New Sociology of Knowledge. John Law, ed. Pp. 264–280. London: Routledge and Kegan Paul.
1987 Science in Action. Cambridge, MA: Harvard University Press.
1988 The Pasteurization of France. Cambridge, MA: Harvard University Press.
Latour, B. and S. Woolgar
1986 Laboratory Life: The Construction of Scientific Fact, 2nd ed. Princeton: Princeton University Press.
Law, J. and J. Hassard
1999 Actor-Network Theory and After. Oxford, UK: Blackwell Publishers.
Lee, J. M.
1996 Longevity & Life Preservation in Oriental Medicine. Seoul: Kyunghee University Press.
Lim, B. M.
2001 Present Status of Oriental and Alternative Medicine related Industries in Korea. Ministry of Health and Welfare. Korea.
Martin, E.
1997 Anthropology and the Cultural Studies of Science: From Citadels to String Figures. *In* Anthropological Locations. Akhil Gupta and James Ferguson, eds. Pp. 131–146. Berkeley, CA: University of California Press.

Miles, A.
1998 Science, Nature, and Tradition: The Mass-Marketing of Natural Medicine in Urbana Ecuador. Medical Anthropology Quarterly 12(2):206–225.
Park, J.
1994 Traditional Medicine in Korea and America. Unpublished doctoral dissertation. Providence, RI: Brown University.
Petryna, A., A. Lakoff, and A. Kleinman, eds. Pickering, A.
1995 The Mangle of Practice: Time, Agency, & Science. Chicago: University of Chicago Press.
Porter, T.
1999 Quantification and the Accounting Ideal in Science. *In* The Science Studies Reader. Mario Biagioli, ed. Pp. 394–406. London: Routledge.
Rajan, K.
2006 Biocapital: The Constitution of Postgenomic Life. Durham, NC: Duke University Press.
Scheid, V.
2002 Chinese Medicine in Contemporary China: Plurality and Synthesis. Durham, NC: Duke University Press.
Star, S.
1991 Power, Technology and the Phenomenology of Conventions: On being allergic to Onions. *In* A Sociology of Monsters?: Essays on Power, Technology and Domination. John Law, ed. Pp. 27–57. London: Routledge.
Sullivan, D. Van der Geest, S.
2006 Anthropology and the Pharmaceutical Nexus. Anthropology Quarterly 79(2):303–314.
Zhan, M.
2001 Does It Take a Miracle?: Negotiating Knowledges, Identities, and Communities of Traditional Chinese Medicine. Cultural Anthropology 16(4):453–480.

Part IV

Political and Moral Economies of Pharmaceutical Research

The Pharmaceutical Studies Reader, First Edition. Edited by Sergio Sismondo and Jeremy A. Greene.
© 2015 John Wiley & Sons, Inc. Published 2015 by John Wiley & Sons, Inc.

The economic value of pharmaceuticals lies chiefly in the knowledge of their usefulness. The costs of production of pills, tablets, capsules, or injectables themselves are usually trivial compared with the costs of extensive research and development operations that lead to them and the costs of the sequence of clinical trials required for their regulatory approval for the treatment of a specific indication. As the production of pharmaceutical knowledge has become increasingly global in its practices, new conflicts have emerged in the ethics and politics of pharmaceutical research.

The articles of this section explore some of the challenges precipitated by the globalization of pharmaceutical research and development. Exploring the sequence of events that made the harvesting of *barbasco* yam of the Oaxaca, Veracruz, and Puebla regions of southern Mexico a crucial step in the global production of steroid hormones, historian Gabriela Soto-Laveaga moves beyond the allegation that pharmaceutical interests in these yams and local ethnobotanical knowledge of their location and harvesting can simply be categorized as a neocolonial form of bioprospecting. Instead, as she argues in Chapter 12, telling the story of *barbasco* in context forces us to attend to complex new forms of agency that knowledge of pharmaceutical chemistry provided for Mexican peasants and North American pharmaceutical executives—although not symmetrically.

The remaining chapters in this section situate the transformation of clinical trials in the late 20th and early 21st centuries, taking shape in different ways across a variety of different geographies. Clinical trials, and randomized controlled trials in particular, are simultaneously treated as a universal "gold standard" for biomedical proof, are very substantial commercial activities, and are often major health interventions in their own right. In Chapter 13, sociologist Jill Fisher explores the increasing gray area between formal understandings of clinical trials as *de jure* experimental formations and the practical sense in which clinical trials have become *de facto* essential structures of health care delivery to some specific populations. In light of this duality, she asks whether the kind of human subjectivity protected by an ethics of informed consent—the cornerstone of contemporary bioethical thinking about clinical trials—is even possible in the current pharmaceutical R&D landscape. In Chapter 14, anthropologist Adriana Petryna describes how the conduct of clinical trials is increasingly mobilized or "offshored" to alternate geographies with looser forms of human subject protection, larger proportions of "treatment naïve" patients, and conditions likely to produce desired results. That trials are increasingly performed by contract research organizations in temporarily pragmatic or convenient locations further problematizes the adequacy of informed consent, as well as the status of trials as biomedical proofs. This analysis is continued by anthropologist Kaushik Sunder Rajan in Chapter 15, in a detailed study of the shift of clinical trials from North America to the Indian subcontinent, with attention to intersecting political, economic, and ethical imaginaries invoked by actors in both India and the United States.

12

Uncommon Trajectories: Steroid Hormones, Mexican Peasants, and the Search for a Wild Yam

Gabriela Soto Laveaga

This article analyzes how evolving pharmaceutical technology, chemical advances, and world politics created the need for an abundant and cheap supply of steroids, and how decisions made in faraway laboratories ultimately determined that a Mexican yam, barbasco, was the best possible raw material. Following this discovery, this article explores how barbasco's exploitation impacted on the Mexican countryside and specifically the men and women hired to gather wild yams. In analyzing, for example, the peasant organizations that emerged, the use of chemical terms by barely literate peasants, and the Mexican government's political strategy to control rural unrest by controlling barbasco production one begins to understand the unexpected consequences of the global search for medicinal plants. In this particular case, the merging of science and peasant life reshuffled social hierarchies in the countryside, granted monetary value to an erstwhile 'weed', and gave a novel reinterpretation to laboratory knowledge and its (social) uses.

> *1934: 'The collection, selling and transport of urine, the search for remains from slaughterhouses and the ordering of a whale were all aimed at the same goal: the production of sex hormones. The making of sex hormones into material realities required the availability of tons of ovaries and testes, as well as millions of liters of urine'.*[1]
>
> —Nelly Oudshoorn

Gabriela Soto Laveaga, "Uncommon trajectories: steroid hormones, Mexican peasants, and the search for a wild yam," in Studies in History and Philosophy of Science Part C 36 (2005). pp. 743–760. Reproduced with permission from Elseiver.

The Pharmaceutical Studies Reader, First Edition. Edited by Sergio Sismondo and Jeremy A. Greene.

1951: 'The cortisone production problem was solved ... it should be noted that the leader in the race was a chemical manufacturer in presumably backward Mexico'.[2]

—Harper's Magazine

If we are not able to follow up our participant-observation studies far enough to take in questions outside the laboratory, we are at great risk of falling back into the so called 'internalist' vision of science.[3]

—Bruno Latour

Introduction

Today the hormones estrogen and progesterone are 'the most widely used drugs in the *history* of medicine':[4] millions of women take hormonal pills, and a hormonal model is widely used to explain the human body. Surprisingly, however, the concept of hormones is, in historical terms, quite recent. The term was not coined until 1905 and it would take nearly three decades before hormones could be mass produced. By the twentieth century scientists had transformed sex hormones from imagined 'secretions' into commodities that could be purchased and manipulated. But before hormones could be neatly boxed and packaged, scientists needed to leave the confines of their laboratories and look for sources, first for organs, then urine, and finally tubers. Ironically, it would be a little known laboratory in Mexico, a country without a domestic chemical research industry of its own, that would eventually solve the supply problem. Indeed, the global demand for steroid hormones was met with the help of the most uncommon of participants, Mexican peasants. This article will analyze this obscure chapter in steroid hormone history and its impact on the history of medicine and of Mexico.

Specifically, this article analyzes how evolving pharmaceutical technology, chemical advances, and world politics created the need for an abundant and cheap supply of steroids, and how decisions made in faraway laboratories ultimately determined that a Mexican yam, *barbasco*, was the best option for raw material. To understand this story within the larger context of its eventual impact on the Mexican countryside, we need to understand what enables the transformation of a local plant from a 'weed' into what was arguably some of the twentieth century's most valuable drugs. By this I do not mean the bit by bit laboratory and marketing process, but rather the historical, political, medical, and social catalysts which urged the scientific community to search for and find barbasco.

Of the various actors responsible for the transformation of the root from plant to medicine, an essential link was the scientists, in particular Russell Marker, who carried their knowledge from American and European laboratories to the places where barbasco grew. But in an amazing reinterpretation of events, in 1975 it was Mexican peasants who claimed that they and not foreign scientists were the ones who controlled the production of hormones, or rather, the raw material needed to produce synthetic hormones. Remarkably, these individuals, who in the eyes of laboratory researchers were the farthest removed from hormone production, later demanded that history acknowledge their role in the very spaces from which they were shunned—pharmaceutical laboratories. No researcher of the time could have envisioned that his quest for a plant substitute for animal sources of hormones would produce structural changes in the Mexican countryside and the birth of one of southern Mexico's most ambitious and organized peasant movements centered on, of all things, a wild yam. By making these proprietary claims, Mexican peasants contested the right of scientists and pharmaceutical companies to own the production and appropriation of scientific knowledge. By disputing the role of pharmaceutical laboratories, Mexican *campesinos* (peasants) challenged the way in which history is told, disseminated, and ultimately written. They brought to the fore the following question: what happens when knowledge which is contained within laboratories suddenly makes its way outside the laboratory walls and filters into the most unexpected of spaces? This paper deals with the uncommon trajectories of drug research. It goes beyond the known researchers, laboratories and events to bring in other pivotal players—Mexican peasants. But to get to that story we must first turn to the laboratories of the early part of the twentieth century. The story of Mexican steroid hormone production begins outside of Mexico in foreign laboratories devoted to the production of sex hormones.

Hormones in the Laboratory

At the beginning of the twentieth century biochemists, clinicians, and laboratory scientists began to study sex hormones.[5] By the late 1930s scientists entering the field of sex endocrinology, however, were confronted with the blunt reality that they were dealing with research materials—testes and ovaries—that were not readily available in sufficient quantities in the laboratory.[6]

Initially, without direct access to starting material, the pharmaceutical industry contracted exclusively with slaughterhouses for the purchase of gonads. This practice, as was described by Nelly Oudshoorn, would lead to future researchers' (gynecologists', physiologists', and chemists') dependence on pharmaceutical companies for a guaranteed supply of animal glands. To further pharmaceutical companies' control of steroid hormone production, by the 1930s the Swiss company Ciba, the German Scherring, and the Dutch Organon had set up a powerful European cartel on patents and cross-licensing agreements.[7] Quite rapidly, then, the study, control, and production of steroid hormones passed from individual chemists to large drug houses.[8] Furthermore, with each discovery the pharmaceutical companies followed up with preparations made to target specific ailments caused by a lack of hormones.

In 1926, when two German scientists discovered that urine was a source of pure hormones, things began to appear brighter for researchers seeking raw material. Pregnant women's urine happened to be far more active than the best ovarian extracts so far obtained and, moreover, 'the supply of urine was both abundant and inexpensive'.[9] Female sex hormones were first isolated in 1929 from the urine of pregnant women, and male sex hormones in 1931 from male urine. In 1938 female sex hormones were also isolated from male urine, confirming earlier beliefs that men and women both possessed female and male hormones.[10] The delay in chemically isolating these substances had been due entirely to the limited availability of raw material since large quantities of active substances, unfortunately, occurred in small doses when dealing with inert matter. Consequently, obtaining appropriate quantities to produce extracts became the main concern.

By the late 1920s therapy with female sex hormones was touted as the remedy for 'menopause, infertility, and problems of the genital organs'.[11] When hormones were marketed as basically 'cure-alls', the demand increased, as did the need for larger quantities of raw material. But despite the enthusiastic reception, researchers were still plagued with the problem of finding cheaper starting material. Scientists determined that to solve this supply problem they would have to step away from preparations made from animal materials. In the search for steroid hormone substitutes, the plant kingdom became the next frontier.

In Search of a Wild Yam

As these hormones were being isolated in laboratories scientists discovered that certain plants contained saponins, a plant sterol, and some, such as Russell Marker, reasoned that vegetable sterols were the solution to hormone production shortages. When referring to Russell Marker, the author of the 1962 reference book *Steroid drugs*, Norman Applezweig, remarked, 'We owe to him, more than to any other man, our ready and low-cost supply of steroid hormones. Without his contributions, we would not have synthetic hormones as we know them today'.[12] How, then, did this American chemist become inexorably tied to the history of Mexico?

Marker knew that sterols were found in the botanical order Liliales—onion, asparagus, and lily families—and the Dioscorea genus, embracing yam, desert yucca, and agave.[16] In particular, Marker was looking for saponin compounds. The structure of sapogenin included 'a long pendulous "side-chain", rather like a tail, attached to the four rings of the molecule',[13] similar to cholesterol, the fatty substance which the body itself uses for making steroids. To make steroids such as progesterone out of cholesterol, the side-chain, then, has to be removed by chemical reaction, and 'this the body can accomplish without difficulty'.[14]

Until then, chemists had been unsuccessful in replicating animal hormones by deriving them from plant material. Marker sought to undo the side-chain, however, and have it simulate progesterone. Within months Marker was able to remove this side-chain using sapogenin from the root of the sarsaparilla plant, called sarsapogenin, and successfully obtain progesterone. In fact, it was this discovery that would place Mexico on the research maps.

The Birth of Syntex

When Marker returned to the United States after having proven that sex hormones could be synthesized using yams, he was given an enthusiastic reception from the research community, but was unable to convince American drug companies that Mexico was the place where a steroid hormone industry should be started. The following quote reflected what were then seen as the many obstacles of working in Mexico on such a 'precarious adventure'.

> The Mexican pharmaceutical industry was virtually non-existent: there were no facilities for processing the black root, and what was more the *cabeza de negro* was hardly the most accessible of source material, for it grew in steamy hilly jungle [sic] where nobody in his senses ever went. And was Mexico politically stable? How could any large company setting up an establishment there be sure of the future?

The reference to Mexico's future economic and political stability hinted at the 1938 oil expropriation in which the Cárdenas government targeted American and British interests.[15] Moreover, other documents made allusion to Mexico as a 'technologically backward nation' whose citizens were 'ill-prepared' to grasp the complexity of organic chemistry. In his memories of that time, Russell Marker comments that even then, president of Parke, Davis & Company, Alexander W. Lescohier, believed that 'nothing useful could be done in Mexico … it was just a waste of money', and decided not to fund Marker's requests for $10,000.[16] Indeed, another chemist's account of the time reinforced the idea of how foreign chemists worked with 'Ph.D. colleagues and well-educated technicians', but in Mexico had to manage a laboratory with 'one college graduate and several charming, but giggly, *señorita*-assistants who had not finished high school'.[17] These images of Mexicans as 'charming' but not a serious site for scientific endeavors would also play a part in how labor at every step of the process was evaluated and remunerated by the drug companies. Finally, a more real obstacle for seeking research funds was the beginning of World War II and so, 'the [American] embassy was advising all Americans to stay out of Mexico at that time ... because no one knew whether Mexico would be in on it on our side or not'.[18] In addition, linked to business, research, and security concerns were those of infrastructure and labor, as the below quote explains.

> The drug companies pointed out that Mexico was a rough country with inadequate transportation and poor industrial facilities. Digging isolated wild plants and hauling tons of unwieldy tubers out of jungles and across mountains was surely doing things the hard way, not to mention the labor problem. No, it was just too farfetched for serious consideration by American businessmen.[19]

Moreover, the labor issue continued to appear time and time again, because the *Dioscorea* roots 'would have to be brought out of the roughest of rough country with no roads save Indian trails and with no potential labor force save untrained and disinterested Indians'.[20] In spite of these hurdles Marker installed himself in Mexico and used a process to collect roots which replicated the region's centuries-old trade networks.

The mechanisms of root collection that Marker's scientific zeal set into motion would endure almost unaltered for nearly four decades. The world's growing demand for steroid hormones derived from diosgenin would require the implementation of a root-picking endeavor which needed thousands of able-bodied persons. Significantly, timely changes in the infrastructure of the Mexican countryside coincided with chemical discoveries in distant laboratories. With the number of unemployed peasants growing in barbasco-rich regions, root-picking became a panacea to which rural people ardently adhered.

Once having obtained large quantities of root, Marker then synthesized more progesterone than had ever been synthesized before, 2000 grams—at the time worth nearly $160,000 dollars.[21] Having obtained the elusive female hormone, Marker now needed a buyer. According to later accounts in scientific journals (*Steroids*, *Chemical Education*, *Journal of the American Chemical Society*), popular magazines (*Life*, *Fortune*, and *Harper's Magazine*) and books on various medical topics Marker unexpectedly showed up at Laboratorios Hormona, S.A.—which marketed natural hormones derived from animal sources among other pharmaceuticals—with, in some versions of this history, two kilos of progesterone, an unheard of quantity at the time.[22] The owners of Laboratorios Hormona, the Hungarian Emeric Somlo and the German Federico Lehmann, were immediately aware of the importance of Marker's achievement.[23] The idea of establishing Syntex S.A., a Mexican company devoted to the industrialization and production of progesterone, was derived from that meeting. Syntex began operating in January of 1944, and in less than a decade it became the major supplier of synthetic hormones to European and American pharmaceutical companies.[24] In a 1951 article, *Fortune* magazine proclaimed that this jungle-root chemical industry was probably 'the most remarkable technological boom ever to come from south of the border'.[25] Marker had almost single-handedly altered the European monopoly of steroid hormone production. Moreover, with his synthesis the price of progesterone dropped to less than one dollar per gram from nearly a $1000 per gram figure.[26] At that point, the scientific world's hormone-seeking gaze shifted from slaughterhouses to the jungles of southeastern Mexico.[27]

By 1949 a raw material better than the initial *cabeza de negro* was found in *barbasco* which, while also a dioscorea, took less time to mature, contained more diosgenin, and was believed to be found in inexhaustible abundance in Mexico's jungles. Whereas *cabeza de negro* took anywhere from six to nine years to mature to significant levels of diosgenin, barbasco contained nearly 6% diosgenin yields in half the time. Earlier concerns with the inaccessibility of barbasco for mass production—due to the labor-intensive collection process of the root—were solved due to Mexico's continued economic instability and political turmoil which made available large numbers of unemployed peasants willing to enter the jungles in search of barbasco. In addition, the method of payment 'upon receipt' of the root had changed to payment in advance. To carry this out, an extensive net of peasant middlemen was now being employed by Syntex. According to a 1951 *Fortune* article these changes took place because 'Mexican villagers were not anxious to go tramping through the jungle gathering strange roots, with only verbal promises of financial gain. Syntex finally had to put up cash in advance and keep up an intricate collection system to keep the *cabeza* flowing'.[28]

Marker abruptly left Syntex less than two years after the inception of his partnership with Somlo and Lehmann. According to later interviews with Marker he departed after Lehmann and Somlo refused to pay him his share of the profits. In retaliation—and in an interesting example of how scientific knowledge is combined with the politics of knowledge—Marker switched and mislabeled reagents. George Rosenkranz, his successor, made the following observations shortly after his arrival at Syntex:

> It soon became obvious that my predecessor, the brilliant, but secretive and suspicious Marker, did not want anybody to know the secrets of his processes ... Reagents and intermediates all carried strange code names. For example, the hydrogenation catalyst was labeled, 'silver'. Solvents were identified by the workers by weight and smell.[29]

In the late 1940s the steroid production process in Mexico was constrained almost in its entirety by a single individual and scientist, Marker. By contrast, in the 1970s, Mexican peasants, wholly unaware of chemical processes, controlled steroid hormone production by regulating the amount and type of wild yams that were extracted.

Shortly after Marker left Syntex he abandoned chemistry altogether and effectively disappeared from public view from 1949 until 1969, when he received an award from the Mexican Chemical Society.[30]

George Rosenkranz and the Study of Chemistry in Mexico

George Rosenkranz, a chemist originally from Hungary, was in Cuba taking advantage of Batista's presidential decree that allowed all emigrants to settle in Cuba, when the owners of Syntex contacted him.[31] Somlo and Lehmann were desperately seeking someone who could continue the work that Marker had so abruptly left behind. For some time and since most Cuban yams yielded only sitosterol, Rosenkranz had been extracting saponins from imported Mexican yams. Once hired by Syntex, Rosenkranz was able to synthesize testosterone and later estrone, using *cabeza de negro*, which up until then had only been available in natural form 'from oceans of pregnant mares' urine'.[32]

Rosenkranz's work in the Mexican chemical industry highlighted the lack of trained Mexican chemists. 'Applying the same solution as in Cuba, [Rosenkranz] started a Ph.D. program' at the National Autonomous University (UNAM).[33] Rosenkranz also actively lobbied to form links between students at Mexico's Instituto de Química on the UNAM campus and Syntex laboratories. The Instituto, developed with the goal of training Mexican chemists to work with steroids specifically derived from barbasco, today continues to be one of the country's leading research centers.[34] As Rosenkranz continued to work on sex hormones extracted from barbasco, world demand would once again shift the focus of the study of hormones and Mexico would once again play a prominent role.

Human Faces Beyond the Laboratories: Mexicans Search for Barbasco

As the world began to clamor for cortisone, the search for barbasco was intensified in the jungles. Interestingly, though barbasco grew in abundance in southern Mexico, it had no commercial value. So, consequently, outsiders needed to come and 'teach' local people about the value of barbasco. Most oral accounts from former root pickers suggest that they learned their trade, either as adults or children, by observing others in their community dig the root. Some older *barbasqueros*, however, recalled that a sample root was brought to the communities by representatives of the laboratories or local middlemen. Locally, barbasco was well known as a fish poison, but it was also considered a pesky 'weed' that invaded corn fields. With its fibrous, branch-like root structure, barbasco competed with the roots of local products, mainly corn and beans. In addition, the uneven ground was a blueprint for frequent and dangerous falls. Furthermore, the oppressive humidity was relentless, commonly reaching highs in the mid to high 90s Fahrenheit. Even standing still made one sweat. A final aggravation for root-pickers was the swarms of tiny insects intent on feasting on uncovered arms and legs. What, then, propelled men, women, and children to enter the jungles by the thousands?

There were several readily apparent enticements. First of all, the root grew in abundance in southeastern Mexico's highly agrarian, underdeveloped, and mainly indigenous regions. Second, in many areas barbasco picking was the only source of income during *tiempos muertos* (dead time), usually from June through September when nothing was harvested or planted, and the area's *plantaciones* were not hiring the usual number of day laborers. Third, the timing of the discovery of cortisone coincided with economic trends throughout Mexico's countryside. Between 1940 and 1960 the number of landless peasants in the countryside grew dramatically. Though there was a modest 11% increase of accessible land in these years the peasant population increased 59% in the same time period.[35] As the number of available field hands grew, the number of work days per peasant decreased from 190 days in 1950 to 100 days in 1960. The worsening employment conditions in the Mexican countryside increased the number of *campesinos* relying on root-picking. By the end of the sixties, barbasco picking was no longer associated simply with *libres*, or men and women without land, but also with *ejidatarios* (land owners). In addition, although the price paid per kilo of barbasco was minimal compared to the profits made on the final product, pickers' earnings were often up to five pesos more than the daily wage paid to a peon.[36] Finally, plantation work was only for adults, but barbasco collection was for everyone. Men, women, and children of all ages looked for barbasco. Single women would go in search of barbasco in groups of four or five, married women would accompany their husbands, and widows could be seen going alone, or with small children. Women with babies or pregnant women would sling them on their back and carry them while they dug into the ground. Once they had found, extracted, and chopped the barbasco root they would shift the child and sling him across their breast and carry the bundle of fresh barbasco on their backs. Having balanced their human and barbasco bundles, women would begin the walk to the nearest collection center. Despite the significant number of women and children pickers, the physical demands of barbasco extraction made the pickers disproportionately male.

As Mexico's peasant crisis became more severe, barbasco became a crucial primary source of income throughout barbasco-rich areas but in particular in the region of Tuxtepec, Oaxaca, where some of the roots with the highest content of diosgenin could be found. Ironically, as the situation of yam pickers worsened, profits from medications derived from the yam began to soar due, in part, to new discoveries at the Syntex laboratories in Mexico City.

Carl Djerassi: Syntex, Cortisone, and an Amazing Mexican Yam

In the early 1950s as more researchers began to experiment with various synthetic alternatives to progesterone, the product derived from Mexican yams continued to be the purest form available. American chemists found the Syntex product between four and eight times more effective than natural progesterone when taken orally.[37] In July, 1951 Upjohn requested from Syntex the unheard amount of ten tons of progesterone at 48 cents per gram (the going rate was $2), and Syntex agreed to manufacture it. It later became known that Upjohn had found a way to convert progesterone into hydrocortisone, which in turn produced the much sought after cortisone. Indeed, by that time cortisone and its derivatives were the most sought after form of steroids and Mexico was the key in its production.[38]

Mexican Syntex would continue to astound the world when, on 15 October 1951, Luis Miramontes, under the tutelage of Carl Djerassi, completed the synthesis of what turned out to be the first oral contraceptive to be synthesized (norethindrone, for short).[39] Contrary to Searle's claims that it synthesized the substance concurrently and independently of Syntex Djerassi, one of the Pill's 'fathers' claims that it was initially Syntex and illustrates it with journal publication dates.[40] In 1956 Syntex ceased to be a Mexican company when Palo Alto-based Ogden Corporation bought it out and shifted its headquarters to California. This action effectively nudged Mexico from the center of hormone production.[41]

By the early 1950s Syntex had become the world's major supplier of synthetic hormones. Effectively a wild yam had revolutionized the world of medicine, but few people then or now stopped to ask themselves how the root made its way from the jungles to be found in powder form in the pharmaceutical laboratories of the leading pharmaceutical companies.

For nearly three decades a steady stream of peasants—an estimated and varying 100,000 by 1970—silently emptied the jungles of barbasco.[42] Between 1955 and 1974, according to Mexican sources 956,569,465 tons of fresh barbasco were gathered from all of southeastern Mexico with a subsequent 7,652 tons yield of diosgenin.[43] But after digging up the root, Mexican peasants still needed to sell it to local buyers and it was during this interaction that local needs encountered, or rather clashed, with scientific knowledge.

Although peasant pickers were key to the extraction of barbasco, there were different levels of middlemen that made the entire process function. Barbasco could not arrive at the laboratories in its raw state (unless specifically used for experiments). The root had to be sliced into slivers, fermented, dried, measured into a labeled sack, and sent to the laboratory (either Orizaba, Veracruz, or Mexico City). Extracting the root from the jungle was the most arduous step of the process, but it was not the final one before exporting the end product to foreign laboratories. This multi-tiered, specialized process reinforced preexisting fortunes by concentrating the power of barbasco collection in the same hands which gave rise to the indigenous middleman.

Not surprisingly, the local barbasco buyer came to replicate on a smaller scale the traditional strongmen in the region. The practice of *enganchar* ('hooking' in laborers by lending them money in exchange for future supplies of barbasco) created a form of debt by which the individual *barbasquero*, or an entire community, was obligated to sell barbasco exclusively to the lender. In addition, the large amounts of money handled by one member of the community, the buyer, began to create class divisions, especially when barbasco buyers (*acopeadores*) acquired horses, built cement houses (traditional homes were made out of wood) and even bought cars with their barbasco commission.[44] Despite the new found power and wealth of many *acopeadores* they, in turn, were responsible to and dependent on the owners of the *beneficios*, or processing plants.

The *beneficio* consisted of large concrete slabs where the fermented root was placed to dry. It was rather astonishing to step out of the thick cover provided by the jungle and encounter a dirt road leading to a paved open space as large as a city block. In the *beneficio*, barbasco was processed and transformed into diosgenin. There were nearly 300 *beneficios* throughout southeastern Mexico. From 1951 to 1975, in the area of Tuxtepec, *beneficios* were privately owned by local individuals or by any of the six pharmaceutical companies working with barbasco in Mexico. During previous crop booms, many *beneficios* had been collection sites for coffee berries and had later been abandoned.

The owner of the *beneficio* would hire salaried men from nearby communities. Some of these *chalanes* eventually learned the trade well enough that they discovered a way to 'purify' the root so that it could yield higher percentages of diosgenin, and since the laboratories not only paid for quantity but also for quality, these men became valuable, local 'chemists'. Chemical knowledge jealously guarded by European and American researchers trickled down into the area of Tuxtepec and became inextricably linked as the main source of labor for landless peasants in the region. Indeed this reinterpretation awarded chemical knowledge a particular twist when locals began to use key chemical terms in every day life to describe their activities.

In September of 1974, President Luis Echeverría decreed that forestry permits for barbasco extraction would no longer be issued to manufacturers of steroids. He claimed that his actions were guided by the 'clamor' from students and barbasco pickers from the states of Veracruz, Oaxaca, Puebla, Chiapas, and Tabasco. Their complaints, he determined, were derived from the 'exploitative price which they received for their natural resource' *and* 'the systemic fraud' from middlemen who bought barbasco for the steroid manufacturing companies.[45] By 1976, Mexico City residents were repeatedly treated to newspaper articles dealing with steroid hormones, transnational pharmaceutical companies, and barbasco.[46] Newspaper articles fostered and reflected the opinion that it was the government's duty to publicly protect barbasco *and* the pickers from pharmaceutical laboratories, in part because control of barbasco represented, 'an important opportunity to unite the [steroid hormone] industry with agricultural production'[47] and harness the profits of a lucrative primary resource. In addition, newspaper articles began to note that what was needed to accomplish these goals was in effect 'state funds'. And, of course, many of these state funds could be attained only from the missing 'Mexican share' of profits of pharmaceutical companies.

Ironically, as the history of barbasco grabbed hold of the nation's imagination, in many regions of Mexico the root was becoming scarce. By 1975 barbasco was losing ground to alternative source materials in the world market; whereas in the late 1950s diosgenin from Mexico's barbasco accounted for 80 to 90% of the world production of steroids, by the early 1970s, this portion had dropped to 40 to 45%.[48] Mexico, it seemed, was unable to increase its production of diosgenin to keep pace with world demand. According to the scholar and Syntex-in-Mexico specialist Gary Gereffi, from 1963 to 1968 the world demand for steroid hormones doubled, but Mexico only increased its diosgenin output by 33%. In addition, from 1968 to 1973 world demand increased another 50% but Mexican diosgenin production increased by only 10%.[49]

There were several reasons internal to Mexico to explain why the country was unable to keep up with the world's demand for diosgenin. First of all, land fit for barbasco production was giving way to commercial agriculture and cattle raising. According to the National Institute for Forestry Research (INIF), in Mexico a total of 7.6 million hectares were suitable for barbasco production but by the 1970s, 80% of that total had already been transformed leaving less than 1.5 million hectares in the six states—Veracruz, Tabasco, Chiapas, Puebla, Oaxaca and Estado de Mexico—where barbasco could still be gathered.[50] More alarming, diosgenin concentration from Mexican barbasco had decreased. As the number of *campesinos* seeking the root augmented, smaller and younger barbasco was picked, inexorably leading to lower percentages of diosgenin.[51] Diosgenin content decreased significantly in some areas from 6 to less than 4%. In addition, barbasco began to disappear completely from certain regions, especially in the area of Los Tuxtlas in Veracruz.[52] The root's disappearance was linked to destruction of its habitat caused by grazing, but also to the increased numbers of peasants who, determined to get the most barbasco, no longer left a piece in the ground so it could regenerate. Most pointedly, despite its enforcement of forestry permits, the state did not have a regulatory body to watch over the extraction of barbasco and it could only 'guesstimate' at what the companies reported as an accurate number. The Ministry of Water Resources (SAG) reported in 1973 that 60,000 tons of barbasco *verde* (green, meaning 'fresh') were extracted per year but despite these official calculations, other agencies such as FONAFE estimated that in that year alone, the number extracted was at least five times that reported.[53] Nevertheless the Mexican government promised that with 'the creation of a state-controlled pharmaceutical industry' the 'irrational exploitation' of both plant and man would end.[54] The solution would be called Proquivemex, a state-subsidized research and development company.

Proquivemex's founding charter guaranteed that the Mexican company would be the only legal exploiter of barbasco.[55] Hence Proquivemex would regulate the collection of barbasco and process the raw root, transforming it into barbasco flour (a diosgenin-rich substance). Transnational pharmaceutical corporations would then not be phased out but would be subordinated to the state company. In addition, the charter also stipulated that Proquivemex could eventually produce its own medications and also rally peasants to demand a fair price for their barbasco.[56]

By 1976 peasant leaders, prompted by teach-ins directed by the 'social arm' of Proquivemex, had appropriated the nationalization of the steroid hormone industry as their own battle because, 'a Mexican product, such as barbasco, must benefit the Mexican peasantry'.[57] Once having understood the importance of barbasco to Mexico and to the world, *campesinos* would stop only when pharmaceutical laboratories that controlled the steroid hormone industry were forced to leave Mexico. For the following months peasants gathered in large and noisy demonstrations throughout the southeast and in Mexico City. Daily newspaper reports began to sprinkle their articles with words such as progesterone, diosgenin, steroids, and degradations to describe the demands of Mexican peasants.[58] Peasants had absorbed the commercial value of these terms and they now used them as currency to attain legitimacy and visibility within Mexican society."

The Mexican government and transnational pharmaceutical companies were caught off guard.[59] But time and politics were in their favor. In spite of general public support the movement to control the steroid hormone industry ended as quickly as it began. At the end of 1976 with the imminent end of Echeverría's populist presidency state funds to projects such as Proquivemex began to wane. Without financial support many of the state-sponsored projects (such as the teach-ins in the jungles) vanished. In the late 1990s the Secretary of the Environment (SEMARNAP) conducted a study to attempt to revive the barbasco trade in the Chinantla of Oaxaca. It would conclude that although barbasco grew in abundance in areas such as the Chinantla local people did not know what barbasco was nor how to gather it. Mexico's legacy in the steroid hormone industry remained hidden from view.

Conclusion

For a barbasco trade to work in Mexico there initially needed to be foreign scientists who could transform the physiological concept of steroid hormones into a material reality that could eventually be *reproduced*. Groups of scientists, physiologists, and pharmaceutical companies far from Mexico made laboratory products into what became specialized drugs.

These faraway experiments, however, propelled Mexico into the center of hormone production when a ready and cheap hormone substitute was found first in *cabeza de negro*, and then barbasco. In order for steroid hormones to exist an entire social and scientific mechanism had to be put to work. First of all, the biological understanding of basic bodily functions was necessary for their production. Once these biological advances had been accomplished, it was then necessary to attempt to tame these processes and obtain as much 'external' material as possible to make the system work. In analyzing these transformations, value is created by scientists and reinforced by pharmaceutical companies. External demands to Mexico suddenly impacted on the country on many levels, from the increased study of chemistry, to the creation of a labor force trained to dig up a root of no value to the locals.

Advances in chemistry pushed researchers to enter social spheres normally not associated with their discipline, that is, women's clinics, barracks, and peasant communities. The result was a complex intertwining of scientific know-how and everyday experiences forced to come together in the search for sex hormones. By giving value, initially to cabeza de negro, and then to barbasco, two different systems of value normally insulated from each other—the scientific model of research and development and the southeastern Mexican peasant's model of production—were brought together. Interestingly, however, the ready and easy supply of barbasco would inevitably alter the market price for steroid hormones and negatively impact on those who labored to harvest the root. In this merging of science and peasant life social roles and obligations would be reshuffled. As the production of barbasco increased, more areas of rural life were altered. It would not be until the presidential term of Luis Echeverría Alvarez (1970–1976) that a series of social, political, and economic events converged to make the nation receptive to the story of the *barbasqueros*. Echeverría would usher in a Mexican welfare state which, by definition, necessitated the renegotiation of the relationship between the state and the peasantry. In Echeverría's political agenda, barbasco would come to symbolize the efforts of that endeavor. Without this political opening, barbasco and its pickers might never have entered the jungle of the Mexican national imagination.

NOTES

1 Oudshoorn (1994), p. 65.
2 Engle (1950).
3 Latour (1983), pp. 141–170.
4 Oudshoorn (1994), p. 9; Emphasis added.
5 In her pivotal work *Beyond nature: Archaeology of sex hormones*, Nellie Oudshoorn outlines the history of steroid hormone research and discovery, and analyzes how in 1920 researchers finally understood many of the body's reactions when the hormone-producing glands malfunctioned (Oudshoorn, 1994). Researchers had also developed a treatment, but the elusive component to treat these maladies was to synthetically replicate hormones for mass consumption.
6 According to researchers of the time, complaints over accessibility to research material grew in the 1920s, when the focus of research shifted from biological function to chemical isolation and identification of sex hormones. Before the advent of increased demand for quantities of gonads in the 1920s, those involved in the study of sex hormones were able to obtain enough material for their own research. For example, gynecologists had easy access to ovaries because in the late nineteenth century it was common practice to remove women's ovaries to control hysteria, irregular bleeding, and even menstrual cramps. Other materials frequently used were the placenta and animal ovaries were used by physiologists, as well as guinea-pigs, rabbits, rats, and mice (Oudshoorn, 1994, p. 67).
7 Mexican hormones (1951), p. 161.

8 In 1941 the US Justice Department ruled that American branches of Ciba, Schering, and Organon could not carry on their monopoly, price fixing, and manipulation of patents of sex hormones in the United States (Mexican hormones (1951), p. 161).
9 Oudshoorn (1994), p. 73.
10 This chemical discovery altered the Victorian conception of biological determinism: basically that nature had determined men's and women's social roles, and that these roles could not be equal or compatible with each other.
11 Oudshoorn (1994), p. 93 and also Clarke (1987). In addition, the market for hormones increased when clinical trials for female sex hormone therapy were extended from the gynecological clinic to the psychiatric clinic and dermatological domain. Women suffering from dysfunctions attributable to the ovaries such as melancholia, schizophrenia, psychoses, depression, eczema, joint disorders, epilepsy, hair loss, diabetes, hemophilia, obesity, rheumatism, irritability, tension, and even eye disorders were all treated with female sex hormones. Since then other social and medical factors have debunked these earlier prognoses. Oudshoorn (1994), pp. 92–95.
12 Quoted in Kreig (1964), p. 256.
13 Vaughan (1970), p.11.
14 Ibid.
15 On 18 March 1938 Mexican President Lázaro Cárdenas signed a decree nationalizing the assets of seventeen oil companies. This act became a symbolic gesture that reinforced Mexico's image as a sovereign nation and placed in the hands of the Mexican government one of the country's most lucrative natural resources. Meyer et al. (2003), p. 582.
16 Marker (1987), pp. 23–24.
17 Kreig (1964), p. 265.
18 Marker (1987), p. 20.
19 Kreig (1964), p. 262.
20 Maisel (1963), p. 45.
21 Lehmann (1973), p. 195.
22 In an oral history Russell Marker asserts that it was the raw material, the root, chopped into 'potato chip' slices which he showed to Somlo and Lehmann and not the actual progesterone (Marker, 1987, p. 24; Djerassi, 1990; Marks, 2001).
23 Gereffi (1983), p. 83.
24 Vaughan (1970), p. 15.
25 Mexican hormones (1951), p. 90.
26 Russell E. Marker, interview by Jeffrey L. Sturchio at Pennsylvania State University, 17 April 1987 (Philadelphia, Chemical Heritage Foundation, Oral History Transcript #0068, p. 20).
27 As late as 1966, however, steroid hormone researchers were still using animal organs as a means of research. For example, A. V. Schally received a generous donation from the meat packer Oscar Mayer in Wisconsin for his research on pig hypothalami. Oscar Mayer slaughtered 10,000 pigs a day and, over time, donated more than one million pig hypothalami to Schally's laboratory. Crapo (1985), p. 45.
28 Mexican hormones (1951), p. 161.
29 Rosenkranz (1992), pp. 409–418.
30 Ibid., p. 412.
31 Ibid.
32 Mexican hormones (1951), p. 90.
33 However, since most students worked at Syntex laboratories, Syntex was soon nicknamed 'University of Steroids' (Rosenkranz, 1992, p. 414).
34 Dr. Ricardo Reyes Chilpa, personal interview, UNAM Instituto de Química, March 1999 and also mentioned in Rosenkranz (1992), p. 414.
35 Bartra (1979), p. 56.
36 In 1970 the average salary paid to *campesinos*, for an entire workday, from five leading barbasco states were as follows: Oaxaca $14, Chiapas $17, Puebla $21, Tabasco $27 and Veracruz $28 (*IX Censo General de Población*, 1970). Quoted in *Proquivemex*, January 19, 1976, Archivo General de la Nación, Proquivemex, Vol. 96, exp. 5, fs. 6. A *campesino* averaged 50 kilos per day. At sixty

cents per kilo (the highest price paid for barbasco) that meant a $30 daily wage, nearly double what a *campesino* made in Oaxaca. Even at forty cents per kilo a picker made nearly six pesos more than the lowest daily wage.

37 Vaughan (1970), p. 20.

38 Gereffi (1983), p. 122.

39 Djerassi (2001), p. 47.

40 Ibid., p. 55.

41 In 1994 Syntex was acquired by the Swiss pharmaceutical giant Roche and the entire research division of Syntex in Mexico was disbanded, closed, and few of its chemists were given credit for their participation in steroid chemistry research. Commenting on this fact, Carl Djerassi wrote in his memoirs, 'Syntex, as a company, and Mexico, as a country, deserve full credit as the institutional site for the first chemical synthesis of an oral contraceptive steroid' (Djerassi, 2001, p. 58).

42 Due to the nature of barbasco collection, the labor force was never accurately tabulated. This is a rough estimate compiled from newspaper articles which cite 25,000 *families*, and from interviews with Alejandro Villar Borja, Eduardo Domínguez, Andrés Correa, and Pedro Ramirez, who list the number as high as 150,000 *campesinos*.

43 These numbers reflect what was reported by the pharmaceutical laboratories and, because of the well known practice of underreporting, these numbers can only be taken as a rough estimate (Asociación Rural de Interés Colectivo, Mexico, 1986).

44 Alejandro Villar Borja and Eduardo Dominguez, personal interviews, February 1999. Pedro Ra&cmacute;&i;rez, personal interview, February 1999. Tlaxcala, Tlaxcala and Toluca, Mexico, respectively. Silvio Rodríguez, personal interview, July 1999. Mexico City.

45 'el precio que recibían por su materia prima, y del engaño que sistemáticamente eran objeto por parte de los intermediarios que compraban este producto, para ser entregado a las Plantas beneficiadoras de las Empresas Fabricantes de Esteroides' (Alejandro Villar Borja Archive, no date, folder: LEA: Creación Proquivemex, Mexico City).

46 Con capital del Estado, el Barbasco dejará de ser fuente de explotació del campesino (1976).

47 Mexicanización de los Esteroides (1976). Pidieron a Echeverría la Nacionalización de Laboratorios Químicos de Esteroides (1976). Nacionalizaremos los esteroides, si presionan las transnacionales (1976). Sale de Mexico el Barbasco para hacer la Pildora (1976).

48 Gereffi (1983), p. 133.

49 From 500 to 550 metric tons (Gereffi, 1983, p. 133).

50 *Excelsior, 30 October* (1974): 'La superficie actual productora de barbasco se reduce actualmente a 1.5 millones de hectáreas, esto lo dijo Ing. Fiacro Martinez del INIF)'.

51 If we recall, barbasco achieves its mature stage between four and six years and companies paid not only for the amount of diosgenin flour, but for its percentage of diosgenin content, 4.2% being the minimum diosgenin content allowed for in purchase contracts.

52 *Excelsior, 30 October* (1974).

53 According to Roberto Peña Razo from FONAFE the number was difficult to calculate, but closer to 300,000 (*Excelsior, 10 October*, 1974).

54 'El ingreso de una empresa paraestatal a la Industria Farmaceutica, Permitira Reducir Precios de Productos Derivados del Barbasco: La explotacion irracional estaba reduciendo la capacidad productiva de Nuestro Pais' (Nuestro Pais, 1976).

55 Proquivemex also hoped to commercialize medical extracts from papaya and the vinca plant.

56 Scientists had warned Echeverría that it was not possible to compete technologically with transnational companies and so it was not prudent to alienate them. 'La situación es lo suficientemente importante para hacer una revisión cuidadosa de la política a seguir en México en relación al barbasco y las hormonas esteroides' (Arturo Gómez Pompa, letter to Gerardo Bueno Zirión, 6 December 1974).

57 Nacionalizar los esteroides (1976).

58 See *El Sol de Mexico, El Universal, Unomasuno*, and *Excelsior* during the months of March 1976, April 1976, and August 1976, for complete coverage of these events.

59 Gereffi (1983), p. 144.

REFERENCES

Applezweig, N. (1962). *Steroid drugs*. New York: McGraw-Hill.

Bartra, Armando (1979). *Notas sobre la Cuestión Campesina, México 1970–1976*. Mexico: Editorial Macehual, S.A.

Clarke, A. E. (1987). Research materials and reproductive science in the United States, 1910–1940. In L. G. Geison (Ed.), *Physiology in the American context 1885–1940* (pp. 323–350). New York: American Physiological Society.

Con capital del Estado, el Barbasco dejará de ser fuente de explotación del campesino. (1976). *El Dia, March*.

Cortisone from giant yam. (1951). *Life Magazine*, 23 *July*, 75–77.

Crapo, L. (1985). *Hormones*. New York: W.H. Freeman & Company.

Djerassi, C. (1990). *Steroids made it possible*. Washington, DC: American Chemical Society.

Djerassi, C. (1992). Steroid research at Syntex: 'The Pill' and cortisone. *Steroids*, *57*(12), 631–641.

Djerassi, C. (2001). *This man's pill*. Oxford: Oxford University Press.

Engle, L. (1950). ACTH, Cortisone, & Co. *Harper's Magazine*, *201*(1203), August, 25–33.

Gereffi, G. (1983). *The pharmaceutical industry and dependency in the Third World*. Princeton, NJ: Princeton University Press.

Hirschmann, R. (1992). The cortisone era: Aspects of its impact. Some contributions of the Merck Laboratories. *Steroids*, *57*(12), 579–592.

Kreig, M. (1964). *Green medicine: The search for plants that heal....* New York: Rand McNally & Company.

Latour, B. (1983). Give me a laboratory and I will raise the world. In K. Knorr-Cetina, & M. Mulkay (Eds.), *Science observed: Perspectives on the social study of science* (pp. 140–170). London: Sage.

Lehmann, F., & Pedro, A. (1992). Early history of steroid chemistry in Mexico: The story of three remarkable men. *Steroids*, *57*(8), 403–408.

Lehmann, Pedro A. (1973). Russell E. Marker: Pioneer of the Mexican steroid industry. *Chemical Education*, 50(March), 195.

Maisel, Albert Q. (1965). *The Hormone Quest*. New York: Random House.

Marker, R.E. (1987). Interview by Jeffrey L. Sturchio at Pennsylvania State University, 17 April. Philadelphia, Chemical Heritage Foundation, Oral History Transcript #0068.

Marker, R. E., Wagner, R. B., Ulshafer, P. R., Wittbecker, E. L., Goldsmith, D. P. J., & Rouf, C. H. (1947). Steroidal sapogenins. *Journal of the American Chemical Society*, *69*, 2167–2171.

Marks, L. V. (2001). *Sexual chemistry: A history of the contraceptive pill*. New Haven: Yale University Press.

Mexican hormones (1951). *Fortune*, *May*, 161.

Meyer, Michael C. et al. (2003). *The Course of Mexican History* (7th ed.). Oxford: Oxford University Press.

Mexicanización de los esteroides. (1976). *El Universal, 13 March*.

Nacionalizaremos los esteroides, si presionan las transnacionales. (1976). *El Universal, 11 March*.

Nacionalizar los esteroides. (1976). *El Sol de Mexico, March* 15.

Nuestro Pais. (1976). *El Heraldo, 12 March*, 15.

Oudshoorn, N. (1994). *Beyond the natural body: An archeology of sex hormones*. London: Routledge.

Pidieron a Echeverría la Nacionalización de Laboratorios Químicos de Esteroides. (1976). *Ovaciones: El Diario de Mexico, 13* March.

Rosenkranz, G. (1992). From Ruzicka's terpenes in Zurich to Mexican steroids via Cuba. *Steroids*, *57*(8), 409–418.

Sale de Mexico el Barbasco para hacer la Pildora (1976). *Excelsior, 14 January*.

Soto Laveaga, Gabriela (2003). Steroid Hormones and Social Relations in Oaxaca. In Casey Walsh et al. (Eds.), *The Social Relations of Mexican Commodities: Power, Production and Place* (pp. 55–79). San Diego: Center for U.S.-Mexican Studies.

Vaughan, P. (1970). *The Pill on trial*. New York: Coward-McCann.

13

"Ready-to-Recruit" or "Ready-to-Consent" Populations? Informed Consent and the Limits of Subject Autonomy

Jill A. Fisher

This article queries the pharmaceutical industry's concept of "ready-to-recruit" populations by examining its recruitment strategies for clinical trials and the types of human subjects who participate in these drug studies. The argument is that the pharmaceutical industry has profited from a system composed of what can more aptly be characterized as *ready-to-consent* populations, meaning populations who do not have better alternatives than participation in clinical trials. Furthermore, through qualitative research, this article aims to highlight some of the limitations of current U.S. federal regulation and to show how these limits signal problems that are not normally discussed in the medical ethics literature about research on human subjects. It does this by examining the impotence of informed consent—both as a concept and as a practice—in light of recruitment strategies and the structural reasons motivating individuals to participate in clinical trials.

During the past two decades, human subjects research has developed into a full-fledged industry with a global presence. Human subjects are needed to test the safety and efficacy of new pharmaceutical products before those drugs or devices can be marketed to the general public. In response to the pharmaceutical industry's demand for human bodies, companies have emerged specializing in finding the right bodies for clinical studies (Epstein, 2007; Fisher, 2005). These companies—contract research organizations (CROs) and central patient recruitment firms—promise increased efficiency in filling clinical trials in order for pharmaceutical companies to get their products to market faster. Although

Jill A. Fisher, "'Ready-to-Recruit' or 'Ready to Consent' Populations? Informed Consent and the Limits of Subject Autonomy," in Qualitative Inquiry 13 (2007). pp. 875–894. Reproduced with permission from SAGE.

The Pharmaceutical Studies Reader, First Edition. Edited by Sergio Sismondo and Jeremy A. Greene.

the implications of these companies for the commercialization of science and for the ethics of human subjects research have begun to be discussed in academic scholarship (Mirowski & Van Horn, 2005; Petryna, 2006), there has not been a close examination of the adequacy of current U.S. federal regulation for safeguarding human subjects within this emergent industry.

This article centers on one particular framing of human subjects—both in the United States and globally—as populations that are "ready to recruit" for clinical trials. This language mobilized by the pharmaceutical industry and ancillary clinical trial companies suggests a view of the public as composed of potential human subjects who can be motivated to participate in clinical trials given the invitation to do so. Moreover, it signifies a strategy by the pharmaceutical industry to capitalize on the political and economic conditions that disadvantage populations around the world. In short, the current clinical trials industry takes advantage of disenfranchised populations by offering these groups limited and problematic access to health care in exchange for their bodies as testing sites for new products (Fisher, 2005).

Discussions about populations being "ready to recruit" for clinical trials have emerged as part of a justification for a broader shift in the sites where the clinical development of pharmaceutical products takes place. Since 1990, the pharmaceutical industry has shifted the bulk of its clinical research away from academic medical centers in the United States to for-profit clinics around the world. This relocation of clinical trials to the private sector has been motivated by the industry's desire to cut drug development costs and speed new products to market (Rainville, 2002). Although the private sector may indeed be a cheaper, quicker place to conduct drug studies, the benefit of this new setting has been framed in terms of the availability of human subjects to participate in clinical research. The underlying logic of this approach has been to stop waiting for potential human subjects to come to clinical trials (i.e., to university hospitals) and instead to take the clinical trials directly to the appropriate patient populations (e.g., to private practices and local hospitals). Thus, the world—in this view—is made up of potential human subjects who, with the right marketing approach, are ready to be recruited into drug studies.

To underscore the importance of this rhetoric surrounding human subjects, this article queries the concept of "ready-to-recruit" populations by examining not only recruitment strategies but also the types of human subjects participating in clinical trials. Specifically, I describe common advertising practices, including a lengthy discussion of a television advertisement designed to recruit potential subjects into an asthma study. Next, drawing on extensive qualitative field research, I relate three case stories of individuals who participated in clinical trials for three very different reasons: the desire to find a cure for an intractable disease, a lack of health insurance, and a source of income.

By attending to the messages—both explicit and implicit—that are embedded in recruitment techniques and by illustrating which specific populations actually participate in drug studies, this article argues that the pharmaceutical industry has profited from a system composed of what can more aptly be characterized as *ready-to-consent* populations, meaning populations who do not have better alternatives than participation in clinical trials. My reframing of the same populations is meant to call into question what operates within the industry as a euphemism for the exploitation of certain groups. Furthermore, this article aims to highlight some of the limitations of current U.S. federal regulation and to show how these limits signal problems that are not normally discussed in the medical ethics literature about research on human subjects. I do this by examining the impotence of informed consent—both as a concept and as a practice—in light of recruitment strategies and the structural reasons motivating individuals to participate in clinical trials.

Recruitment and Informed Consent

Informed consent as the key to decision making for participation in medical research arose through U.S. federal regulation designed to protect the rights and welfare of human subjects. Emerging in 1981 after nearly a decade of congressional hearings responding to public outcry over abuses of human subjects, U.S. regulation aimed to eliminate the deception and coercion of Americans participating in research (Faden & Beauchamp, 1986). The panacea for correcting the problems of the past was symbolized by informed consent and the ethical principle of respect for persons (i.e., autonomy) on which it is based. According to many ethicists, informed consent is the primary basis for determining that a research study is ethical (e.g., Caplan, 1998). Both the federal regulation and the ethical principle are premised on the assumption that individuals act as autonomous beings who make measured decisions about participating in research on the basis of information given to them. Although social scientists as well as feminist bioethicists have criticized this position by arguing that the ethics of human subjects research is much more complex than consent alone (e.g., Corrigan, 2003; Halpern, 2004; Sherwin, 1996; Wolpe, 1998), informed consent and the principle of autonomy have remained the foundations of ethical discourse and practice, especially in the policy-making context.

In fact, the U.S. federal regulation has changed very little in the past 25 years. Informed consent continues to be seen as sufficient protection for human subjects. Perspectives on informed consent, however, have not been entirely static. A recent recommendation from several advisory bodies to the government has been to reenvision informed consent not as a form to be signed but as a process (Institute of Medicine, 2002). The clinical trials industry itself has internalized this new rhetoric surrounding consent and strongly advocates for informed consent to be an ongoing process, one that will aid in the recruitment and—equally important—the retention of human subjects (Anderson, 2004). In this industry view, informed consent should be strategically mobilized in such a way to persuade individuals to enroll in studies and to inform them of their responsibilities to pharmaceutical companies (Fisher, 2008).

Another model of informed consent that has been conceptualized by bioethicists envisions human subjects as collaborators in the research process. Robert Veatch (1987), who has significantly contributed to developing this position, advocates for patients and human subjects to be in partnership with physicians and researchers:

> The patient as a partner needs to know all those things that a reasonable person would want to know in order to decide whether to participate in the partnership. Reasonable persons who are potential partners in a venture may want to know certain risks and potential benefits, but they may also want to know information that has no bearing whatsoever on potential risks. They may want to know something about the purposes of the study, maybe even something about the theory underlying the innovation. It is no longer a matter of benefits and harms—to either the subject or society—but rather what it takes to decide whether tobecomes an active partner in an important enterprise. (Veatch, 1987, p. 9)

This position—as well as other instantiations of it developed by feminist bioethicists (e.g., Sherwin, 1998)—is radical in that it attempts to take the ethical principle of autonomy a step beyond consent to encourage human subjects to engage actively in the research enterprise.

Although a collaborative model of research can be highly successful in investigator-initiated studies where the researchers who have conceptualized the project are directly interacting with human subjects, pharmaceutical clinical trials prove more challenging because the physicians conducting the studies are rarely the ones who have designed them. In addition, pharmaceutical studies emphasize subjects' passive compliance over active investment. Apart from these challenges to meaningful collaboration in pharmaceutical research, the partnership model requires that subjects themselves accept an active role in the research process if offered. This is seldom the case in practice.

In addition, despite reevaluations of the purpose and practice of informed consent, there is generally little recognition of when the process of informing as well as consenting begins. Policy makers and many ethicists assume that informed consent begins when prospective human subjects are directly given information about the research, usually the informed consent form. In other words, informed consent is generally thought to begin in clinical trials when individuals undergo what is called a "screening and consent visit" in the clinic. During this time, those individuals discuss the research with study staff and receive a lengthy informed consent form to sign and date.

What these views of informed consent do not take into account, however, is that most prospective human subjects have already decided to take part in clinical studies before receiving the informed consent forms (Fisher, 2005). This indicates that the process of consent actually begins *before* potential human subjects are informed about the purpose, risks, and benefits of any given study. Thus, the importance of recruitment cannot be underestimated given that potential human subjects are making decisions about participating in clinical trials before they know the details of the studies for which they will volunteer.

Recruitment methods for clinical trials vary from physician referrals to highly specific databases of patients to mass media advertising (Anderson, 2004). With the privatization of clinical trials, recruitment has increasingly been viewed as a science, and many niche-market companies have established themselves as experts in finding human subjects for clinical trials (Epstein, 2008). Like direct-to-consumer advertising for marketed drugs, advertising for clinical trials has increased dramatically in the past decade and has consequently increased the visibility of these studies in the United States. In large cities around the country, clinical trials have become a part of everyday life through the public face that advertising for these studies has created. Advertisements appear across a range of venues and media from public transportation and newspapers to radio and television.

The proliferation of clinical trial advertising has reached the point where individuals' understanding of, and expectations about, medical research is rooted in the messages infused in these advertisements (Fisher, 2005). This is, of course, no accident and is, in fact, part of the process of privatization that clinical trials have been undergoing since the early 1990s. These ads can be said to be not only tools for recruiting human subjects into *specific* clinical trials but also for increasing the public's awareness about participating in clinical trials more generally. This is particularly important to consider when examining the role of recruitment on informed consent.

Analysis of Advertisements

Advertising strategies as part of clinical trial recruitment serve to shape potential human subjects' decisions to participate in pharmaceutical drug studies. More important, the most prevalent advertisements in the mass media for clinical trials depict common illnesses that tend to be chronic and rarely life threatening. Ads for depression, anxiety, insomnia, and arthritis studies appear with much more frequency than ads for cancer or HIV/AIDS clinical studies. Print ads emphasize that human subjects participating in clinical trials will receive medical evaluations and "study medications" or "investigational medications" at no cost.

These ads tend not to communicate very much information but encourage interested parties to "call today!" or "give us a call" at local or toll-free numbers. In contrast, radio and television advertisements are often composed of story lines in which characters inform each other about the possibility of participating in clinical trials. This genre of advertisement communicates on multiple levels about what can be gained and for whom by enrolling in a drug study.

The U.S. Food & Drug Administration (FDA) regulates the content of all advertisements used for recruitment into clinical trials, and it is the responsibility of local or centralized institutional review boards (IRBs) to review each proposed advertisement before it can be made public. Despite this oversight, ads often (intentionally) undermine existing protections for human subjects through the information they do or do not supply. In fact, marketing techniques can be said to privilege a "ready-to-consent" orientation toward recruitment.

One television advertisement for an asthma study epitomizes how misleading information gets communicated about clinical trials. In this ad, two women—one African American and one White—run into each other in a grocery store and discuss an asthma clinical trial for their family members. The following is the text of the television commercial:[1]

[W1 = White woman, W2 = African American woman, VO = male voice-over]

W1: Hi, Nicki.
W2: Hey, girl, how's things?
W1: Pretty good, except for my youngest Sherry.
W2: What's the matter with Sherry?
W1: Oh, it's her asthma. She can't go anywhere without her inhaler, and it embarrasses her so much.
W2: My husband Anthony, he's the same way, and he's been using his inhaler since he was 12.
W1: Well, has he tried any other treatments?
W2: Honey, he's tried all kinds of things!
W1: What are you going to do?
W2: You know, I convinced him to go into an asthma research study.
W1: You did what?!
W2: Well, I saw this TV ad. They said they were studying an investigational asthma medication, so I wrote down the 800 number, and I gave them a call.
W1: And?
VO: If you're 12 or older and suffer from asthma, call 1–800-XXX-XXXX to enroll in a clinical research study. Participants receive free examination, study medicines, lab and breathing tests, and carfare. Have your medications with you when calling.
W1: Hey, can I get that number? Maybe I can get Sherry enrolled.
W2: I'll call you with it as soon as I get home.
VO: 1–800-XXX-XXXX.

The text of this advertisement alone cannot communicate the enthusiasm of the two women at having a potential solution for their ill family members' problems. In addition, during the voice-over, the text "free examination," "free study medicines," and "free lab and breathing tests" float over a backdrop of fresh produce. In each case, the word *free* is repeated on the screen and appears in a much larger font than the other words.

This ad is particularly interesting because the layered meanings that are communicated about clinical trials are infused with representations of gender, race, and class. What is immediately striking about this advertisement is that the women depicted do not have asthma and are not the population targeted for recruitment into the clinical trial. This is not the same as saying that they are not the target population for the advertisement itself.

In fact, as wives and mothers, they are indeed the right demographic for the marketing message. The implied message is that it is up to women, who care about the health and well-being of their families, to "convince" those in their charge to enroll in clinical studies.

It is also not merely a coincidence that there is an African American woman depicted in this advertisement and that she is the woman who is informing the other about the study. This representation is meant to project to African American viewers that clinical trial participation is the right choice for them too.[2] As for the meanings communicated about class, the television commercial implies that clinical trials are options for middle-class Americans, not just the poor who sign up to be guinea pigs or the rich who are looking for an alternative cancer therapy. Overall, the implicit message of the ad is that participation in research studies is legitimate, even safe enough for children.

The maternal theme is important in that it underscores the ineffectualness of current asthma medications from both medical and psychosocial perspectives. Specifically, one woman's daughter and the other's husband cannot go anywhere without their inhalers, and this is embarrassing to them. The problem is twofold: (a) The inhalers are not physiologically effective because they treat the symptoms rather than the disease, and (b) the inhalers are not socially effective because they are embarrassing—or at least the symptoms of asthma are embarrassing, and the inhaler represents these symptoms. This double failure of standard asthma treatment becomes the women's responsibility for their loved ones.

Seen through the lens of the women seeking better asthma treatments for their families, the advertisement suggests that the study medicine will have better results, both physiologically and psychosocially. The implied promise is that the drug under investigation will be efficacious, safe, and better for asthma sufferers. Although this product may indeed be a better treatment for asthma, the television commercial is misleading because it implies a set of results that are the very purpose of the study itself.

The intent of this optimistic framing of the study medicine is for potential human subjects (or their loved ones) to assume that clinical trials—and this one in particular—do offer magic bullet cures. And, equally important in the ad copy, these results can be had at absolutely no cost to those who participate in the research study. What goes unmentioned in the advertisement—and others like it—are the use of placebo versus active drug, the potential risks to the human subjects, and the logistical burden of participating (both for the subjects themselves and for family members accompanying them to study visits).

The irony about clinical trial recruitment is that there are more disclaimers given to viewers as part of direct-to-consumer marketing of FDA-approved drugs and their side effects than there are of investigational products, which may prove to be neither safe nor efficacious after clinical testing. Thus, from a regulatory perspective, the information communicated in advertisements for marketed drugs is required to be more balanced than the information about clinical trials. Given the American public's general savvy about prescription drugs and general ignorance about drug development, the difference in advertising practices must be understood as problematic. This is particularly disturbing because the information contained in ads for clinical trials is much more digestible and straightforward than information in informed consent documents. As a result of these and other recruitment strategies, it should be no surprise that advertising can have a profound impact on the decisions of potential human subjects (even after they have read informed consent forms). Yet an analysis of marketing to recruit human subjects is ungrounded without a discussion of the human subjects who do participate in clinical trials. To illustrate some limitations on informed consent, the next section will examine three cases of study volunteers' decision making about enrolling in three very different pharmaceutical clinical trials.

Participation and Informed Consent

The trends in the United States surrounding participation in pharmaceutical clinical studies can be mapped onto differences in gender, race, and class (Fisher, 2008). Early clinical testing of new products, called Phase I research, generally aims to determine the safety (read: toxicity) of investigational drugs in healthy humans and to establish appropriate dosage in humans for subsequent testing. These types of studies are overwhelmingly filled by low-income, minority men who participate in clinical trials in exchange for money.[3] In contrast, later clinical evaluation of pharmaceuticals (Phases II and III) aims to test the efficacy of these products.[4] Enrollment in these studies tends to be composed of individuals without health insurance and particularly White women.

In a very real sense, clinical trials have come to serve as a limited and problematic resource for disenfranchised groups. What this means in the context of the argument here is that structural variables are often much stronger determinants of participation in clinical trials than are the details of specific studies. What matters to most potential human subjects is that they will receive the monetary compensation or a form of access to health care; the risks of the study are usually of little interest to them, except in the extremely rare cases that informed consent forms are explicit about the possibility of death as a "side effect." Many individuals who have participated as human subjects in drug studies report that what mattered to them much more than the risks of the study were the logistics (Fisher, 2008). When there are frequent study visits or long in-patient confinements, many individuals cannot make the clinical trial fit into their lives and must decline participation.

If potential human subjects are not particularly concerned about the details contained in informed consent forms and if most of their information comes from recruitment sources such as mass media advertisements, human subjects are making decisions to participate in studies on the basis of their impressions of what benefits clinical trials will have for them. To explore this point further, I take three examples of human subjects who have participated in pharmaceutical clinical trials. Each case highlights a different type of motivation for participation in these studies: (a) patients with progressive diseases, (b) individuals without health insurance, and (c) healthy individuals seeking income. Together, these cases illustrate that decision making regarding participation in clinical trials is more complex than is modeled in the federal regulation, which assumes ideal "autonomous" individuals weighing the pros and cons of particular studies.

Case 1: Progressive diseases

During my fieldwork in the southwestern United States on the clinical trials industry, I had the opportunity to sit in on an informed consent visit for a study to test the safety of an experimental treatment for Alzheimer's Disease. The potential human subject was a 75-year-old Latina woman, accompanied by her middle-age son. They had found out about the study through a print advertisement in a local newspaper. The ad had emphasized that human subjects could continue to take their prescribed Alzheimer's medication while taking part in the study and receiving a "study medication."

The tone of the informed consent visit was educational. The physician conducting the study spent an hour with the woman and her son to explain the disease itself and the history of the product being tested. The most important information given about the study was that the product had previously been tested in humans and had caused the development of encephalitis in many of the participants, leading to death in several cases. The current 1-year study consisted of a retooled version of the drug, and the purpose was solely to test its safety. The mother and son were told that the study would not have any therapeutic value and that the primary motivation for participating should be altruism.

After the physician finished presenting the information, he asked whether either the son or the woman had any questions. What occurred during the subsequent conversation was revealing about the assumptions that potential human subjects (and their family members) have about medical research. The son began by telling the physician how important it was to him to find an effective treatment for his mother. Although this would likely be true for any individuals watching their parents deteriorate from Alzheimer's, the son had turned to clinical research because he had recently buried his father who had suffered for many years from the same disease. The possibility of losing his mother in the same slow way was unacceptable to him. His goal, in his explanation as to why he responded to the advertisement, was to find a treatment that would curb the progression of his mother's Alzheimer's disease.

In response to the son's explanation, the physician carefully reiterated that participants would not receive any therapeutic benefit from the study. He explained that although the study included a rigorous evaluation, including magnetic resonance imaging (MRI) at the outset to establish the diagnosis of Alzheimer's disease, there would be no further tests during the course of the year to assess the amount of deterioration participants had experienced because of their illness. Despite being assured that the study would do nothing to improve his mother's condition, the son actively continued to search for a therapeutic benefit for his mother.[5] For example, he hypothesized that his mother might experience an improvement in her illness if the treatment was later proved to be efficacious. He posited that even if the purpose of the study was not to help his mother, the drug could still work to that effect. The physician quickly told him that in order for the drug to have any effect, it would have to be administered regularly, and this study included only one dose and lengthy follow-up.

After much more exchange between the physician and the son, it appeared that the son had indeed accepted that his mother would not improve from participating in the clinical trial. Instead of using this opportunity to thank the physician and leave, the son settled on the diagnostic benefits of participating in the study as sufficient reason for his mother to enroll. His mother had only the most basic health coverage through Medicare, and he was attracted to the idea that she would be able to have a very expensive MRI performed. Even though he had responded to the ad because he hoped for a miracle cure for his mother, the son had his mother sign the consent form to enter a study that would have no therapeutic benefit and would have significant risks. It seemed that the son had made up his mind that his mother would participate in the study prior to hearing the details. What the informed consent visit achieved was to give him new reasons for justifying her participation.[6]

Case 2: Health insurance status

A White woman in her late forties volunteered for a clinical trial to test the efficacy of a product to treat a condition known as "overactive bladder." When I interviewed her, she had been enrolled in the clinical trial for approximately 6 months, and she described these few months as life changing. Before seeing an advertisement about the study, she said that she was well aware that she had a medical condition that needed treatment. As someone who worked hourly jobs most of her life, she had not had any form of health insurance since becoming an adult. She described for me the embarrassment that overactive bladder had caused, leading her to pay out of pocket to see a physician and get a prescription for treatment. After filling the prescription for a brand-name drug, she decided that she would

use the treatment sparingly. Because it was so prohibitively expensive, she would not be able to fill it as often as she should. During the next few months, she had several "accidents" at work, resulting in her losing her job and the little means she had to fill the prescription. She was out of work for several months when the first "miracle" happened.

She recalled hearing an advertisement on the radio that she felt described her perfectly. According to her, the ad stated that a clinic was seeking participants for a 6-month evaluation of an overactive bladder drug for individuals currently not taking any medications for this condition. Not only would the study offer free medical evaluations and "medicines," but it also promised a stipend. Because she was no longer employed, the small income she would receive confirmed even further that the study was indeed "perfect" for her. She immediately called the toll-free number and was scheduled to screen for the study. In response to my questions, she told me that she could not recall much of what was discussed in the informed consent form, including any of the risks of the trial. What she remembered was feeling concerned that she might not get the treatment because some participants would receive a sugar pill. She went on to say that these worries were unfounded because she is sure that she got the drug; her symptoms cleared up entirely, and she experienced "dry mouth," a common side effect of the drug.

As the trial elapsed, she began to worry about the end of the study. She dreaded losing access to the drug because of her continued inability to pay for any treatment herself. To make matters worse, she had been able to find a new job and feared losing it if she was no longer being "treated." At the beginning of the 6th and what was to be the final month of the study, the second "miracle" happened. The study coordinator told her that the pharmaceutical company had decided to extend the study by an additional 12 months and asked her if she would be interested in continuing her participation. She described this news as immediately lifting an incredible burden. She said that the clinical trial had been life changing and its extension a godsend. In her estimation, clinical trials were the perfect option for people without health insurance suffering from medical problems. This case indicates that information about risks contained in the consent form did not matter compared to having limited access to a "treatment" that she otherwise could not afford.

Case 3: Healthy human studies

I interviewed a Latina woman in her early thirties who described her interest in volunteering for a healthy human study as motivated by the desire for additional income. She was a single mother with a fairly low-paying job, and she thought that volunteering for a well-paying clinical trial would do a lot to provide additional money to see her through a few months. She called the toll-free number and was informed about several studies for which she prequalified—based on sex, age, and so on—and could select one for which to screen. She told me that the woman on the phone told her about a vaginal endometriosis study, and this study appealed to her because she had once been diagnosed with endometriosis, and it was something she knew a little bit about. She also felt from her personal experience that women's health problems are not as well understood as they should be and that being in *that* study would not only benefit her economically but that it was something she could feel proud of participating in too.

When she arrived at the clinic to screen for the study, she was given a lengthy informed consent form to read and paperwork about her medical history to fill out. She also received a presentation with a group of other potential subjects by one of the staff. She told me what she could not understand was why the woman presenting the information kept talking about attention deficit disorder when she was there for an endometriosis study.

She interrupted the staff person to clarify, and she was told that she was, in fact, in the process of screening for an attention deficit disorder (ADD) study. When she told the woman that it was not the study she had signed up for, the woman assured her that she was equally qualified for the ADD study. She told me she hesitated only for a moment. She asked how much the ADD studied paid, and because it was the same amount ($2,300), she signed the form. When I asked her, she said she did not know what the risks of the ADD study might have been and had no idea how those risks might have compared with any risks in an endometriosis study. She said that what was important about volunteering for a study was the original motive—the income she could earn—not any reasons associated with any particular study. Although she indicated that she would have been more "proud" to have participated in the endometriosis study, those details were somewhat interchangeable compared to the bottom-line stipend amount that motivated her primary interest in participating in a clinical trial. Informed consent did not matter much in the face of financial need.

These three cases are meant to illustrate the disconnect between the reasons why individuals participate in clinical trials and U.S. federal regulation to protect human subjects. Holding autonomy and informed consent as the model for ethical practice, federal regulation places decision making about study participation within a vacuum, stripping it of all social contexts (Corrigan, 2003; Fisher, 2006b). Qualitative approaches to evaluating why individuals enroll in clinical trials are critical for understanding how structural conditions shape those decisions.

A healthy critique of the ethical principle of *autonomy* does not, of course, imply that individuals cannot and do not exert agency in relation to the clinical trials industry. Individuals are clearly savvy about the choices that they make about whether to participate in studies. In fact, those who participate in healthy subject studies are incredibly insightful about the exchange in which they are engaged with the pharmaceutical industry. Instead, what I am arguing is that the principle of autonomy—and the formal procedure of informed consent—is insufficient to protect individuals from research abuses.

Conclusion

This article has introduced some of the ways in which current U.S. regulation fails to protect human subjects in pharmaceutical clinical trials. By highlighting recruitment strategies that confer both explicit and implicit meanings and expectations about study participation, I have argued that the information that potential human subjects receive about clinical trials is often misleading and that this initial information is more salient than anything contained in informed consent forms. The irony of the regulation (or lack thereof) surrounding recruitment for clinical trials is that marketers have more freedom in crafting messages about investigational drugs than do marketers in advertising FDA-approved prescription drugs to consumers. The second part of this article drew on field research to illustrate some reasons why individuals participate in clinical trials and how these motivations (i.e., intractable disease, lack of health insurance, economic need) appear vastly more important to subjects than information contained in informed consent forms.

Bioethicists and policy makers have proposed new models of informed consent for revitalizing the process and making consent more robust. Proposals have included more mainstream ideas, such as de-emphasizing consent forms and stressing ongoing information and opportunities for consent, to more radical models, such as advocating for partnerships between researchers and subjects. Responding to the impotency of informed consent forms to communicate effectively to potential human subjects, these alternative models seek to engage subjects in more dialogue throughout the course of their involvement in clinical trials.

A limitation of all these proposed models for consent is that they are unable to account for imbalances of power, not only between researchers and subjects but also among groups and institutions within society. By focusing on *how* subjects participate but ignoring *why* they participate, current informed consent models artificially circumscribe subjects' decisions within a dyadic vacuum of clinical relationships. More important, this focus operates to hide the broader implications of pharmaceutical research and the insufficiency of informed consent as a mechanism to lessen the burden of research on disadvantaged groups.

What must become the focus of attention is that clinical trials have become a way for people to earn some income or have access to the medical establishment. Current federal regulation does not acknowledge these facts in its guidelines on "vulnerable populations" or in its rules for good clinical practice. Although I am not arguing for a prohibition against recruiting the uninsured or the poor for clinical trials, I am calling for a reevaluation of the *structural conditions* in the United States that make clinical trial participation necessary for these groups. In the congressional investigations in the 1970s on the use of prisoners for medical research, for example, U.S. Senator Edward Kennedy coupled his call for human subjects protection with a call for prison reform. In his view, the avidness with which prisoners participated in studies (for money, for reduced sentences, for better food, etc.) signaled that something was wrong with the penal system (Hornblum, 1998). Likewise, today's environment surrounding clinical trial participation signals gross problems with our health care system and with our distribution of economic and social opportunities for American citizens and others. These issues become more urgent as clinical trials are increasingly globalized and affect diverse groups. It should be a priority to ameliorate the conditions that have contributed to the creation of populations of disenfranchised individuals who are ready to consent to pharmaceutical clinical trials regardless of the risks.

NOTES

1 This advertisement can be viewed online at http://www.trialbuilder.com/tv_friends_56.html. Last accessed on November 16, 2006.

2 There has been some debate about the willingness of African Americans to participate in clinical trials. Some research has claimed that as a group, African Americans are suspicious of researchers because of past cases of exploitation (e.g., Corbie-Smith, Thomas, & St. George, 2002; Gamble, 2000). A smaller body of research has suggested that African Americans are no more or less suspicious of clinical research than are Whites, but that their lower level of participation is due to less access and knowledge of studies or is due to the attitudes of African American physicians toward clinical trials (e.g., Brown & Topcu, 2003; Lynch, Gorelick, Raman, & Leurgans, 2001). I think both types of claims oversimplify past and present prejudices and structural reasons for African Americans' participation or nonparticipation. I also find it problematic that these types of studies often assume that participation in clinical trials is unequivocally in the best interest of this or any group. For discussions about the politics of inclusion of minorities in clinical studies, see King (2000) and Epstein (2004).

3 Payment for participation in Phase I studies is determined by whether the study is in- or outpatient, the length of the study, the number of doses of the investigational drug, and the potential risks associated with the product. Advertisements for Phase I trials often announce that studies will "pay up to" $3,500, and most studies pay more than $1,000. It is important to note that these studies, although generally safe, do have debilitating or fatal results, including a March 2006 Phase 1 study in London (Rosenthal, 2006) and a 2001 study at Johns Hopkins (Halpern, 2004).

4 Efficacy is determined in most industry-sponsored clinical trials by comparing the investigational drug to a placebo. This means that products under development have to be shown only to be better than nothing (i.e., a sugar pill) to receive approval by the FDA. In some cases of severe illness, it is impossible to randomize patients to a placebo arm of the study, but most pharmaceutical

companies prefer placebo-controlled trials because they are considerably cheaper and because it is much easier to show efficacy (Fisher, 2005; Petryna, 2006).

5 Belief in a therapeutic benefit to clinical studies when there is none is referred to as a "therapeutic misconception." See Appelbaum and Lidz (2008) for an important review of the literature and recommendations for minimizing these beliefs in human subjects. Elsewhere, I develop the concept of *procedural misconceptions* to highlight the ways in which clinical contexts can create false expectations about research in human subjects (Fisher, 2006b).

6 Although my inclination is to problematize the paternalism that I witnessed in the relationship between the mother and son, it was impossible for me to determine the degree to which the woman had already been affected by Alzheimer's disease. What is probably more worthy of discussion is the physician's acceptance of the son's role as decision maker without evaluating the competency of the woman to make decisions for herself. For an interesting example of public controversy surrounding consenting on others' behalf, see Chun and McEneaney (2006), who discussed the case of New York City orphans who were enrolled in HIV clinical trials with the consent of the city authorities.

REFERENCES

Anderson, D. L. (2004). *A guide to patient recruitment and retention.* Boston: Thomson CenterWatch.

Appelbaum, P. S., & Lidz, C. W. (2008). The therapeutic misconception. In E. J. Emanuel, R. A. Crouch, C. Grady, R. Lie, F. Miller, & D. Wendler (Eds.), *The Oxford textbook of clinical research ethics.* New York: Oxford University Press.

Brown, D. R., & Topcu, M. (2003). Willingness to participate in clinical treatment research among older African Americans and Whites. *The Gerontologist, 43*, 62–72.

Caplan, A. (1998). *Due consideration: Controversy in the age of medical miracles.* New York: John Wiley.

Chun, M., & McEneaney, E. H. (2006, August). *Personhood and the balance of risk and benefit: Analyzing the participation of foster children in clinical trials.* Paper presented at the meeting of the American Sociological Association in Montreal, Canada.

Corbie-Smith, G., Thomas, S. B., & St. George, D. M. M. (2002). Distrust, race, and reasearch. *Archives of Internal Medicine, 162*, 2458–2463.

Corrigan, O. P. (2003). Empty ethics: The problem with informed consent. *Sociology of Health and Illness, 25*, 768–792.

Epstein, S. (2004). Bodily differences and collective identities: The politics of gender and race in biomedical research in the United States. *Body & Society, 10*, 183–203.

Epstein, S. (2007). *Inclusion: The politics of difference in medical research.* Chicago: University of Chicago Press.

Epstein, S. (2008). *The rise of "recruitmentology": Clinical research, racial knowledge, and the politics of inclusion and difference. Social Studies of Science.*

Faden, R. R., & Beauchamp, T. L. (1986). *A history and theory of informed consent.* New York: Oxford University Press.

Fisher, J. A. (2005). *Pharmaceutical paternalism and the privatization of clinical trials.* Unpublished doctoral dissertation, Rensselaer Polytechnic Institute, Troy, NY.

Fisher, J. A. (2006a). Co-ordinating "ethical" clinical trials: The role of research coordinators in the contract research industry. *Sociology of Health and Illness, 28*(6), 678–694.

Fisher, J. A. (2006b). Procedural misconceptions and informed consent: Insights from empirical research on the clinical trials industry. *Kennedy Institute of Ethics Journal, 16*(3), 251–268.

Fisher, J. A. (2008). *Medical Research for Hire: The Political Economy of Pharmaceutical Clinical Trials.* New Brunswick, NJ: Rutgers University Press.

Gamble, V. N. (2000). Under the shadow of Tuskegee: African Americans and health care. In S. M. Reverby (Ed.), *Tuskegee's truths: Rethinking the Tuskegee syphilis study* (pp. 431–442). Chapel Hill: University of North Carolina Press.

Halpern, S. A. (2004). *Lesser harms: The morality of risk in medical research.* Chicago: University of Chicago Press.

Hornblum, A. M. (1998). *Acres of skin: Human experiments at Holmesburg Prison.* New York: Routledge.

Institute of Medicine. (2002). *Responsible research: A systems approach to protecting research participants.* Washington, DC: National Academies Press.

King, P. A. (2000). The dangers of difference. In S. M. Reverby (Ed.), *Tuskegee's truths: Rethinking the Tuskegee syphilis study* (pp. 424–430). Chapel Hill: University of North Carolina Press.

Lynch, G. F., Gorelick, P. B., Raman, R., & Leurgans, S. (2001). A pilot survey of African-American physician perceptions about clinical trials. *Journal of the National Medical Association, 93*(12), 8S–13S.

Mirowski, P., & Van Horn, R. (2005). The contract research organization and the commercialization of scientific research. *Social Studies of Science, 35*(4), 503–548.

Petryna, A. (2006). Globalizing human subjects research. In A. Petryna, A. Lakoff, & A. Kleinman (Eds.), *Global Pharmaceuticals: Ethics, markets, practices* (pp. 33–60). Durham, NC: Duke University Press.

Rainville, B. (2002). Strategic outsourcing with contract research organizations: Targeting corporate goals. *Drug Information Journal, 36*(1), 77–81.

Reason, P., & Bradbury, H. (Eds.). (2006). *Handbook of action research.* Thousand Oaks, CA: Sage.

Rosenthal, E. (2006, April 8). British rethinking rules after ill-fated drug trial. *New York Times.* Retrieved from http://www.nytimes.com/2006/04/08/world/europe/08britain.html?ex=1180411200&en=7f53f64a1a24dca7&ei=5070

Sherwin, S. (1996). Feminism and bioethics. In S. M. Wolf (Ed.), *Feminism & bioethics: Beyond reproduction* (pp. 47–66). New York: Oxford University Press.

Sherwin, S. (Ed.). (1998). *The politics of women's health: Exploring agency and autonomy.* Philadelphia: Temple University Press.

Veatch, R. M. (1987). *The patient as partner: A theory of human-experimentation ethics.* Bloomington: Indiana University Press.

Wolpe, P. R. (1998). The triumph of autonomy in American bioethics: A sociological perspective. In R. DeVries & J. Subedi (Eds.), *Bioethics and society: Constructing the ethical enterprise* (pp. 38–59). Upper Saddle River, NJ: Prentice Hall.

14

Clinical Trials Offshored: On Private Sector Science and Public Health

Adriana Petryna

This article addresses the offshoring of clinical trials to middle- and low-income countries, and the complicated ways in which they have become integral to public health and quality of care in these contexts. It focuses on the operations of United States-based contract research organizations (CROs), which make up a specialized global industry focusing on the recruitment of human subjects and investigators; they are key players in an outsourced world of clinical development 'service providers'. To get an on-the-ground understanding of the offshored clinical trial, the author worked with regulators, health services administrators, and research clinicians in Eastern Europe and Latin America, two clinical trial market 'growth regions'. By addressing the strategies of evidence-making that inform clinical trial offshoring, this article identifies the context-specific calculations by which experimental groups are being identified. It also addresses aspects of the clinical trial operational model, in which the failure to predict safety outcomes or a paradigm of expected failure is being exported along with the offshored trial. By highlighting the uncertainties of clinical research, this article points to gaps in systems of human protection as it considers new forms of accountability in private sector science and public health.

Clinical Trial Environments

Currently, an estimated 50,000 clinical trials are being run worldwide. Over 40% of these new studies are taking place in so-called nontraditional research areas—countries that are experiencing epidemiological change associated with declining health resources but that have

Adriana Petryna, "Clinical Trials Offshored: On Private Sector Science and Public Health," in BioSocieties 2 (2007). pp. 21–40. Reproduced with permission from Macmillan Publishers.

The Pharmaceutical Studies Reader, First Edition. Edited by Sergio Sismondo and Jeremy A. Greene.

little share in the world's pharmaceutical market.[1] The bulk of these trials are commercially sponsored, and they range from gene therapy studies for rare diseases to studies for treatments for more common disorders; from studies of compounds mimicking existing drugs to studies in search of secondary uses for them.

Poland, for example, registers an average of 400 new trials annually and the neighboring Czech Republic 300. Most of these trials are phase III trials; they require large and diverse populations and are carried out before a drug is launched onto the market. Dr Renata Novak, a businesswoman managing clinical trials in the Czech Republic for a North American company told me that since that country has one of the highest rates of colon cancer in the world, it has become a hub for colon cancer studies. In most cases, data from such trials will be used to gain approval from the US Food and Drug Administration (or FDA) or the European Agency for the Evaluation of Medicinal Products (EMEA). People outside major drug markets enroll in these trials to access state-of-the-art technology and care. Dr Novak estimated that, so far, one in 100 Czechs (or 100,000 people) have participated in clinical trials, which are now, in her words, 'a normal part of health-care delivery'.

In another example, Poland, which until recently had one of the highest rates of cardiovascular-related death in the world, has developed impressive preventive apparatuses to reverse this trend. The country's leading heart institutes and public hospitals have become preferred destinations for trials of therapies ranging from hypertension treatments to invasive surgical procedures. Hospital administrators so welcomed these trials that, by the late 1990s, the National Institute of Cardiology in Warsaw was 'awash in thrombolytics', or clot-busting drugs, according to one businessman coordinating trials in Poland. He told me, 'Not a single ampule was purchased because each patient who needed that treatment got it from a clinical trial.'

This article addresses the offshoring of clinical trials to middle- and low-income countries and the complicated ways in which they have become integral to public health and quality of care in these contexts. Clinical trials are social institutions, and the question of whether to carry them out, where and how is a political one. These politics bear the stamp of a patterned set of practices inherent to the pharmaceutical industry as it has evolved in North America and elsewhere—I specifically have in mind the history of research among minorities and so-called cooperative patients and professional guinea pigs, and the power the industry exerts over evidence-making and drug regulatory policy.[2]

I analyze US-based contract research organizations (CROs), which make up a specialized global industry focusing on the recruitment of human subjects and investigators and on clinical research. They are crucial players in an expanding business world of outsourced clinical development 'service providers'. This world includes everything from patient recruitment firms to investigative sites, investigative site management organizations, academic research organizations, patient data mining companies, data-capture software vendors and commercialized institutional review boards (IRBs).

Several of the largest of these CROs are located in the northeastern United States pharmaceutical corridor. Pharmaceutical and start-up biotechnology companies often rely on CROs to implement and manage global clinical trials according to a given research protocol. In coordinating clinical trials in the United States and abroad, they provide guidance through complex regulatory and legal environments and data management and statistical services. CROs also supply on-the-ground monitoring services to assure their pharmaceutical clients and regulators that clinical research was conducted according to accepted technical standards; that it complies with national and international ethical guidelines concerning biomedical research in humans; and that the data has integrity and is free from fraud.

The new clinical trial environments that CROs help to tailor are adaptable, mobile and, to some extent, parasitic. They insert themselves in ongoing and unresolved conflicts over market reforms and the role of public institutions in local societies. At any given moment they can move somewhere else. National health and regulatory experts have high stakes in attracting clinical trial investments to their countries and keeping them there. These experts play a key role in shaping the public's understanding of clinical trials—their benefit to patients and to public health systems more generally. To get an on-the-ground understanding of the offshoring of clinical trials, I carried out a comparative ethnographic inquiry in two of the fastest growing regions for clinical trials (Latin America and Eastern Europe), working with trial coordinators, study monitors and local investigators in these regions and where, to some extent, clinical research plays an increasingly important (though generally under-acknowledged) role in public health services provisioning.[3]

In the summers of 2003 and 2004, I interviewed scientists affiliated with the Brazilian drug regulatory body (ANVISA) and academic-turned-industry-sponsored researchers of the Unit of Clinical Research of the University Hospital in a major city in southern Brazil. Also, in summer 2005 I observed the work of the Polish office of a mid-sized CRO (which I will call Pharmexel). I was particularly concerned with how scientific integrity is maintained and ensured in these new markets, as well with conveying the ethical reflections and critiques of the diverse scientific actors involved.

By addressing the strategies of evidence-making and the legal and ethical precepts that govern commercial clinical trials, I shed light on the context-specific calculations by which experimental groups are being constituted and the value systems that bring doctors and patients into these trials. My long-term engagement with trial practitioners also points to the gaps in current systems of human subjects protection, both international and national, and I specify the kinds of harm that, despite the oversight of institutional review boards and informed consent, are nonetheless being produced.

In the first part of this article, I highlight some of the regulatory, economic and technical reasons underlying the acceleration and offshoring of clinical trials. I discuss key events that recently framed the public debate over medical research in contexts of public health crisis. In 'zones of crisis', protection and safety considerations are weighed against immediate health benefits or the knowledge to be gained. Ethics and method are modified to fit the local context and experimental data required. And this 'ethical variability' becomes a core value and a presumed course of action in the global testing of pharmaceuticals (Petryna, 2005). In the second part of this article, I address the clinical trial operational model and debates about its inability to gauge drug safety and risk (FDA, 2004). According to many of my informants, safety problems are detected only after-the-fact; and this retrospective detection speaks to a fundamental abandonment of the scientific method to characterize harm. The CRO perspective allows an appreciation of the persistent problems and uncertainties underlying the clinical research enterprise, and it points to gaps in oversight and responsibility. The operations through which efficacy and safety data happen become ethnographic contexts from which to observe the benefits and risks of private sector science as it is rapidly integrated into public health systems in emerging drug markets.

Pharmaceutical Capital: Contract Research in Brief

So, what drives the demand for larger pools of human subjects? First, as I mentioned earlier, simply the sheer number of trials being run. The advent of blockbuster drugs with sales of over a billion dollars annually has led to the profitable 'me-too drugs' business. With minimal pharmacological alteration, these drugs build on or mimic blockbuster drugs and are not especially innovative. Second, to satisfy US regulatory demands, increasingly large numbers of patients must be included in clinical trials to prove long-term safety, especially of drugs designed to be widely prescribed. Third, some drug categories—like antihypertensives to control blood pressure and statins to control cholesterol—are expanding dramatically as new compounds are developed. Competition to get drugs approved and marketed steps up the search for subjects. Fourth, there is significant growth in the number of new chemical entities—patents are inundating the United States Patent Office for compounds that have yet to undergo clinical testing (CenterWatch, 2005).

Shifts in the very science of drug development also impact subject recruitment. As new molecules are discovered, more experiments are taking place (before the formal phases of human testing) to determine their clinical and market viability. Also, the available pool of human subjects in major Western pharmaceutical markets is shrinking. 'Treatment saturation' is making Americans and Western Europeans increasingly unusable from a drug-testing standpoint (see Gorman, 2004). As the late Hein Besselaar, the grandfather of the contract research industry, put it to me in an interview in 2004, 'People in the West live on pills. You have the 50-year-old who takes three or four different medications. Someone living in Eastern Europe may be on one medication for high blood pressure or whatever, but certainly not three or four.' In other words, our bodies produce too many drug-drug interactions and are less and less able to show specific drug effectiveness, making test results less statistically significant.

The roots of a specialized contract research regime are traceable to the post-Second World War pharmaceutical expansion, when a fee-for-service industry evolved in response to a demand for more safety testing in animals. In the early 1970s, a few CRO-like consultancies were established as adjuncts to the pharmaceutical labor force. As a former executive explained to me:

> They were a cottage industry, people working out of garages with a few computers—scientists who came out of the industry with experience and said I can take on some of this data management work or trial monitoring on a contract basis. But pharma did not trust these people with anything large or complicated.

By the early 1980s, pharmaceutical companies were regularly outsourcing laboratory and clinical services, including the monitoring of investigational sites and the data produced. Mega-trials and me-too drugs came into vogue, and CROs promised expertise and reduction in time and cost.

By the mid 1990s the research enterprise was booming and many CROs went public. The pharma capital to be made was in clinical research. As one industry executive told me in 2003: 'Fifty-five billion dollars go into research and development. Forty billion of that is in development. And of that forty billion probably 60% is spent on phase II and III trials. So big money is there'.

Today, the CRO industry claims that it provides for roughly 40% of the number of clinical research personnel engaged in drug development activities.[4] Most CROs are involved in locating research sites, recruiting patients and, in some cases, drawing up the study design and performing analyses. Sometimes they work directly with primary health-care facilities, hospitals or consortia of therapeutic specialists. Some even have their own centralized ethical review boards.

Clinical trials are divided into four phases. Phase I studies rely on roughly 20–80 healthy volunteers and determine the tolerable dose range of a new drug. Phase II studies evaluate efficacy and safety in 100–300 subjects who have the disease or condition to be treated. Phase III studies generate more safety and efficacy data. They are generally multicentered and can involve up to 10,000 people in 10–20 countries. This phase is the most time-consuming and expensive.[5] Phase IV studies provide further safety and efficacy information after the drug has been marketed, and they can involve millions of people.

Constructing Global Subjects

The expansion of pharmaceutical testing worldwide is not only driven by industry motives. During my field research in the mid to late 1990s on the social and political aftermath of the Chernobyl nuclear disaster, I observed a rapid growth of pharmaceutical markets in Ukraine and its neighboring countries (Petryna, 2002). Some physicians who tended to Chernobyl victims told me how anxious they were to learn how to do trials and to attract clinical trial contracts both because of the abundance of various untreated diseases and because the scientific infrastructures on which the physicians were dependent were quickly deteriorating without new public funding. This mix of ongoing public health crisis and the needs and interests of local scientific communities was leading to a reconceptualization of patients and their value.

CROs see Eastern Europe as a particularly good recruitment site. Postsocialist healthcare institutions are conducive to running efficient trials because they remain centralized and have a reasonable scientific infrastructure. Given the unmet demand for specialized care, patient enrollment is said to be quick. High literacy rates in these areas mean that subjects offer more 'meaningful' informed consent, thus minimizing potential problems with auditors. Large Latin American cities such as São Paulo are also considered premium sites because, as one recruiter told me, 'Populations are large. It's a question of how many patients I can get within a limited area, which reduces travel cost.'

Some regions and countries are more attractive than others because of the abundance of what is commonly known as 'treatment naïveté', a term that refers to populations that (apparently) have not been diagnosed or treated for a particular condition. Treatment-naïve populations are considered 'incredibly valuable', as one researcher told me, because 'these populations offer a more likely prospect of minimizing the number of variables affecting results'. That people in low-income countries also might be taking several drugs or treatments, often unsystematically, has not deterred companies from identifying particular contexts in those countries as sites in which the 'naïve' might be found, in a poorer region or provincial hospital, for example.[6]

The increasing choice of Third World citizens to be subjects of global drug trials parallels their poverty status. Even if the trend in drug trial expansion can be justified in terms of potential health benefits, pursuing disadvantaged populations that have (as yet) little or no legal recourse in case of harm involves troublesome ethics. The baseline conditions that would make a universal ethics applicable and enforceable worldwide are highly uneven. Critiques of such experimental regimes focus heavily on procedural issues—clinical conduct and informed consent—as if harm could be exclusively located within a traditional model of physician-induced neglect. As efforts are made to expose violations of individual bodily integrity, social scientists also need to chart how people are categorized and gathered into these experimental regimes, and why protective mechanisms are at times unable to intervene. We also need to look at the value patients bring to these regimes and what is owed to them, such as continued treatment once a trial is over.

The controversy over placebo use in Africa in 1994 during trials of short-course AZT treatment to halt perinatal transmission of HIV was a watershed in the debate over ethical standards in global clinical research.[7] Here I take it as a watershed of a different sort: of how subject populations are generated at the intersection of regulatory deliberation, commercial interest and crises (upon crises) of public health. In this well-known case, some US researchers argued that giving less than standard care to those on the placebo arm of the study was ethically responsible, even if in the United States the standard of care was available. Critics viewed the use of a placebo arm as highly unethical. Research in developing countries, therefore, was being held to a different standard than in the developed world.[8]

Harold Varmus of the National Institutes of Health (NIH) and David Satcher of the Centers for Disease Control (CDC), which, among other institutions, authorized and funded the AZT trial, claimed that the trial was ethically sound. They cited local cultural variables and deteriorated health services as making the delivery of the best standard of care infeasible. It would be a paternalistic imposition, they argued, for critics in the United States to determine the appropriate design of medical research in a region under such stress, and it was within the jurisdiction of local and national authorities to decide on appropriate research conduct and treatment distribution.

Ethical imperialism or ethical relativism? These were the terms of the debate. The first position builds its case on histories of marginalized communities that were coerced or misled into experiments and greatly suffered as a result. Historians point to other communities, such as those of the 'cooperative' patients and professional guinea pigs, that complicate these histories of coercion (Marks, 2002). The second position (ethical relativism) relativizes ethical decision-making as a matter of sound science, but it fails to consider the uptake of this relativizing move in corporate research contexts. For me, the AZT trial and the debates that followed it highlight the role of crisis in the consideration of variability in ethical standards in human research. Some crises have led, perhaps inescapably, to experimentation. But one can ask: are crises states of exception or are they the norm? To what extent does the language of crisis become instrumental, granting legitimacy to experimentation when it otherwise might not have one?

The debate over the ethics of the AZT trial prompted the sixth revision of the Helsinki Declaration, which deals with 'all aspects of human biomedical research and provides guidelines for research involving human subjects'.[9] The 2000 revision stated that placebos should not be used when standards of treatment are known: 'The benefits, risks, burdens, and effectiveness of a new method should be tested against those of the best current prophylactic, diagnostic, and therapeutic methods.' If the ethics were unambiguous, the regulatory weight of the declaration was not. Pharmaceutical companies, already expanding operations abroad and calculating the economic advantages of placebo use (placebos lower costs and, many argue, placebo trials produce more unambiguous evidence of efficacy), were eager to learn from regulators about the legal enforceability of the declaration while finding ways to continue using the placebo.

Dr Robert Temple, the influential former director of the Center for Drug Evaluation at the FDA, clarified the rules of the global drug development game. He undercut the regulatory significance of the declaration and threw his support behind placebo advocates. He referred to the Guideline for Good Clinical Practice, issued by the International Conference on Harmonization (ICH-E10, 2001) in the early 1990s, as the alternative and more relevant guideline on the ethics of placebo use. This ICH brought together regulatory authorities of Europe, Japan and the United States with industry experts, and it made clinical data from international research sites transferable and acceptable to regulatory bodies in these major markets. This guideline states, 'Whether a particular placebo controlled trial of a new agent will be acceptable to subjects and investigators when there is a known effective therapy is a matter of patient, investigator, and IRB judgment, and acceptability *may differ* among *regions and ... populations chosen*' (Temple, 2002: 213, emphasis added). In other words, the ethical standard for research in the world was variability.

In fact, Dr Temple's backing of the placebo trial was informed by a concern about the integrity of scientific data. The alternative to the placebo control is the active control trial. With active controls—in which a new drug is compared with a standard one—one has to worry about an increased chance of study defects that may invalidate the data, such as poor patient compliance and the use of concomitant medications on the part of the patient that can obscure effect. The treatment-naïve are preferable subjects given this logic. It is precisely because they are often poor and supposedly do not have access to medical treatments that they are considered more foolproof and valuable research subjects.

One researcher I interviewed said the FDA's response to the Helsinki Declaration revision 'made research efficiency a priority and this was in line with what industry wanted'. The murky ethics of placebo use could be circumvented by offering what is known as equivalent medication—not necessarily the best or standard treatment, but whatever is at hand as a best local equivalent. 'Do I give them a sugar pill or vitamin C?' as he cynically asked me. In the meantime, the study will be ethical, the data will have integrity and, sadly (in some cases), the patients will remain treatment-naïve.[10]

In accounting for the link between regulation and the making of ethics in human research, historian Harry Marks writes, 'It is as if ethical discourse and the regulations governing research exist in two parallel universes which share some common elements but do not connect' (2000: 14). But I would argue that the aftermath of the AZT trials demonstrates how connected those universes are and how regulatory decision-making at the transnational level encourages the evolution of 'local' and 'ethically variable' experimental terrains.[11]

To attract pharmaceutical investments, the regulatory agencies of many countries soon signed up to the International Conference on Harmonisation (ICH). Signing up meant these countries would begin the costly work of setting up agencies that could standardize and monitor the conduct of trials in their countries. They would also build ethical review boards to ensure the rights and protections of patients. This process was slow, yet the subjects involved in international clinical trials grew from 4,000 in 1995 to 400,000 in 1999. These numbers are low, as they refer to new drug applications (NDA) only.[12] Indeed, they are *very* low, considering the kinds of experimental activities that are not registered and hence not officially accounted for.

The largest increase in clinical trial participation occurred in Eastern Europe and Latin America. This global growth has brought with it a new set of unknowns over the circumstances of research and concerns over possible exploitation of foreign subjects. In 2001, the Office of the Inspector General, a body that carries out periodic reviews of the FDA, told that agency after careful review that, in spite of its active promotion of the search for sites and subjects elsewhere, the FDA is not able to protect human subjects in research elsewhere. The Office of the Inspector General recommended that the FDA support and in some cases assist in establishing local ethical review boards.

This approach leans heavily on IRB oversight and toward a liability model of accountability: let's name the responsible local parties (in some cases set them up first), and surely they can gather information and make right decisions, surely they can stop inappropriate research from taking place. A working legal system is assumed. Much is also assumed about who is and isn't the agent of abuse, most typically defined as the medical investigator.

As the rapid and semiregulated growth of clinical trials was under way, scandals arose that exposed the structural flaws and real absences of institutionalized protective structures in a hastily globalized system. Consider the now infamous case of Trovan, a widely prescribed antibiotic that had been taken off the market in the United States because it was found to have serious liver side effects. A 1996 Nigerian trial was supposed to show that Trovan could be used to treat meningitis, but the protocol was not approved by a US ethics committee and received inadequate review in the host country. Lawyers for Nigerian plaintiffs moved against Pfizer in the deaths of 11 children, who were among the trial participants. The trial happened during a massive outbreak of bacterial meningitis in the context of a civil war. Some children were given Trovan in a form never tested on humans before; others were given a lowered dose of a proven therapy for meningitis (ceftriaxone) that, according to the legal complaint allowed researchers to show that Trovan was more efficacious. The plaintiffs' lawyers claimed that this lower dosing caused the children's deaths.

They suggested an array of complicitous interests in making the children accessible for research that includes Nigeria's rulers, Ministry of Health officials, local hospital administrators, FDA regulators who authorized an unapproved drug's export to Nigeria for humanitarian purposes, and company researchers who redirected children waiting for standard treatments to their own experiment.

Even if there had been a functional ethical review of US industry-sponsored research, the tragedy might not have been prevented so long as these interests were not on the side of protection but, overwhelmingly, on the side of making populations accessible for research. As this brief sketch of the legal sparring shows, ethical regulation is a realm of contingent practice, and the allocation of protection for human subjects is far from settled.

Keeping the Clinical Trial Market in Poland

Drug companies invest almost half a billion dollars in clinical research in Poland each year. The medical director of a major pharmaceutical firm operating in Poland told me in 2005 that Central-Eastern Europe is the 'second largest producer of clinical data' after the United States. I followed clinical trials staff and scientists of one CRO to its Warsaw affiliate to see how clinical trial environments are tailored and operationalized. Here it is not a matter of looser standards or circumvention of FDA regulations, but about how such environments are tinkered with to be sustainable and profitable over a long run.

I first met Dr Jan Mazur[13] when he visited the US headquarters of Pharmexel. Mazur leads this mid-sized CRO's clinical trial services strategy and expansion across Central-Eastern Europe. He came to speak to Pharmexel's marketers about the region's high data productivity.

During his presentation, Mazur provided data about his country's dire health predictors and its poorly financed health-care and universal health insurance systems. He juxtaposed this data to information about the high quality of clinical research and Poland's adaptation to international standards. The message to get to potential clients was clear: they will not fail in recruiting and they will have reliable data. Mazur also conveyed clinical trial success stories; they all involved what are known in the industry as 'rescue studies'. The term applies to studies that start in one location and, because of poor recruitment, are moved to another location midway through the trial. So, for example, it takes one year for 50 investigative sites in Western Europe to recruit 200 rheumatoid arthritis patients. Whereas five central-European sites recruit the exact same number in just two months.

When I arrived in Poland, however, Mazur's success stories turned out to be a bit more complicated. One such story involved a placebo-controlled study for a diabetes drug. The study's inclusion criteria required previously untreated (or treatment-naïve) patients with 'very high' blood-sugar levels. In Western Europe, subject recruitment for the study was exceedingly low. And in Poland, Dr Mazur expressed anxiety about pressures to recruit 'dangerously sick patients'. He told me, 'If you are newly diagnosed, you cannot possibly have such high blood-sugar levels!' He was referring to 'normal' medical contexts, where diabetics would be diagnosed and treated at much lower blood sugar levels. He seemed to suggest that timing of diagnosis was everything. There was room to maneuver and therein lie potential abuses.

Dr Mazur explained to me that the study drug was not significantly different from what was already on the market, but the patients were chosen in a way that made small therapeutic differences more obvious (it was a me-too). He was able to slightly modify the inclusion criteria to recruit patients with a slightly less severe condition—in his words, to make 'non-existent patients' come into existence. Because of the 'complexity' of this protocol, the CRO also hired its own on-site physicians to review each and every patient already randomized—to make sure they are actually *eligible* for the trial. 'It becomes very difficult to exclude other causes for the same symptoms and signs, and the wrong people may get into the trial. It's a safety issue.' Dr Mazur was extremely conscientious, and his company valued him for it. But I could not help but wonder what others in the same position may or may not choose to do.

The 'complex' studies Dr Mazur spoke of were predominantly rescue studies for me-too drugs. These were not gene therapy or cardiac intervention trials—trials that we might normally associate with more complexity—but trials for drugs that constitute the majority of the drugs that are FDA approved today (Angell, 2006). Taming complexity seemed to be an unwelcome part of his expertise, but one he had to deploy, lest he jeopardize Poland's privileged position in the clinical trials global market. But who is responsible for the danger in the me-too protocol? The drug manufacturer always had the option of taking the protocol elsewhere—to another CRO, to another country—if Pharmexel decided to reject it. The company's added efforts to make protocols do-able and safe (by hiring their own physicians, for example) were driving up their costs.

Hidden harms—sometimes, there is no rescue from them. Consider the recent troubles with rofecoxib (Vioxx) a drug that belongs to a class of drugs that is now known to increase the risk of heart attacks. A meta-analysis of rofecoxib trials that appeared in *The Lancet* revealed that evidence of cardiovascular risk from the drug was known before September 2004, when Merck withdrew the drug from the market (Juni *et al.*, 2004). The drug maker offshored clinical research to Eastern Europe in the mid 1990s, before able study monitors like Dr Mazur arrived *en masse* on this up-and-coming clinical trial scene. Vioxx underwent testing in countries such as Poland, which, as I mentioned, have seen some of the highest rates of cardiovascular-related deaths in the world. *The Lancet* article suggests that contexts with different background risks can lead to a misclassification or underappreciation of coronary events, which, in turn, 'could have biased results in trials that did not include external appraisal of safety outcomes' (the use of monitors, for example).[14]

I spoke to several Polish and Russian investigators who ran Vioxx studies and they, understandably perhaps, denied any problem at their sites. But, for Dr Mazur, the protocol itself carries background risk. He said companies can choose the most cost-effective tools to observe and record patients' symptoms (for instance, using cheaper pain-scales rather than more expensive laboratory exams to verify drug-related symptoms or effects). But this is not a matter of simply saving on costs. His colleague in the United States went further and told me that, 'adverse events are not just inadequately reported, but harm in general is under-hypothesized'. Its acknowledgement may be deferred or in his words, simply 'engineered out'. And, if harms are revealed (in the post-marketing stage, for example), they can be attributed to environmental or individual causes rather than to the study drug.

'Pharmaceuticals are the New Gold'

There are also socio-economic harms at stake in globalized clinical testing. For the past three summers, I worked with academic researchers in the newly built Unit of Clinical Research of the University Hospital in a major city in southern Brazil. The team, led by Dr Paulo Picon, was critical of the ways pharmaceutical companies and CROs were influencing the course of medical research and public health in Brazil. Dr Picon and his team were analyzing the efficacy and dosage requirements of new drugs entering the market. They were particularly concerned with drugs that do not promise to cure or extend life, but simply lower some non-clinical indicator, such as the reduced virological response promised by the hepatitis C drug, peginterferon. Some new drugs cost 20 times more than existing treatments, and these researchers are showing that their efficacy is not much better. 'The industry is pressuring the state to purchase these drugs,' Dr Picon said, and he added: 'Pharmaceuticals are the new gold.' He went on to compare a gram of peginterferon to a gram of gold:

> One gram of gold costs 50 reais, $24. Today, one gram of peginterferon costs 4.4 million reais 2 million dollars ... one gram. With this one gram you can treat 110 patients and you might prevent, you *might* prevent one liver cirrhosis. One cirrhosis in 110 patients ... you *might* prevent.

Desperate patients demand these treatments, as the country's constitution guarantees the right to universal health care. They are modeling their efforts after successful movements by AIDS patients in Brazil and the United States (Biehl, 2006; Epstein, 1996).[15] Today, this combination of patient activism and commercial science is leading to what anthropologist Joao Biehl (2006) calls a 'pharmaceuticalization of public health', raising vital questions about public health priorities, financing and equity. These university researchers are creating a kind of counter-science, designing protocols that show that lower doses of certain drugs are equally efficacious and cost less. They are also working with local prosecutors and educating judges to make sure that this alternative evidence will have some legal weight.

In September 2005, a group of clinicians active in industry-sponsored research and working in another hospital, told me of a problem they are currently facing. They were conducting a clinical trial to test the efficacy of a new therapy for a rare genetic disorder. Advanced-stage patients who had never received any treatment were recruited, according to the study's strict inclusion criteria.

The well-respected director of the genetics service was eager to secure the contract for the trial because of the resources it would bring to the service. Without his colleagues' knowledge, he agreed to the sponsoring company's demand to reserve the right to withdraw the drug at any time—this was written into the consent forms that the patients signed. Informally, however, the company agreed to provide medication for two years, and it continued to do so for a third year. The drug worked well. But, without notice, the company pulled the study drug. A company representative hinted to the clinicians that Brazil was too slow in registering the drug. Company lawyers had contacted the patients to spur a patient activist group to pressure the government to buy these drugs (which can cost up to $200,000 per patient annually). This effort failed. Later, I learned that the company running the trial had been sold. Whatever had led to the withdrawal, the clinicians involved had no institutional and legal recourse. There was no more treatment. Within four years, their advanced-stage patients would most likely die.

As clinicians expressed their concerns over patient care, they highlighted the contractual uncertainties that pervade the world's clinical trial scene and how an obligation to minimize harm can be undercut. Accounting for such uncertainties requires moving beyond 'doctor–patient' relations or 'investigator misconduct'. Their experience points to urgent problems of responsibility buried beneath the 'paper ethics' of the globalized trial, and the ethical variability that leaves ample room for contingent or opportunistic behaviors.

This case illuminates the unevenness of institutional powers in the now-global landscape of experimentation, as well as the lack of local coordination and negotiating ability. While the benefits deriving from the globalized clinical trial were clearly conceptualized by the various parties involved, one variable that was not well thought-out was the harm that could occur if the study treatment was withdrawn. Moreover, no one is helping patients to formalize their interests (other than the trial sponsor). A modeling of the value that patients actually bring to the trial (and ultimately, to the drug) would be illuminating too. Also, patients' informed consent should be supplemented with informed *contracts* on the part of local investigators.

The significance of clinical research for the welfare of large numbers of people is growing (Kahn *et al.*, 1998), but the benefits deriving from globalized research are unevenly distributed. Current institutional ideas about patient protection remain rather narrowly construed, and the harm dimension (how harms are produced in the broader contexts of experimentation) needs specification. Clinical trials are large-scale and multi-variable systems. But, as this article shows, uncertainty pervades their inputs and outputs and—as the paradigm of expected failure suggests—threatens the integrity of the system itself. Biased protocol design can 'engineer up' the success of the trial, but approaches to detecting safety problems remain inadequate. The ability to choose treatment-naïve subjects creates efficient results, free of statistical noise, but even here my CRO informants expressed serious doubts about the generalizability of data—for example, how can results derived from treatment-naïve groups ever be generalized to populations in treatment-saturated markets?—as well as concerns about ineffective and unsafe drugs entering the market. This article also explored the technical practices by which companies can make harms go away, and the role of offshoring in this regard. These practices go hand in hand with the absence of governmental institutions capable of monitoring the entrance of ineffective drugs into the market and their long-term side effects, not to mention that, in many countries, patients still lack legal recourse for harms incurred during and after trial participation.

Industry and regulatory concerns about ethics seem to matter currently at the level of the data—more specifically, at the level of ensuring the 'integrity of data'. Why invest in a foreign site, if one is uncertain whether the data collected there will even be usable in the US drug approval process? This, I believe, is currently driving the push for the establishment of more local ethical review boards in new sites. Was there informed consent? Did the local investigator agree to accept all responsibility in cases of harm? Did the local ethical review board review and ok the protocol? At stake is the making of an airtight documentary environment assuring the portability of foreign-derived data. Furthermore, when the focus of the experiment is on portability of data, the uncertainties of context and patient-related variables are engineered out. And this in itself is a risk that may show up later as a harm.

Whether they work directly for the clinical trial industry as scientists and study monitors, or are occasionally on its payroll as recruited investigators, my informants in the United States, Brazil and Poland show how harm detection can be deferred and patient protection compromised. Rather than positioning themselves as isolated entrepreneurs being 'squeezed down by costs' or as passive stewards of a clinical trial machine, they reaffirm the need for a sounder science and of stretching the capacities of clinical trials as health-care interventions—medical research and care go hand in hand. They champion a different sort of market-oriented pharmaceutical contract, one that goes beyond a proceduralized form of ethics and that can value patients again. As the turf war among pharmaceutical sponsors for human subjects rages on, I have drawn on their diverse perspectives to consider how accountability is brought to bear on the offshored clinical trial and the challenges it raises for global public health.

NOTES

1 Among the 10 leading global pharmaceutical markets, the United States ranks first and holds a 60.5% share. Germany, France, Italy, the UK, Spain and Belgium also rank among the top 10. Combined, they hold a 21% share, followed by Japan (15.1%), Canada (2.4%), and Australia (1.1%) (http://www.imshealth.com). The Office of Inspector General, Department of Health and Human Services, states that 'among the countries that have experienced the largest growth in clinical investigators [for commercially sponsored trials] are Russia and countries in Eastern Europe and Latin America' (2001: i).

2 For critiques of the United States system for developing, testing, and using prescription drugs, see Abramson (2004), Angell (2005), Avorn (2004), Goozner (2004), Kassirer (2004); Moynihan and Cassels (2005).

3 According to CenterWatch, an investigator is:
A medical professional, usually a physician but may also be a nurse, pharmacist or other health care professional, under whose direction an investigational drug is administered or dispensed. A principal investigator is responsible for the overall conduct of the clinical trial at his/her site.
A study monitor is:
[a] person employed by the sponsor or CRO who reviews study records to determine that a study is being conducted in accordance with the protocol. A monitor's duties may include, but are not limited to, helping to plan and initiate a study, and assessing the conduct of studies. Monitors work with the clinical research coordinator to check all data and documentation from the study.
Reference: http://www.centerwatch.com/patient/glossary.html#5

4 This estimate is given by the Association for Clinical Research Organizations (http://www.acrohealth.org/trends.php). ACRO is the main lobbying and trade organization for the world's largest CROs.

5 When I refer to clinical trials in this article, I am mainly referring to Phase III trials.

6 On 'irrational' treatment uses, see Etkin (1999). On the circulation of pharmaceuticals within the lifeworlds of the urban poor in Delhi, see Das and Das (2006).

7 For different perspectives on this controversy, see Angell (1988, 1997, 2000), Bayer (1998), Botbol-Baum (2000), Crouch and Arras (1998), de Zulueta (2001), Farmer (2002), Lurie and Wolfe (1998, 2000), Rothman (2000).

8 Marcia Angell (2000), for example, said that practices like the use of a placebo arm were reminiscent of the Tuskegee experiment, in which, for decades, African-American men were followed to observe the natural course of their untreated syphilis.

9 The Helsinki Declaration has been modified five times since its first edition in 1964. It deals with 'all aspects of human biomedical research, providing guidelines for investigators to follow in research involving human subjects' (Guess *et al.*, 2002: 19).

10 Another researcher echoed the sense that concerns have shifted from justice to efficiency-based standards in global research when he told me that ethics is a 'workable document. ... Equivalent medication in Eastern Europe is not the same as equivalent medication in Western Europe, so you could work the Helsinki Declaration.'

11 A recent review (Kent *et al.*, 2004) found that ethical guidelines that specify best proven therapy are routinely being violated, regardless of decisions made by local or international scientists and regardless of funding sources.

12 An NDA is an application to the FDA to obtain a license to market a new drug in the US.

13 This is a pseudonym.

14 The quote continues: 'the inclusion of an independent endpoints committee should be the rule, and exceptions to this rule should be justified (2004:2025).'

15 Indeed, there has been a shift since the 1980s with the integration of desperate patients suffering from cancer and AIDS into 'fast-track' research. Acknowledging this group of special patients called for flexibility within medical institutions with regard to the process of evaluating the effectiveness of therapies through clinical trials. In terms of drug access Brazil's free dispensation of combined anti-retroviral treatments has been hailed as a model of AIDS intervention in a low-income country.

REFERENCES

Abramson, J. (2004). *Overdosed America: The broken promise of American medicine*. New York: HarperCollins.

Angell, M. (1988). Ethical imperialism? Ethics in international collaborative clinical research. *New England Journal of Medicine, 319*, 1081–1083.

Angell, M. (1997). The ethics of clinical research in the Third World. *New England Journal of Medicine, 337*, 847–849.

Angell, M. (2000). Investigators' responsibilities for human subjects in developing countries. *New England Journal of Medicine, 342*, 967–968.

Angell, M. (2005). *The truth about the drug companies: How they deceive us and what to do about it.* New York: Random House.

Angell, M. (2006). Your dangerous drugstore. *New York Review of Books, 53*(10). URL (accessed February 2007): http://www.nybooks.com/articles/19055

Avorn, J. (2004). *Powerful medicines: The benefits, risks, and costs of prescription drugs.* New York: Knopf.

Bayer, R. (1998). The debate over maternal-fetal HIV transmission prevention trials in Africa, Asia, and Caribbean: Racist exploitation or exploitation of racism? *American Journal of Public Health, 88*, 567–570.

Biehl, J. (2006). Pharmaceutical governance. In A. Petryna, A. Lakoff, & A. Kleinman, (Eds), *Global pharmaceuticals: Ethics, markets, practices.* Durham, NC: Duke University Press.

Botbol-Baum, M. (2000). The shrinking of human rights: The controversial revision of the Helsinki Declaration. *HIV Medicine, 1*, 238–245.

Crouch, R.A., & Arras, J.D. (1998). AZT trials and tribulations. *Hastings Center Report, 28*, 26–34.

Das, V., & Das, R.K. (2006). Pharmaceuticals in urban ecologies: The register of the local. In A. Petryna, A. Lakoff, & A. Kleinman, (Eds), *Global pharmaceuticals: Ethics, markets, practices.* Durham, NC: Duke University Press.

de Zulueta, P. (2001). Randomised placebo-controlled trials and HIV-infected pregnant women in developing countries: Ethical imperialism or unethical exploitation? *Bioethics, 15*, 289–311.

Epstein, S. (1996). *Impure science: AIDS, activism, and the politics of knowledge.* Berkeley: University of California Press.

Etkin, N. (1999). The rational basis of 'irrational' drug use: Pharmaceuticals in the context of development. In R.A. Hahn, (Ed.), *Anthropology in public health: Bridging differences in culture and society*, 165–182. New York: Oxford University Press.

Farmer, P. (2002). Can transnational research be ethical in the developing world? *The Lancet, 360*, 1301–1302.

FDA (Food and Drug Administration) (2004). *Innovation/stagnation: Challenge and opportunity on the critical path to new medical products.* March. Washington, DC: Dept of Health & Human Services.

Geertz, C. (2000) [1984]. Anti anti-relativism. In *Available light: Anthropological reflections on philosophical topics*, 42–67. Princeton, NJ: Princeton University Press.

Goozner, M. (2004). *The $800 million pill: The truth behind the cost of new drugs.* Berkeley: University of California Press.

Gorman, J. (2004). The altered human is already here. *New York Times*, 6 April: F1.

Guess, H.A., Kleinman, A., Kusek, J.W., & Engel, L.W. (Eds) (2002). *The science of the placebo: Toward an inter-disciplinary research agenda.* London: BMJ Books.

Juni, P., Nartey, L., Reichenbach, S., Sterchi, R., Dieppe, P.A., & Egger, M. (2004). Risk of cardiovascular events and rofecoxib: cumulative meta-analysis. *The Lancet, 364*, 2021–2029.

Kahn, J.P., Mastroianni, A.C., & Sugarman, J. (1998). *Beyond consent: Seeking justice in research.* Oxford: Oxford University Press.

Kassirer, J.P. (2004). *On the take: How medicine's complicity with big business can endanger your health.* Oxford: Oxford University Press.

Kent, D., Mwamburi, M., Bennish, M., Kupelnick, B., & Ioannidis, J. (2004). Clinical trials in sub-Saharan Africa and established standards of care: A systematic review of HIV, tuberculosis, and malaria trials. *Journal of the American Medical Association, 292*, 237–242.

Lurie, P., & Wolfe, S.M. (1998). Unethical trials of interventions to reduce perinatal transmission of the human immunodeficiency virus in developing countries. *New England Journal of Medicine, 337*, 853–855.

Lurie, P., & Wolfe, S.M. (2000). Letter to the National Bioethics Advisory Commission regarding their report on the challenges of conducting research in developing countries (HRG Publication #1545). URL (accessed January 2007): http://www.citizen.org/publications/release.cfm?ID=6746

Marks, H. (2000). *Where do ethics come from? The role of disciplines and institutions.* Paper presented at the Conference on 'Ethical Issues in Clinical Trials', University of Alabama at Birmingham, 25 February.

Marks, H. (2002). *Commentary. 3rd Annual W.H.R. Rivers Workshop*, 'Global Pharmaceuticals: Ethics, Markets, Practices', Harvard University, 19–21 May.

Moynihan, R., & Cassels, A. (2005). *Selling sickness: How the world's biggest pharmaceutical companies are turning us all into patients.* New York: Nation Books.

Office of the Inspector General, Department of Health and Human Services (2001). *The globalization of clinical trials: A growing challenge in protecting human subjects.* Boston, MA: Office of Evaluation and Inspections.

Petryna, A. (2002). *Life exposed: Biological citizens after Chernobyl.* Princeton, NJ: Princeton University Press.

Petryna, A. (2005). Ethical variability: Drug development and the globalization of clinical trials. *American Ethnologist, 32*, 183–197.

Rothman, D. (2000). The shame of medical research. *New York Review of Books, 47*(19), 60–64.

Temple, R. (2002). Placebo-controlled trials and active controlled trials: Ethics and inference. In H.A. Guess, A. Kleinman, J.W. Kusek, & L.W. Engel, (Eds), *The science of the placebo: Toward an interdisciplinary research agenda*, 209–226. London: BMJ Books.

15

The Experimental Machinery of Global Clinical Trials: Case Studies from India

Kaushik Sunder Rajan

Clinical trials constitute the drug development component of the process of therapeutic development. There is no way that any new drug molecule can come to market without a series of trials for safety and efficacy in animals and humans. Clinical trials therefore constitute the *experimental machinery* of biocapital: they are necessary to conduct before a drug comes to market, are particularly elaborate in the context of the U.S. regulatory framework, and are in themselves cost-intensive and high-risk with no guarantee of success. India, in this story, envisages itself as a major experimental site. Clinical trials, therefore, provide a lens through which to study the globalizing dynamics of biocapital in terms of the cost and biomedical rationales for outsourcing trials to developing country sites like India.

Clinical trials constitute the set of practices required to certify a new drug molecule as safe and efficacious for the market. This set of practices serves in its rationale as a regulatory watchdog to prevent the market from being flooded with unsafe or spurious medication.

The stages of clinical trials are as follows: First, there is preclinical toxicological testing of a potential new drug molecule. This is usually performed on animals, in order to determine whether the molecule being tested is safe enough to put into a living system. This is followed by dosage studies, in order to come up with a metric that relates the dose of the drug being administered to safety and efficacy. Predictably, the efficacy of a drug increases with its dose, but so too does its toxicity, so the attempt is to find an optimum range of doses within which efficacy is maximized without compromising safety too much. If acceptable dose ranges can be determined within animals, then it proceeds to a three-phase trial in humans. Phase I trials

Kaushik Sunder Rajan, "The Experimental Machinery of Global Clinical Trials: Case Studies From India," in Aihwa Ong and Nancy Chen (eds.) Asian Biotech: Ethics and Communities of Fate. Durham, NC: Duke University Press, 2010. pp. 55–80. Reproduced with permission from Duke University Press.

The Pharmaceutical Studies Reader, First Edition. Edited by Sergio Sismondo and Jeremy A. Greene.

are conducted on a small number of healthy volunteers to test the basic safety of the drug (since drugs that seem safe in animals may yet show adverse effects in humans). Phase II involves scaled-up, larger efficacy and safety trials on one hundred to three hundred patients. Phase III trials are large-scale, randomized trials that may be conducted on a few thousand people, usually patients suffering from the ailment for which the therapy has been developed. These trials are usually coordinated across multiple centers, often (increasingly) globally.

Most trial sponsors are biotechnology or pharmaceutical companies because drug development in the United States (and in most parts of the world) is largely undertaken by the private sector. This means that the biomedical and experimental rationales for clinical trials are completely entwined with the market value that these companies see from the drugs that eventually get developed, and with the market risk that attends the drug development process. Parenthetically, there is no epistemic reason why the drug development process should be so completely in the private sector, though this has become a naturalized facet of the biomedical economy, and is one of the factors that has allowed the seamless appropriation of health as an index whose value can be purely evaluated in terms set by the market. According to the Healthcare Financial Management Association's newsletter, "Twenty years ago, 80% of clinical research trials were conducted through academic medical centers. In 1998, estimates indicated the number of academic medical centers as investigator sites had dropped to less than half."[1] Health research and production is thus progressively captured by capital, and now needs to be seen as a semiautonomous sector of capital. The organizational complexity of clinical trials has however meant that it has been difficult for pharmaceutical companies to manage them, leading to the emergence of an entirely new industry segment devoted to the management and administration of clinical trials. These companies, called clinical research organizations (CROs), are now an integral part of the overall biomedical economy.

Clinical trials provide comparative insights into the study of biocapital across multiple sites globally. My own work focuses on India and the United States, two countries that are interconnected through flows of capital, infrastructure and expertise, especially through the investment of nonresident Indian entrepreneurs repatriating a "culture of innovation" back to India. In this context, a host of CROs are emerging in India to conduct these trials, thereby providing a contracted service for (largely Western) biotech and pharmaceutical companies. If clinical trials are the experimental machinery of biocapital, then India, in this story, envisages itself as a major experimental site. Clinical trials, therefore, provide a lens through which to study the globalizing dynamics of biocapital in terms of the cost and biomedical rationales for outsourcing trials to developing country sites like India.

The Indian Clinical Trials Landscape

In this essay, I outline some of the dynamics of clinical trials in India, especially in terms of the huge amounts of capacity building taking place in anticipation of the movement of global trials there. I am interested in briefly mapping the various institutional actors and political economic dynamics at play in this arena. But I am particularly interested in showing how *ethics* is fundamental to the experimental machinery of global clinical trials as it touches down in India. It provides an engine to create ethical subjects involved in conducting clinical trials (CRO managers, employees, and researchers), but also allows the seamless creation of, and expropriation of, Third World experimental subjects, who are, I argue, "merely risked." Capacity building is certainly technological and institutional; but I want to focus on the various human capacities that are generated and/or taken advantage of as part of this experimental machinery. Ethics in the globalizing world of biotechnology is situated;

and my interest lies in understanding the ways in which these situated ethics both structure and respond to pharmaceutical logics of value generation.

The movement of clinical trials to international (non-U.S.) locations started in earnest in the mid-1990s. Adriana Petryna cites figures that point to a dramatic growth in the number of international human subjects recruited into these trials, from 4,000 in 1995 to 400,000 in 1999.[2] A recent study by the consulting firm A. T. Kearney shows that roughly half of the 1,200 clinical trials conducted in 2005 in the United States had an international trial site.[3] In the 1990s, most of this international growth occurred, as Petryna notes, in countries that had agreed to harmonize standards in commercial drug testing with those set by the International Conference on Harmonization (ICH) guidelines. These included primarily Latin American and Eastern European countries, but interestingly not India. Over the past four years, however, India has been one of the most aggressive sites of clinical research infrastructure establishment and growth.

Indian actors currently see the country as providing an extremely attractive destination for outsourced clinical trials from the West. Contract research in the Indian pharmaceutical industry is already robust, and was estimated by the Chemical Pharmaceutical Generic Association to be worth between $100 and 120 million in 2005, while growing at 20–25% per year.[4] Indian actors are eagerly anticipating the further influx of global clinical trials into the country. Who are these actors, and what are their anticipations based upon?

The most central, perhaps, are members of the burgeoning CRO industry. These are the most immediate beneficiaries in terms of revenues and profits of trials coming to India, and are therefore keen to create conditions whereby the influx of these trials can grow in a sustained and streamlined fashion. CROs are the major drivers of the ramp-up in clinical research infrastructure, and are particularly influential in building a regulatory framework for the conduct of trials. It is estimated that there are approximately one hundred CROs of reasonable size operating in the country at the moment.

The Indian pharmaceutical industry is another interested party. It is in the process of retooling its business model in the wake of India becoming a signatory to patent regimes imposed by the World Trade Organization (WTO). Indian patent laws prior to WTO allowed Indian pharmaceutical companies to reverse-engineer generic versions of drugs that had product patent protection in the West. Such reverse engineering is now not possible under a WTO regime for the duration of a drug's patent (twenty years). This has forced a number of leading Indian drug companies into a business model driven by research and development, whereby they, like their Western counterparts, engage in the much riskier process of novel drug discovery and development. Clinical trials become constitutive of this business model, because one cannot develop novel drugs without subjecting them to this elaborate regime of safety and efficacy testing. In other words, the Indian pharmaceutical industry has itself served as a spur to the CRO industry. Becoming signatory to the WTO has also potentially made India a more attractive clinical research destination from the perspective of Western trial sponsors seeking to outsource global trials, since their intellectual property is better protected under such a regime.

What is surprising, however, is the immediacy with which clinical trial activity has sprung into life in India post-WTO. In many ways, the real spurt in business, regulatory and training activity around clinical trials in India started around the same time that India started implementing a WTO-based patent regime (January 1, 2005). That initial spur did in fact come from the Indian pharmaceutical industry as it started retooling its business models in anticipation of a WTO regime.

Ranbaxy has been responsible for the growth of the Indian clinical research industry in more ways than one. Its business model is currently twofold—first, to aggressively increase its presence in global generics markets (including the United States), and second, to try and discover its own therapeutic molecules that it might license to multinational pharmaceutical companies in exchange for the payment of various milestone-related royalties. In both cases, developing clinical testing facilities became very important for the company, and Ranbaxy was one of the first Indian pharmaceutical companies to develop an inhouse CRO. It also started outsourcing trials, thereby spurring the development of a CRO industry. In addition, Ranbaxy ended up being a source of much clinical research expertise. Three of Ranbaxy's main clinical researchers left the company in 2000 to create Wellquest in Bombay (itself a CRO seeded by another major Indian pharmaceutical company, Nicholas Piramal), while two other scientists from Ranbaxy were the cofounders of another major CRO, Lambda, in 1999. In this way, certain sections of the Indian pharmaceutical industry have generated clinical research work themselves, and have provided the capital and expertise required for the industry to take off. These events again make it too simple to suggest that clinical research capacity is purely being built as a consequence of the desire of "the West" to outsource trials to cheap Indian locations, though Indian actors are certainly betting on such a desire materializing in more research contracts.

A third actor consists of the regulatory agents and agents of the state. The immediate regulatory agency in India is the Drug Controller General of India (DCGI), a nominal equivalent of the U.S. Food and Drug Administration (FDA). The DCGI was, until a few years ago, a fairly peripheral presence on the Indian regulatory landscape, but is now in the process of recreating itself as a serious regulatory agenda-setting organization.

Yet another actor consists of educational and training institutes for clinical research. Building the human resource capability to conduct and monitor trials in India is a key challenge, and a number of entrepreneurial ventures are engaged purely in training the labor force required to undertake this work. Finally, there are the physicians who actually conduct the trials, who in the Indian context have a relatively marginal presence compared to the CRO industry in setting the infrastructural and regulatory agenda for the conduct of such research.

There is a striking and universal interest among these actors (though not to the same extent as among physicians) not just in building clinical research infrastructure in India but also in promoting India as a clinical trial destination globally. The experimental potential of Indian populations as trial subjects melds seamlessly into the market potential that CROs perceive from an influx of these trials into India, and this convergence is facilitated by a larger historical moment that sees the Indian state branding and marketing itself to investors at global forums. Investments in the nation-state articulate with investments in biomedicine to result in capacity building for clinical trials.

Some of the enthusiasm around clinical trials within India is mirrored in the West by agents who might outsource clinical trials to the country. However, for the most part, the surge in clinical trials contracts to India is still in the realm of anticipation and potential. The infrastructure building occurring in India is very real; but it is a bet on future outcomes that, like any other speculation, may or may not pay off. Understanding the clinical trial situation in India involves understanding both the enthusiasms and the reservations that exist on the part of Western agents who may wish to contract trials out to India.

The anticipation of global clinical trials coming to India is based on the expectation that it would in various ways serve the interests of Western trial sponsors (especially U.S. biotech and pharmaceutical companies) to outsource these trials to India. This expectation is, at one level, a general market expectation—a recent McKinsey report, for instance, estimated that clinical research in India will be a one-billion-dollar industry by 2010.[5] These types of estimations are consequential in setting certain expectations as well as certain actions on the part of both Indian and Western actors in motion.

These expectations are based on the various perceived advantages involved in taking clinical trials to India. They include, among other factors, a cost advantage—estimates suggest that taking trials to India could save overall clinical trial costs by 30–50% for a multinational company, based on lower labor and infrastructure costs. There is also a perceived recruitment advantage—it is assumed that patients would be easier to recruit into trials, especially treatment-naïve patients. A major problem for drug companies conducting trials in the United States is that Americans are so therapeutically saturated—they tend to be on so many drugs that it is very difficult to determine the efficacy of the experimental drug being tested without having to confront a whole range of drug-drug interactions that muddy the data considerably.

There are other factors to consider while thinking about the attractiveness of a country as a clinical trials location. A recent report by A. T. Kearney, which provided an "attractiveness index" for countries as clinical trials destinations, considered three factors, in addition to cost efficiency and patient pool: "regulatory conditions," "relevant expertise," and "infrastructure and environment." These are indeed three key areas that Indian actors are focusing on as part of their capacity-building efforts; nonetheless, Kearney already ranks India as the second most attractive destination for clinical trials outside the United States after China. India scored much higher than the United States in terms of patient pool and cost efficiency, but lower on the other three counts.[6]

However, the scenario is more complicated than one in which Western multinational companies are trying to tear the door down to exploit cheap Indian populations. If anything, it is an open question as to how badly Western companies would want to outsource especially early-stage clinical trials to India. There are obvious advantages to doing so in terms of cost and the ease of volunteer recruitment; there are also downsides in terms of the relative difficulty of monitoring trials (which is very important to do properly if the data generated is to pass muster with the FDA), and in terms of the potential public relations disaster that could attend an early-stage clinical trial gone horribly wrong in a Third World context. Indeed, the Kearney report points out that in August 2005, the top twelve pharmaceutical companies reported conducting 175 ongoing trials in Germany (attractiveness index of 4.69) and 161 in the United Kingdom (attractiveness index of 5.0), compared to 26 in India (attractiveness index of 5.58). In 2004, Pfizer invested roughly $13 million into clinical trials in India, which, while sounding like a lot of capital investment, can be put in perspective by the fact that its total global R & D expenditure was $8 billion. Perhaps more than pharmaceutical companies themselves, it is Western CROs who see real value in outsourcing some of their (already outsourced) activity to other countries. Therefore, while there are convincing market rationales for taking trials to India, and an already strong movement of these trials there through the multinational CRO industry, much of the capacity building in clinical research in India is still a bet on potential future value that Indian CROs see from outsourced trials rather than a reaction to a movement of trials that has already occurred.

Capacity building here means something far more extensive than building experimental infrastructure for conducting clinical trials, which is perhaps the easiest component of capacity building for clinical trials in a country like India, where material and financial resources do not constitute anymore the rate limiting step. This most basic aspect of capacity building also generates the least amount of concern among Indian actors trying to attract trials into the country. Other aspects of capacity building include the development of the data management, human resource and, especially, regulatory infrastructures. I elaborate briefly upon the first, before talking about regulatory infrastructure building in some detail.

Data management infrastructure

One important part of the clinical trials procedure concerns experimentation—the actual process of putting experimental drug molecules into animals and humans in order to test efficacy and toxicity. The "meaning" that comes out of these trials, however, is in the data generated in these experiments; processing and managing this data is an incredibly complicated task. This mass of data is eventually the basis for the crucial end point of the regulatory process, the *package insert*. The package insert is the label that gets put on the package of any approved drug, indicating the uses for which the FDA has legally approved a drug. Much of this data is generated by the trial sponsors themselves, and as biotech and pharmaceutical companies increasingly outsource trials to CROs, by the CROs. Annotating and presenting this data in an intelligible form to the FDA is a crucial part of the clinical trials procedure.

Independent of establishing India as an experimental site is concomitant capacity building to make India a destination of choice for managing data relating to clinical trials. This is enabled by India's strong software capabilities, which already have helped it emerge as a major site for outsourced back-end information technology (IT) service work. According to Michael Arlotto, senior vice president for corporate development at Quintiles, the North Carolina–based multinational CRO, his company sends almost three-quarters of its *global* trial data to be processed in Bangalore.[7]

Not surprisingly, Indian companies have started up that focus their business model purely on the data management aspect of clinical trials. An early example of such a small homegrown start-up is the Hyderabad-based Sristek, which initiated operations in clinical trial data management in 2002, before the intense capacity building of the post-WTO era. Sristek's cofounders themselves had no background in the life sciences or health care—one was a mechanical engineer, while the other had an MBA degree. What they leveraged was their expertise in software applications, and the existence of a human resource infrastructure for those applications.[8]

Sristek's trajectory points to the constitutive importance of data management as part of the clinical research endeavor. But Sristek too is not immune to the overwhelming potential of experimental clinical research, and is indeed in the process of reinventing itself as a CRO that can also conduct trials in addition to manage trial data. Sristek's story simultaneously points to the independent importance of data management practices in clinical research, and to the ways in which the lure of experimental clinical trials overdetermines the clinical research landscape in India today.

Regulatory infrastructure

Perhaps the most elaborate challenge in terms of building infrastructure for clinical trials is building an adequate regulatory infrastructure. Certainly, if India is to get global trials, it is essential for its regulatory infrastructure to be much stronger than it is currently. In her work on clinical trials, Adriana Petryna has argued for a state of "ethical variability," suggesting that ethical practices of clinical trials resolve differentially in First World locales and Third.[9] While in practice it is quite possible that the implementation of ethical guidelines ends up being more stringent in the First World than in the Third, it is important to be attentive to the very serious attention that is being given to ethics by both the Indian regulatory agencies and the CRO industry there. Equally, it is important to be attentive to what constitutes such an ethics, and what gets left out.

An ethical trial protocol primarily concerns itself with the collection of informed consent. This includes the entire apparatus that surrounds the production of the consent process, especially an institutional review board (IRB) infrastructure. These ethical practices were enshrined in guidelines that the Indian government laid out for good clinical practice (what is known as GCP) in 2001. In 2005, these guidelines were converted into law, termed Schedule Y of the Indian Drugs and Cosmetics Act, which insists upon GCP. Interestingly, the Indian laws are the only ones in the world where the violation of GCP is deemed a criminal rather than a civil offense. At the same time, global trials that are valid in the eyes of the FDA need to be harmonized to what are known as ICH protocols (ICH being the acronym for "International Conference on Harmonization of Technical Requirements for Registration of Pharmaceuticals for Human Use"). Therefore, Indian regulators are currently involved in a massive standardization process, driven by the Indian CRO industry, which seeks to harmonize Indians laws with ICH protocols. In the letter of the law, then, Indian ethical guidelines, legally enshrined, are likely to be at least as stringent as ethical guidelines for the conduct of clinical research in the United States, and in some ways, more so.

Members of India's CRO industry bristle at the suggestion that clinical trials move to India because it is possible to cut ethical corners there. Such suggestions have been part of the debate on the movement of clinical trials to India, and acquired salience and legitimacy because of an article published by two prominent Indian physicians, Samiran Nundy and Chandra Gulhati, in the prestigious *New England Journal of Medicine* that equated clinical trials in India to a "new colonialism."[10] CRO leaders are acutely aware of the need to build a positive media image for their industry, and are very invested in pointing out the ways in which Schedule Y goes beyond the good clinical practice demanded in ICH guidelines. Specifically, Schedule Y is concerned with ensuring extra care in gathering informed consent from illiterate subjects and in considering what might constitute "ethical" compensation for poor subjects recruited into trials (the logic here being that lucrative remuneration for participation in clinical trials can actually act as a coercive incentive for poor people to participate in early-stage trials). One Mumbai-based CRO executive, Arun Bhatt, was typically emphatic about the importance of Schedule Y and good clinical practice: "We are new. We don't want to play with the evolution of ethics."[11]

Outside the enforcement potential of Schedule Y, however, a larger regulatory body with the scope of the FDA is still absent. As mentioned earlier, the Drug Controller General of India (DGCI) is the nominal equivalent of the FDA, but one whose purview is still relatively limited to approving drugs for market or for import into the country. Part of the regulatory efforts under way in India at the moment consist in building a more substantial regulatory body with oversight powers that parallel those of the FDA, and whose conduct can further be harmonized with that of the FDA.

Ethics, legally enshrined and contractually enforced, is integral to the capacity-building efforts around clinical research in India. Members of the CRO industry are the biggest drivers of building an ethical regulatory infrastructure. Nonetheless, the form that ethics takes (which is, quite literally, the informed consent form) does not mitigate the fundamental structural violence of clinical trials performed in Third World contexts. I will elaborate upon this in the next section. The clinical research landscape in India is more complicated than just neo-colonial exploitation of Indian populations as "guinea pigs" by rapacious multinational interests, where cutting corners is the norm and ethics is easily sacrificed. Indeed, the problematic is far more interesting, and involves analyzing the desire on the part of Indian state and corporate actors for India to become a global experimental site, as well as considering how a complete and formal attentiveness to ethics can nonetheless lead to structurally violent and exploitative structures of global biocapital.

A Critique of the Global Biomedical Economy: Expropriation, Exploitation, and the Structural Violence of Biocapital

I suggested in the previous section that Indian actors, especially the CRO industry, are seriously concerned with ethics, which gets legally enshrined in what is referred to as good clinical practice. GCP, however, is primarily concerned with proper protocols for collecting informed consent at the time of trial enrollment, and with the adequate monitoring of clinical trials in the various centers at which they are conducted. In this section, I want to lead my overview of the clinical research landscape in India toward a critique of biocapital.

Consider, for instance, the Hyderabad-based CRO Vimta Laboratories. Vimta is in many ways considered the gold-standard Indian CRO. Founded in 1991, it is one of India's oldest CROs. It is the only CRO that is publicly traded on the Bombay Stock Exchange, and the only CRO in the country that has been audited twice by the FDA (passing both times with flying colors). The clinical research manager of a U.S.-based company that I talked to suggested that Vimta was exactly the sort of company she would consider collaborating with if she were to look for an Indian partner with which to conduct trials.

Vimta's concern with and process for collecting informed consent is exemplary of the insistence of GCP in the Indian context. I visited Vimta as a part of my fieldwork. The first room I was shown was the waiting and screening room, which looks like the waiting room of a railway station, where trial subjects come in and are given their consent forms and a basic questionnaire to fill out in order to determine whether they are qualified to participate in the trial. The walls of the waiting room are empty, except for a single bulletin board that outlines all the risks that could accrue to participants in a clinical trial; it is written only in English. I was told that in order to participate in a trial, the subjects have to be literate (though not necessarily in English), and they are invariably male (Vimta only enrolls females if the trial sponsor specifies a need for female subjects).

Beyond the waiting room is a long corridor, with many rooms where different types of medical examinations are conducted on trial volunteers. I learned while being walked through this corridor that the consent forms the subjects sign in the waiting room are specifically for the medical screening procedures—if the subjects are selected to participate in the trial, they sign a separate form, which is particular to the trial they are enrolled in. A number of the trials conducted at Vimta are Phase I trials on healthy volunteers. Recruiting subjects into Phase I trials has, as I mentioned earlier, become increasingly difficult in the United States. I was told that volunteer retention is much better in India than in the States because "people trust doctors here." Interestingly, although recruiting healthy people to have risky molecules administered to them is such a challenge, the entire setup seems to emphasize "selection"—it is almost as if getting enrolled into a trial is a test that only those who are fit enough can pass. Moreover, the subjects are only ever referred to as "volunteers," suggesting no doubt their autonomous rational agency, the same agency that gets contractually codified through the consent form.

Such deep and, I believe, serious concern with informed consent and GCP, reflected both in national laws and in the practices of companies such as Vimta, does not however even touch upon the question of *access to drugs*. By this I mean the following: in the United States, clinical trials at least implicitly suggest a social contract between a few people who are put on potentially risky medication in order to garner a larger social good, the development of new therapy. People recruited into Phase I trials tend to be less well-off in the United States as well, so that the social contract is never a pure liberal contract between rational individuals in what John Rawls would call an "original position" of assumed equality.[12] Nonetheless, there is an animating liberal sentiment that absolutely presumes that therapy, if developed, will eventually be accessible (on the market, for a price—so it does raise issues of affordability and distributive justice; but those are issues that in principle can be addressed through liberal welfare state mechanisms). In the Indian context, by contrast, there is no guarantee that an experimental drug tested on an Indian population would even have to be marketed there after approval (let alone made available at an affordable cost). There have been no moves on the part of the Indian state to insist upon this through, for example, mechanisms like compulsory licensing regulations. The likely outcome therefore is a situation where Indian populations are used purely as experimental subjects, without the implicit social contract of therapeutic access at the end of the day.

This issue of access to drugs is a live question in the Indian physician community, leading to critiques such as Nundy and Gulhati's referenced earlier. A leading Delhi-based psychiatrist in a prominent private hospital (who preferred anonymity) told me, for instance, that "while we understand the need for conducting trials, there is need for more uniform regulatory control."[13] This is not someone who is outside the circuits of clinical research, but rather someone who conducts a number of psychiatric trials in two centers where he has affiliations. Most of the trials such prominent physicians conduct, however, are Phase III trials on patients they are treating, which puts their practice into a different ethical calculus (having to do with pastoral care) than that of CROs who are looking to increase Phase I trials on healthy volunteers (which is a concern purely with experimental subjectivity). The relationship of trials to access to drugs is, for this physician, an acute question, especially for the Phase III trial subjects who may need to continue taking the experimental medication that is tested upon them if it is shown to have positive effects. In India the only mechanisms that exist to ensure such access, however, come from the policies of the companies sponsoring the trials, or from the concerns of the center conducting the trial. This physician told me: "In the last two trials [we conducted], the companies have said they'll try and make drugs available [after the completion of the trial]. We are yet to see if that will happen. If it doesn't happen, then we will only participate with companies who give an absolute commitment [to making drugs available]."[14]

While this physician and the hospitals where he is based might be willing to take such an uncompromising position on linking clinical experimentation to therapeutic access and pastoral care, such a linkage is less likely to figure in the calculus of CROs, especially those focused on early-stage trials, since their source of value lies directly in increasing the number of trials they can conduct rather than in seeing tangible therapeutic benefits in patient populations. This physician told me that while there is intense debate within the psychiatric community in India over the relationship of clinical trials to drug access, there is hardly any conversation between physician investigators and regulators or the CRO industry.

This subjection to experimental regimes without an insistence on concomitant therapeutic access does not seem to occur primarily through the reluctance of Western pharmaceutical companies to market drugs in India. No one in the Indian CRO industry whom I have talked to, and no one who is actively involved in coming up with GCP guidelines, felt that it was necessary to insist that drugs tested in India be marketed in India, in spite of the fact that the question of the relationship between clinical trials and access to drugs is a live topic of discussion amongst the Indian physician community. "Ethics," therefore, is provisional and partial, and at this point refers mostly to concerns with informed consent.[15]

Uncoupling experimental subjectivity from therapeutic access, which (through acts of omission) occurs at a legal and regulatory level, configures Indian experimental subjects in law and in practice for the cause of health, but locates them outside a regime of pastoral care. In other words, these experimental subjects contribute in some nebulous sense to health by making themselves available as experimental subjects, but this is in no way necessarily linked to their own healthiness, or to the healthiness of other Indians who might get access to new medication as a consequence of the risks to which they are subjected. The nature of these risks was brought home to me during my tour of Vimta, when I was shown a room, at the time darkened and secluded, with only four beds in it. This, I was told, is the intensive care unit where trial subjects are admitted and administered to in case of adverse events. The room looked like a medical emergency room that might exist in a factory to attend to accidents on the factory floor. It emphasized not just the high-risk nature of experimental subjectivity, but that being a trial subject is, specifically, high-risk *labor*.

Such experimental subjects, outside the circuits of pastoral care (and therapeutic consumption), come to be *merely risked*. But the very circuits of pastoral care and therapeutic consumption that these subjects fall out of *can only be constituted in the first place* through the existence of such "merely risked" subjects. These experimental subjects provide the conditions of possibility for the global (primarily Western) neo-liberal consumers of therapy.

While the experimental subject, I argue, is a condition of possibility for biosociality and the neoliberal therapeutic consumer, there is an additional point that I wish to make, which is the *structural impossibility* of such a figure being a *political* subject. This does not mean that experimental subjects cannot politically mobilize; there are many conditions under which they conceivably could. But those conditions would be purely contingent, and one of the contingencies that would most likely lead to a political subjectivity for these subjects (either organized or otherwise) would be through pain and/or death, for instance through a likely scandal that would result from a serious adverse event in a clinical trial. The way in which the experimental subject *does* get figured is *ethically*. And the ethical figuration occurs through informed consent.

This merely risked experimental subject is subject to *logics of expropriation* that are constitutive of the structural logics of biocapital that I am trying to trace. These are bodies that are made bioavailable to global circuits of experimentation, circuits that are driven by value logics of pharmaceutical capital. Indeed, the very global scale of these circuits of experimentation gets constituted because of the value-considerations of capital. Without the cost rationales for outsourcing trials to Third World destinations, the globalization of clinical trials would not have become such a dynamic imperative—clinical trials have, after all, been an important part of the American drug development landscape for something in the vicinity of half a century before the rapid move to take these trials abroad started in the mid-1990s. And without the property mechanisms, harmonized and enforced globally through the WTO, that provide patent protection to multinational pharmaceutical interests, this imperative of globalizing capital would not have had the security to realize its aspirations. Similarly, capital considerations drive the Indian CRO industry to aggressively build infrastructure in India to attract these trials, to increase trial recruitment, and to uncouple these considerations from any serious concern with therapeutic access.

In this situation, the partial ethics that gets enshrined through GCP, far from mitigating the structural violence of capital, serves instead to make it possible. It does so through the instrument of the liberal contract that is embodied in the informed consent form. Just as wages becomes the materialized contractual form through which individuals are "freed" from serfdom and converted into workers in industrial capital, so too does the informed consent form "free" experimental subjects from being coerced guinea pigs by providing them with the autonomous agency that such a contract signifies. A concern with ethical variability suggests that somehow the problem with globalizing clinical trials is that ethical enforcement is likely to be less stringent and vigilant in the Third World than in the First. My attempt here has been to show that, in contrast, it is precisely the harmonization of ethical standards globally that provides the conditions of possibility for the experimental subjection of the "merely risked" Third World subject; and further, this harmonization of ethics goes hand in hand with the harmonization of property regimes globally. These two parallel movements—the contractual codification of ethics combined with the exclusionary instruments of property—together provide global capital with the security to turn even healthy Indian populations into experimental subjects, who are both merely risked and free to choose to be so.

The structural violence of clinical experimentation starts with the fact that it is a procedure that requires, in part, the risking of healthy subjects in order to be set in motion. In other words, the very epistemology of clinical trials is risk-laden—both for the subjects who get experimented upon, and for the companies who invest huge amounts of money in a therapeutic molecule that may or may not eventually come to market and realize that investment. It is a structural violence that gets exacerbated by preexisting global structural inequalities, which result in more bioavailable bodies for less cost in Third World locales than in First World ones. In other words, the structural violence of human experimentation is exacerbated by the structural violence of globalization—the former violence is epistemic, the latter historical. The third layer of structural violence is imposed in the form of the liberal contract, which, just as a wage does in industrial capital for the worker, frees the experimental subject to make his body available for experimentation.

The question to be asked of this third layer is one that is central to Marx in his analysis of capital and regards the conditions of possibility that enable the availability of workers for capital (or in this case, experimental subjects for clinical trials) in the first place. In "The So-Called Primitive Accumulation," Marx shows that this becomes possible only through pre-existing acts of violence that force people into proletarianization.[16] These acts of violence are absolutely historically specific, but they do show a consistency of form. So, for instance, subject recruitment into Phase I clinical trials in India occurs, on the face of it, through newspaper advertisements. The public face of trial recruitment cannot, however, suggest the conditions that make it attractive for individuals to consider the in fact quite lucrative inducement of risking oneself as an experimental subject.

For example, I have written elsewhere about Wellquest, which is located in the mill districts in Mumbai.[17] I learned from scientists at Wellquest that most of the trial subjects recruited by the CRO happened to be unemployed mill workers who had lost their jobs due to the progressive evisceration of the textile industry in Mumbai over the last thirty years. The details are too elaborate to go into here; suffice to say that the mill districts are currently populated by more than 200,000 unemployed mill workers, many of whom are waiting for the payment of back wages. They are already, therefore, subjected to the violence of deproletarianization that has occurred consequent to the death of a sector of manufacturing capital. The workers' tenements, mainly located along with the mills in the districts (and known as *chawls*) are under threat of being torn down, so that in addition to losing wage and livelihoods, these workers are now in danger of losing their shelter as well. A number of unemployed mill workers have turned into street hawkers in order to earn a living, but there is an organized state and middle-class campaign against the hawkers, who are deemed noisy and polluting, and perhaps most important, accused of taking up valuable parking space.[18] There is no way to understand the dynamics of clinical experimentation in the mill districts of Mumbai without understanding all these prior moments of violence that act as an inducement to sign an informed consent form. First, the mill workers are removed from their factories. Then they are removed from their dwellings. Then they are removed from the streets. Only thus do they acquire the freedom to become autonomous trial "volunteers."

Much of my argument rests on the fact that clinical experimentation in the Indian context is not linked to therapeutic access. It is, however, certainly possible to imagine such a situation; and if this linkage is not brought about either by the activist intervention of advocacy groups fighting for access to drugs or by the intervention of the state insisting on a biopolitical rationale of the public good/public health, then it is most likely to be brought about by market mechanisms at the point at which India is perceived as a potential market for therapeutic consumption. In such a scenario, one can quite easily imagine the coexistence of experimental subject expropriation (i.e., those who fall out of the market because they do not have the purchasing power to buy drugs) in the context of high amounts of therapeutic marketing within India itself.

If we are to understand biocapital from the perspective of pharmaceutical companies' logic, then what is at stake is not therapeutic access in the cause of health, but increasing therapeutic consumption in the cause of value. In parallel, from the perspective of CROs, clinical trials in the cause of therapeutic access are not at stake, but rather clinical trials in the cause of value. The global articulation of pharmaceutical and CRO logics of value generation structures and over-determines an enterprise that purports to be about pastoral care in terms of expropriation and exploitation. It is important therefore to privilege an analysis of value, rather than assume from the outset that biopolitics, or pastoral care, is what is at stake.

At the same time, I wish to highlight my ethnographic overview of clinical trials in India to resist a too-quick denunciation of clinical trials on ethical or moral grounds. There are many incongruities that are vital to stay attentive to, not least the hyperattentiveness to ethics and regulation of clinical practice by the Indian state. The structural violence of global clinical trials, at least in its manifestations in India, is not due to a lack of ethics, but rather because value, captured by logics of capital and mediated through the pharmaceutical and CRO industries, overdetermines the practices that emerge.

NOTES

1 See Tracy Lewis, Jerome Reichman, and Anthony So, "The Case for Public Funding and Public Oversight of Clinical Trials," *Economists' Voice* 4, no. 1, art. 3 (2007). For the Healthcare Financial Management Association's figures, see http://www.hfma.org/publications/margin_newsletter/CompetitiveFinancialAdvantages.htm (no longer available).

2 Petryna, "Drug Development and the Ethics of the Globalized Clinical Trial," Institute of Advanced Studies, Occasional Paper Series, 6.

3 A. T. Kearney, "Make Your Move: Taking Clinical Trials to the Best Location," *A. T. Kearney Report*, http://www.atkearney.com/ (accessed January 3, 2007; no longer available).

4 As cited by the Indian Brand Equity Federation on its Web site, http://www.ibef.org/industry/pharmaceuticals.aspx (accessed January 3, 2007). These figures include contract work that is generated domestically as well by foreign sponsors, and includes not just clinical trial activity but also the contract manufacturing of active pharmaceutical ingredients.

5 *NASSCOM—McKinsey Report* (NASSCOM, 2002), http://www.nasscom.in/.

6 A. T. Kearney, "Make Your Move."

7 Michael Arlotto, personal conversations, January 25, 2006.

8 I am grateful to Ramesh Meesala, one of Sristek's cofounders, for extensive conversations about his company's trajectory.

9 Petryna, "Drug Development and the Ethics of the Globalized Clinical Trial" and "Ethical Variability."

10 Samiran Nundy and Chandra Gulhati, "A New Colonialism?—Conducting Clinical Trials in India," *New England Journal of Medicine* 352, no. 16 (2005): 1633–36.

11 Arun Bhatt, interview with the author, February 24, 2006.

12 John Rawls, *A Theory of Justice* (1971; Cambridge, Mass.: Belknap, 2005).

13 Delhi-based psychiatrist, interview with the author, February 27, 2006.

14 Ibid.

15 It is possible that this situation might be changing, DCGI called a meeting of key clinical research stakeholders on July 17, 2008, to consider possibilities of further amendments to Schedule Y. I was not present at that meeting, but have heard from people who were that one of the issues discussed was the question of access to experimental drugs. I cannot speculate as to the motives for this, or how this will translate into regulatory or legislative measures (and neither could my informants). Suffice to say, this discussion is occurring more than three years after the earlier regulation was drafted around GCP. Even if some attention to drug access is given now, it will happen significantly after the codification of regulation pertaining to informed consent.

16 In Karl Marx, *Capital: A Critique of Political Economy*, vol. 1, ed. Frederick Engels, trans. Samuel Moore and Edward Aveling (1867; London: Penguin, 1976), pt. 8.

17 Sunder Rajan, "Subjects of Speculation: Emergent Life Sciences and Market Logics in the US and India," *American Anthropologist* 107, no. 1 (2005): 19–30. Also see *Biocapital*, chap. 2.

18 For an account of the violence against hawkers in Mumbai, see Arvind Rajagopal, "The Menace of Hawkers," in *Property in Question: Value Transformation in the Global Economy*, ed. Katherine Verdery and Caroline Humphrey (New York: Berg, 2004).

Part V

Intellectual Property in Local and Global Markets

The Pharmaceutical Studies Reader, First Edition. Edited by Sergio Sismondo and Jeremy A. Greene.
© 2015 John Wiley & Sons, Inc. Published 2015 by John Wiley & Sons, Inc.

Over the past three decades, the multinational pharmaceutical industry has played an extraordinarily active role in the development of a nearly global legal framework for intellectual property, and for drug patents in particular. At the beginning of the 20th century, many countries excluded drugs from the sphere of patentability or allowed patents only on their processes of production. In the 21st century, a drug patent grants its owner exclusive rights to manufacture and market that drug for at least 20 years in every country that has signed onto the 1994 Agreement on Trade-Related Aspects of Intellectual Property Rights, or TRIPS. Patent holders now have greater power to prevent others from copying their drugs, extend their monopolies through creative patent filing and re-filing, and exert control over the movement and pricing of their drugs. Yet conflicts continue to break out on many fronts. In particular, many pharmaceutical patents are challenged and overturned, and after patents expire, new contests over intellectual property can erupt regarding trademarks and the similarity or difference of competing generic products.

Central to arguments for today's patent regime is the claim that strong intellectual property rights promote innovation, whereas allowing copying results in stagnation. In Chapter 16, sociologists Maurice Cassier and Marilena Correa explore one contest over patents and international pricing. In 1996, the Brazilian government proposed to provide antiretroviral medications free of charge to citizens living with HIV/AIDS. As part of price negotiations with international drug producers, Brazil threatened to declare a health emergency and empower other companies to produce and sell the drugs at lower prices ("compulsory licensing"). To add teeth to its threat, Brazil funded national laboratories to develop the know-how to produce copies of the drugs. In this chapter, Cassier and Correa uncover some of the innovation work of copying pharmaceuticals: developing new skills, new production processes, and new similar drugs.

In Chapter 17, anthropologist Stefan Ecks looks at how one pharmaceutical company responded to a successful local challenge of one of its patents. The Swiss-based firm Novartis failed to convince Indian regulators that its own near-copy, called Glivec, of one of its earlier cancer drugs deserved a fresh patent. As a result, Indian companies were free to sell their less-expensive versions of the drug within the country. Novartis paired a legal challenge to this with an economic one: giving Glivec away for free to low-income Indian patients. Its strategy undercut competitors, allowing the company to maintain some control over the price and distribution of the drug, especially outside India.

In the final chapter of this volume, anthropologist Cori Hayden displays a multiplication of kinds of similarity and difference in copies as Mexican pharmacies adapt to changing international standards for generic drugs. Chapter 18 begins with a description of the Mexican pharmacy chain Farmacias Similares that sells only drugs that are "similar" to brand-name drugs, or to use the drugstore's slogan, "the same but cheaper." As with Ecks' account of pharmaceutical copies in India, conflicts around patent violations in Mexico are not simply conflicts between private companies and public interests, but international versus local pharmaceutical regimes of pharmaceutical standardization, each claiming to be aligned with some public interests.

16

Intellectual Property and Public Health: Copying of HIV/AIDS Drugs by Brazilian Public and Private Pharmaceutical Laboratories

Maurice Cassier and Marilena Correa

Brazilian public and private laboratories' experience in copying antiretrovirals (ARVs) since 1993 has been a technological learning process that in some cases has produced innovations. Reproducing drugs and synthesizing their active principles involves the combination of information available in patent documents and the partial rediscovery of certain know-how through laboratory manipulations. Chemists have to reconstruct the numerous "cat leaps" in patent documents, and in so doing often improve on the published processes or formulae. Generics laboratories are also able to use this knowledge base to invent new formulae, combinations of existing molecules, or to discover new molecules. Since 2000, the five laboratories studied have filed about ten patents on ARVs. The authors pieced together this technological learning process by interviewing chemists at generics laboratories, using methods of the sociology of science.

Introduction

On 2 June 2005, the Constitutional, Judicial and Citizenship Commission of the Brazilian House of Representatives unanimously passed a bill to place HIV/AIDS drugs beyond the scope of patentable objects.[1] Member of Parliament Roberto Gouveia justified this reform of the 1996 Brazilian intellectual property law in the following terms: '*Patents have to be*

Maurice Cassier and Marilena Correa, "Intellectual property and public health: Copying of HIV/AIDS drugs by Brazilian public and private pharmaceutical laboratories," in RECIIS 1 (2007). pp. 83–90. Reproduced with permission from RECIIS (Revista Eletrônica de Comunicação, Informação & Inovação em Saúde).

The Pharmaceutical Studies Reader, First Edition. Edited by Sergio Sismondo and Jeremy A. Greene.

suspended if they run counter to the interests of public health'. Three weeks later, on 23 June, the Health Minister announced a compulsory licence authorizing the federal government laboratory Far Manguinhos, of the Oswaldo Cruz Foundation in Rio de Janeiro, to undertake the production of a combination of two antiretroviral (ARV) molecules without authorization from the patent holder. These measures of exclusion of patentability or suspension of patents specifically concerning AIDS drugs were a consequence of the failure of the Health Ministry's negotiations with three international pharmaceutical laboratories (Abbott, Merck, Gilead). The Ministry had hoped to obtain price reductions on four patented antiretrovirals that accounted for four-fifths of Brazil's AIDS programme expenditures. The international laboratories had also refused to grant voluntary licences to those Brazilian laboratories that had requested them, especially the Far Manguinhos federal laboratory. The granting of a compulsory licence and consequent local production of these drugs by Brazilian laboratories was seen to have a twofold public health and industrial advantage for Brazil. With respect to public health, generic versions were expected to cost half of what patented proprietary drugs did. With respect to industry, Brazilian public- and private-sector laboratories would thus be able to use their production and research capacities developed since the mid-1990s in the field of ARVs to fight AIDS. However, a few weeks later the Brazilian Health Ministry backed down on its decision to use the compulsory licence and announced that it had reached a satisfactory compromise with Abbott on the price of the drug in question, Kaletra. Leaders of the AIDS programme and NGOs deplored this decision, which they believed would compromise the continuity of local production of generic drugs and the viability of the programme for the free distribution of tritherapies in Brazil.[2] These conflicts over intellectual property on antiretrovirals have been recurrent in Brazil since 1996, when the country embarked on a programme of universal distribution of HIV/AIDS drugs and local production of generic drugs.[3]

In this paper we consider the conditions of emergence of this generic industry at the intersection of public health policy, intellectual property rights, and industrial policy in the chemical and pharmaceutical fields. The first section shows how local production of generics corresponds to the policy of universal access to HIV/AIDS drugs implemented by the Health Ministry since 1996. The second section presents the very particular situation that prevailed as regards intellectual property in Brazil prior to 1996, that is, the unpatentable status of drugs, which allowed licit copying of ARVs. In the third section we examine the practice of copying drugs in Brazilian pharmaceutical laboratories and the technological learning accompanying it. The fourth section studies the innovation processes likely to be triggered by copying: either the further development of pharmaceutical manufacturing processes or copied drug formulae, or the launching of new research projects on new families of ARVs, which benefit from the knowledge base acquired during the copying phase. The fifth section considers the situation created by the 1996 new patent law which, on the one hand, banned the copying of new generations of antiretrovirals and, on the other, enabled Brazilian laboratories to protect their discoveries of new molecules and new drug formulations. Finally, the conclusion reverts to the exceptional situation in Brazil regarding HIV/AIDS drugs, which originally could be copied freely and then were patentable from 1997. Today these drugs are a subject of controversy, over the granting of compulsory licences and over their possible new exclusion from patent law.[4] We also show that patents play a dual role in this history, as instruments of reservation of inventions and vehicles of technology transfer. This experience furthermore provides interesting material for reflection on the role of intellectual property asymmetries that are justified by both public health policies and industrial development.[5]

Public Health Policy and Local Production of Generic Drugs

In Brazil's experience in combating AIDS, with its approach based on universal access to treatment and on the copying of antiretrovirals by Brazilian pharmaceutical laboratories, the most singular feature is the entanglement of public health policies and industrial drug policies. This mixture distinguishes Brazil from India, where the generic drug industry has developed in the strict framework of market incentives.[6] In November 1996, the Brazilian State President passed a law instituting 'the free distribution of drugs for HIV/AIDS carriers'.[7] This presidential decree, which granted an exceptional status to the AIDS epidemic, put AIDS drugs beyond the scope of the market, since they were to be bought and distributed freely by the Health Ministry via the public health system. The decree also provided for the creation of a commission to define the list of drugs that could be classified as tritherapies. This list was to be revised annually 'to take into account the advancement of scientific knowledge and new commercialized drugs'. The most original fact is that the Brazilian State did not stop at this role of distributing goods considered to be essential. It also became a 'health entrepreneur' via the work of government pharmaceutical laboratories, which embarked on the local production of antiretrovirals. These public laboratories are a highly original institution in Brazil. They are either the property of the Health Ministry, as in the case of the Technological Drug Institute of the Oswaldo Cruz Foundation in Rio de Janeiro, known as Far Manguinhos, or the property of local States.[8] In 1996 the heads of government laboratories and the Health Ministry agreed to launch a programme for the copying of ARVs, aimed at sharply reducing the price of these drugs that absorbed a huge proportion of the Ministry's budget. The development of production of generic or similar drugs in Brazil was intended to reduce the amounts of patented molecules bought from leading international laboratories and to force prices down.[9] The AIDS programme had the effect of reviving public pharmaceutical laboratories' production. The federal laboratory Far Manguinhos, largely inactive in the early 1990s, multiplied its production by seven and its income by 20 in the period from 1995 to 2002. It acquired a special production line for ARVs, certified by the Brazilian drug agency ANVISA in September 2002. Far Manguinhos reinvested its profits in research, recruited chemists from industry and academia, and acquired research equipment and facilities. Today this laboratory is a technical platform that serves as a reference for the Brazilian pharmaceutical industry.

From 1993, several laboratories in the private sector also undertook the copying and production of ARVs for fighting HIV/AIDS. In that year a small pharmaceutical chemistry laboratory, a start-up founded by chemists from the Federal University of Rio de Janeiro, started to copy AZT. Two other laboratories, located close to the University of Campinas and the University of Sao Paulo, initiated their programme for copying AZT and protease inhibitors in 1994 and 1996. The last privately-owned laboratory to launch into the ARV field did so in 2000 at the request of Far Manguinhos, which needed raw material for its production of ARVs. The two organizations, one public and the other private, are bound by a technology cooperation contract. For private-sector laboratories working in this field, the Health Ministry's purchases were a promise of markets, at least before the government procurement system turned towards Indian and Chinese laboratories at the expense of local producers. Private laboratories are sometimes requested directly by the Health Ministry to develop ARV synthesis technologies, especially when the Brazilian government wants to pressure international laboratories into reducing their prices. The government is still able to rely on private generics producers to replace the products of an international laboratory that withdraws from Brazil: "*For Ganciclovir, when Roche stopped supplying the Brazilian government, the government asked us whether we would be able to develop this drug in*

Brazil. We answered: we'll develop the synthesis, and we helped the government to develop the lyophilization methodology" (laboratory director).

Government pharmaceutical laboratories have a limited industrial capacity in pharmaceutical production. They are able to carry out only the final manufacturing phase, that is, formulation and production of the drug, not the synthesis of its active principles. These they buy from Brazilian, Indian or Chinese laboratories in the private sector. There is thus a complementarity between public-sector laboratories, specialized in formulation, and commercial laboratories, which supply the raw materials. In the case of certain antiretroviral molecules, public- and private-sector laboratories cooperate and exchange knowledge and technology.[10] In some cases, laboratories in the two sectors compete when they formulate the same drugs.

The Unpatentable Status of Drugs in Brazil from 1945 to 1996: A Licit Copying Regime

Brazilian public- and private-sector laboratories' engagement in the copying of HIV/AIDS drugs was possible owing to the particular status of drugs as 'public goods' in Brazil from 1945 to 1997. In 1945 President Getulio Vargas decreed the non-patentability of pharmaceutical products, with the twofold public health and industrial development objective. The idea was to stimulate the production of drugs for the most serious diseases in the country, and to encourage the creation of a local pharmaceutical industry to produce substitutes for foreign imports. This exclusion was reinforced under the military government in 1971. The new industrial property law excluded both manufacturing processes and pharmaceutical products from patenting, with the aim of promoting technology transfer and strengthening a sector that was essential for the local population.[11] The copying of drugs patented abroad was therefore perfectly legal.

The policy of copying ARVs for HIV/AIDS was a continuation of experiments in reverse engineering in the seventies and eighties. During the 1980s, the Health Ministry set up a system of tax incentives and financial advantages to encourage the copying of drugs and the production of pharmaceutical raw materials by the pharmaceutical and chemical industry.

This legal situation favourable to the copying of foreign inventions and the creation of a pharmaceutical industry to replace drug imports lasted until 1996. Paradoxically, Brazil amended the legal status of drugs in February 1996, just a few months before the law on universal free access to HIV/AIDS drugs was passed. Consequently, local production of antiretrovirals could concern only the first generation of drugs, patented before 1996. The second generation of ARVs, protected by patents, could be copied only under compulsory licence.

Copying and Technological Learning

Brazilian and Indian generics laboratories' practice of copying drugs[12] has been a subject of intense international controversy. Brazil has been accused of 'piracy', even when copying was legal in that country, since it reproduces drugs without paying the R&D costs involved in inventing them. Reverse engineering has also been criticized as a redundant and futile activity because it reproduces what has already been invented elsewhere. In November 2002 GlaxoSmithKline summed up copying as a wastage of resources: "*The remaining engineers in the pharmaceutical industry in India have, at least until recently, spent their time on reverse engineering to circumvent existing 'process' patents (i.e. reinventing the wheel) rather than on innovation … India's history demonstrates how a weak IP system can at best lead to waste of R&D effort on re-engineering* … .[13]

Our survey on chemists directly involved in the ARV copying projects of Brazilian public- and private-sector laboratories and on people in charge of intellectual property and technology transfers[14] shows, on the contrary, a process of technological learning or the phenomenon of learning-by-doing that results from copying. The practice of copying ARVs involves the creation and acquisition of knowledge by Brazilian chemists and results in the development or enhancement of these laboratories' R&D capacities. In certain cases this new knowledge base is used to open research projects on new families of ARVs.

Consider the work of chemists who embark on the copying of an ARV. The process starts with bibliographic research, first on international patents and then on scientific articles or articles published in professional journals. Here the researchers exploit the documentary use value of patents, which varies, depending on the molecule. The Far Manguinhos federal laboratory's engagement in ARV production, for instance, started with a detailed analysis of the patents concerned. This research, carried out by an experienced chemist, revealed problems in highly specific syntheses as well as bottlenecks in the procurement of certain reagents. In a privately-owned laboratory a chemical engineer was entirely devoted to reading and synthesizing patents, and to identifying the steps that would be difficult to reproduce. Reading patents involves a process of interpretation and transposition. It is therefore necessary to adjust the processes described in the patent to local conditions of production that are not strictly equivalent to those described in the invention. The knowledge contained in the patent is fundamentally incomplete, due to the owner's restrictions and, more generally, to the absence of know-how required to apply the described technology. Chemists in generics laboratories, who lack the patent owner's know-how, therefore have to undertake the patient reconstruction of the technology. For that purpose, they draw on information found in publications, knowledge obtained from other generics producers (Far Manguinhos chemists have visited their suppliers' factories in India several times), and the expertise of university chemists who advise them. Basically, they have to complete the patent by laboratory research to reconstruct certain processes or analyse the drugs or raw material obtained commercially. Step-by-step, products have to be characterized and synthetic processes reproduced. The difficulty of this reconstruction, between patent documents, scientific articles and reverse engineering itself, varies depending on the complexity of the molecules and the documentary use value of the patents. It took a generics manufacturer in the private sector two years to reproduce the synthesis of Ritonavir, a protease inhibitor. One year was spent on reaching the laboratory scale and another year on the scale-up. In the process, the laboratory did of course learn a great deal on the same families of molecules. The R&D manager explained:

"*For Ritonavir, developing the synthesis took us two years; for Lopinavir, six months, because Lopinavir and Ritonavir have partly similar structures; similar types of chemistry and expertise; it's much easier today to develop new syntheses*".

Generics producers also had to reconstruct the references or standards of the molecules that they copied. Since these were patented molecules, their chemical references were not divulged in the international pharmacopoeias. For example, the Far Manguinhos laboratory produced references of these molecules for its own use – quality control in the factory – and for the Brazilian pharmacopoeia. The quality service of a private-sector generic drug producer devised its own analytical methods to control its production and obtain approval from ANVISA, the national drug agency. Copying thus produces reports, data files, test methods and abundant documentation for internal or public use.

The production of generic AIDS drugs triggered the creation or improvement of the R&D capacities of both public- and private-sector laboratories. Consider the example of the Far Manguinhos federal laboratory. It recruited chemists from industry and universities and acquired a large amount of research equipment, financed by the profits from ARV sales. The result is a technical platform that serves as a reference for the Brazilian pharmaceutical industry. Since this laboratory had to buy raw materials for its drugs from commercial Indian, Chinese or Brazilian laboratories, it first had to equip itself with a large analytical department for performing characterization tests on the molecules. These tests were then routinely used to control the quality of the raw material purchased. Although it was not equipped to carry out chemical syntheses on an industrial scale, Far Manguinhos then created a synthesis laboratory in which it reproduced steps in synthesizing processes for the purpose of characterizing molecules or developing synthesis procedures to be transferred to industry. Finally, the public laboratory formed a team to formulate drugs, for transfer to other Brazilian public-sector laboratories. Within a few years, between 1996 and 2002, Far Manguinhos had created an R&D laboratory for analyses, syntheses and formulations, which accounted for close to 30% of the laboratory's staff (215 researchers out of a total of 739 employees).

The ARV copying programme has also been accompanied by knowledge trading and even technology transfer contracts between laboratories in the public and private sectors. Consider the following two examples. In the first case, the government laboratory carried out a bibliographic study and developed the complete synthesis of a molecule that was then transferred to an industrial laboratory, which took care of the scale up and production. In the second case, the federal laboratory and the industrial laboratory negotiated an agreement on several operations: the federal laboratory would buy raw material from the industrial laboratory, which would transfer to it the drug formulation technology in its possession. The two partners also agreed to cooperate on an R&D project on a new family of anti-proteases identified by the Federal University of Rio de Janeiro.

Copying thus leads to local production of knowledge generated by the study of patents and laboratory manipulations. Patents constitute an important vehicle of technology transfer, although they are fundamentally incomplete. Knowledge is traded between generics producers who specialize in the different phases of drug production or enter into partnerships. This knowledge created by copying is likely to be transferred to other laboratories. The Far Manguinhos federal laboratory transfers its technologies to other Brazilian laboratories and the director has offered the technology acquired by Brazilian chemists to laboratories in eastern and southern Africa.

Copying and Pharmaceutical Innovations

We have observed some degree of continuity between pharmaceutical copying and innovation. In the laboratories studied, copying leads to innovation in various ways. The first is incremental innovation, which derives directly from the copied activity: generics producers improve the synthesis routes or formulations of the drugs that they copy. These adjustments can lead to patents relating to improvements (formulations) or are kept secret (new synthesis routes). The second way is more radical innovation that can lead to the development of new drugs, for instance by combining several existing molecules, by discovering new properties in the polymorphous molecules of the copied molecule, or by identifying new families of antiretroviral drugs. For example, the Far Manguinhos laboratory analyses the polymorphs of existing antiretroviral drugs to discover new therapeutic properties. It is also involved in research projects on new families of antiretroviral drugs derived from research initiated in-house or in academic laboratories. In the latter case, a patent has been filed jointly with the Federal University of Rio de Janeiro on a new protease inhibitor. These research projects on new molecules, which no longer rely on the copying of foreign inventions, benefit from these laboratories' technological learning during the imitation phase. The reproduction of existing molecules has been accompanied by the creation of R&D teams and by the acquisition of competencies on antiretroviral molecules, which can be applied to new research projects. We witnessed this dynamic in one of the industrial generic drugs laboratories that we studied, which started by copying ARVs before developing its own molecules, in partnership with São Paulo University.

The new molecules discovered by university laboratories or the new formulations invented by generic drug producers are patented. For example, a new family of protease inhibitors, discovered by a university chemist and developed by the Far Manguinhos laboratory, was patented by the Federal University of Rio and the Health Ministry's laboratory. The patent covers Europe, the United States, Japan, Chile, India and South Africa. This patent should enable the university and the government laboratory to control the diffusion and industrialization of the invention. Generic private laboratories have registered patents on new formulations, on their preparation processes – e.g. for protease inhibitors – and on the new molecules that they have identified. New synthesis routes based on chemical engineers' very specific know-how, and which represent a source of productivity gains for generics producers, are generally kept secret.

Technological improvements or new molecules discovered by Brazilian generic drug producers benefit from the new law on intellectual property in terms of which pharmaceutical products and processes can be patented. The Far Manguinhos federal laboratory intends to use its patents to control and regulate the drug market. In most cases it will leave other laboratories or firms to industrialize new drugs and to produce raw materials, and will use its patents to transfer its technologies towards Brazilian laboratories. More generally, with or without patents, Far Manguinhos has a systematic policy of technology transfer towards private industry. Processes developed on a laboratory scale – a scale of one kilogram – are simultaneously sent to the firms concerned.

Brazilian universities also have intellectual property policies and in some cases a particular person is responsible for monitoring patent applications and technology transfers.[15] For example, a Federal University of Rio team of chemists patented several new molecules as part of a strategy to valorize academic research and to transfer and control technology. A Brazilian university network exists to promote intellectual property and diffuse transfer tools. In the course of their activity of copying generics, Brazilian generic drug producers apply for patents relating to improvements, or patents on new molecules, when they wish to develop pharmaceutical research aimed at inventing new products, generally in cooperation with university laboratories. These innovation projects on new molecules are nevertheless still at a very early stage.

Conflict Between the Brazilian Health Ministry and International Laboratories: Negotiations on Prices and Compulsory Licences

Although the 1996 patent law serves to protect new molecule inventions, it also excludes the possibility of copying new generations of antiretrovirals. The production of Brazilian generic AIDS drugs is expected to decline as soon as the drug 'cocktails' adopted by the Health Ministry for its tritherapies have included the new patented molecules. As more of these new patented molecules are included in the treatments opted for by the Ministry, the market for copied drugs will gradually shrink.

On three occasions, in August 2001, September 2003 and June 2005, the Brazilian government brandished the threat of a compulsory licence on patented ARVs during price negotiations with international laboratories. The four second-generation ARVs bought by the Health Ministry accounted for 80% of the AIDS programme's budget and patent holders refused to grant the price reductions requested. In June 2005, for example, the Health Ministry threatened to have the generic equivalent of Abbott's Kaletra manufactured by the Far Manguinhos federal laboratory for almost half the price of the proprietary drug.[16] The threat was credible in so far as the government laboratory had extensive experience in the antiretroviral field and had prepared reverse engineering of the drug at the Health Ministry's request. Since the preparation of a compulsory licence requires reverse engineering on the licensed molecule, the Health Ministry directly requests public- and private-sector laboratories to prepare the synthesis of specific molecules. This preparatory work of knowledge acquisition is crucial to the Brazilian government, for it can decide on a compulsory licence only if the country's chemists are able to manufacture the generic molecule at a satisfactory price. Finally, in July 2005 the Health Ministry announced a compromise on the prices of Kaletra and gave up the option of a compulsory licence and the production of generic versions. One of the leaders of the Ministry's AIDS Programme criticized this decision that reduced the scope of local generics production: '*ARVs copied here are used less and less with the appearance of new treatments*'. In fact, despite several threats, Brazil has never implemented this type of compulsory licence.

Parallel to this battle over compulsory licences, members of parliament supported by NGOs proposed another, more radical solution: the amendment of the 1996 law on intellectual property, so that ARVs would be excluded from patents. On 2 June 2005 the Constitutional, Judicial and Citizenship Commission of the Brazilian House of Representatives unanimously passed a bill placing HIV/AIDS drugs outside the scope of patentable objects.[17] This article, that ratifies the exceptional status of AIDS, is explicitly designed to guarantee the viability of the Health Ministry's AIDS programme. The aim is not only to reduce the prices of ARVs, but also to ensure that their local production can continue. This exclusion of ARVs from patents could, however, prevent the patenting of new molecules discovered by researchers in the public and private sectors.

Conclusions

The Brazilian experience in copying HIV/AIDS drugs illustrates a number of points. First, it highlights the exceptional status of drugs as regards intellectual property. Considered as public goods, drugs could be copied freely in Brazil until 1996. Although they again fell under patent law in that year, they remained 'essential goods' with respect to the norms of public health policy. In 1996, a few months after the new intellectual property law had been passed, a presidential decree proclaimed universal free access to drugs for HIV/AIDS carriers. To implement this policy the government mobilized public-sector pharmaceutical laboratories to produce generic drugs. These public health objectives entered into conflict with the patentable status of new generations of antiretroviral drugs as soon as the prices of the new molecules weighed too heavily on the Health Ministry's budget. Hence, the numerous conflicts with the proprietary laboratories and controversies over compulsory licences since 2001. This limit on patent rights is inscribed in the new patent law and can apply if the patented product is not produced locally within three years. In 1999, a Presidential decree strengthened the possibilities of compulsory licences 'for the public interest' and especially for public health. In September 2003 a new Presidential decree specified the conditions for the application of a compulsory licence for national emergency reasons, in the public interest. Intellectual property of ARVs had to compromise with public health norms. Finally, the Health Ministry's public incentives concerning AIDS were decisive in reviving the production of generic drugs in Brazil.

Second, this experience also reveals the possibilities opened by an asymmetry in the intellectual property rights of different countries, for public health objectives and technological transfer and learning.[18] In this respect, compulsory licences can be considered from the angle not only of public health policies but also of technology transfer. The 30 August 2003 WTO agreement on the application of the Doha Declaration contains an article which 'recognizes' and encourages 'technology transfer' between generic drug importing and exporting countries.[19] The Brazilian President's September 2003 decree concerning compulsory licences was designed to compel patent holders to transfer the know-how in their possession. Preparation of compulsory licences is itself a phase in the acquisition of knowledge and technological learning, via the analysis of patent documents, reverse engineering in laboratories, exchanges between public- and private-sector laboratories, and Brazilian chemists' visits to Indian and Chinese generic drug producers.[20]

Third, the complexity of patents is revealed. Patents are tools to protect inventions and ban copying, to the detriment of generics producers. They are also vehicles for technology transfer when copying is declared legal either because the drug is excluded from patentability or because the patents in question are subject to a compulsory licence. Lastly, patents are double-edged instruments for pharmaceutical firms in Brazil. On the one hand, if ratified, the reform to intellectual property law, passed by the House of Representatives in June 2005, will exclude ARVs from patents and promote the extension of the market to copying. On the other hand, it will prevent laboratories in the public and private sectors from patenting improvements or new molecules. A generics producer that manufactures the active principles of existing ARVs and that discovers new ARVs could face this dilemma.

Finally, the Brazilian experience offers an original solution to the alternative proposed by Paul Romer in an essay on the knowledge and development economy: using ideas invented elsewhere or producing one's own ideas.[21] In an article Romer compares two contrasting models: that of Mauritius which uses ideas from elsewhere by encouraging foreign investments; and that of Taiwan which encourages the domestic production of knowledge by increasing its investments in R&D. Brazilian generics laboratories represent another model consisting of the use of foreign inventions through reverse engineering and the local production of innovations derived directly or indirectly from copying: directly when the copying of drugs is accompanied by additions and improvements that are likely to be patented, and indirectly when the generic laboratories reuse knowledge acquired during the copying phase to launch new research projects. Two pharmaceutical laboratories out of the five that we studied developed this trajectory, from copying to research on new drugs. Apart from the knowledge production implicit in copying, it also leads to the creation or extension of R&D laboratories. These are mainly analytical laboratories – to characterize and control raw material – and synthesis and formulation laboratories. The production of generic drugs for the AIDS programme furthermore revived reflection and initiatives towards the reconstruction of a pharmacochemical industry in Brazil by the State, private industry and universities.[22]

NOTES

1 This law amends Article 18 of the Brazilian patent law on exclusions from patentability: 'The following are not patentable: [...] drugs as well as the processes for obtaining them, specifically for the prevention and treatment of AIDS', Law N° 22/03, June 2005.

2 Interview with C. Gossas, Brazilian AIDS Programm, September 2005.

3 There have been three crises concerning compulsory licences for ARVs: August 2001, September 2003 and June 2005. On all three occasions the Health Ministry brandished the threat of a compulsory licence but finally backed down when agreement was reached on the prices of ARVs bought from the leading international laboratories.

4 This exclusion is discussed in the bill passed by the House of Representatives in June 2005.

5 On this question the reader is referred to the work of the British Commission on Intellectual Property Rights, 'Integrating Intellectual Property Rights and Development Policy', London, September 2002.

6 Cf. the work of Jane Lajouwe on the Indian pharmaceutical industry: 'The introduction of pharmaceutical patents in India: Heartless Exploitation of the Poor and Suffering ?', NBER Working Paper N° 6366, January 1998.

7 Decree 9.313 of 13 November 1996. Note that universal access to health services is a constitutional right in Brazil (Article 196 of the 1988 Constitution).

8 Brazil has 18 government laboratories. Six are involved in the production of ARVs for the AIDS programme.

9 Between 1996 and 2001, public-sector laboratories' production resulted in a 71% drop in prices, on average, compared to the prices of molecules purchased from international labs.

10 This type of technology exchange and cooperation in the field of ARVs concretizes a recommendation in a World Bank report on the pharmaceutical sector in Brazil: 'Public Policies in the Pharmaceutical Sector: A Case Study of Brazil', Jillian Clare Cohen, January 2000, 25 pages.

11 However, the investments of Brazilian privately-owned laboratories were inadequate to meet this objective. In 1988 foreign laboratories controlled two-thirds of the market.

12 The two are linked by trade, as Indian laboratories supply Brazilian ones with raw materials.

13 Commission on Intellectual Property Rights' Report on Integrating Intellectual Property Rights and Development Policy – Comments from GlaxoSmithKline, November 2002, 15 pages.

14 We collected 45 interviews in 2002, 2003 and 2004. We also visited the R&D laboratories and industrial sites of these different pharmaceutical laboratories. This survey was financed by the ANRS (*Agence française de recherché sur le sida*) the French national agency for AIDS research.

15 The number of patents filed by Brazilian universities has grown substantially since 1997.

16 The government laboratory would have produced a generic version of Kaletra for 68 cents, instead of Abbott's Kaletra at $1.17.

17 The law amends Article 18 of the Brazilian Patent Act that covers exclusions from patentability. In terms of this law the following are not patentable: '... drugs and the processes required to obtain them, specifically for the prevention and treatment of AIDS', Law n° 22/03, June 2005. This law subsequently still has to be passed by the Senate and ratified by the State President.

18 This situation has a long history in the pharmaceutical field. For instance, at the beginning of the century researchers at the Poulenc laboratory in France took advantage of the non-patentable status of drugs in France to systematically copy German pharmaceutical patents. Cf. Cassier, 2004, 'Pharmaceutical patents and public health in France: opposition and specific drug appropriation devices, 1791–2004', *Entreprises et Histoire* n° 36. See also the example of chemistry and pharmaceuticals in Switzerland in the nineteenth century and early twentieth century, 'The patent controversy in the 19th conference on 'History and Economics of Intellectual Property Rights', 3–4 June 2005, Paris.

19 'Implementation of the Doha Declaration on TRIPS and public health', 28 August 2003, World Trade Organization.

20 Conflict over compulsory licences for Efavirenz and Nelfinavir in September 2003 was preceded by a mission by Brazilian chemists to India and China.

21 'Two strategies for economic development: using ideas and producing ideas', P. Romer, Proceedings of the World Bank Annual Conference on Development Economics, 1992.

22 In 2003 several seminars were held in Brazil on the topics 'Health-related Innovation Projects' (Oswaldo Cruz Foundation, 9–10 June 2003) and 'The Industrial Complex in Health' (BNDES, Ministry of Development, Industry and Foreign Trade, 5–7 May 2003). In 2005 and 2006, the Academy of Science organized a cycle of conferences on the theme of pharmaceutical policy and innovation. See also the report 'ARV production in Brazil' by Antunes and Fortunak, 2006.

17

Global Pharmaceutical Markets and Corporate Citizenship: The Case of Novartis' Anti-Cancer Drug Glivec

Stefan Ecks

This paper analyses a remarkable transformation of global capitalism in recent years: that corporations claim to be 'good citizens' and are driven by higher aspirations than profits alone. It focuses on the lawsuit brought by the drug company Novartis against the Indian government over the patent for the anti-cancer drug Glivec. Novartis' attack on Indian patent law caused an international outcry. Opponents of Novartis argued that the company was trying to destroy essential provisions in the Indian law that keep drugs affordable even after the country signed up to the World Trade Organization's agreement on Trade-Related Intellectual Property Rights (TRIPS). With reference to 'the constitutional obligation of providing good health care to its citizens', the High Court in Chennai, India, dismissed Novartis' challenge in August 2007. While health activists celebrated the court's decision as a victory for anti-corporate citizens, this article argues that Novartis won a more important battle elsewhere: to protect its profits in European and North American markets. The article shows how claims to 'citizenship' were mobilized by both anti-Novartis and pro-Novartis groups, and how Novartis' global corporate citizenship programme succeeded even when it seemed to fail.

'Citizenship' has emerged as a key concern at the intersections between critical theory, medical anthropology and science studies (Jasanoff, 2004). Over the past few years, a number of terms have been coined. Adriana Petryna (2002) and Nikolas Rose (2006) speak of 'biological' citizenship, to grasp how bodily suffering becomes a resource through which people stake welfare claims in times of neoliberal reform. Studying HIV/AIDS activists in

Stefan Ecks, "Global Pharmaceutical Markets and Corporate Citizenship: The Case of Novartis' Anti-cancer Drug Glivec," in BioSocieties 3 (2008). pp. 165–181. Reproduced with permission from Macmillan Publishers.

The Pharmaceutical Studies Reader, First Edition. Edited by Sergio Sismondo and Jeremy A. Greene.

Burkina Faso, Vinh-Kim Nguyen (2004) introduced 'therapeutic' citizenship to highlight patients' claims to global organizations. João Biehl (2004) speaks of 'biomedical' citizenship to define HIV/AIDS patients in Brazil who submit themselves to state health surveillance, as opposed to people on the margins who die without leaving a trace in the official statistics. This article employs another term, 'pharmaceutical citizenship', to ask about the relations between life-saving drugs and legal, political and social rights. In relation to global corporate citizenship, pharmaceutical citizenship foregrounds how companies are claiming to be 'good citizens' by giving access to their products, and, in turn, how health activists are quoting citizens' rights to hold companies responsible for supplying drugs to everyone in need.

Today's pronouncements on global corporate citizenship seem like a realization of what Marcel Mauss (1997 [1925]) advocated several decades ago. In his celebrated work, *The Gift*, Mauss not only discusses *potlatch*, *kula* and *hau*, he also lays out his vision of a fair future for industrial societies. The purpose of Mauss's analysis of so-called archaic forms of exchange is to show that they hold a lesson for industrial capitalism: that social solidarity is far more important than individual profit maximization. Instead of separating clearly between domains of pure commodities and pure gifts, Mauss advocates hybrid forms of morally embedded exchanges.

One of Mauss's conclusions is that archaic, pre-capitalist forms of exchange should be seen in parallel with reformed capitalism. In *The Gift*, Mauss asks us to reflect on an archaic past to rediscover the future of industrial societies. What Mauss calls 'corporate solidarity' (*solidarité corporative*) had already been made reality by some businessmen of his era. Corporate solidarity, honour and unselfishness were the leading principles through which the economy should be constantly improved and 'humanized':

> Thus, we can and we must return to the archaic, to the elements; we will rediscover the motives of life and of action that are still known to numerous societies and classes: [for example] the joy of giving in public.... It is even possible to conceive what a society would be like where parallel principles prevailed. To a certain degree, a morality and economy of this type already works among the free professions of our great nations. Honour, unselfishness, [and] corporate solidarity are no vain words, nor are they against the needs of labour. Let us humanize other professional groups as well, and let us constantly improve them. That will be a great progress made, as Durkheim has often advocated. (Mauss, 1997 [1925]: 263, my translation)

Hence it is possible to read Mauss's *The Gift* as an early manifesto in support of corporate citizenship. The 'joy of giving in public' that reform-minded capitalists are celebrating puts them—more or less—on a par with the north-western chiefs who organized potlatches for the benefit of all.

Mauss can be taken up on his claim that it is *ethically* wrong to separate between self-interested exchanges and non-interested gift-giving. What I want to argue in the following is that to clearly separate between pure commodities and pure gifts is more ethical than to advocate hybrid gift-commodities—especially if seemingly pure gifts in one domain distract from big profits made elsewhere. The example I want to discuss here is that of Novartis' court case against the Indian government over the patent of its anti-cancer medicine Glivec. Let me start with a summary of the legal case.

Novartis *versus* the Government of India

Glivec (or Gleevec) is used to treat Chronic Myeloid Leukaemia (CML) and Gastrointestinal Stromal Tumours (GIST). The drug does not give a permanent cure from cancer, but only stalls its progress. That means that the drug needs to be taken *lifelong*. Without a continuous supply of Glivec, a patient's life expectancy is extremely short.

Novartis first patented Glivec's active ingredient, imatinib mesylate, in 1993 (Novartis, 2007b). At that time, India did not grant such patents on drug molecules. In 1972, the Indian government adopted a patent regime that only protected the *process* of drug manufacturing, but not active ingredients. In practice, this meant that any drug molecule, even if patented in other countries, could be reverse-engineered and generically produced in India. Over the past decades, these patent laws allowed the Indian pharmaceutical industry to become the world's leading producer of cheap generic medicines. By protecting different production processes, the old patent regime led to a situation where thousands of companies could compete with each other with practically identical products. A side effect of this intense competition is that drug prices in India are generally much lower than in other countries, including most countries in the developing world (Hayden, 2007; Tripathi *et al.*, 2005).

All of this is now changing. India joined the WTO in 1995, which forces the country's drug industry to follow the agreement on Trade-Related Intellectual Property Rights (TRIPS). Before signing this agreement, India negotiated a 10-year transition period, which is now expired. Since 2005, the Indian Patents (Amendment) Act has been fully implemented.

In 1997, Novartis started to apply for patents for a second version of the drug, the so-called beta crystalline form of imatinib mesylate. In India, the patent application was received under 'mailbox' provisions. During the 10-year transition period, Indian patent offices accepted applications to be reviewed after 2005. In 2003, Novartis was awarded a preliminary five-year period of Exclusive Marketing Rights (EMR) for Glivec. Before that, nine Indian pharmaceutical companies (among them Cipla, Natco, Hetero and Ranbaxy) sold imatinib mesylate at around Rs 96,000 (ca. £1,125) per patient per year, which was around 90% cheaper than the Novartis brand (Berne Declaration, 2006). Even after the 2003 EMR ruling, three Indian companies were allowed to produce and sell the drug in India, as well as to export it to other countries (Novartis, 2007b).

In January 2006, Novartis was denied an Indian patent for Glivec. In August 2006, the company took legal action against this decision. The legal conflict revolved around the undecided question of 'whether secondary patents obtained after 1995 for a new chemical entity patented before 1995 can be used to prevent generic companies from producing the drug' (Chaudhuri, 2005: 69). The Chennai Patent Office rejected Novartis' application for the beta form of imatinib mesylate primarily under Section 3(d) of the Indian Patents (Amendment) Act of 2005 (Government of India, 2005). This section states that variations of known molecules will be treated as 'the same substance, unless they differ significantly in properties with regard to efficacy'. This clause, which is not explicitly part of WTO agreements, aims to prevent companies from 'ever-greening' expiring patents and from getting new patents on molecules that are small variations of already existing drugs. In the case of Glivec, the Patent Office found that it was neither new nor significantly more effective than what was already patented pre-1995.

Novartis, in turn, argued that the beta version of Glivec is significantly better than the previous version (for example, that it has much better bioavailability). The second argument was more fundamental: Novartis argued that Section 3(d) is 'unconstitutional and in breach of India's obligation under TRIPS'.[1] Lawyers for Novartis invoked Article 14 of the Indian Constitution, which guarantees equal protection of all citizens by the laws of the country. They argued that the dismissal of its patent application violated Novartis' citizen rights.

In a press release dated 15 February 2007, Novartis (2007f) backed its claims with the recommendations of a report commissioned by the Ministry of Commerce on India's compliance with TRIPS. This report was prepared under the chairmanship of Dr R.A. Mashelkar, a former Director-General of the Council of Scientific and Industrial Research (CSIR) and one of the country's most prominent scientists. Mashelkar's report advised that it is incompatible with TRIPS to limit the grant of new patents to New Chemical Entities (NCEs) or

New Medical Entities (NMEs). If the patent offices wanted to turn down 'ever-greening' patent applications, this could be done through a proper application of existing rules and did not require Section 3(d).

Novartis filed this case against various governmental bodies: the Union of India, the Controller General of Patents and Designs, and the Chennai Assistant Controller of Patents and Design. But the company also sued a Mumbai-based NGO called the Cancer Patient Aid Association (CPAA), which had been fighting several legal disputes over Glivec already (Pharmabiz, 2004). A number of Indian pharmaceutical companies, such as Ranbaxy and Cipla, have also entered the court case alongside the CPAA and the governmental offices.

In April 2007, part of the legal battle shifted to a new arena. The Indian government, sensing that the Glivec case is only the beginning of a surge of similar cases, established the Intellectual Property Appellate Board (IPAB) to deal with contested patent applications. The Glivec patent application was the first case to be submitted to this board in September 2007. To date, no decision has been reached because of continual struggles about how this committee should be run (Pharmabiz, 2008). However, the primary question of whether Section 3(d) is TRIPS-compliant remained in the Chennai High Court (Pharmabiz, 2007a).

In August 2007, the Madras High Court dismissed Novartis' challenge. The court's decision had several layers. The court decided that it was not entitled to rule on WTO compliance questions. Instead, the WTO's own Dispute Settlement Body should decide this matter. It further ruled that Section 3(d) of the Indian Patent Act was not in violation of the Indian Constitution, as Novartis had claimed. Turning the tables on Novartis' invocation of constitutional rights, the court rejected the petition with reference to 'the constitutional obligation of providing good health care to its citizens'.

Pharmaceutical Citizens *versus* Novartis

Novartis' attack on the Indian government caused a furore among health activists, who felt that the company was destroying legal provisions that try to keep drugs affordable even after the country joined TRIPS. They held that, if the lawsuit succeeded and Section 3(d) was eliminated, many more 'old' drugs would be in line to get new patents. This would have far-reaching consequences for global drug prices, because healthcare in the developing world was relying on India's exports of cheap generics. Under a product patent regime, generic competition is restricted and a patent-holding company can exploit its monopoly to charge high prices. Without state-funded health provisioning, high drug prices mean that poorer people cannot afford all the drugs they need. The activists' shortcut analysis for this scenario is 'patents kill', and that, without Section 3(d), patents will kill even more. The 'life and death' argument by activists is particularly pressing in relation to HIV/AIDS drugs (Redfield, 2005). Since India is one of the world's main suppliers of inexpensive anti-retrovirals, any tightening of patent laws would dramatically decrease their availability and affordability. Instead of giving lifesaving drugs to those who needed them, Novartis was taking them away for no other reason than capitalist profit maximization.

Novartis' legal challenge to the Indian laws triggered the formation of a broad alliance of international action groups. By March 2007, more than 70 NGOs from around the world were lobbying Novartis to withdraw the case. For example, the UK-based aid organization Oxfam (2007) started an e-mail campaign against Novartis, personally addressed to its CEO, Daniel Vasella. At Novartis' annual general meeting on 6 March 2007, Berne Declaration (2007), a Swiss NGO, appealed to Novartis to drop the case. They stated that more than 350,000 people from across the globe had written to Novartis asking them to back down. Berne Declaration also staged a demonstration outside Novartis' Basel headquarters. A (black) woman lay in a sickbed holding a poster that urged Novartis to drop its case in India. A (white) member of the NGO was standing beside her with a mock packet of 'ProfitPills' which promised: 'Guaranteed: out of reach for poor people'.

Médecins Sans Frontières (MSF) has been one of the most vocal organizations to protest against Novartis. In its campaign, MSF (2007) argued that 'the lives of millions are at stake!!' not just in India but across the world. As a leading producer of generic medicines, India had, according to MSF, become the 'pharmacy of the world', and aid programmes crucially relied on generic versions of lifesaving drugs. MSF worried that the availability of generic HIV/AIDS medicines is threatened if patents hinder Indian companies from producing them. According to MSF, if Novartis won the case, 'millions of people across the globe could have their sources of affordable medicines dry up'. In a video clip produced by MSF, a dark-skinned person is about to take a pill before two hands in rubber laboratory gloves snatch away first the single pill, then the whole pack. A voiceover urges the viewer to 'call on Novartis to drop the case!' (Médecins Sans Frontières, 2007). The clip depicts the exchange between the corporation and patients neither as gift exchange nor as commodity exchange. Instead of saying that the company *gives* drugs to patients, it argues that it *takes* drugs away from patients who already hold them in their hands. Novartis' position as the rightful owner of drug patents is subverted in favour of a view of patients as rightful owners of drugs that are being stolen.

On 7 February 2007, my colleague Soumita Basu and I attended an NGO stakeholder meeting on the Novartis case in Kolkata. The meeting was organized by a Kolkata-based journalist who said that he had first come across the problem of patent laws while working on a documentary on pharmaceutical companies. He held that it was completely obvious that TRIPS is causing huge price rises for drugs. The only question was how to organize a protest movement.

Invited to the meeting were about 30 representatives of several health-related NGOs, activist lawyers, academic researchers, as well as party members of the CPI-M (Communist Party of India [Marxist]), which celebrated 30 years of uninterrupted rule in the state of West Bengal in 2007 and of CITU (Centre of Indian Trade Unions, closely aligned with the CPI-M). The walls of the meeting room were decorated with posters that equated the fight against Novartis with the fight against British colonial rule, especially with the 'Quit India Movement' of 1942. Just as the British were asked to withdraw from India, so global pharmaceutical companies were asked to 'WITHDRAW ALL PATENT APPLICATIONS'.

Among many passionate speeches, one given by a representative of MSF India described how intense competition between Indian generic producers and multinationals had driven down drug prices. In the field of HIV/AIDS medicines, generic competition from India, 'the pharmacy of the world', had pushed down prices by up to 99% from what they cost when they were first launched in patented form. She also pointed out that the aid efforts of international NGOs such as MSF crucially rely on the availability of cheap Indian generics. On the Glivec case, she said that it was the Cancer Patients Aid Association, a group of *citizens*, who first opposed Novartis through pre-grant opposition: 'They challenged Novartis in the Chennai patent office, proving that it was an old drug. That shook up Novartis! They didn't expect this.'

In a remarkable turn of events, Mashelkar made headlines again a few days later on 19 February 2007, when he announced the official withdrawal of the report by the Technical Expert Group on Patent Law. The trigger for this unprecedented step was that the report had come under allegations of plagiarism. As Mashelkar stated in a letter, 'certain technical inaccuracies in the Report ... have inadvertently crept in' (quoted in Srinivas, 2007). These 'inaccuracies' consisted in the verbatim lifting of passages from an academic paper published by Shamnad Basheer (2006), an intellectual property lawyer based in Oxford and Washington DC.

On 28 January 2007, Basheer had published a blog in which he argued that the Mashelkar Report plagiarized his earlier paper (Basheer, 2007). This announcement was swiftly used by activists to make an even more serious allegation: that the integrity of the whole Mashelkar committee was compromised by multinational pharmaceutical interests. An open editorial by Chan Park and Achala Prabha (2007) in the *Times of India* alleged that Basheer's 2006 paper was funded by Interpat, a lobby group of multinational pharma companies—Novartis being one of them. (In fairness, Basheer argued in his blog that Mashelkar plagiarized only parts of his paper but came to different overall conclusions.) The authors of the editorial are affiliated to the Lawyers' Collective (2007a), an NGO which gives legal counsel to CPAA in the Chennai court case. Hence the Lawyers' Collective was aligned with the Indian pharmaceutical companies who are working with CPAA in the case. To be sure, this alliance between activist lawyers and Indian companies was not straightforward and remained fragile. But both groups shared an interest in Novartis losing the case.

It is evident that Mashelkar's withdrawal of the Report had happened even *before* the public letter of 19 February, and just in time for the court hearings on 15 February. Mr Lakshmikumaran, the counsel for two of the Indian companies, Ranbaxy and Hetero, stated in court that the Mashelkar Report was now withdrawn and that there was no reason to consider its recommendations any further (Lawyers Collective, 2007b). It seems that on that day, the anti-Novartis alliance knew more about the compromised status of the Report than Novartis, who, on the same day, published a press release that quoted Mashelkar.

From February onwards, Indian Left Front parties mobilized a national campaign against Mashelkar and argued that it was not enough to withdraw the Report, but that the committee had to be disbanded (Purkayastha, 2007). On 15 March 2007, it was announced that the central government had allowed Mashelkar's Technical Expert Group on Patent Law issues to submit a revised version of its report (Pharmabiz, 2007b). Just days later, Mashelkar announced his resignation as chairman of the committee (Pharmabiz, 2007c).

By the time that the Chennai High Court dismissed Novartis' legal challenge, the company seemed to have lost the battle for public opinion as well. After the court ruling in August, there was still a possibility that Novartis could take the case to the WTO in Geneva. However, company representatives soon declared that this would not happen. According to S. Srinivasan, a long-term activist for affordable drugs, Novartis hesitated to move the case on to Geneva 'because of the bad publicity it will create' (Srinivasan, 2007: 3687). Moving the case to Geneva and risking even more bad publicity was not an option.

Up to this point, the Glivec story might be seen as a success for anti-corporate citizens. It was a citizens' group that opposed Novartis' patent application in the Chennai Patent Office. It was civil society organizations such as MSF that gathered global support against the corporation. It was an assemblage of lawyers, journalists, and political activists that forced the withdrawal of the Mashelkar Report and shamed one of India's most eminent scientists into stepping down. It was activists who delivered a blow to Novartis' public image long before the legal case was decided. It might seem, therefore, that Novartis' global corporate citizenship programme failed spectacularly. But this would be too quick a conclusion.

Pharmaceutical Citizens *Pro* Novartis

Novartis works hard to position itself as one of the world's most ethical and respectable companies. In 2006, Novartis was named 'Super Sector Leader' for healthcare in the Dow Jones Sustainability Index (DJSI) and was ranked as the world's second most respected pharmaceutical company by *Barron's*, a US business magazine (Novartis, 2007d). Being successful and being ethical are not seen as conflicting goals: the company's motto is 'Caring and Curing' (Novartis, 2007c).

The Novartis website contains extensive material on the company's global corporate citizenship (GCC) programmes. Novartis states that its ethics of 'caring and curing' rest on four 'pillars': first, to provide patients with high-quality drugs; second, to conduct business in an ethical way; third, to be a 'good neighbour' among people and communities; and fourth, to protect the environment (Novartis, 2007c). Central to Novartis' GCC agenda are its access-to-medicine programmes. The provision of free Glivec to patients who could otherwise not afford it is flagged up in the company's *GCC Review* of 2006 (Novartis, 2007c). It tells the story of Shawn Watts, a South African patient who could not afford to pay for Glivec out of his own pocket. Through the Glivec International Patient Assistance Program (GIPAP), Novartis 'made it possible for the young South African to have a continual supply of the drug that has saved his life' (Novartis, 2007c: 5). The GCC brochure further points out that GIPAP has helped more than 20,000 patients in 80 countries. In 2006, the company provided drugs with a market value of US $362 million, which is nearly half the budget for all its access-to-medicine programmes. Besides drugs, GIPAP also fosters leukaemia support groups and supplies disease and treatment information. The conditions for getting access to GIPAP India are that the cancer diagnosis is confirmed by a doctor and that a patient can prove his or her inability to pay for Glivec. The criteria for this are that a patient earns less than Rs 336,000 (GB £4,000) per month and is not reimbursed by his employer, by health insurance or by other sources (Novartis, 2006b).

There has been a continuous rise in access programmes like GIPAP in recent years. According to a publication by the US lobby group PhRMA (Pharmaceutical Research and Manufacturers of America, 2003), pharmaceutical companies are by far the biggest charitable donors. In 2001, drug companies contributed nearly 34% of all donations by US companies. The report also points out that, between 1998 and 2002, the number of US patients receiving medicines through corporate access programmes has increased from 1.5 million to 5.5 million (Pharmaceutical Research and Manufacturers of America, 2003). Access-to-medicine schemes are likely to grow further in the future and can be expected to become an important factor in developing countries as well.

In a video clip published by Novartis (2007a), Ranjit Shahani, head of Novartis India, juxtaposes 'two Indias'. One of the Indias was 'sprinting', while the other was 'crawling'. While India's economy was booming and people's standards of living were rising, there were many people who could not afford to pay for drugs. Novartis' access-to-medicine programmes were filling this gap. In India, Novartis' GIPAP was administered through an international NGO called The Max Foundation (TMF). Through TMF, Novartis was giving Glivec to '99%' of all patients diagnosed with CML or GIST (around 6,700 Indian patients were enrolled in GIPAP in December 2006; see Novartis, 2007b). Shahani claims that, without GIPAP, there was 'no hope', and 'most of these patients would not be there' any more. The statement ends with an appeal to protect drug patents. Without patents, there was no incentive to invest in innovative drugs, and without innovative drugs, the future of 'our children and our children's children' was threatened.

Almost all of Shahani's claims have been disputed. Shahani himself, in response to criticisms by the CPAA, once mentioned the first serious limitation of the programme: 'it is access to specialist healthcare facilities in our country which is more of an issue insofar as CML and its diagnosis is concerned' (quoted in Pharmabiz, 2005a). In other words, '99%' of all patients include only those who are diagnosed by a sufficiently competent doctor. In Shahani's estimate, only 4,000 of about 15,000 cases in India are diagnosed and referred to GIPAP in this way. Another point of controversy is the condition that many patients might be disqualified from GIPAP because they are, in principle, covered by schemes such as the

Employee State Insurance Scheme (ESIS). Although this is a form of health insurance, this state fund would never pay for an expensive drug like Glivec (Pharmabiz, 2005b).

However far the reach of GIPAP in India really is, Novartis is building up a large constituency of pro-corporate citizens who can hardly fail to feel somewhat indebted to the company. In a video clip, Viji Venkatesh, Head of MaxStation India, describes patients' reactions to Novartis' generosity: 'they cannot believe their eyes and their ears' (Novartis, 2007e). It does not come as a surprise, then, that only days after the left-stakeholder meeting, there was another civil society meeting on Glivec in Kolkata, this time in favour of Novartis. A volunteer training workshop organized by TMF in Kolkata on 10–11 February 2007 was turned into a 'Gratitude Meeting' and provided a forum to criticize anti-Novartis activists. A banner on the speaker's lectern read 'Novartis saved our lives' and patients spoke about how the free access to the anti-cancer drug was their only chance of survival. Similar events were staged in other Indian cities. For example, on 13 February 2007, GIPAP recipients presented a map of India scribbled full of signatures at the Novartis offices in Mumbai. On 9 February 2007, TMF started to organize a global signature petition that asked patients and their relatives to sign the following statement: 'I am alive and living with dignity thanks to Novartis and its Glivec International Patient Assistance Program, GIPAP' (Max Foundation, 2007).

With around 5,300 signatures by March 2007 (Novartis, 2007b) and hardly any resonance in the news media, this campaign looked pale compared to the anti-Novartis action organized by NGOs, which attracted a great media response and hundreds of thousands of supporters. But the pro-patent, pro-Novartis activism of this cancer patient group served a crucial role in the case in the Chennai High Court.

Y.K. Sapru, founder and chairman of the Cancer Patients Aid Association (CPAA), asserted in court that Novartis violates the 'fundamental right to life and health' of its citizens guaranteed by the Indian Constitution. He argued that 'the non-availability and non-affordability of any form of Imanitib Mesylate to CML patients is violative of rights of the CML patients under Articles 14 and 21 of the Constitution'. The National Sample Survey 1999–2000 had shown that Indian households have extremely high out-of-pocket expenses for healthcare, and that about 75% of these expenditures go to buy drugs. Many people lived in poverty, there was hardly any insurance available and the government did not spend much on healthcare. In this situation:

> … it is important that patents are not granted for frivolous drugs, as it would increase the cost of medication and make it out of reach of the majority of people in the country, thereby violating their right to life and health as guaranteed under the Constitution of India. Section 3(d) of the Patents (Amendment) Act, 2005 does prevent frivolous patents from being granted. (Cancer Patients Aid Association, 2006)

Novartis could counter this argument through its global corporate citizenship achievements. In a Writ Petition (No. 24754, cited in Lawyers Collective, 2007a), Novartis underlined that it is running GIPAP, 'one of the most generous and far reaching Patient Assistance Programmes ever developed'. The Petition further states that Novartis 'gives 99% of Glivec free of cost'. GIPAP made it difficult, if not impossible, for the anti-Novartis alliance to argue that cancer patients are dying purely because of corporate greed. Hence activism by MSF and other organizations revolved entirely around the wider fall-out of a change to the Indian patent law and not around cancer patients.

It is also crucial to understand why Novartis emphasized the role of The Max Foundation. This NGO gives invaluable support to Novartis' claims to be a good corporate citizen. First, TMF administers GIPAP in India, allowing Novartis to appear as a distant benefactor that does not directly influence patients. It also protects Novartis from being blamed if anything goes wrong with the programme. Second, events like the 'Gratitude Meeting' and signature campaigns could never be organized directly by Novartis. The pro-corporate support from suffering citizens lends a level of ethical credibility to Novartis' insistence on patent rights that no pronouncement from their own PR office could match. Already in April 2005, CPAA alleged that GIPAP was nothing but a 'Trojan Horse to weaken possible challenges to its market exclusivity in India'. However, the moral high ground about whether GIPAP covered all patients in need or not was won by Novartis.

To maintain a *difference* between the company and the NGO is vital. The exercise would fail if not-for-profit activities appeared as tainted by corporate interests. At the same time, it would be wrong to think that Novartis simply 'bribes' citizens into supporting its corporate interests. There is no reason to doubt that all the cancer patients who support Novartis are 'authentic'. For them, there is a strong incentive to be thankful for medicines which they could never buy themselves.

It is not without irony that, in the run-up to the Chennai case, Novartis' CEO himself seems to have suggested that the CPAA was a *pro*-corporate group of citizens sponsored by Indian generic manufacturers: 'Vasella said that generic companies are often behind patient groups in India, and said he would not be surprised if they gave money to the groups' (Gerhardsen, 2006). The CPAA has vehemently denied this charge and even sent a defamation notice against Vasella, demanding US$ 500,000 in damages (Cancer Patients Aid Association, 2007).

I think it is fair to say, however, that NGOs like CPAA foster *pro*-corporate forms of citizenship. The Glivec case was *not* about for-profit corporations battling not-for-profit civil society organizations. Instead, it was a battle between an alliance of players who believed that product patents should be strictly protected, and an alliance who believed that patents should not, or only minimally, be upheld. On the one side, Novartis was allied to the patient group TMF and, for a while, aligned with Mashelkar's Expert Group on patent laws. On the other side, NGOs were aligning themselves with large *Indian* pharmaceutical corporations who had been producing generic imatinib at a fraction of Novartis' price. The anti-Novartis alliance was not anti-corporate; it was only battling against the monopolies ensured by patents.

To be precise, the anti-Novartis lobby was not even against patents as such, but only against high drug prices charged by patent-holding corporations. If Novartis had marketed Glivec at an affordable price from the beginning, the Chennai court case would have never happened. If transnational health activists praise India as the 'pharmacy of the world', this is not because the Indian state is *producing* affordable generics, but because the Indian state gives free rein to *privately owned*, *for-profit* drug companies to compete with each other in a minimally regulated market (see Jeffery *et al.*, 2007).

Behind the high-minded ethical and legal debates in the Glivec case lies an essential economic question: why does Novartis prefer to give away Glivec *for nothing* in India, if it could at least charge as much as its generic competitors? Since when does it make economic sense to make *no* profits rather than, at least, *some* profits?

Give to the Poor to Take from the Rich

Novartis is the world's third-largest pharmaceuticals company and, with its Sandoz division, the world's second-largest manufacturer of generics. In 2006, Novartis reported a net sales rise of 15% to reach US $37 billion and a rise of net income by 17% to reach US $7.2 billion (Novartis, 2007g). Sales of Glivec are a key contributor to the company's profits: the drug generated sales of more than US $2.5 billion in 2006 and was the second highest-selling brand among all Novartis products. Net sales of the drug were US $630 million in the US and over US $1.9 billion in the rest of the world (Novartis, 2006a: 6). The drug is also expected to be a blockbuster over the coming years. The company plans to file for a new patent for imatinib in the treatment of Glioblastoma Multiforme in 2008. According to a book written by Vasella and Slater (2003), Glivec is a 'magic bullet' that rewrites medical history. Even if it may not rewrite medical history, it surely rewrites Novartis annual sales statistics.

As with practically all patent-protected drugs, the only markets that really make a difference are in developed countries, especially in the United States and in the European Union. Glivec is no exception. Given the high price of the drug, it would be an exaggeration to say that the Indian market for Glivec is 'small'—rather, it is practically non-existent. Not even the generic versions of imatinib by Indian companies were priced at an affordable level. The retail price of the generic imatinib was just below Rs 100,000 per patient per year. Compare this sum to Rs 25,825, the annual *per capita* income of Indians in 2005–6 (Bhandari and Kale, 2007) and it will be immediately clear that generics were just as unaffordable for out-of-pocket payers as the Novartis brand. Since the drug does not give a permanent cure from cancer, but only manages to halt its progress, it must be taken lifelong. A middle-class family might be able to scrape together the money needed for a year's worth of treatment, but could never afford it for a lifetime.

It is likely that NGOs like CPAA could procure imatinib at an even lower price through direct deals with generic manufacturers. NGOs can negotiate discounts of up to 90% below the retail price of generics if they go directly to producers and cut out wholesalers, retailers and other middlemen (see Ecks, 2007). But such NGO activities cannot cover the whole country and barely make a difference to the overall situation. In this view, the charge by health NGOs that drug prices will *become* unaffordable because of patents is only partly true: most of the costly drugs, including anti-cancer drugs, are *already* unaffordable to most individual patients, but will *also* become unaffordable to NGOs.

Be this as it may, the question remains why Novartis does not sell Glivec at a price that can be paid by Indian patients, but rather provides it at no cost. A partial answer to this question comes from Novartis' *Annual Report 2006* (Novartis, 2006a), which states that GIPAP is part of the company's efforts to extend its share in Public-Private Partnerships (PPPs) with a 'dynamic' pricing structure. The company estimates how much, if anything, can be charged for a drug in a local market. At the bottom of the scale are countries like India, where GIPAP works like a traditional donation scheme that gives drugs free of cost. Countries which can afford to pay more are only offered 'shared contribution' models, where Novartis supplies Glivec at a lower price if local payers, such as state hospitals, private health insurers or NGOs, pick up part of the bill. Such schemes are said to be changeable at any moment according to circumstances: 'access programs are able to adapt to changing healthcare policies' (Novartis, 2006a: 65). In the long run, Novartis plans to charge the same (high) price in all countries: 'these initiatives are evolving as a result of recognition by payors of the value of a therapy, as well as countries' rising ability to pay' (2006a: 65). In short, India is still too poor to be charged even a share of the price, but this will change if the economy continues to grow.

Another reason to give Glivec away, instead of going for at least a share of the costs, could be that Novartis wanted to eliminate competing Indian versions. If GIPAP is as comprehensive in India as Novartis claims, there is no one left who would buy the pills from Indian producers. Simultaneously, generic imatinib cannot yet be exported to European or North American markets like, for example, generic Prozac, for which the original patent is expired. Even before patents were enforced in 2005, Indian companies could only legally export to markets where patents were already expired. In all of the 35 countries where Novartis still holds a patent for Glivec, generic versions cannot be sold. For example, the US patent for Glivec is valid until 2013 and no generic competition is allowed there until then. If there is no Indian market, if there is only a small export market, and if there is an ongoing legal insecurity about the status of the patent (*Economic Times*, 2008), it is obvious that Indian companies are losing interest in producing Glivec altogether. Indeed, this is what seems to have happened over the past years. In 2004, major companies such as Cipla, Sun, Ranbaxy and Intas stopped producing generic imatinib (Express Pharma, 2004). The 2006 editions of CIMS (*Current Index of Medical Specialities*), an index of drugs available in the Indian market, did not list a single generic producer of imatinib mesylate.

Another reason to hand out Glivec to Indian patients free of charge is to build up a constituency of vocal citizens in favour of Novartis' Indian patent claims. Novartis' global GIPAP exists since 2001. The Max Foundation took up its work in India only in 2004. It is hardly a coincidence that the access programme was started right after Novartis first won the Exclusive Marketing Rights for Glivec and when generic competitors were restricted. That GIPAP aimed to avoid a public relations disaster for Novartis if thousands of cancer patients were to die because they could not afford Glivec is hardly far fetched. Hence CPAA's charge that GIPAP is a 'Trojan Horse' to weaken attacks on Novartis' market exclusivity is entirely plausible. If these same patients also raise their voices and start a signature campaign in favour of Novartis' court case, that is all the better for shareholder value. Nikolas Rose (2006: 142) argues that pharmaceutical companies sponsor patient support groups to keep in good standing with the public and to advertise its products. What Novartis achieved goes far beyond this: the pro-Novartis patients became a vital part of the corporation's legal struggle in India.

Yet it is not, as CPAA and other activist groups hold, the market *in India* that is at stake for Novartis. A drug as expensive as Glivec was never meant to make any profits in India. With Glivec, Novartis found itself in a situation where almost no one could afford its product and where a number of competitors were offering the same substance at a much lower price. Perhaps the best the company could do was to give away the drug in India for free to win two battles *elsewhere*: first, to protect its image of a 'good citizen' in Europe and North America; second, to maintain the high price level in European and North American markets.

According to the Kolkatan economist Sudip Chaudhuri (2005: 323), global companies do not offer drugs at lower prices in India for fear of two kinds of leakage. On the one hand, they fear a 'physical leakage' of drugs from low-price to high-price markets. On the other, 'they may actually be more worried about the information spillovers—the knowledge about lower prices in developing countries generating demand for lower prices in developed ones' (2005: 323).

Patent-holding drug companies argue that high drug prices are necessary to recuperate the high costs of research and development of new medicines. At the same time, the marginal costs of producing pills are extremely low. Unlike cars or other commodities that are expensive to make, giving away a few million pills is not costly. Because of the low marginal costs, the price of a pill does not reflect the cost of manufacturing, but the cost of discovering, testing and marketing it. For Novartis, the high *value* of Glivec needs to be represented in its high price, and this needs to be done consistently across global markets. If Glivec was sold at a fraction of its global price in India or elsewhere, the two kinds of leakage mentioned by Chaudhuri (2005) would be inevitable. Even if the physical spillover could be stemmed, the information spillover could not. Whoever would buy Glivec in Europe or North America at the high price set by Novartis would feel cheated—and whoever feels cheated might start some kind of European or American citizens group against corporate greed and drug patents.

I would argue, then, that global corporate citizenship is not a brake on free-wheeling capitalism, but rather a strategy of extending and accelerating it by new means. Different from what Bourdieu (1998) might have predicted, GCC is not 'a programme for destroying collective structures which may impede pure market logic', but a programme aimed at *fostering collective structures* that enhance profitability, such as pro-corporate patient activism. It does not destroy social bonds to give free rein to capitalism in all spheres of life, but it creates new social bonds to *distract* from less obvious market mechanisms. It does not spread a kind of 'Darwinism' that rewards winners and discards losers, but it rewards some of the poor to reap even bigger rewards from the rich.

In this sense, I think it would be more ethical by corporations to tone down the claim of being a 'good citizen' and to state in simple capitalist terms why they are doing what they are doing. If medicines such as Glivec are not 'free gifts' but part of a global pricing strategy, this should not be disguised through a rhetoric of good citizenship.

Failing that, I would suggest that global health activists could start another signature campaign among European and North American citizens that could read: 'We are happy to pay sky-high prices for patented drugs even if we know that the same drugs are cheaply available in developing countries.' In the (unlikely) case that such a campaign would succeed in getting a few million signatures, the future of affordable drugs in the developing world might be truly secured. This would be a form of global solidarity that Marcel Mauss might have liked as well, even if it clearly separates gifts from commodities.

NOTE

1 The full statement of Novartis case is contained in Chennai High Court Writ Petition No. 24754 of 2006; for a short version, see Novartis (2007b).

REFERENCES

Basheer, S. (2006). Protection of regulatory data under Article 39.3 of TRIPs: *The Indian context.* London: Intellectual Property Institute. URL (accessed January 2008): http://www.ip-institute.org.uk/pub.html

Basheer, S. (2007). The Mashelkar Committee Report on patents: Placing it in context OR reading the lines and not 'between' them. *Spicy IP*, 28 January. URL (accessed January 2008): http://spicyipindia.blogspot.com/2007/01/mashelkar-committee-report-on-patents_28.html

Berne Declaration. (2006). Novartis challenges the Indian Patent Law. 9 October. URL (accessed January 2008): http://www.evb.ch/en/p25011414.html

Berne Declaration. (2007). Statement of the Berne Declaration at Novartis' AGM. 6 March. URL (accessed January 2008): http://www.evb.ch/en/p25012134.html

Bhandari, L., & Kale, S. (2007). *West Bengal: Performance, facts and figures (Indian States at a glance 2006–07).* Delhi: Pearson.

Biehl, J. (2004). The activist state: Global pharmaceuticals, AIDS, and citizenship in Brazil. *Social Text, 22*, 105–132.

Bourdieu, P. (1998). Utopia of endless exploitation: The essence of neoliberalism. *Le Monde Diplomatique*, December. URL (accessed January 2008): http://mondediplo.com/1998/12/08bourdieu

Cancer Patients Aid Association. (2006). Affidavit in response to Novartis, Writ Petition No. 24759, 9 September, High Court Chennai.

Cancer Patients Aid Association. (2007). CPAA sends defamation notice to Novartis. 30 January. URL (accessed March 2008): http://www.cpaaindia.org/aboutus/PublicEyeAwards.htm

Chaudhuri, S. (2005). *The WTO and India's pharmaceuticals industry.* New Delhi: Oxford UP.

Ecks, S. (2005). Pharmaceutical citizenship: Antidepressant marketing and the promise of demarginalization in India. *Anthropology & Medicine, 12*, 239–254.

Ecks, S. (2007). Comment on C. Hayden, A generic solution? *Current Anthropology, 48*, 490–491.

Economic Times (India) (2008). Natco Pharma up 5% as SC stays Novartis hearing. 29 January. URL (accessed April 2008): htpp://economictimes.indiatimes.com/stocks_in_news_home/Natco_Pharma_up_5/articleshow/2740369.cms

Express Pharma. (2004) Generic companies withdraw imatinib mesylate. 6 February. URL (accessed April 2008): http://www.expresspharmaonline.com/story.php?&idno=436

Gerhardsen, T.I.S. (2006). Novartis persists with challenge to Indian patent law despite adversity. URL(accessed March 2008): http://www.ip-watch.org/weblog/index.php?p=430&res=1280_ff&print=0

Government of India, Ministry of Law and Justice. (2005). The Patents (Amendment) Act. URL (accessed 15 January 2008): http://www.patentoffice.nic.in/ipr/patent/patent_2005.pdf

Hayden, C. (2007). A generic solution? Pharmaceuticals and the politics of the similar in Mexico. *Current Anthropology, 48*, 475–495.

Jasanoff, S. (2004). Science and citizenship: A new synergy. Science and Public Policy, 31, 90–94.

Jeffery, R., Ecks, S., & Brhlikova, P. (2007). Global assemblages of pharmaceuticals: Rethinking TRIPS and GMP. *Biblio, 30* (3), 45–52.

Lawyers Collective. (2007a). http://www.lawyerscollective.org/%5Eamtc/%5EPatent_Oppositions/gleevec/gleevec-15-2-07.asp (last accessed 27 July 2007).

Lawyers Collective. (2007b). http://www.lawyerscollective.org/%5Eamtc/Mashelkar_Committee/news_&_updates/news1.asp (last accessed 27 July 2007).

Mauss, M. (1997 [1925]). *Sociologie et anthropologie*. Précédé d'une introduction à l'œuvre de Marcel Mauss par Claude Lévi-Strauss. Paris: Quadrige/Presses Universitaires de France.

Médecins Sans Frontières. (2007). People before patents: the lives of millions are at stake!! Online petition. URL (accessed January 2008): http://www.msf.org/petition_india/international.html

Novartis. (2006a). *Annual Report 2006*. URL (accessed January 2008): http://www.novartis.com/downloads/investors/reports/AR06_E_web.pdf

Novartis. (2006b). Novartis v Union of India, Writ Petition No. 24754 of 2006, High Court, Chennai.

Novartis. (2007a). About Novartis: Ranjit Shahani. URL (accessed April 2008): http://youtube.com/watch?v=wNhijTE6dxo

Novartis. (2007b). About Novartis: History of Glivec in India. URL (accessed January 2008): http://www.novartis.com/downloads/about-novartis/glivec-history-india.pdf

Novartis. (2007c). *Corporate citizenship review*. URL (accessed March 2008): http://www.novartis.com/downloads/about-novartis/CCR_English.pdf

Novartis. (2007d). Corporate Citizenship News. URL (accessed January 2008): http://www.novartis.com/about-novartis/corporate-citizenship/news/2007-01-07_influential_sustainability.shtml

Novartis. (2007e). Novartis provides free access to patients globally. Video clip, 9 March. URL (accessed January 2008): http://www.youtube.com/watch?v=_3w81df3KwI

Novartis. (2007f). Novartis seeking clarity in Indian patent laws: A critical incentive for long-term R&D investments into better medicines for patients. *Business Wire India*, 15 February. URL (accessed January 2008): http://www.businesswireindia.com/PressRelease.asp?b2mid=12008

Novartis. (2007g). Novartis strategic healthcare portfolio drives sustained strong performance with record full-year results in 2006. Novartis media release, 18 January.: URL (accessed March 2008): http://cws.huginonline.com/N/134323/PR/200701/1098754_5.html

Nguyen, V. (2004). Antiretroviral globalism, biopolitics, and therapeutic citizenship. In A. Ong, & S. Collier (Eds), *Global assemblages: Technology, politics, and ethics as anthropological problem*, 124–144. Oxford: Blackwell.

Oxfam. (2007). Email pharmaceutical giant Novartis. URL (accessed July 2007): http://www.oxfam.org.uk/what_you_can_do/campaign/mtf/actions/novartis.htm

Park, C., & Prabha, A. (2007). Patent wrong. *Times of India*, 12 February. URL (accessed January 2008): http://timesofindia.indiatimes.com/OPINION/Editorial/LEADER_ARTICLE_Patent_Wrong/articleshow/1593525.cms

Petryna, A. (2002). *Life exposed: Biological citizenship after Chernobyl*. Princeton, NJ: Princeton UP.

Pharmabiz. (2004). SC admits cancer patients' petition against granting EMR for Gleevec. 11 August. URL (accessed March 2008): http://www.pharmabiz.com/article/detnews.asp?articleid=23237&sectionid=44

Pharmabiz. (2005a). Letter to the Editor. 15 April. URL (accessed January 2008): http://www.pharmabiz.com/article/detnews.asp?articleid=27114&sectionid=44

Pharmabiz. (2005b). Editorial: Pricing cancer drugs. 20 April. URL (accessed March 2008): http://www.pharmabiz.com/article/detnews.asp?articleid=27192&sectionid=47

Pharmabiz. (2007a). IPAB postpones hearing of Novartis Glivec case to July 2. 18 June. URL (accessed March 2008): http://www.pharmabiz.com/article/detnews.asp?articleid=39348&sectionid=44

Pharmabiz. (2007b). Mashelkar gets 3 months to correct report on Patent Law issues. 15 March. URL (accessed March 2008): http://www.pharmabiz.com/article/detnews.asp?articleid=37997&sectionid=19

Pharmabiz. (2007c). Dr Mashelkar resigns as TEG chairman. 17 March. URL (accessed March 2008): http://www.pharmabiz.com/article/detnews.asp?articleid=38046&sectionid=17

Pharmabiz. (2008). SC stays hearing of Glivec case by IPAB sans technical member. 29 January. URL (accessed March 2008): http://www.pharmabiz.com/article/detnews.asp?articleid=42735&sectionid=44

Pharmaceutical Research and Manufacturers of America. (2003). Pharmaceutical companies lead the way in corporate philanthropy. URL (accessed January 2008): http://www.phrma.org/files/2004-01-20.884.pdf

Purkayastha, P. (2007). Novartis and Mashelkar: Tripping up on patents. *People's Democracy, 31* (10), 11 March. URL (accessed March 2008): http://pd.cpim.org/2007/0311/03112007_snd.htm

Redfield, P. (2005). Doctors, borders, and life in crisis. *Cultural Anthropology, 20* (3): 328–361.

Rose, N. (2006). *The politics of life itself: Biomedicine, power, and subjectivity in the twenty-first century*. Princeton, NJ: Princeton UP.

Srinivas, A. (2007). 'Certain inaccuracies have crept in': A contrite but defiant Mashelkar withdraws his patent report. *Outlook Magazine*, 5 March. URL (accessed January 2008): http://www.outlookindia.com/fullprint.asp?choice=2&fodname=20070305&fname=Mashelkar+%28F%29&sid=1

Srinivasan, S. (2007). Battling patent laws: The Glivec case. *Economic and Political Weekly*, September 15, 2007, 3686–3690.

The Max Foundation. (2007). Press release: Gratitude meetings. 9 February. URL (accessed March 2008): https://www.maxaid.org/Default.aspx?trgt=newsstories&choice=70

Tripathi, S.K., Dey, D., & Hazra, A. (2005). *Medicine prices and affordability in the state of West Bengal, India: Report of a survey supported by World Health Organization and Health Action International*. URL (accessed January 2008): http://www.haiweb.org/medicineprices/surveys/200412IW/survey_report.pdf

Vasella, D., & Slater, N. (2003). *Magic cancer bullet: How a little orange pill may rewrite medical history*. New York: HarperCollins.

18

Generic Medicines and the Question of the Similar

Cori Hayden

Mexico is currently Latin America's largest and fastest-growing pharmaceutical market, with total sales in 2003 estimated at $8.2 billion U.S. dollars. *Farmacias Similares* and other discount chains are now making inroads into that market, a fact that has prompted concerted resistance from the trans-national industry and its trade representatives in Mexico. Meanwhile, a proliferation of kinds of similarities and a proliferation of competitors means that *Farmacias Similares* now faces the unenviable task of insisting that the main product they sell, under an increasingly well known name, does not actually exist. "*Similares*" is a commercial name – the name of their chain – but they argue that they do not produce "similar" medicines.

The newly visible market for generic medicines in Mexico, and particularly the rapid growth of the now-ubiquitous pharmacy chain *Farmacias Similares*, provokes important questions both for pharmaceutical politics and for the social studies of science, technology, and medicine. Mexico is currently Latin America's largest and fastest-growing pharmaceutical market, with total sales in 2003 estimated at $8.2 billion U.S. (Espicom Business Intellligence, 2003). *Farmacias Similares* and other discount chains are now making inroads into that market, a fact that has prompted concerted resistance from the transnational industry and its trade representatives in Mexico. *Farmacias Similares* are at the center of a rapidly growing web of organizations and associations overseen by recently-declared Presidential candidate Víctor González Torres, whose enterprises include not only the increasingly lucrative pharmacy chain and his own generics company (*Laboratorios Best*), but also the crusading National Movement Against Corruption, which is currently targeting the *Seguro Social*; the

Cori Hayden, "Generic medicines and the question of the similar," Cinvestav, Jan-Mar. (2006). pp. 50–60. Used with permission from Cori Hayden.

The Pharmaceutical Studies Reader, First Edition. Edited by Sergio Sismondo and Jeremy A. Greene.

non-profit social assistance organization *Fundación Best*; and an umbrella group overseeing these and several other affiliated organizations, which goes by the name of *Grupo por un País Mejor*.

One might argue, perhaps, that González Torres is attempting to establish a parallel health care system to that provided by the state: for, alongside the *Farmacias*, he has established over 1,000 low-cost health clinics, primarily in *barrios populares*, as well as a new health plan (the *SimiSeguro*) which seems designed to compete directly with the federal government's own *Seguro Popular* (a plan that seeks to extend health coverage to those left out of the main public sector institutions, eschewing the language of "citizens" who have a right to health care in favor of the notion of consumers who bear "individual responsibility" for the consumption of health services). With his own forays into the provision of health care, González Torres has, undoubtedly, become an important player in what may well be a reconfiguration of pharmaceutical and health politics in Mexico.

At the center of the self-declared Simi revolution is an understanding of "those who have the least" not just as an "underserved population" but as an untapped market (and, it might seem, as a potential electoral base). A key factor in this move, in turn, is the proliferation of cheaper copies of name-brand pharmaceuticals, known and sold variously as *similares*, *genéricos*, and *genéricos intercambiables* (similars, generics, and interchangeable generics). The differences between these terms are important, as will be discussed below, but in broad terms generics can be defined as copies of drugs based on the same active substance as the patented, name-brand "original." For example, Schering-Plough's antihistamine Clarityne® is based on the molecule or active substance Loratadina; once the patent on Clarityne® expires,[1] any company can manufacture and market its own drug using Loratadina, which can be purchased from a wide range of suppliers across the world. Dr. Simi is certainly not the only purveyor of such cheaper medicines in Mexico. Many other chains such as *Farmacias del Ahorro* and *Farmacias de Dios* as well as smaller corner pharmacies now stock generic drugs alongside their brand-name counterparts. But arguably it has been the *Similares* enterprise – and their increasingly familiar refrain, "*Lo mismo pero más barato!*" ["The same, but less expensive!"] – which has done the most to popularize the idea that a medication can have a cheaper, generic substitute. For example, a widely prescribed hypertension medicine that sells for roughly 300 pesos/month in its original, branded form is available from *Similares* for 30 pesos/month.

A New Market?

The owner of *Farmacias Similares*, Víctor González Torres, is among other things the great grandson of the founder of *Laboratorios Best*, a company that was established in the 1950s to manufacture generics for sale to the *Instituto Mexicano de Seguro Social* (IMSS) and the other public sector health services.[2] In fact, from the 1950s until very recently, the public sector was the lifeblood of the small generics industry in Mexico, which currently consists of approximately 50 small- to medium-sized companies.[3] After González Torres took over leadership of *Laboratorios Best*, he started his own transport and packaging companies for *Best* products. In 1997, he announced the opening of the first branch of his *Farmacias Similares* – a chain that would sell only copied drugs. It was a novel commercial strategy; at that time, the vast majority of drugs on sale in private pharmacies were patented, name-brand medications, and in fact 90% of the value of the Mexican pharmaceutical market was generated by the sale of brand-name medicines. Some of the drugs sold by *Similares* are manufactured by *Laboratorios Best*, which, like other generics companies, purchases active substances from suppliers (domestic and foreign) and assembles and packages the drugs in their own factories, adding their own brand-name (for example, "Bestafen" is *Best's* brand of ibuprofen). In 2004, 50 of the roughly 300 medicines sold in *Farmacias Similares* were produced by their own *Laboratorios Best*; the pharmacy chain purchases the rest of its inventory from other generics companies, both Mexican and foreign.

The arrival of *Farmacias Similares* in 1997 was not, of course, an isolated event. In 1997 and 1998, following several years of drug supply problems within IMSS and relatively unchecked increases in the costs of the patented drugs on sale in most pharmacies, the Secretary of Health opened the way for such a development by embarking on a series of efforts to stimulate a broader demand for, and supply of, cheaper pharmaceutical alternatives beyond the *Seguro Social* and other public institutions. This multipronged effort has included public education and advertising campaigns and a new prescription decree that required, starting on January 1, 1998, that public sector physicians name the active substance of the drug in a prescription, rather than simply prescribing a brand name. This may seem like a minor intervention but as pharmaco-economist Raúl Molina Salazar has noted, when you change prescription practices you actually start breaking monopolies.[4] Argentine economists described a similar policy in that country in 2002 as a direct challenge to neoliberal or de-regulationist prescription policies (Tobar and Godoy Garraza, 2003). And in fact this question has implications for medical education itself; at least one of Mexico's leading university pharmacology departments is now re-emphasizing basic pharmacology and encouraging medical students to think beyond the brand names that are peddled to them in relentless visits from transnational drug company representatives (see also Lakoff, 2004 on Argentina).

The Similar and the "Similar"

Significantly, the government has also established new regulatory categories and testing regimes through which to manage the domain of the pharmaceutical copy. We might ask, now, what do the terms "similar", "the same", and "the generic" convey? They are, it must be emphasized, not simply different or vernacular names for the same thing. Initially, regulatory provisions spoke of *medicamentos genéricos* (those packaged for the public sector and labeled only with the name of the active substance, a presentation familiar to anyone who has received medicines from the *Seguro Social*) and *genéricos de marca* (branded generics: those labeled with a generics' company's own brand name, for sale to the wider public through pharmacy chains, such as *Farmacias Similares*' own Bestafen (ibuprofen)). But recently, yet another regulatory category has come into circulation: the interchangeable generic (*genérico intercambiable*, or *GI*): that which meets strict tests for "bioequivalence." *This* label for "the same" requires not only that the drug contain the same active substance as its patented counterpart, but that it be absorbed by human bodies in the same way, and at the same rate as the original. This absorption rate is its "bioavailability" or *biodisponibilidad*. Bioequivalence (*bioequivalencia*) is expensive to prove (the cost is roughly $100,000 per product), requiring a double-blind clinical trial in 24 healthy patients over 3 months. It thus also requires authorized institutions such as hospitals to be available to conduct such tests. Simple *medicamentos genéricos* do not require this kind of testing, nor, by implication, do they require the mobilization of these new institutional and infrastructural linkages.[5]

Where does the ascendance of the *GI* as a category leave the "similar"? Many people in Mexico talk about "similars" as a kind of drug, and many smaller pharmacies, alert to the growing commercial success of Dr. Simi, advertise that they, too, sell "medicamentos similares." And in fact the *Secretaría de Salud* (Ministry of Health) has implicitly endorsed this category by allowing medicines to be marketed under such a name. But *Farmacias Similares* and *Laboratorios Best* associates are not particularly happy with this development, for a few reasons. First, and ironically, given that they are making a hefty profit on copied drugs, they now complain about the pirates who plague *them* (such as the storefront in a small town outside of Toluca, sporting the hand-painted sign, "*Farmacias Simylares*").

But, more broadly, *Similares* associates might find reason to regret their initial inspiration regarding the name of their pharmacy chain. They now find themselves trying, at every opportunity, to differentiate the *Similar* brand from the idea of the merely similar, insisting in interviews and in public symposia that there is actually no such thing as a "similar" drug. Certainly, this is true in regulatory terms: there is no official regulatory category or testing regime for "similars." But many people familiar with the science of pharmacology will argue that there is a quasi-technical definition of a "similar drug": it is one that has the same biological activity as a patented original (for example, an anti-inflammatory drug such as Advil) but that is *not based on the same active compound*.[6] Víctor González Torres insists that the products he sells in his pharmacies (again, either produced by *Best* or purchased from other generics companies) are based on the same compounds as the patented originals, and indeed a growing number of products on *Similares*' shelves do actually bear the label of *Genérico Intercambiable*. But this fact has not protected the chain from the effects of an intriguing self-inflicted wound. Dr. Simi's flagship enterprise now faces the unenviable task of insisting that the main product they sell, under an increasingly well known name, does not actually exist. "*Similares*" is a commercial name — the name of their chain — but they argue that they do not produce "similar" medicines. As the chief chemist for *Laboratorios Best* told me in a 2004 interview, "Now everyone says we sell *medicamentos similares* ... it's not true! They're branded medicines, made by national laboratories."

Generics and the Social Studies of Science and Technology

These entwined concerns about the definition and viability of the generic, the similar, and the national raise interesting questions. For at stake with generics is not, precisely, "novel" research and development nor the related question of linkages between basic research and the industrial sector, but rather the manufacture, distribution, and sale of copies. And yet, the question of the "viability" of the copied drug — and, by extension, of a domestic generics industry — brings us directly to the question of Mexico's scientific and technical networks (see Bueno and Santos, 2003), and the relationship between a domestic pharmaceutical sector and transnational developments revolving around the often competing poles of public health and "free trade" (González Luna, 2004). From the point of view of the social studies of science and technology, a number of issues can be highlighted here.

1. *Opening the 'black box' of the pharmaceutical*

The question of what might count as "the same" or "*lo mismo*," in *Similares*' terms, has emerged as a matter of enormous popular, regulatory, economic, and political interest, and it has opened up an even more basic, previously "black-boxed" question as a newly popular topic of conversation: of what, precisely, does a pharmaceutical consist? How can a drug really be "the same" and still be 70% cheaper than its branded counterpart? (Conversely, to ask the political-economic question, what exactly accounts for the high cost/"value" of a brand?) Moreover, as science studies scholars might ask, what regimes of testing, knowledge production, and legitimation (such as those required for *GI* designation) are coming to life in these ongoing debates over the legitimacy of different actors within the pharmaceutical sector?

2. *Pharmaceutical research and development as a project of "the nation"*

Farmacias Similares and the broader shifts of which they are a part must also be seen in light of a century-long history of efforts within Mexico to create a viable domestic pharmaceutical research, development, and manufacturing sector. Keeping in mind the rich body of social science and historical work on the *Instituto Médico Nacional* (*IMN*) at the turn of the 20th century (Cházaro, 2000-2001; Hersch Martínez, 2000), or President Luis Echeverría's efforts to promote national pharmaceutical self-sufficiency in the mid-1970s (Lozoya, 1976; Soto Laveaga, 2003), we might note that the *Similares* project has tapped into — but also radically transformed — an illustrious history of pharmaceutical nationalism in Mexico. In the mid 1970s, for example, Luis Echeverría's efforts to shore up a fracturing body politic made the state a key source of support for science and technology, and the main protagonist in a series of efforts to reinvigorate an authentically Mexican pharmaceutical sector. Appeals to "*lo nacional*" have been an important rallying cry for *Farmacias Similares*, whose early publicity schemes emphasized that Mexican companies can indeed produce high quality drugs, and that the nation can thus break foreign companies' grip over the health of the "*pueblo mexicano*."

3. *The state and the market, or, the public and the private*

But González Torres' own brand of pharmaceutical nationalism differs very strongly from previous, state-led efforts in Mexico. González Torres, whose generics company once survived solely on sales to the public sector, now refuses to sell any medicines to the *Seguro Social*, while he calls on the private sector and a growing web of "civil society" organizations (many of which are of his own making), to do the work of providing health care to "those who have the least." As we might glean from his self-description — "*I'm Che Guevara in a Mercedes!*"— González Torres is explicitly leading a businessman's revolution, one that he is now actively exporting to Guatemala, Costa Rica, Argentina, and elsewhere in Latin America.

Indeed, while Dr. Simi makes appearances across the Americas, it is worth noting that the politics of the generic is not everywhere the same. Perhaps the strongest contrast is that which can be seen between Mexico's private sector-led generics revolution and the widely-hailed efforts in Brazil to ensure universal access to HIV/AIDS medicines since the mid-1990s, in which a strong, state-run biomedical sector and generics industry have played an important role. The Brazilian model suggests how generics may be part of a re-assertion of an enterprising state's notion of public health against prevailing transnational trade and intellectual property regimes (Biehl, 2004; Molina Salazar, Rivas Vilchis, and Escobar, 2003). In contrast, in Mexico, and certainly in the hands of Dr. Simi, generic drugs seem to be part of an ongoing privatization of health care, in which the burden of medication costs shifts ever further towards individual consumers, and particularly the poor. This is the population, reconfigured as a "market," for which Dr. Simi and the federal government's *Seguro Popular* seem, in fact, to be competing. In the generics/Simi wars we see a powerful battle afoot not just or even primarily between "transnational" (private) and "national" (public) interests, but simultaneously between embattled public sector health institutions and an increasingly powerful and arguably populist consumerism. With Echeverría's 1970s Mexico, Díaz's *Instituto Médico Nacional*, and even post-1996 Brazil in mind, we should not be surprised that core questions over belonging, social exclusion, and the consolidation of national techno-scientific infrastructures should be waged through the politics of the pharmaceutical. But as Víctor González Torres and his alter ego, Dr. Simi, shows us all too vividly, we would do well not to assume too much about the shape that this pharmaceutical politics might take.

NOTES

1 The period of monopoly protection is twenty years according to the terms of Mexico's entry into the TLC/NAFTA.
2 The González Torres family is illustrious on more fronts than one: one of Víctor's brothers is the founder of the Green Party of Mexico, and another sibling was the founder of a competing pharmacy chain, *Farmacias del Ahorro*.
3 Patricia Facci, interview, 25 July 2005.
4 Interview, March 3, 2004.
5 The *GI* is not simply a straightforward matter of "quality" and biome- dically-validated markers for guaranteeing consumer safety. As science studies scholars have long argued, viability, quality, and "robustness" are simultaneously technical and political/social issues, and the category of the *GI* is no exception. Its institutionalization is something for which the transnational industry trade associations have militated (not only in Mexico but across Latin America), in part, some argue in Mexico, as an added and costly gatekeeping barrier to pharmaceutical legitimacy for smaller domestic companies.
6 Jaime Tortoriello, interview, February 17, 2004.

REFERENCES

Biehl, Joao. 2004. "The Activist State: Global Pharmaceuticals, AIDS, and Citizenship in Brazil." *Social Text 22* (3):105–132.

Bueno, Carmen and María Josefa Santos, coords. 2003. *Nuevas tecnologías y cultura*. México, DF: Universidad Iberoamericana.

Cházaro, Laura. 2001/2002. "La fisioantropometría de la respiración en las alturas, un debate por la patria." *Ciencias* 60-61: 37–56. Special Issue: La Imagen de los Indigenas en la Ciencia. Mexico City: UNAM.

Espicom Business Intelligence Limited. 2003. World Pharmaceutical Markets Series, Report on Mexico: April 11.

González Luna M., Sergio 2004. *Los medicamentos genéricos: un acierto patente. Inovación y libre competencia en la industria farmaceútica nacional*. México DF: Editorial Porrúa.

Hersch Martínez, Paul. 2000. *Plantas medicinales: relato de una posibilidad confiscada*. México DF: Instituto Nacional de Antropología e Historia, Serie Antropología Social.

Lakoff, Andrew. 2004. "The Private Life of Numbers: Audit firms and the Government of Expertise in Post-Welfare Argentina," in Stephen Collier and Aihwa Ong, eds. *Global Assemblages: Governmentality, Technology, Ethics*, New York: Blackwell.

Lozoya, Xavier. 1976. El Instituto Mexicano para el Estudio de las Plantas Medicinales. A.C. (IMEPLAM). *In Estado Actual del Conocimiento en Plantas Medicinales de México,* edited by Xavier Lozoya and Carlos Zolla, 243–255. México, D.F., Folios.

Molina Salazar, Raúl, José F. Rivas Vilchis, and Ma. de los Angeles Escobar. 2003. "Financiamiento y acceso al tratamiento del VIH/SIDA: el caso de Brasil y México." In José F. Rivas Vilchis and Raúl Molina Salazar, eds., *Politicas Farmaceúticas y Estudios de Actualizacíon de Medicamentos en Latinoamérica*, pp. 75–92. Organización Mundial de la Salud, Fundación Oswaldo Cruz, and the Universidad Autónoma Metropolitana-Iztapalapa.

Molina Salazar, Raúl, José F. Rivas Vilchis, and Rubén Román Ramos. 2003. "Industria farmaceútica mundial: principales características." In José F. Rivas Vilchis and Raúl Molina Salazar, eds., *Politicas Farmaceúticas y Estudios de Actualizacíon de Medicamentos en Latinoamérica*, pp. 11–26. Organización Mundial de la Salud, Fundación Oswaldo Cruz, and the Universidad Autónoma Metropolitana-Iztapalapa.

Soto Laveaga, Gabriela. 2003. "Steroid Hormones and Social Relations in Oaxaca," in Casey Walsh, Elizabeth Emma Ferry, Gabriela Soto Laveaga, Paola Sesia, and Sarah Hill, eds., *The Social Relations of Mexican Commodities: Power, Production, and Place,* pp. 55–79. La Jolla, California: Center for U.S.-Mexican Studies.

Tobar, Federico and Lucas Godoy Garraza. 2003. Políticas para mejorar el acceso a los medicamentos. Notas desde el caso argentino. In José F. Rivas Vilchis and Raúl Molina Salazar, eds., *Politicas Farmaceúticas y Estudios de Actualizacíon de Medicamentos en Latinoamérica,* pp. 75–92. pp. 27–40. Organización Mundial de la Salud, Fundación Oswaldo Cruz, and the Universidad Autónoma Metropolitana-Iztapalapa.

Index

The Pharmaceutical Studies Reader, First Edition. Edited by Sergio Sismondo and Jeremy A. Greene.